W9-AAL-437

FAST TALK &
FLUSH TIMES

FAST TALK &
FLUSH TIMES

The Confidence Man
as a Literary Convention

William E. Lenz

University of Missouri Press
Columbia, 1985

Copyright © 1985 by The Curators of the University of Missouri
University of Missouri Press, Columbia, Missouri 65211
Printed and bound in the United States of America

Library of Congress Cataloging in Publication Data

Lenz, William E.
  Fast talk and flush times

  Bibliography: p.
  Includes index.
    1. American fiction—19th century—History and
criticism. 2. Trickster in literature. 3. Deception in literature.
4. Swindlers and swindling in literature.
I. Title.
PS374.T7L46   1984   813′.3′09355   84–2200
ISBN 0–8262–0450–3

B+T; 21.00

18,306.

for my father (1917–1977),
a fast talker par excellence

ACKNOWLEDGMENTS

To Leo Mark, who at Amherst College first introduced me to Melville's *Confidence-Man*, I obviously owe an intellectual debt that cannot adequately be repaid in rhetorical currency. At the University of Virginia, Harold H. Kolb, Jr., and Alan B. Howard patiently encouraged, challenged, and sharpened the original study that has grown into this book. David Levin, Stephen Railton, and Joseph Kett contributed numerous suggestions for improving the manuscript, and Gary Lindberg of the University of New Hampshire generously shared with me his insights on the confidence man. Hennig Cohen of the University of Pennsylvania deserves special mention as a disinterested reader who sent a young scholar pages of detailed questions. John Cummins, my chairman and good friend, and Maria Ferri and Lisa Tronzo, my untiring assistants, contributed innumerable hours to *Fast Talk*.

For technical assistance and photographic reproduction I am indebted to Robert Cooley, my colleague at Chatham College, and Marcia Grodsky of the University of Pittsburgh; the Darlington Memorial Library of the University of Pittsburgh allowed me to include the Baldwin and Harris illustrations from their collection. In somewhat different forms, portions of *Fast Talk and Flush Times* have appeared in *Colby Library Quarterly*, *The Markham Review*, *University of Mississippi Studies in English*, *The Old Northwest*, and in *One Hundred Years of "Huckleberry Finn": The Boy, His Book, and American Culture*; I wish to thank the editors for permission to reprint material from their pages. The Chatham College Central Research Fund provided a summer grant to aid in the final preparation of the manuscript. And of course the largest debt I owe to my wife, whose continuous support gave me the confidence I so often needed.

W.E.L.
Chatham College
Pittsburgh, Pa.
1 April 1984

CONTENTS

Acknowledgments, vii

1. The New
Country, 1

2. The Early Tradition
of Confidence Games, 29

3. The Emergence of the
Confidence-Man Convention, 57

4. Four Variations of
the Confidence Man, 97

5. The War, Mark Twain, and the
Flush-Times Confidence Man, 147

6. From the New Country
to the Twentieth Century, 185

Appendix: The Confidence Man in
Nineteenth-Century America, 205

Notes, 209

Bibliography, 221

Index, 233

The whole life of an American is passed
like a game of chance.

> —Alexis de Tocqueville,
> *Democracy in America* (1835)

Arrest of the Confidence Man. —For
the last few months a man has been
travelling about the city, known as the
"Confidence Man;" that is, he would go
up to a perfect stranger in the street,
and being a man of genteel appearance,
would easily command an interview.
Upon this interview he would say, after
some little conversation, "have you
confidence in me to trust me with your
watch until to-morrow;" the stranger, at
this novel request, supposing him to be
some old acquaintance, not at the
moment recollected, allows him to take
the watch, thus placing "confidence" in
the honesty of the stranger, who walks
off laughing.

> —*New York Herald*, 8 July 1849

1 THE NEW COUNTRY

You have nothing but your character . . .
in a new country to depend upon.

—Captain John Farrago

The American has, in fact, yet no
character.

—Hugh Henry Brackenridge

The confidence man, a distinctly American version of the archetypal trickster, rises from the historical conditions of the boom and bust "flush times" and begins to have a literary life of his own in the 1840s. The term *confidence man*, which first appears in public discourse in 1849 as a description of what the *Literary World* called a "new species of the Jeremy Diddler,"[1] had by 1857 achieved currency as "one of the indigenous characters who has figured long in our journals, courts, and cities."[2]

Like the Elizabethan fool, Shakespeare's scheming Falstaff, or Robert Greene's cabalistic cony-catchers, the American confidence man embodies forces of disorder, transition, and unrest, just as he shares with Odysseus, Satan, and Till Eulenspiegel the skill of manipulating appearances. The American confidence man, however, emerges as a local rather than a mythic figure; he relies not on supernatural powers or charms or courts but on the fluid nature of society in the New World with its unique opportunities for self-government, self-promotion, self-posturing, and self-creation. He appears to trace his ancestry most directly from the ambiguities of the New World, which had earlier given rise to the regional images of the peddler, the Yankee, and the rustic Jonathan. Yet he does not spring from the natural landscape of New England but from an imaginative territory called by a host of nineteenth-century writers the "new country," exploiting the thinly settled and ill-defined regions along the frontier. Although the

confidence man draws upon these and other antecedents, he
is defined by the nineteenth-century flush times, by the continually evolving new country, by his shifty language in the
service of fun, and by a cardinal motive—personal profit. To
him, the question posed by Melville's wooden-legged man—
"How much money did the devil make by gulling Eve?"[3]—is
itself a sleight-of-hand trick designed to distract attention
from his enterprise. Prowling fictional and historical works
during the antebellum flush times, the confidence man dis-
dains mere jokes and pranks, avoids eastern cities and criminal partners, shuns all tools but his own rhetoric. In border
states where identity is often only a matter of assertion, he
plays upon the need for confidence, the suspicion of dishonesty, the dream of easy riches, and his victims' certainty of
their superior shrewdness. Temporary comic master of the
new country, the confidence man seeks and wins the confidence of everyone he meets, then betrays that confidence for
his own advantage.

The New World

The New World did not become the new country overnight,
but it did from the first appear to foster shiftiness. Almost by
definition, the New World represented the unknown, a psychological as well as a physical locale that seemed to embody
at best ambiguity and at worst disorder. As William C. Spengemann argues, "By obtruding upon the elegantly simple cos-
mology of the late Middle Ages an unanticipated, amorphous,
and therefore unassimilable 'fourth part of the world,' the discovery [of America by Columbus] gradually removed the world
as a whole from the authoritatively defined state of being it
had enjoyed before 1500 and thrust it into a highly uncertain
state of becoming."[4] For over one hundred years accounts of
the New World were rhetorical voyages of discovery and exploration, attempts to represent the unconventional in conventional terms for an interested but often skeptical Old World
audience. Thus Christopher Columbus called the people he
found "Indians" and claimed that on his third voyage he had
nearly sailed to the earthly paradise.[5] What motivated Colum-

bus was in part his desire projecting itself as wish-fulfilling fantasy onto the unknown, in part his practical need to justify expensive voyages, and in part his recognition that he was a lone witness in what Wayne Franklin terms the "explorer's universe," an ambiguous expanse of possibilities "where word is deed" and where a report constitutes reality.[6] Sixteenth- and seventeenth-century promotion literature often exploited the dreams and the real or imagined needs of the Old World, picturing the New as a land of flowing milk and honey; the uncertainty of New World conditions made manipulation or misrepresentation possible and—as profit was involved—likely. In *A Further Account of the Province of Pennsylvania* (1685), William Penn makes explicit one of the primary reasons for colonization: so that "those that are Adventurers, or incline to be so, may imploy their Money, to a fair and secure Profit."[7]

If the New World existed as a speculative utopia in the minds of some promoters, it often appeared a terra incognita harboring chaos to early settlers. In an attempt to establish order and control over the vast wilderness around them and the potential wilderness within, the *Mayflower* pilgrims chose to "Covenant and Combine" themselves "into a Civil Body Politic."[8] The optimistic vision of the New World as the Garden of Eden competed with a simultaneous perception of the New World as the last stronghold of Satan. Despite the continued efforts of Puritan colonists to create perfect Bible communities, it soon became apparent that the devil was hard at work in New England, leading men into temptation and inciting Indians to violence. Fragile communities like Plymouth Plantation offered new opportunities for saints and sinners alike. As William Bradford noted in 1642, "Marvelous it may be to see and consider how some kind of wickedness did grow and break forth here, in a land where the same was so much witnessed against and so narrowly looked unto, and severely punished" (*OPP*, 316). The frequency of sinners—and the extreme forms of sin—in the colony Bradford explains through conventional biblical allusions (*OPP*, 321–22), yet he is clearly disturbed by the indeterminacy of identity engendered by the New World. How can one perceive the true nature of John Lyford, Thomas Morton, Isaac Allerton, and Thomas

Weston, to say nothing of the Arthur Peach Gang or the infamous Thomas Granger? How can any claims be ultimately authenticated or denied? The uncertainty of identity aids John Lyford, for example, a possibly counterfeit minister who repeatedly plots against Bradford and uses his position to seduce young women (*OPP*, 147–69). Cotton Mather in 1699 finds Lyford's repentances and recommissions more difficult to understand and judge, and devotes an entire chapter of the *Magnalia Christi Americana* to "Wolves in Sheeps' Cloathing," men who impersonate ministers for profit.[9] As the case of "Teague" makes clear, in which an Irishman's ability to read allows him to masquerade as a priest (*MCA*, 541), the question of New World evil is not fully answered by saying, as Bradford does of Lyford, that the community was "bitten" (*OPP*, 210). For Mather, these "impostors" raise complex questions about the nature of identity, language, and perception in America, and he is unable simply to condemn and dismiss Lyford, "Teague," Dick Swayn, Eleazer Kingsberry, and others as devils. Their number, moreover, suggests an increase in subaltern shape-shifters that Mather feels at pains to examine. The dangers New England faces are less clear and more subtle than in Bradford's day, Satan's presence is more ambiguous and more difficult to identify in absolute terms; men who present themselves as ministers may be minions of the devil, and even sermons—God's Word interpreted—may prove to have been stolen (*MCA*, 541).

To look at a few examples of more obviously pecuniary shiftiness, we might turn to John Winthrop's *Journal*. In 1639 the fine of £200 was levied against Robert Keaine for unfair profitmaking, an occasion that caused John Cotton to lecture upon some "false principles" of New World commerce: "That a man might sell as dear as he can, and buy as cheap as he can. . . . That, as a man may take the advantage of his own skill or ability, so he may of another's ignorance or necessity."[10] The question of what constitutes a fair profit still troubled men like the Quaker John Woolman in 1756, causing him to disencumber himself of numerous clients and thus of much tempting profit.[11] Another Quaker, Peter Collinson, wrote to his friend William Bartram the naturalist in 1763 condemning the avaricious nature of Americans in general and finding particular fault with the shameless deceit of the infamous Pennsylvania "Walking Purchase" of Indian lands: "We, every manner of way, trick, cheat, and abuse these Indians with impunity. . . . I could fill this letter with our arbitrary proceedings, all the colonies through; with our arbitrary, illegal taking their lands from them, making them drunk, and cheating them of their property."[12] Francis Daniel Pastorius, the founder of Germantown, prayed that God would rid Pennsylvania of such human "chaff" as the "coiners of false money and other persons."[13] In "The Sot-Weed Factor" (1708), Ebenezer Cooke satirized the prevalence in Maryland of deception, dishonesty, unscrupulousness, and licentiousness.

> Many Canniballs transported o'er the Sea
> Prey on these Slaves, as they have done on me.
> May they turn Savage, or as *Indians* wild,
> From Trade, Converse, and Happiness exild,
> Where no Man's Faithful, nor a Woman Chast.[14]

These complaints pale by comparison with the wholesale looting practiced by John Robinson; during his eighteenth-century governmental career Robinson drained more than £100,000 from the treasury of Virginia through schemes including the recirculation of paper notes he was required to destroy.[15] The lucrative customs of land-grabbing, speculation in specie, smuggling, vote-buying, and bribe-taking have been well documented throughout the colonies, while the Georgia legislature itself played a game of fast and loose with the 1795 sale of Yazoo land for millions of dollars.[16] In this atmosphere, new fortunes could be quickly amassed, though it was equally true that the New World could as rapidly strip the newly rich of their wealth.

The New World also sanctioned the complementary impulses of self-definition and self-promotion. The art of putting the best appearance forward can be seen in the competing versions of events recorded by William Bradford in *Of Plymouth Plantation* and by Thomas Morton in *The New English Canaan*, while Captain John Smith's *General History of Virginia*, William Byrd's *History of the Dividing Line*, and Benjamin Franklin's *Autobiography* are not only public accounts but also personal documents advancing complimentary images of their authors. The self-posturing of Franklin, moreover, cre-

ated an imitable model for Americans continuing throughout
the nineteenth century. Franklin's methods, intentions, and
attitudes therefore bear close examination. They reveal themselves in his defense of the minister Hemphill, who to Franklin's delight preached practical sermons on the virtue of good
works.

> One of our Adversaries having heard him preach a Sermon that
> was much admired, thought he had somewhere read that Ser-
> mon before, or at least a part of it. On Search he found that
> Part quoted in one of the British Reviews, from a Discourse of
> Dr. Forster's. This Detection gave many of our Party Disgust,
> who accordingly abandoned his Cause and occasion'd our
> more speedy Discomfiture in the Synod. I stuck by him how-
> ever, as I rather approv'd his giving us good Sermons compos'd
> by others, than bad ones of his own Manufacture.[17]

Here in Franklin's wry defense of Hemphill we can begin to
see the development of practical benevolence superceding the
Puritan conception of absolute morality. It is a gradual process,
as is shown by those who desert Hemphill, but it is steady.
Just as Mather could recognize more human complexity in the
motivations of a seducer than Bradford, so too can Franklin
see with more detachment the act of sermon-stealing. To
Franklin, Hemphill is no descendant of Mather's "Wolves."

The self-conscious irony implied by moral relativism leads
Franklin himself to assume the appearance of virtues when he
cannot muster their reality, to burn his lamp at night later
than his rivals, and to translate Cotton Mather's *Essays To Do
Good* into a secular program of self-improvement. Richard B.
Hauck, noting that Franklin "could con the troops into attending prayer meetings, or he could con the separated colonies into rebellion," concludes that Franklin is a confidence
man.[18] Hauck overlooks Franklin's benevolence and self-
deprecating sense of play, qualities which distinguish him
from deceivers like Governor Keith, who in the *Autobiography* encourages Franklin to travel to England with the promise
of the governor's letter of credit, a promise he has neither the
intention of keeping nor the funds to make good (93–94).
Whether Franklin cajoles citizens into public works or assists
Quakers to provide money for community defense, his pro-

motions further the goal of social betterment; though he may puff and prance and strut, claiming more personal credit or purity of motive than is his due, the public receives the value of each project.

In addition, Franklin's shape-shifting—when he casts himself as Silence Dogood, Poor Richard, or the star of the *Autobiography*—is a literary activity designed, as he notes of the *Almanac*, to convey "instruction" (164–65). What is important about these personae is not that they are misrepresentations or "false" images, but that through them we can see the tendency of Americans to view themselves with increasing detachment. As Daniel Hoffman points out, by the mideighteenth century "the power of transformation, of self-transformation, is no longer seen as malevolent."[19] Franklin's self-posturing—unlike Morton's or Lyford's—promotes the values of social responsibility and individual industry necessary to nationbuilding. He also marks a divergence from the seventeenth-century attitude that fiction is by definition evil; to improve the self in autobiography is not the work of the devil any more than to counterfeit the language of Silence Dogood is to join the ranks of Mather's "impostors."

These changes in attitude find popular expression around the turn of the century in Royall Tyler's clever Jonathan (*The Contrast*), in the emerging figure of the Yankee, in Hugh Henry Brackenridge's satiric portraits of Americans in *Modern Chivalry*, in Ann Stephens's *Jonathan Slick in New York*, in Seba Smith's Jack Downing, in Thomas Haliburton's Sam Slick, in the oral tales of Mike Fink, Pete Featherton, and Davy Crockett, and in the pages of newspapers like John Neal's *The Yankee*. These appearances share four characteristics: they reveal a new acceptance of fictionmaking as not immoral, they record a new ambivalence toward shiftiness expressed through humor, they register interest in the varieties and vagaries of language, and they suggest the desire stimulated by successful expansion, development, and revolution to create national symbols of American identity. Instructively, each figure is, like Franklin, in part an exercise in self-caricature; Americans have become willing to accept not the saints of Bradford or Mather but self-consciously ironic fictional characters as their literary representatives. Constance Rourke, one of the best readers of the relation between American character and American humor, finds the two intertwined.

> "The comic," says Bergson, "comes into being just when society and the individual, freed from the worry of self-preservation, begin to regard themselves as works of art." With his triumphs fresh and his mind noticeably free, by 1815 the American seemed to regard himself as a work of art, and began that embellished self-portraiture which nations as well as individuals may undertake.[20]

As Rourke demonstrates, figures like the Yankee began as regional types, then evolved into emblems of American character recognized here and abroad. They mark the end of the colonial New World and the start of the American new country, manifest the initial stirrings of the flush-times confidence man, and wryly proffer dead-pan answers to J. Hector St. John de Crèvecoeur's famous question, "What then is the American, this new man?"[21]

The New Country

The impulse toward self-definition visible in the writings of William Bradford, Thomas Morton, John Smith, J. Hector St. John de Crèvecoeur, and Benjamin Franklin, and in the figure of the Yankee and other native types, culminated in the self-assertive visionary rhetoric of the Declaration of Independence.

> We hold these truths to be self-evident, that all men are created equal, that they are endowed by their Creator with certain unalienable Rights, that among these are Life, Liberty and the pursuit of Happiness.

The Declaration and the Revolution clearly set the stage for a new phase of self-definition, what Gary Wills calls the actual invention of America.[22] Although the choice of 1775, 1776, 1783, 1789, or 1800 might be arbitrary, it seems certain that between 1775 and 1815 Old World and colonial perceptions of the New World changed radically. Daniel Boorstin contends that "America grew in the search for community."

> Between the Revolution and the Civil War the young nation flourished not in discovery but in search. It prospered not from

> the perfection of its ways but from their fluidity. It lived with
> the constant belief that something else or something better
> might turn up. . . . Americans were glad enough to keep things
> growing and moving. When before had men put so much faith
> in the unexpected?[23]

Yet alongside this new faith in possibilities grew up a concomitant distrust of the unknown and a desire for the comforts of the familiar. Brilliantly analyzing the rising popular iconography of the Revolution, Michael Kammen charts the development of this complementary impulse: "What is most interesting about the 1820s, perhaps, is the fact that many Americans became engaged, in various ways, upon a quest for political order, social stability, and national identity."[24] In this view Americans sought to make coherent sense of the Revolution, to consolidate its gains and defuse its antisocial energies, to shape the thirteen colonies of the New World into a democratic republic of thirteen united states, a palpable "new country."

The search for identity and order in the early nineteenth century is evidenced by the popularity of Mason Locke Weems's *Life of Washington* (1800); the biography of General Francis Marion, the "Swamp Fox," by Weems and Peter Horry (1810); the *Life and Adventures of John Paul Jones* (1807); William Wirt's *Patrick Henry* (1817); and a host of other Revolutionary War biographies and histories. Taken as a group, works like these codify a vanished past, certify it as heroic in stature, disseminate what Kammen views as a common cultural myth, and form a convenient bridge (especially for post-Revolutionary generations) between the past and the present (and future). Localized events become transformed into a national mythos. The same process is at work in the rapid cultural acceptance of the Yankee, and more directly visible in the immediate triumph of Washington Irving's "Rip Van Winkle" and "The Legend of Sleepy Hollow." The story of Rip Van Winkle does more than fulfill the male fantasy of escaping a shrewish wife and a life of labor; it effects through fiction the disorienting transition from George III to George Washington, dismissing by its nonthreatening fairy-tale form and the humorous detachment of its ironic narration Americans' real or imagined anxieties about life in the new republic. Rip learns—

and conveys to the reader—that his life in the United States will remain essentially the same; any changes—in flags, names, or political institutions—are either superficial or for the better: Rip Van Winkle achieves freedom and ease at Doolittle's Union Hotel.

"The Legend of Sleepy Hollow" has a similar implicit function. The tale first distinguishes between the progressive present and the legendary past, reducing the colonial era and the Revolution to fireside stories or superstitions. Irving views Ichabod Crane's interest in the musty volumes of Cotton Mather's witchcraft accounts as an eccentricity that marks his credulity and, almost tangentially, suggests to the reader the irrelevance or failure of Puritanism. The headless horseman that terrorizes the susceptible schoolmaster, moreover, is not a dreadful presence from the Revolutionary past with which men of the present generation must once again struggle but the projection of Ichabod's overexcited fancy, a manifestation of his own nonutilitarian nature. Brom Bones demonstrates through his manipulation of Ichabod Crane's nightmare that by 1819 (or even by 1789, the ostensible date of the story) Americans should have relegated both Puritan and Revolutionary fears to the realm of history and legend; witches, ghosts, and Hessians haunt only the dreamy—children, women, and Ichabod Crane. The pragmatic nineteenth-century man, like the hearty and industrious Brom Bones, lives in the present, sees the past as superstition, and makes practical use of a hoary specter, harnessing its fantastic energy to vanquish a rival. Brom Bones's comic representation of the ghostly Hessian's head as a pumpkin creates a disjunction between past and present through which the potential terror of a real Hessian trooper is disarmed.

Second, as in "Rip Van Winkle," Irving presents as models for the reader individuals who have become reconciled to nineteenth-century life. Although Brom Bones obviously triumphs over the anemic schoolmaster, marries Katrina Van Tassel, and becomes a gentleman farmer, it is easy to forget that Ichabod Crane may have adjusted to the modern age and achieved a different measure of success. Just before the closing frame Irving's narrator (Diedrich Knickerbocker) recounts that Ichabod appears to have moved to New York City, been admitted to the bar, flirted with politics and the press, and now presides as justice over the Ten Pound Court. By suggesting this destiny for Ichabod Crane, Irving narratively asserts that success is possible for all kinds of men in America, that a heterogeneous society offers flush times to those who will only look to the present and not remain possessed or obsessed by the past.[25] Two diametrically opposed regional types are made into successful fictional emblems of national identity, just as the colonial past and the Hudson River Valley are made into cultural synecdoche for the United States. To identify with either the prankster or the pranked is to discover a viable role to emulate.

One consequence of the success of post-Revolution historical and fictional works seems to have been the reinforcement of a perhaps unconscious geographical demarcation between East and West. Biographies like those of Washington created national myths of (and primarily for) the original thirteen colonies, just as Irving's stories turned the Hudson River into the shared property of American citizens. Along the eastern seaboard established cities symbolized the high culture achieved by the new republic, while to the west (or often to the north or south) existed the new country. Henry Nash Smith writes in *Virgin Land* that "until the very end of the eighteenth century the West beyond the Mississippi was so shadowy and remote that it could be pictured in almost any guise that might occur to a writer's imagination."[26] Without wishing to put undue pressure on the success of Ichabod Crane, it is instructive to recall that he begins a new life in New York City: Ichabod Crane is no Daniel Boone (and neither is Brom Bones a pioneer though he appears more rustic). Irving displays an eastern bias that prevailed for years, the definition of eastern culture against western "wilderness" that seems a corollary of the initial codification of national identity in terms of the Revolutionary past and the early nineteenth-century search for order.

If the Hudson River functions as a familiar locus of order (even producing its own native school of painting), then the Mississippi River serves as a symbol of disorder. The two rivers are in imagination—and for at least a generation in fact—worlds apart. The works of Hugh Henry Brackenridge, Philip

Freneau, William Cullen Bryant, Edgar Allan Poe, James Kirke
Paulding, Washington Irving, and even James Fenimore
Cooper cast the Trans-Allegheny region as howling wilderness
or untapped Eden. As these and a host of lesser writers attempted to create a "native American literature" (as it was
commonly called), a body of work that would compare favor-
ably with the literary heritage of Europe, they sought to dispel
the Old World image of Americans as coonskin-capped savages and therefore produced fictions that were often derivative
in technique, emphasizing the sophistication of the (eastern)
writer, and that in content either sanitized the vast territories
beyond the Allegheny range or reduced their complexity
through conventional labels including the *West*, the *frontier*,
and the *new country*. In the late eighteenth century Crèvecoeur recorded the moral and psychological results of this geo-
graphic division, displaying in his *Letters* an anxiety about the
effects of "the great woods,"[27] while as late as 1849 the Swiss
scientist Arnold Guyot insisted on a form of cultural geography: "Is it not on the shores of the Atlantic that life is developed to its most active, most intense, and most exalted form?
Is this merely a chance consequence of the accidental debar-
kation at that point of the colonists of the Ancient World? No,
gentlemen, brilliant as may be the prospects the West may
aspire to from the exuberance of its soil, life and action will
always point toward the coast."[28] The *West*, the *frontier*, and
the *new country* were essentially iconographic constructions
similar in function to the earlier *New World*, conventions
serving to separate the writer from the terra incognita and to
domesticate the unknown in the act of naming. The geo-
graphic vagueness of these tags formed a large part of their
literary utility. As Edwin Fussell contends,

> Especially in early nineteenth-century American thought and
> expression, the term West is not only all-inclusive but it per-
> petually vacillates between what might be called an absolute
> meaning (location) and what might be called a relative mean-
> ing (direction), the first of which is entirely arbitrary while the
> second is dependent upon the time, the location, and the lin-
> guistic habits of the speaker. . . . The American West is almost
> by definition indefinite and indefinable, or at least changing,
> pluralistic, and ambiguous in significance.[29]

To Hugh Henry Brackenridge the new country is at once the new republic, the sparsely settled region of western Pennsylvania, and the ambiguous, fluid modes of American behavior. And to most nineteenth-century Americans, as Ray Allen Billington demonstrates, the new country and the frontier existed in their minds and vocabularies as a place of uncertain but suspected opportunities for self-advancement.[30] But to effect this exploitation by both settlers and writers, the new country first had to become at least partially known.

The exploration of the new country forms yet another aspect of the nineteenth-century quest for identity, order, and stability. In 1803 the Louisiana Purchase added more than one million square miles to the United States, dwarfing the territories of the Old Southwest and Old Northwest. In addition to stimulating migration into these regions, Jefferson's acquisition of Louisiana and the subsequent expeditions authorized to explore it captured the American imagination with its newness. Lewis and Clark (1804–1806) reported on the new territories to a fascinated eastern audience, bringing back glowing accounts of the possibilities for trapping and trading in the nearly virgin land. Yet Thomas Freeman, Zebulon Montgomery Pike, and Major Stephen H. Long made less successful western expeditions, and in 1823 Long created the myth of the "Great American Desert" that was to plague the Great Plains for decades.[31] These men did not tame the new country but imported notions of its wildness to the East in much the same manner as Crèvecoeur.[32]

Even as migration made these regions secure and stable, the new country remained a land of ambiguous promise, potential hostility, and uncertain social order in the minds of writers. In *Travels in New England and New York* (1821–1822) Timothy Dwight warns pioneers not to be led astray by fantasies: "In certain stages of society the expectations of enterprising men may, with little difficulty, be raised to any imaginable height. Fortunes, they will easily believe, may be amassed at a stroke, without industry or economy, by mere luck, or the energy of superior talents for business."[33] Dwight also cautions the unwary about land speculators and itinerant peddlers, going so far as to claim that "men who begin life with bargaining for small wares will almost invariably become sharpers. . . . Their sobriety is exchanged for cunning, their honesty for imposition, and their decent behavior for coarse impudence."[34] Condemning the immorality and roughness he finds common in his travels, Dwight echoes the arguments and accusations of Crèvecoeur, William Byrd, Charles Woodmason, Timothy Flint, Alexis de Tocqueville, Caroline Kirkland, James Hall, and James Fenimore Cooper. Timothy Flint compiles a list of speculators, robbers, and hostile Indians in his *Condensed Geography and History of the Western States or the Mississippi Valley* (1828), James Hall dramatizes historical river pirates and bloodthirsty savages in his fictionalized *Legends of the West* (1832), while James Fenimore Cooper provides unsettling portraits of backwoodsmen through Richard Jones in *The Pioneers* (1823) and Abiram White in *The Prairie* (1827). Cooper, in fact, offers a model of the ambiguous attitudes held by nineteenth-century Americans. The "*new* States" could nurture a hero as admirable as Natty Bumppo, but they could also produce "swarms of that restless people" who, like Abiram White, are "deluded by their wishes." In addition, Cooper recognizes that Natty Bumppo must die without heirs in *The Prairie*, passing on to Paul Hover last words of advice that are at best ambivalent:

> Much has passed atween us on the pleasures and respectableness of a life in the woods or on the borders. I do not now mean to say that all you have heard is not true; but different tempers call for different employments. You have taken to your bosom, there, a good and kind child, and it has become your duty to consider her, as well as yourself, in setting forth in life. You are a little given to skirting the settlements; but to my poor judgment, the girl would be more like a flourishing flower in the sun of a clearing, than in the winds of a prairie. Therefore forget anything you may have heard from me, which is nevertheless true, and turn your mind on the ways of the inner country.[35]

Truth, like identity and morality, appears to be a relative concept only temporarily fixed.

In the quest for national identity, which often seems as much a linguistic search as a literal one, the value of the new country resides in its ability to contain and express contradictory truths. As used by Hugh Henry Brackenridge, Daniel

Drake, Johnson Jones Hooper, Joseph Glover Baldwin, George Washington Harris, Herman Melville, Mark Twain, and William Dean Howells (to list a few), the term *new country* throughout the nineteenth century subsumes the definitions of the *frontier* and the *West* advocated by Ray Allen Billington and Edwin Fussell;[36] it is potential, opportunity, change itself. "In America," the panorama painter John Rawson Smith declaimed, "the country itself is ever on the change, and in another half century those who view this portrait of the Mississippi will not be able to recognize one twentieth of its details."[37] An Ohio Valley pioneer in the 1830s noted that the settlers themselves embodied contradictions: "The people of the west, viewed as individuals, resemble the inhabitants of almost every clime; but taken as a whole, they are unlike every people under heaven. . . . Everything is new, just coming into existence."[38] These sentiments form a nineteenth-century refrain, as in the words of a new arrival in Michigan: "Language, ideas, manners, customs—all are new."[39]

The new country functions throughout the century as a psychic landscape, a projection of American hopes and fears. On the one hand, as Daniel Boorstin argues,

> a great resource of America was vagueness. American uncertainties, products of ignorance and progress, were producers of optimism and energy. Although few acknowledged it, in the era between the Revolution and the Civil War this vagueness was a source of American strength. Americans were already distinguished less by what they clearly knew or definitely believed than by their grand and fluid hopes.[40]

The sense of possibility could stimulate development and industry. Before midcentury the Cumberland Road, the Erie Canal, the Baltimore & Ohio Railroad, and myriad other transportation projects triggered large-scale migrations to the West and brought the flush times to the new country. Americans could build a new and better life in the Old Southwest or Old Northwest, believing that the newness of the land and the process of migration would transubstantiate their dreams into realities; when after 1820 a man could buy as little as eighty acres at $1.25 per acre, it seemed obvious to thousands of pioneers that the nineteenth-century way to wealth lay to the west. Especially following the panics of 1819, 1837, 1857, and

1873, Americans anxious to leave behind lagging economic conditions or personal failures traveled to the new country, creating a unique state of affairs Boorstin calls settlement before discovery. Migration meant rebirth, renewal, and personal success. The pioneer participated in a vast creative enterprise that was at its best uplifting and fulfilling. In books like Caroline Kirkland's *A New Home—Who'll Follow?* (1839) the spirit of enthusiasm is contagious, and even when she criticizes the roughness of conditions in Michigan or the morals of her neighbors, she remains guardedly optimistic about the new country.

On the other hand, new settlers *were* traveling into the unknown and often keenly felt the pressures of uncertainty. The very conditions that encouraged migration, development, and confidence also fostered speculation, boosterism, and suspicion. The new arrival without land, job, or home made easy prey for the unscrupulous. The greenhorn might, like the comic butt of George P. Morris's story "The Little Frenchman and His Water-Lots" (1839), be tricked into buying worthless swampland or a homestead controlled by determined squatters.[41] Squatters comprised two-thirds of the population of Illinois in 1828, and claim-jumping and preemption were widespread. Moral and legal confusion reigned. In *Western Clearings* (1845) Caroline Kirkland describes the distrust and animosity "new-country-folks" held toward "land-sharks," "land-lookers," and "land-hunters"; the reason for conflict she locates in competition during the "madness of speculation"—"land-fever." "The whirl, the fervor, the flutter, the rapidity of step, the sparkling of eyes, the beating of hearts, the striking of hands, the utter *abandon* of the hour, were incredible, inconceivable. . . . He who had no money, begged, borrowed, or stole it; he who had, thought he made a generous sacrifice, if he lent it at cent per cent."[42]

In the 1850s in Kansas, land fever, speculation, and chicanery became so intense, reports Albert D. Richardson, that "it was not a swindle but a mania. The speculators were quite as insane as the rest."[43] To the acute observer Alexis de Tocqueville this climate was to be expected, directly attributable to the moral character of pioneers.

> Those Americans who go out far away from the Atlantic
> Ocean, plunging into the West, are adventurers impatient of
> any sort of yoke, greedy for wealth, and often outcasts. . . .
> *There is nothing of tradition, family feeling, or example to
> restrain them.* Laws have little sway over them, and mores
> still less.[44]

The new country often appeared a fictional territory inhabited
by picaros.

The anxieties engendered by this atmosphere were height-
ened by historical conditions: Indian wars, bank failures, or
market declines could extinguish the dreams of both speculator and settler overnight. In addition to these potential dangers, the memory of past reversals lingered in the popular
imagination; if an individual had not suffered bankruptcy
himself, he had at least felt the effects of national panics.
Though all were well today, could ruin be far behind? For the
flush times seemed naturally to be followed by hard times, the
fluctuations from boom to bust forming an apparently inevitable historical cycle. The specter of failure—side by side with
the dream of success—haunted the new country. Just as uncertainty served as one antidote to optimism, so too did the
transient's vulnerability mar the dream. Despite the threat of
robbers, swindlers, hostile Indians, illness, accident, extremes
of climate, and self-delusion, migration continued, fueled by
either the optimism of a boom or the pessimism of a bust, by
the rumors of gold in 1849 or of diamonds in 1872, by the offer
of cheap homesteads in 1862 or of free Indian lands in 1889,
and primarily throughout the century by the persistent belief
that the new country would in fact make one's fortune. As one
early nineteenth-century pioneer phrased it, "this is a land of
plenty, but we are proceeding to a land of abundance."[45] Pessimism kept alive the myth of the Great American Desert at
the same time that optimism fostered the myth of the American Paradise.

The Confidence Man

The alternating attitudes of optimism and pessimism found
reconciliation in conventional images like that of the new
country. The inclusiveness or vagueness of this term mini-

mized the discrepancies between known and unknown, imposed rhetorical order on potential chaos, and structured the uncertain into a familiar literary form. Through the Adamic act of naming, the wildness of the new country was partially domesticated, constraining the unknown to function as both an emblem of American fears and a repository of American aspirations. As a convention the new country safely channeled anxiety and desire.

In the early nineteenth century Americans embraced George Washington and Davy Crockett as representative ideals. As archetypes of heroic American character, they symbolize the ability of Americans to organize, interpret, and survive the unknown, to form the unformed into stability and order. As imitable models, however, George Washington and Davy Crockett seem to represent antithetical attitudes: Washington was enshrined in serious works as the first American president, the father of the United States, an educated intellectual, and a paragon of honesty; Crockett was celebrated in humorous subliterature as a frontier individualist, a citizen of the backwoods, a know-nothing of horse sense, and a model of shiftiness.[46] Together they seem to form an uneasy resolution of conflicting aspects of American identity; in the cities of the East, honesty is the best policy, while in the new country of the West, dishonesty and cunning are to be employed.

In Cooper's Natty Bumppo these contradictory virtues are clearly dramatized in one individual: be true when you can, and always in the clearings, but be tricky when you must, and especially in the wilderness. In addition to advocating two antithetical modes of behavior, which as we have seen Leatherstocking categorizes as two truths, Natty Bumppo embodies a vanished ideal, one that Cooper's novels demonstrate to be inadequate to post-1820s conditions. (Both Leatherstocking and Washington die before 1800, and Crockett becomes a martyr at the Alamo in 1836). All three are in fact anachronistic idealizations, not reconciling but avoiding anxieties produced by the evolving new country. Washington clearly has little to do with this territory, and Crockett—despite his legislative serivce—is, like Leatherstocking, bound in the popular imagination to the wilderness of bears, Indians, and individual acts of heroism. With increasing migration to, settlement of, and development within the new country, backwoods archetypes like Crockett and Leatherstocking continue to battle elemental forces; they are, however, an expression of a nostalgic impulse, and by the 1840s must make room for other figures representing new social conditions. Crockett himself offers a clue to the form one new figure will take; the common denominator among the Crockett tales, annuals, biographies, and autobiographies is humor.

Daniel Boorstin persuasively argues that the same qualities that make Crockett and other frontier heroes heroic also make them comic.

> The pervasive ambiguity of American life, the vagueness which laid the continent open to adventure, which made the land a rich storehouse of the unexpected, which kept vocabulary ungoverned and the language fluid—this same vagueness suffused both the comic and the heroic. Both depended on incongruity: the incongruity of the laughable and the incongruity of the admirable. In a world full of the unexpected, where all norms were vaguely or extravagantly defined, readers of the Crockett legends were never quite certain whether to laugh or to applaud, whether what they saw and heard was wonderful, awful, or ridiculous.[47]

Two points need to be emphasized about these popular superheroes. First, Davy Crockett remains throughout the century a hero of the wild, a man who singlehandedly unfreezes the sun on the coldest day of the year; his apotheosis at the Alamo in 1836 fixes him in a mythic realm well beyond the experience of all but a few Americans. Second, the humor of incongruity and exaggeration, so much a part of the Crockett tradition (and so absent from the Leatherstocking novels), develops in the subliterature of the Old Southwest and functions as a means of displacing anxieties. Humor reconciles Americans to the 1840s new country.

As American society developed in the Old Southwest, the uncertainties of the new country became less elemental than social. In the 1840s, for example, fear of war with Indians seemed less likely than war with Mexico, while cyclones seemed less threatening than economic cycles. In this newly uncertain new country, conditions inverted traditional archetypes and engendered an antihero of society, the confidence man. Emerging as a local phenomenon in the humorous fic-

tions of the Old Southwest, the confidence man personifies
the ambiguities of the new country in a nonthreatening form.
He gives substance to the ambivalent American attitudes toward the flush times by enacting in his "snaps" individual
dramas of boom and bust. Through artful fast talk he elicits
the confidence of opportunistic optimists, manipulating the
counters of confidence, optimism, opportunity, and greed until his victims are fleeced. Like the new country, the confidence man seems to offer wealth, comfort, and success to
those sharp enough to seize these elusive rewards; that he consistently betrays the confidence placed in him, that he appears
buoyed by optimism while his gulls seem pulled under by
skeptical pessimism, that his victims function as representative Americans, express deep nineteenth-century anxieties
about the possibility of realizing the dream of success in the
new country and about the integrity of public myths of moral
American character. The reader laughs at the confidence
man's ingenuity, at his delight in profitable masquerade, at his
victims' infinite avariciousness, at their easy manipulation,
and, for a moment, admits and enjoys an anti-Adamic and
anti-Edenic image of himself and of the new country.

Johnson Jones Hooper introduced to the nation one of the
first fully articulated confidence men in *Some Adventures of
Captain Simon Suggs*. Simon Suggs struck a responsive chord
in 1845 when he advised that "IT IS GOOD TO BE SHIFTY IN A
NEW COUNTRY."[48] As elaborated by Hooper, the confidence
man is a representative man of a marginal society; Simon
Suggs exploits a new country characterized by greed, hypocrisy, and shiftiness. The confidence man's roles form a catalogue of flush times activities: Suggs's career includes bouts
as card sharp, speculator, politician, war hero, Indian fighter,
camp-meeting enthusiast, and slave trader. Hooper's confidence man acts as an index to nineteenth-century anxieties:
he realizes in a comedic structure an increasing cultural nervousness about such broad issues as the future of the new
country, the multiplicity of identity, the difficulty of distinguishing reality from appearance and morality from hypocrisy,
and the cultural ramifications of manifest destiny and urbanization; analyzed more narrowly, the confidence man gives
voice to a long list of specific fears including that of war (with

Mexico, with England, or among states), of increased Indian hostilities (as well as of Indian extermination), of public protestations of morality and the private practice of immorality, of repeated panics and national failure, of the implications of mob rule inherent in Jacksonian democracy, of a conflict between the increasing powers of the federal government and the rights of states, and of the sectional, economic, and social tensions caused by slavery.

Captain Simon Suggs gives shape to these anxieties; Johnson J. Hooper imposes the order of comedy upon the chaos of these cultural fears, temporarily resolving them for the reader, dispelling them in laughter. In the humorous successes and failures of the confidence man, the reader perceives a fictional model of boom and bust, one that allows him to reconcile antithetical attitudes of hope and fear, confidence and suspicion, and optimism and pessimism. The reader is safely distanced from the immorality of the confidence man and his victims by being aligned with Hooper's ironic, cultured narrator. With the exception of the frame-narrator, all Hooper's characters are "low," morally despicable types who inhabit a degenerate, fictive new country. Within this controlled fictive arena, Simon Suggs unmasks through masquerade and fast talk the hypocrisy and greed of his victims; carefully distanced from these shenanigans—by point of view and by a language unavailable to Hooper's characters, to name two devices—the reader can enjoy the artful antics of the confidence man in Hooper's fiction while condemning similar snaps in reality. As Hooper shares with the reader the mechanics of Simon's games, the reader is enlisted as the confidence man's silent partner. The novelty of this position dulls the reader's judgment of the confidence man and momentarily encourages the reader to laugh at the fleecing of self-serving or self-righteous gulls. To participate imaginatively in such humorous confidence games allows the reader to envision the worst image of Americans within the safe confines of comic fiction and to discharge the anxieties this image creates through laughter at the apparent poetic justice dispensed by the confidence man in Hooper's narrow focus on a highly exaggerated, stylized, corrupt new country. The specters of ambiguity, immorality, and betrayal are raised by the fiction and are dispelled

by the technique of a tightly controlled humorous world. Like
a tall tale of a backwoods hero lassoing and riding a cyclone, a
confidence man story images and domesticates the reader's
real fears.

The difficulty in isolating the confidence man as a literary
convention occurs for a variety of reasons: the figure rises to
prominence in a period marked by literary experimentation,
the "American Renaissance"; the confidence man develops
through the interaction of fictional and historical sources and
remains in the American mind as a cultural as well as a literary convention; the convention evolves within the informal,
regional genre of Southwest humor; throughout the nineteenth century, writers continue to employ characters like the
Yankee, the prankster, and the peddler, which had contributed
to the formation of the confidence man; and modern scholars
have been too quick to label all "shifty" American characters
"confidence men," an act of retrospective naming that blurs
the distinitions of form and function which literary historians
should seek to clarify.

Gary Lindberg, in the most recent and most comprehensive
study of American confidence men, concludes that the confidence man is a central but covert culture hero. Despite admirable analyses of shifty promissory language and gesture in
numerous sources from Emerson and Thoreau to Melville and
Barth, Lindberg throws such a large net that he fails to catch
the essential conventional nature of the American confidence
man as a distinct literary form. Susan Kuhlmann limits the
usefulness of *Knave, Fool, and Genius: The Confidence Man
As He Appears in Nineteenth-Century American Fiction* by
linking such diverse characters as Chaucer's Canon, Hooper's
Simon Suggs, and James's Madame Merle and by treating peripheral figures (owing more to other modes) like Hawthorne's
Westervelt as having a central place in the confidence man
tradition. Richard B. Hauck similarly groups John Smith, Benjamin Franklin, Simon Suggs, and Elmer Gantry and ultimately subsumes these varied types under the rubric of "the
absurd." Warwick Wadlington focuses exclusively on the ne-
gotiation of confidence between author and reader in Melville,
Twain, and West, while John Blair moves abruptly from Melville to five twentieth-century authors to chart "a cycle of

moral revaluation" in *The Confidence Man in Modern Fiction*.[49] Although most admit that the New World intensified both physical and metaphysical uncertainties, and that the flush times bred predators in many forms, critics have been unable or unwilling to distinguish between a universal pattern of blustering fast talk or deceitful manipulation and its particular American variation—the confidence man as a humorous literary convention, representative, master, and survivor of the nineteenth-century new country. Tricksters, promisers, shape-shifters, and rogues appear in many genres and periods, but the American confidence man emerges as a distinct literary convention defined by the new country, the 1830s and 1840s flush times, the genre of Southwest humor, and initially a cardinal motive: pursuit of personal profit.

P. T. Barnum serves as a useful point of reference in discussing American attitudes toward confidence, shiftiness, and the new country. His life from 1810 to 1891 nearly parallels the rise, fall, and reemergence of the confidence man as a literary convention, and his autobiography, in which he revealed his motives and techniques, was a popular bestseller for forty years following its publication in 1855. Barnum achieved the success, wealth, influence, and public notoriety dreamed of by fictional confidence men like Hooper's Simon Suggs, Baldwin's Ovid Bolus, and Melville's Cosmopolitan; adopting roles of increasing visibility and prominence—from peddler to editor to showman to legislator—he adapted himself as few literary confidence men could to changing conditions throughout the nineteenth century. Envisioning America as a continually self-renewing, exploitable new country, Barnum operated within a tradition given explicit statement by Brackenridge in *Modern Chivalry*: "Si populus vult decipi, decipiatur";[50] or, in Barnum's own more popular style, "When people expect to get 'something for nothing' they are sure to be cheated, and generally deserve to be."[51] Though he claimed to be no more than an honest showman, to the nineteenth century he appeared a culture hero, a public symbol of humbug, humor, profit, and success. At the height of his career, Barnum had his emblematic nature analyzed by a perceptive Englishman: "Barnum is not an ordinary showman. . . . He stands alone. Adopting Mr. Emerson's idea, I should say that Barnum

is a representative man. He represents the enterprise and energy of his countrymen in the 19th century, as Washington
represented their resistance to oppression in the century pre-
ceding."[52] Neil Harris, in a fine study of the showman, con-
curs and argues that Barnum's autobiography should be read
as "a text on the social functions of illusion and the role of a
deceiver in an egalitarian society."

> Credulity and deceit, disguise and sincerity, hypocrisy and
> idealism, art and artifice were subjects of critical importance
> in a society that had abandoned traditional rituals of accredi-
> tation. Antebellum Americans worshipped both equality and
> achievement. . . .
>
> Barnum's exaggerations and confessions, his humbugs and
> deceits, were the dreams of many Americans who could not
> try them. His audacity in donning the mantle of morality ap-
> pealed to Americans convinced that the older boundaries of
> human behavior were no longer valid, but who dared not over-
> step these limits themselves. Barnum was not merely a Trick-
> ster . . . he had become one of the lightning rods of the Amer-
> ican imagination, drawing off the anger of the gods from the
> community's sins to himself. And his wealth and success sug-
> gested that divine wrath did not always punish outrageous in-
> dulgence.[53]

In this context Barnum seems analogous to Simon Suggs and
his compatriots. Within nineteenth-century America's moralistic, industrious society, they function as antiheroes who
humorously and harmlessly pervert, invert, manipulate, or ex-
aggerate its official values and goals. They embody and vent,
not unlike the Elizabethan fool, anxieties Americans share
about the future, the new country, and themselves.

The similarities between P. T. Barnum and Simon Suggs are
often striking. Both seek to profit from artful fast talk and self-
promotion; delight in humorous strategems and skillful manipulations; make book on the defensive virtues of skepticism, cynicism, and distrust; maintain an apparent optimism
and boldly survive; and successfully market the novelty of the
new country to an eager audience. Barnum's successes, bank-
ruptcies, and adaptations trace as well the familiar pattern of
boom and bust, while his technical disclosures of his own
humbugs—and the complicity he demanded of the public
(which should judge for itself)—continued debate of the mer-

its, motives, limits, and determinability of shiftiness and honesty, appearance and reality, that had long been part of discussions on the American character. Charles Dickens echoed the confusion in the minds of many Europeans about American identity when he isolated at the heart of Americans a sense of "universal distrust": "You will strain at a gnat in the way of trustfulness and confidence, however fairly won and well deserved, but you will swallow a whole caravan of camels, if they be laden with unworthy doubts and mean suspicions."[54] Barnum effectively resolved contradictory attitudes by demonstrating that Americans perceived no conflict; credulity and skepticism, immorality and morality, pseudo-science and science, humor and profit were through style inextricably linked and mutually supportive. Uncertainty held the special attraction of novelty, and the challenge to discriminate personally between fiction and fact appears to have been irresistible in the land of self-reliant democratic individualism. The new country, P. T. Barnum, and Simon Suggs all encouraged Americans to trust and test their own abilities, offering as a reward confirmation of one's superiority in an ideally classless, protean society. Neil Harris speculates that "concentration on whether a particular show, exhibit, or event was real or fake, genuine or contrived, narrowed the task of judgment for the multitude of spectators. It structured problems of experiencing the exotic and unfamiliar by reducing that experience to a simple evaluation."[55] Walter Blair and Hamlin Hill add that figures such as Barnum and Suggs reveal the American admiration of expertise, technique, and success without moral reflection.[56] In fact, nineteenth-century Americans seemed especially to enjoy successful cons; they enjoyed the direct challenge to their intellects and sensibilities, the chance to debunk and unmask fraud, the lively controversy aroused, the ingenuity of hoaxes and harmless tricks, and, perhaps most important and most particularly American, they enjoyed that which was new.

In 1843 Barnum anonymously offered New Yorkers the opportunity to witness a real, wild-West buffalo hunt at Hoboken, New Jersey, free of charge. Although Barnum did contract in advance with the ferry-boat captains (who did a land-office business between New York and New Jersey) to split their fares with him that day, and although the buffalo herd was less wild than woolly, the service he performed in introducing city folk to these mythic denizens of the new country was appreciated by most in attendance. N. P. Willis reported that one passenger on a returning ferry warned those just coming in that the event was " 'the biggest humbug you ever heard of!' Willis added, that the passengers on the boat with him were so delighted, that they instantly gave three cheers for the author of the humbug, whoever he might be."[57] The audacity of the performance, not to mention its scope, makes it fascinating and hence successful. Thus might be explained Barnum's success in displaying Joice Heth, the supposedly 161-year-old nurse of George Washington, or the fabulous Feejee Mermaid mummy, which had the head of a monkey and the lower body of a fish. And like the confidence man who piques the interest of his audience by flashing real gold before their eyes, Barnum often presented real wonders, including Jenny Lind, the "Swedish Nightingale," Chang and Eng the Siamese twins, "General" Tom Thumb, and the enormous Jumbo the elephant, to command attention.

Yet if Barnum seems analogous to Simon Suggs, under closer scrutiny he is more the showman he professed to be than the confidence man modern critics insist he is. In his own exposé of nineteenth-century frauds, *The Humbugs of the World* (1865), Barnum unironically lectures Americans on the need for confidence, concluding that the man without confidence does not recognize "that every sham shows that there is a reality, and that hypocrisy is the homage that vice pays to virtue."[58] Without taking Barnum too literally, just to be safe, it seems nevertheless true that the essence of P. T. Barnum is to be found in the more accurate analogy to Johnson Jones Hooper. Susan Kuhlmann implicitly makes this connection in her chapter "The Fictive Imagination as a 'Useful Art,' "[59] but she fails to follow its implications to conclusion. Fictionmaking was an acceptable form of deceit in the nineteenth century, yet Barnum and Suggs appear in the final analysis to be second cousins while Barnum and Hooper appear genuinely to be first. The showman is like Hooper in complete control of his performers; he offers the public a familiar, clearly limited arena—Barnum's American Museum and

Hooper's *Adventures of Captain Simon Suggs*—in which to delve for amusement and for escape from the monotony of reality. The confidence man, on the other hand, promises reality in the form of tangible profit. Barnum's point of view is Hooper's, one the audience essentially shares from a comfortable distance outside the aesthetic structure: questions of morality are left behind upon entering the American Museum and *Simon Suggs*; for the duration, the audience agrees to subscribe to the playful rules of a ritual, conventional game. Through the security of a controlling point of view, both Barnum and Hooper engage and maintain attention; their often ironic tone and their mockery of their performers further strengthens the bond between showman-author and audience. In each case the public is restrained from condemnation through this invitation to superiority, through the insistence on the humor and harmlessness of the spectacle, and through the revelations of manipulation freely given by Barnum in his autobiography and by Hooper throughout. The confidence man depends on secrecy and anonymity; the showman and author trade on notoriety and exposure.

In addition, Barnum and Hooper bring the ambiguities and oddities of the new country to a national audience: Joice Heth, Colonel Fremont's "woolly horse," and the western buffalo hunt have this in common with the shifty Simon Suggs, hardshell preachers, and land speculators. Unlike the confidence man, Barnum and Hooper make no attempt to enlist the greed of the public; both provide entertainment for a set price. And finally, the world of Barnum's American Museum is clearly a fantastic creation, an aesthetic world which, like Hooper's fictional world, poses as an alternative universe. Both establish what Johan Huizinga terms a "play-ground," within which "an absolute and peculiar order reigns."[60] Huizinga argues in *Homo Ludens*:

> Into an imperfect world and into the confusion of life [play] brings a temporary, a limited perfection. . . .
> The element of tension in play . . . plays a particularly important part. Tension means uncertainty, chanciness; a striving to decide the issue and so end it. . . . Though play as such is outside the range of good and bad, the element of tension imparts to it a certain ethical value in so far as it means a testing of the player's prowess.[61]

The tension and uncertainty experienced by Barnum's and Hooper's audience is of a different order than that felt by Simon Suggs's victims; the audience consciously and deliberately seeks out the experience and consents to it, while the victims of the confidence man are unwilling and unknowing participants in his performance. And of course at any moment Barnum's spectator can leave the American Museum just as Hooper's reader can put down *Simon Suggs*, whereas the fictional Simon Suggs inhabits a restricted, self-enclosed realm that has no exit and is self-referential.

Without I hope appearing to play fast and loose myself, I have been insisting on the distinction between fictional confidence men and historical confidence-man-like analogues. Though fiction-writer and showman may in fact be acceptable cultural versions of fictional confidence men in the nineteenth century (or vice versa), and though historical figures are useful in locating the popular appeal of characters such as Simon Suggs, it is important to see that the confidence man evolves as a distinct convention of American literature and must be studied as an aesthetic form within that culture to which it is a response and of which it is an expression. To quote Melville's narrator in *The Confidence-Man*, "It is with fiction as with religion: it should present another world, and yet one to which we feel the tie."[62]

2 THE EARLY TRADITION OF CONFIDENCE GAMES

> Here's for the plain old Adam, the
> simple genuine self against the whole
> world.
>
> —Ralph Waldo Emerson, *Journals*

> All falsehoods, all vices seen at
> sufficient distance . . . become
> ludicrous.
>
> —Ralph Waldo Emerson, "The
> Comic"

Hugh Henry Brackenridge's *Modern Chivalry* (1792–1815) and Augustus Baldwin Longstreet's *Georgia Scenes* (1835) survey the loose tradition of tricksters and confidence games that contributed to the creation of the American confidence man as a literary convention symbolizing the southwestern flush times. *Modern Chivalry* recapitulates the traditional literary forms available to writers in their attempts to apprehend the new country, while *Georgia Scenes* reveals the struggles of nineteenth-century writers to develop new literary techniques and new stereotypes of American character. During the twenty years that separate these works there emerged a growing acceptance of American shiftiness, an increasing literary independence, and an informal new genre of American fiction.

Modern Chivalry

In *Modern Chivalry*, Hugh Henry Brackenridge offers a catalogue of early American confidence games which have their roots in sources as diverse as Elizabethan drama and Puritan demonology. He pictures the new country as encouraging ambiguity, confusion, corruption, and autotheism, and he presents the confidence game as a satiric model of democratic society. In addition, Brackenridge expresses common anxieties of educated Americans about the future of the new republic during its transition from Puritan theocracy to political democracy.[1] Even as it exposes discrepancies between the real and ideal in American society, *Modern Chivalry* allows the reader to discharge in laughter the tensions this gap creates by employing the traditional and therefore reassuring form of the humorous picaresque.

In chapter 1, Capt. John Farrago is mistaken for a biter by a gaggle of jockeys. Brackenridge plays on the reader's recognition of Farrago as a harmless Don Quixote to suggest the equivocal nature of identity in the new country. The jockeys—stock characters in the *Spectator* tradition, "a class of people not far removed from the sagacity of a good horse"[2]—reinforce this theme by their belief "that there is no trusting appearances" and that Farrago must be something other than a gentleman: "For they could have no idea, that a man could come there in so singular a manner, with a groom at his foot, unless he had some great object of making money by the adventure. Under this idea, they began to interrogate him with respect to the blood and pedigree of his horse" (7). Their assumption that pedigree determines value spurs Farrago to lecture.

> —Gentlemen, said he, it is a strange thing that you suppose that it is of any consequence what may be the pedigree of a horse. For even in men it is of no avail. Do we not find that sages have had blockheads for their sons; and that blockheads have had sages? (7)

Captain Farrago's argument is rigorously democratic, yet the implications of his reasoning escape notice: pedigree and appearance, two criteria used to determine identity and value in the Old World, are untrustworthy in the New. Like each horse, each man must be tested individually. The jockeys, who come to believe Farrago not a clever sharper but a pedantic fool, fail to recognize that he proves cause for their initial suspicions. That he is neither a biter nor a fool establishes in this first episode the uncertainty of identity, the slipperiness of language, and the limitations of perception. His misapprehension as a biter suggests several things about American society: first, the figure of the biter is familiar to the reader; second, the problem of ascertaining identity, made more difficult by the mobility of an increasing population, is so acute that it is commonly assumed that every stranger is a biter; and third, by the late eighteenth century the biter is no longer merely a historical exemplum of vice but a device of the fiction writer. Neither moral nor immoral, the biter is a rhetorical construction that has independent aesthetic value; as if to confirm that the biter is in fact a literary device, Farrago is only a biter in the jockeys' imaginations and, for an instant, in Brackenridge's prose.

The reader's guide on this journey is Brackenridge's narrator, an observer of American eccentrics who goodnaturedly admonishes Farrago, Teague, and the other characters in a normative language instilling confidence; classical and homespun maxims dot his narrative, confirming his position as a cultured rationalist. As the captain examines the institutions of the new republic, he also explores its literary possibilities, incorporating sermons, tracts, historical sketches, and tall tales in his picaresque. Although his survey of literary genres echoes Farrago's tour, the narrator is no American Quixote but an enlightened gentleman whose morals, humor, and discretion mirror those of his intended audience.

In a typical adventure, Captain Farrago is approached by an entrepreneur who wishes to masquerade Teague as a Kickapoo Indian chief. "I confide in your good sense," the sharper tells the captain, "and have occasion for your servant" (56); Irishmen, Dutchmen, and other men with accents counterfeit Indian leaders, make treaties with federal commissioners, and divide the goods intended to prevent Indian warfare. "Is it possible," Farrago asks, "that such deception can be practised in a new country?" (56). This confidence game suggests that appearances are untrustworthy, that Americans make profits from immoral activities, that the republic's officials are either knaves or fools, and that the occasional biters of earlier periods have become organized and commonplace: "These things are now reduced to a system; and it is so well known to those who are engaged in the traffic, that we think nothing of it. . . . This being the case, it can be no harm to make a farce of the whole matter; or rather a profit of it" (57). The treatymaker exhibits a characteristic interest of the age in mechanics rather than morals: recognizing the discrepancies between appearance and reality, language and act, intention and result, he seeks not to unite them in Puritan fashion into one moral vision or truth but to exploit these differences for personal profit. Concerned with creating his own way to wealth, he considers financial success proof of the virtue of manipulation.

Brackenridge pictures the processes of democratic government as appearances that mask elaborate confidence games. Style, rather than substance, is all-important on the frontier; as if in perverse imitation of Benjamin Franklin, the treatymaker puts on the appearance of good works, satisfying both himself and the legislative guardians of democracy. He is able to masquerade Irishmen as Indians because identity is uncertain, because language is merely style, and because everyone has come to the new country with "some great object of making money by the adventure" (7). In this society, Farrago the idealist is deluded, while the sharper follows the norm in pursuit of the real—money. Americans neither want nor need the unpleasantness of truth, but seek the smooth assurance of style.

Captain Farrago is himself fascinated by the sharper's style, inquiring how Irish can be passed off as Kickapoo, and reveals the ease with which a man of morals can become caught up in discovering practical solutions. He recognizes that the treatymaker is not confused or disheartened by the ambiguities of the frontier, that he confidently puts them to a personally rewarding purpose, and that his scheme is a systematic program—not unlike Franklin's—for insuring survival and wealth. To dissuade Teague from becoming a partner in the swindle, the captain adopts a version of the confidence game: he, too, manipulates through misrepresentation, picturing to Teague the pain he will endure by being scalped, rather than the profit he will enjoy scalping the government.

> "There has been a man here with me, that carries on a trade with the Indians, and tells me that red-headed scalps are in great demand with them. . . . The taking off the scalp will not give much pain, it is so dextrously done by them with a crooked knife they have for that purpose. The mode of taking off the scalp is this; you lie down upon your back; a warrior puts his feet upon your shoulders, collects your hair in his left hand, and drawing a circle with the knife in his right, makes the incision, and, with a sudden pull, separates it from the head, giving, in the mean time, what is called the scalp yell. The thing is done in such an instant, that, the pain is scarcely

felt. He offered me an 100 dollars, if I would have it taken off
for his use, giving me directions, in the mean time, how to
stretch it and dry it on a hoop. . . . He talked to me something
of making you a king of the Kickapoos, after the scalp is off;
but I would not count on that so much; because words are but
wind." (58–59)

This is not unlike Bradford representing Thomas Morton as a
devil, or Captain John Smith embellishing the dramatic story
of his rescue by Pocahontas. Teague, who believes Farrago's
words to be more than wind, is easily deceived: "Dear master,
vid you trow me into ridicule, and de blessed shalvation of my
life, and all dat I have in de vorld, to be trown like a dog to de
savages, and have my flesh torn out of my head . . . for an 100
dollars or the like?" (59).

The answer is "Of course not"—Farrago is like Franklin a
benevolent deceiver, one who subjects Teague to imaginary
pain in order to protect society from actual harm. The captain
adopts the sharper's method to create a literary image of a
common fear—that of being scalped—to instruct Teague as
Brackenridge instructs the reader. Farrago's minute description is amusing to the reader, for unlike the bog-trotter, he
knows it is merely a tall tale. As fictional analogues of the
reader's own anxieties, these literary confidence games function as humorous devices to divert attention from horrifying
possibilities to harmless, rhetorical resolutions. The dangers
of violence and fraud are defused because the reader concen-
trates on the clever technique of the treatymaker, the Hogarth-
like terror of Teague, the precise language of Farrago, rather
than on the reality of scalping. In equally precise terms Captain Farrago details the limitations of marriage, the pulpit, the
stage, the legislature, and other occupations to which Teague
aspires but for which he is unqualified. Myth, literature, religion, and empiricism mix without distinction in the captain's
entreaties: a seductive landlady becomes in language an
American Circe, an old hag planning to transform Teague
magically into a pig prior to castrating him (96–97). Frightened by these vivid images, the Irishman seems a comic version of Thomas Morton or John Lyford.

Farrago's humorous tale-telling is related to the treatymaker's and, more closely, to Brackenridge's. Like the author of

Modern Chivalry, the captain creates fictions in order to instruct; both concur that "it can be no injury to deceive a man to his own advantage" (246). What Farrago fails to understand, and what Brackenridge satirizes, is that like most of his countrymen, Teague reckons advantage in dollars. A blind lawyer who argues with the captain over Teague's service to a fraudulent conjurer "in the semblance of Belzebub" intones two laws that govern the new country: "Doubtless it was a fraud upon the public; but the people themselves became a party, by consulting the wizard. . . . But in foro conscientiae, it might be a question of whether it was wrong to trick people that were willing to be tricked. Si populus vult decipi, decipiatur"; and "But in a republican government, the trade or employment of a man, is but little considered. The great matter is, the profits of it. Does it make the pot boil? If the bog-trotter finds his account in the service, and makes money, the world will wink at the means" (502–3). The lawyer offers the American trickster as the real American Adam.

Brackenridge follows closely Farrago's attempt to reconcile this perception with the ideals of democracy. In book 2 of *Modern Chivalry*, a controversy arises that echoes Cotton Mather's warning of "Wolves in Sheeps' Cloathing" and Franklin's defense of the minister Hemphill.

> Two men appeared, the one of a grave aspect, with a black coat; the other without the same clerical colour of garb; but with papers in his pocket which announced his authority to preach, and officiate as a clergyman. The man with the black coat, averred, that coming over together, in a vessel from Ireland, they had been messmates; and while he was asleep one night, being drowsy after prayers, the other had stolen his credentials from his pocket. The man in possession of the papers, averred they were his own, and that the other had taken his coat, and by advantage of the cloth, thought to pass for what he was not. (99)

The two preachers dramatize ironically the captain's pronouncement that "you have nothing but your character . . . in a new country to depend on" (17). Farrago proposes that each preach a sermon, and "let him that expounds the scripture the best, be adjudged the clergyman" (99). The two discourses present a contrast in styles as distinct as that between the captain's and Teague's. The performances divide the people, but the captain resolves the issue in a suggestive manner.

> Gentlemen, said he, the men seem both to have considerable gifts, and I see no harm in letting them both preach. There is work enough for them in this new country; the first appears to me, to be more qualified for the city, as a very methodical preacher; but the last is most practical; and each may answer a valuable purpose in their proper place. (104)

The solution is itself most practical, for it recognizes that two styles may serve one purpose, and that the impostor's enthusiasm may be as important in taming the frontier as the ordained minister's credentials. Imaged tensions are discharged in laughter at his sermon, a recitation of Adam and Eve's genealogy, and in admiration of the captain's solution; the reader knows that the episode is, after all, a fiction. Brackenridge, however, not only exploits the appearances of New World tricksters but also explores the implications of their presence in American culture as creators of fictions. Of *Modern Chivalry* Brackenridge writes: "Now it may be said, that this is a fiction; but fiction, or no fiction, the nature of the thing will make it a reality" (22). If fictions do become realities, then Farrago's solution of the minister-impostor is neither successful nor amusing. It is clearly unfair, not to mention unchristian, to certify the impostor as a "practical" man of God; his congregation will be at least ill-served. Farrago's decision smacks of condescension and elitism, and, as in his misrepresentation to Teague of the treatymaker's intentions, it suggests a certain sadistic pleasure the captain takes from giving people he considers foolish what he thinks they deserve. If Americans are willing to be tricked, and willingly accept mere style as the substance of reality, then Captain Farrago is himself willing to give them style—with a vengeance. At this point Farrago has internalized the pattern of confidence games he deplores in American society and becomes the object of satire for more than his quixotic behavior; he manipulates for personal profit, receiving the sensations of perverse, vicarious pleasure as his reward.

Brackenridge expresses more than the fear that politicians, lawyers, doctors, and other citizens are dishonest profiteers

and that American society encourages corruption in every
profession; *Modern Chivalry* dramatically gives shape to
Brackenridge's fear that beneath the appearances of order in
society lie the realities of chaos. If style has become separated
from substance, as Brackenridge insists in his introduction[3]
and as *Modern Chivalry* demonstrates, then meaning—certainty of identity, intention, reference—cannot be determined. In the face of this epistemological uncertainty, Brackenridge focuses his fiction through a conventional literary
character whose stock-in-trade is the confusion of appearance
and reality, the substitution of language for fact—the archetypal trickster. Embodying the ambiguities of border states—
between civilization and wilderness, the rulers and the ruled,
style and substance—the trickster, especially in humorous
guises like the Lord of Misrule or Till Eulenspiegel, plays confidence games that temporarily unleash the spirit of disorder
and, as they are defined and sanctioned by society, displace
unarticulated cultural fears of impending chaos. Brackenridge's repeated use of the confidence game appears in this
light an attempt to domesticate the deepest fears of enlightened Americans through a constraining, recognizable, comic
literary structure. *Modern Chivalry*, however, dramatizes the
inability of Americans to discover adequate bases for judgment and calls into question the ability of Brackenridge's own
fiction to offer certainty or reassurance. As the new country
does not have the well-defined social structures of the Old
World, the confidence games of *Modern Chivalry* express cultural anxieties about the American frontier, political corruption, practical democracy, social mobility, and the limits of
perception that cannot wholly be resolved in humorous fiction. The literary conventions of the Old World prove inadequate to the New.

In 1839 the editor of a monthly literary magazine could say
of *Modern Chivalry*, "Twenty years ago this work . . . was the
humorous textbook of all classes of society."[4] The dismissive
tone reflects a change in the attitudes of Americans toward
confidence games, a change that was visible in the disappearance from polite literature of humorous and harmless expressions of American shiftiness. Nonetheless, the questions
Brackenridge raises in his union of Old World techniques,

American materials, and confidence games again demanded expression in the southwestern flush times of another new country.

*   *   *

In the period following the publication of *Modern Chivalry*, the confidence game vanishes from American fiction as a critical model of democratic society. The cry for American writers to create a "Columbian" literature intoned by Philip Freneau, Charles Brockden Brown, Joel Barlow, and others encouraged laudatory and unambiguous literary images of America. The desire to be recognized by a skeptical European audience as successful practitioners of a valuable art led American writers to imitate Old World models: thus the *Red Book* of John Pendleton Kennedy and Peter Hoffman Cruse, which brought satiric essays and verse on American subjects to Baltimore, was consciously modeled on eighteenth-century British periodicals like the *Spectator*. In this literature, an acceptable American characer might be the time-worn sentimental rogue or picaro, but certainly unacceptable would be a self-serving American biter who might appear representative of the new republic.

Yet in the oral tales and informal fictions sprouting on the southwestern frontier, American tricksters retained the sharp social bite present in *Modern Chivalry*. This evolving tradition, however, remained submerged beneath the dominant literary establishment of polite letters in the 1820s. The generation of Americans coming of age in the "Era of Good Feeling" for the most part exchanged self-criticism for self-congratulation and sought in fiction unthreatening realizations of American independence, merit, and achievement. In the wake of the collapse of Federalism, American defeats in the War of 1812 (in which Washington, D.C., was burned), and the suspension of specie payments heralding the Panic of 1819 and a national depression, American culture could not accommodate Brackenridge's satiric tricksters in its national literature. The Monroe Doctrine of 1823, proclaimed following President Monroe's reelection without opposition, is perhaps the most obvious example of the American desire for a reassuring and confident national rhetoric. In the popular imagination the War of 1812 became a series of stunning military victories for individual American leaders, a transformation reflecting the power of the need for American optimism. After all, by 1820 William Henry Harrison and Andrew Jackson seemed to have put an end to Indian hostilities, and between 1810 and 1830 the population of settlers beyond the Appalachians quadrupled; to most Americans the Indian inhabitants of the frontier seemed abstract literary images. The popular response in the 1820s anticipates that following the Civil War: Americans embraced literary stereotypes as true representative men, transformed American guilt into optimistic idealism, and relegated American biters to simplistic, secondary fictional roles. Critical expressions of American shiftiness, ambiguity, and defeat were overshadowed by the popular need—intensified by the legacy of the American Revolution—to confirm as realized the national dreams of security, certainty, and success. Ambivalence within the new republic found expression in "The Legend of Sleepy Hollow," "Rip Van Winkle," and the Leatherstocking novels: Irving opposes two competing orders in Ichabod Crane and Brom Bones and dramatizes disorientation in Rip Van Winkle; Cooper chronicles the loss of the noble wilderness and the death of Natty Bumppo as a direct result of the advance of ignoble civilization. The American public, however, chose to ignore (or could not admit) the anxieties about class, morality, democracy, and the new country clearly present in the works of the "American Goldsmith" and the "American Scott."

*   *   *

In 1822 William H. Gardiner urged his countrymen to create a native American literature, fashioning the events of their history into romantic images of national identity: "We have long been of opinion that our native country opens to the adventurous novel-writer a wide, untrodden field, replete with new matter admirably adapted to the purposes of fiction." Noting that "the characters of fiction should be descriptive of classes, and not of individuals," he devotes several pages to the great variety of "specific character" found in the United States, listing such representative types as the proud Virginian, the Dutch burgomaster, and the uncivilized Indian. Comparing the covenanters immortalized by Scott to "those sterner puritans" whose journey into the wilderness remained yet unexplored, Gardiner suggests that three American epochs "are peculiarly well fitted for historical romance;—the times just succeeding the first settlement—the aera of the Indian wars, which lie scattered along a considerable period—and the revolution." "What would not the author of Waverly," he challenges, "make of such materials?"[5]

Gardiner's summons, appearing in the prestigious *North American Review*, explicitly accepts conventional literary forms; he heralds Cooper as the American Scott and praises *The Spy* as forming "the foundations of American romance." In this view, nineteenth-century American literature will be "American" because its settings will be American, though its techniques clearly will be European. In addition, Gardiner implicitly rejects figures of democratic corruption, vice, and duplicity as inappropriate, unworthy, and uncharacteristic of this native art.

James Kirke Paulding's "The Yankee Roué" reveals the union of New and Old World elements as clearly as it marks the fate of shifty American characters.[6] More roué than Yankee, Stafford Sheffield inherits a fortune and sets out to prove his worth by seducing another man's wife. The roué's desire to adopt European social manners, undemocratic attitudes, and ungodly morals leads him to shoot himself in the foot in a duel and to a dissolute end in the Bowery. Paulding teaches a lesson that smacks of the humorless tracts of his contemporary, Mason Locke Weems. Like Weems's *God's Revenge Against Gambling. Exemplified in the Miserable and Untimely Deaths of a Number of Persons of both Sexes, who had Sacrificed their Health, Wealth, and Honor at Gambling Tables*, "The Yankee Roué" imitates the stereotypes of British sentimental and didactic fiction. Stafford Sheffield is a two-dimensional exemplum, a Europeanized aberration whose destruction reaffirms the American values of industry, frugality, honesty, and morality. In fact, to his native land Paulding attributes nothing more than his birth: the tale could without damage have been located entirely in Europe, retitled "The Youthful (or "Parisian" or "London") Roué."

Henry Junious Nott's "The Counterfeiters" owes just as little to Mills's Gap, North Carolina. Although nominally the plot concerns a conflict between rough mountaineers and civ-

ilized valley farmers, the mysterious Martin Brownfield—
called a "feudal baron" by the narrator—plays the soured English highwayman to perfection. If Brownfield practices an
American confidence game with counterfeit money, it is
eclipsed by the story of Brownfield's daughter's love for the
prosecuting magistrate's son. In true sentimental style,
Brownfield kills his own son, mistaking him for his enemy's,
and, without further mention of counterfeit money, begs his
daughter from his deathbed to marry the magistrate's son.

Collected in *Novelettes of a Traveller*, Nott's tale shows the
influence of eighteenth-century English periodical literature
(not to mention *Romeo and Juliet*). In similar fashion the
"Biographical Sketch of Thomas Singularity, Journeyman
Printer," also included in *Novelettes*, displays its descent from
periodical and picaresque fiction, borrowing from American
soil only its ostensible location. At best Thomas Singularity's
misadventures with snakes, bees, and women appear diluted
versions of Teague O'Regan's.

In 1835 Alexis de Tocqueville acutely observed that literary
forms of the Old World, veneered with American names and
settings, served as appropriate literature for the New World.

> Not only do the Americans constantly draw upon the trea-
> sures of English literature, but it may be said with truth that
> they find the literature of England growing on their own soil.
> The larger part of that small number of men in the United
> States who are engaged in the composition of literary works
> are English in substance, and still more so in form. Thus they
> transport into the midst of democracy the ideas and literary
> fashions which are current amongst the aristocratic nation
> they have taken for their model. They paint with colors bor-
> rowed from foreign manners; and as they hardly ever represent
> the country they were born in as it really is, they are seldom
> popular there.[7]

Anticipating Tocqueville's complaint, Gardiner chides "the
graceful and humorous author of Knickerbocker and the
Sketch Book" for not making use of more American sources
and suggests that "the Indians themselves are a highly poeti-
cal people"; as the savage warrior "is no mean instrument of
the sublime and terrible," "we see not why those superstitions
of theirs . . . may not be successfully employed to supersede
the worn out fables of Runic mythology."[8]

The response to Gardiner's suggestion in nationalistic journals can be gauged by the popularity of Lydia M. Child's "The
Indian Wife," Sarah J. Hale's "The Frontier House," and James
Hall's "The Backwoodsman." Each sketch reduces the inhabitants of the frontier to literary stereotypes offering the polite
reader the luxuries of sorrow, terror, and superiority. The Indian appears as either an agent of evil or a sentimentalized
hero living in harmony with nature; the backwoodsman likewise becomes alternately a rough comic barbarian or a courtly
gentleman. When these characters assume center stage they
lose their American traits and are transformed into eighteenth-century European archetypes of noble pathos and honorable vengeance. In Child's "Indian Wife," Princess Tahmiroo
has been married for her father's wealth by the unscrupulous
trader Florimond de Rancé. The name suggests that Americans are not party to such vile acts and functions to displace
any guilt Child or her readers have for taking Indian lands.
Unable to witness the sale of her ancestral lands and the es-
trangement of her newly Europeanized daughter, Tahmiroo
paddles over the Falls of St. Anthony, choosing death for herself and her young son. Four years later James Hall's "Indian
Wife's Lament" (also in *Legends of the West*) follows another
wife and children over the Falls of St. Anthony, this time in
eighteenth-century couplets. Both Hall and Child may have
drawn upon historical as well as literary sources; Wordsworth,
whose "Complaint of a Forsaken Indian Woman" appeared in
Lyrical Ballads (first printed in the United States in Philadelphia in 1802), urges the reader to "see that very interesting
work, Hearne's *Journey from Hudson's Bay to the Northern
Ocean.*" Sentimental characterizations like Mrs. Child's are
indebted to European literary stereotypes. As Roy Harvey
Pearce explains in *Savagism and Civilization: A Study of the
Indian and the American Mind*, noble savages alternate with
heartless butchers in early national fiction. In Hale's "Frontier
House"—as in the numerous popular Pocahontas plays—both
images uneasily coexist: bloodthirsty Indians spare the family
of a woman who offered them kindness in the past. More
frequently, though, literary Indians, as in Hall's "The Backwoodsman," display no mercy: they carry off a young bride-to-
be on her way home from a camp-meeting; their brutal inten-

tions are matched by the ferocity of the "Patriarch of Kentucky," who refuses sleep or thanks until each Mingo is killed. Pearce concludes that "by the first quarter of the century . . . Indian nobility and ignobility, Indian virtues and vices, had to be at once admitted and praised and dispraised for what they were, qualities tied together and delimited by the special nature of Indian society."[9]

At the same time that Thomas Singularity played his impolite tricks and polite backwoodsmen vanquished savage Indians, Mike Fink drank barrels of rot-gut whiskey, made love to willing country girls, and joyfully cracked together human skulls. Around campfires, in local "doggeries," and at any official meeting, the exploits of Fink and his contemporaries were recounted. The popularity and importance of these oral tales throughout the nineteenth century is testified to by the metaphoric observations of the acutely perceptive Andrew Lang: "All over the land men are eternally 'swopping stories' at bars, and in the long endless journeys. . . . How little, comparatively, the English 'swop stories'! . . . The stories thus collected in America are the subsoil of American literary humour, a rich soil in which the plant . . . grows with vigour and puts forth fruit and flowers."[10] These stories were short, often recounting a single incident, and were meant to be told in one sitting. Acts of tremendous strength, incredible marksmanship, and devilish cunning form the base of this oral tradition, in which the frontier appears inhabited by neither roué nor noble savage but by a breed known as "half man, half horse, and half alligator."[11] No hastily repainted European scenery, the frontier functions as a central character in many narratives, an entity competing fiercely with backwoodsmen. The Ohio Falls that Mike Fink rides in a broadhorn, the frozen sun that Davy Crockett oils with a bear, the rivers that suddenly flow backward in a tale of Pete Featherton—these landscapes challenge the imagination.

These features of the frontier environment naturally formed material for campside yarns, in which the triumph of regional heroes over swollen rivers, deep snows, and savage Indians reaffirmed each man's abilities and temporarily minimized in fiction the day-to-day hazards of frontier life. The oral tale was set temporally in the present or recent past and spatially in a nearby region. The teller, who had usually witnessed the event himself, vouched for its truth personally, thereby guaranteeing implicitly repetitions of superhuman achievements. As opposed to the romance, which as Gardiner explains converts the familiar into a theater of remote antiquity, the oral narrative domesticates elements in everyday life that are terrifying or bizarre. To do this storytellers often made light of danger, or made light of the consequences resulting from the worst imaginable accidents; humorous exaggeration was a main ingredient in oral art, apparent in the tornado ride of Davy Crockett down the Mississippi River, or in the ram-butting match that finally scattered the brains of Jack Pierce. Whether victor or victim, the narrator of the tale survives. He also gives form to chaotic experiences, proclaiming his existence as he laughs at adversity. He is able to laugh because of the control he establishes by means of the dramatic frame, the conventional form of most frontier tales, within which the rough action occurs. With the storyteller introducing and concluding the tale, all manner of activity—earthy, brutal, supernatural—can take place in between, safely distanced from the listener. Tocqueville again demonstrates his perceptiveness of the patterns—literary as well as social—evolving in the new country.

> Accustomed to the struggle, the crosses, and the monotony of practical life, [Americans] require rapid emotions, startling passages,—truths or errors brilliant enough to rouse them up, and to plunge them at once, as if by violence, into the midst of the subject. . . . Style will frequently be fantastic, incorrect, overburdened, and loose—almost always vehement and bold.[12]

This loose narrative form, antithetical to that found in early nineteenth-century annuals and reviews, encouraged the creation of mountain-size heroes who spoke outrageous dialect and withstood unbelievable challenges. And as tales were swapped at informal gatherings, each teller in turn would try to top the last, embellishing and exaggerating to the utmost reach of his powers of invention. Half a century after Tocqueville, Henry Adams reflected in similar fashion that "border society was not refined . . . and little idea could be drawn of the character that would at last emerge. The Mississippi boatman and the squatter on Indian lands were perhaps the most distinctly American type then existing, as far removed from the Old World as though Europe were a dream."[13]

The frontiersman, epitomized in the oral tales of Davy Crockett, Daniel Boone, Mike Fink, and others (not to mention Natty Bumppo, as well), became an accepted image of national identity, one intrinsically linked to images of the American landscape and the conventions of fireside art. Part picaro, part rogue, part Indian, and part animal, he embodied both the wildness of the historical frontier and the superhuman qualities necessary to survive it. The storyteller, not restricted by the expectations of a formal literary audience, freely indulged his fantasies and fears, creating symbolic American characters within distinctly American settings and forms. The hunt, the fight, the contest, the swap: these were the activities of the frontiersman, archetypal actions made American in oral lore.

Oral tales began to appear in local newspapers in the 1820s as humorous filler contributed by amateur writers. William T. Porter, editor of the popular and successful weekly *New York Spirit of the Times*, boasted in 1837 that "from Maine to Florida, from the St. Lawrence to the Missouri, a thousand gifted pens are employed in imparting novelty and interest to our columns."[14] Stories of frontier exploits kept the form and flavor of their oral sources to insure "novelty and interest," and, as Walter Blair notes, "to go one step farther in catching the pleasant quality of a fireside yarn, many of the correspondents . . . put their mock oral tales into an evocative framework."[15] Duplicating in print a common ritual of the frontier, these tales brought to an expanding and an increasingly educated regional audience a sense of identity and community.

Georgia Scenes

Augustus Baldwin Longstreet's *Georgia Scenes, Characters, Incidents, &c. in the First Half Century of the Republic* (1835) is typical of the regional literature that began to give form to the passions, anxieties, and doubts suppressed in earlier fiction. The first collection from the Old Southwest to reach a national audience, its eleven editions demonstrated that the rural life of the Old South was of interest to New Yorkers as well as Virginians and that unidealized frontier materials could be adapted to literary forms flexible enough to preserve their native freshness. Dominated by the rhetoric of an Addisonian narrator, Longstreet's tales are nonetheless often populated by rough-hewn backwoodsmen who prance, snort, and bellow in a vernacular guaranteed to attract attention. In *Georgia Scenes* the frame technique establishes an aesthetic distance between the author and his dialect-using characters that is essentially comic; the reader joins the cultured narrator in laughing at the rude talk and crude manners of the country folk he describes. This structure emphasizes an even greater moral distance, one not always found in oral tales, and reveals that the audience is presumed to be morally aligned with the proper narrator (and author) in contrast to the vernacular characters. The "half man, half horse, half alligator" is an oddity— the well-bred narrator is the moral and perceptual center of the story. Though he may enjoy watching the antics of Georgia b'hoys, fighting, drinking, and practical joking are clearly not the occupations of a Whig gentleman.

They are, however, the occupations of Longstreet's characters. As the first in a line of southwestern writers, Longstreet developed frontier stereotypes and narrative techniques that record the boom and bust flush times, express Whig anxieties about the practice of Jacksonian democracy, and reveal the influence of oral, journalistic, and literary traditions. In *Georgia Scenes* the figure of the American sharper begins to emerge from the violence, cruelty, and opportunism characteristic of this new country.

"The Character of a Native Georgian" reflects Longstreet's dependence on conventional literary devices like the prankster. Ned Brace "seemed to live only to amuse himself with his fellow-beings, and he possessed the rare faculty of deriving some gratification of his favorite propensity, from almost every person whom he met, no matter what his temper, standing, or disposition."[16] Impossible to claim as wholly an American innovation, the "Native Georgian" yet reveals the growing interest in distinct characterization begun with Royall Tyler's

Jonathan, and though certainly related to Addisonian eccentrics like Sir Roger De Coverly and Will Honeycomb, in name alone he is more suggestively American; *Ned Brace* has neither the euphony nor the affectation of *Pindar Cockloft*. His tricks likewise bear a more American stamp than those of Thomas Singularity or Brom Bones.

In a ritual of good-fellowship, each traveler salutes a Savannah barkeeper with his name before entering the public house; Ned Brace's alarmed refusal to speak his name aloud, offering instead a soiled and illegible scrap of paper to the proprietor, suggests in humorous form the fragility of American hospitality, the self-assertiveness of individual identity, the uncertainty inherent in a mobile population, and the importance Americans place on forthrightness and personal conformity. Ned's joke of withholding his name, like that of mashing his food into a mush or drinking coffee and tea together, violates unwritten social conventions and comically exposes the uncertainty and distrust lurking just below the surface of American confidence. Ostensibly a sketch of an eccentric in the *Spectator* tradition, "The Character of a Native Georgian" cuts across the grain and demonstrates the vulnerability of society in the new country. Amusing though it is as Ned preys upon "the beau in the presence of his mistress, the fop, the pedant, the purse-proud, the over-fastidious and sensitive" (31), the tone of the sketch shifts when Ned disrupts a fire brigade for a lark: as Savannah burns in the background, Ned stops the passage of water to the blaze, insisting on quenching his thirst with an entire bucket of water. No denunciation follows; although the narrator closes this frame, he shares with Ned an ambiguous moral position: both exist on the same imaginative level, and walk off "on our way homeward" virtually hand in hand.

The preface to *Georgia Scenes* acknowledged Longstreet's problem of establishing control over ambiguous frontier materials.

> I cannot conclude these introductory remarks, without reminding those who have taken exceptions to the coarse, inelegant, and sometimes ungrammatical language, which the writer represents himself as occasionally using, *that it is lan-*

guage accommodated to the capacity of the person to whom
he represents himself as speaking. (iv, Longstreet's emphasis)

The emphasis in this admonition implies intention, but Longstreet's ambiguous rhetoric creates more problems than it
solves. Ignorance of the implications of using frontier materials and new narrative techniques occasionally led him to tor-
tured syntax, uncertain aesthetics, and aberrant ethics.

"Georgia Theatrics," the first Georgia scene, postulates a
solution to both moral and artistic imperatives. The narrator
opens the frame with an explanation of the "Dark Corner" of
Lincoln.

> I believe it took its name from the moral darkness, which
> reigned over the portion of the county, at the time of which I
> am speaking. If in this point of view, it was but a shade darker
> than the rest of the county, it was inconceivably dark. If any
> man can name a trick, or sin, which had not been committed
> at the time of which I am speaking, in the very focus of the
> county's illumination, (Lincolnton), he must himself be the
> most inventive of the tricky, and the very Judas of sinners. (5)

His tone is at once amused, condescending, and self-righteous,
and the Latinate diction and measured cadences of his speech
establish his superiority to the moral wilderness around him.
Completely in control while contrasting the area's moral and
natural condition, the narrative voice assures as it describes
the charms—"undulating grounds," "luxuriant woodlands,"
"sportive streams," "vocal birds," "blushing flowers"—of a
perfect pastoral. This eighteenth-century idyll is suddenly
shattered.

> "Boo-oo-oo! Oh, wake snakes, and walk your chalks! Brim-
> stone and——fire! Don't hold me, Nick Stoval! The fight's
> made up, and let's go at it. ——my soul, if I don't jump down
> his throat and gallop every chitterling out of him, before you
> can say 'quit'!"
>   In Mercy's name! thought I, what band of ruffians has se-
> lected this holy season, and this heavenly retreat, for such
> Pandaemonium riots! I quickened my gait, and had come
> nearly opposite to the thick grove whence the noise had pro-
> ceeded, when my eye caught indistinctly, and at intervals,
> through the foliage of the dwarf-oaks and hickories which in-
> tervened, glimpses of a man, or men, who seemed to be in a

violent struggle; and I could occasionally catch those deep
drawn, emphatic oaths, which men in conflict utter, when
they deal blows. (6)

The contrast between narrator and character is rhetorical,
temporal, and moral—the narrator is separated from and
clearly condemns the battle he perceives; the dialect used by
the combatants emphasizes the rough-and-tumble nature of
the frontier, which relies on lawless brutality to maintain a
semblance of order: "'Enough! My eye's out.' . . . 'Now, blast
your corn-shucking soul . . . come cutt'n your shines 'bout me
again, next time I come to the Court-House, will you!'" (7).
Presented dramatically, the details are horribly realistic and
serve not only as a historical record of backwoods language
but also as an indictment of backwoods morality. Reader and
narrator deplore the fight, horrorstruck at its consequences.
From similar moral positions, both view brawling as distaste-
ful, uncivilized, and unchristian—senseless violence at its
worst. Both are, as well, implicitly threatened by the proximity of the struggle; the narrator of "Georgia Theatrics" is only
one step away from joining the fracas (though, admittedly, that
step is a long one). However, by a kind of narrative sleight of
hand, Longstreet makes the violence disappear into comedy.

"Come back, you brute! and assist me in relieving your fellow
mortal, whom you have ruined for ever!"
    My rudeness subdued his embarrassment in an instant; and
with a taunting curl of the nose, he replied "You needn't kick
before you're spur'd. There a'nt nobody there, nor ha'nt been
nother. I was jist seein' how I could 'a' *fout*." So saying, he
bounded to his plough, which stood in the corner of the fence
about fifty yards beyond the battle ground.
    And would you believe it, gentle reader! his report was true.
All that I had heard and seen, was nothing more nor less than
a Lincoln rehearsal; in which the youth who had just left me,
had played all the parts, of all the characters, in a Court-House
fight. (7–8)

The threat vanishes, or rather its existence is forcibly denied, so that the author appears to disengage himself from the
savagery described. Longstreet's moral position is unassailable—he condemns from a safe distance the characters who
would use violence, and, as the fight did not actually occur,
denies that his hands are dirtied by the tale's minuteness of

"Georgia Theatrics" (from Burton,
Cyclopaedia, 1858).

detail. His stuffy narrator, like the duelling roué who shoots himself in the foot, becomes an object of derision; he, not the author, overheard, misapprehended, and overreacted. And he, not Longstreet, may appear the voyeur. Seen in this way, "Georgia Theatrics" constrains the violent elements of the frontier as the apparent threat is removed by the denial, ex post facto, of its reality.

In action "Georgia Theatrics" resembles the typical misadventures of oral tales. In language, however, its narrator recalls the eighteenth-century affectations of Messrs. Boozle and Noozle in Longstreet's "The Ball." "Georgia Theatrics" forcibly yokes together their self-consciously inflated literary style and the painfully realistic vernacular description of a frontier fight. Despite the fact that no violence is actually committed, the narrator seems not an objective gentleman but an effeminate, foppish moralist, a southwestern Ichabod Crane whose bookish rhetoric is more appropriate to a georgic like Thomson's "The Seasons" than a robust Georgia scene. In fact, "Georgia Theatrics" has no conclusion: the implications of the incident extend uneasily beyond the visionary abilities of the narrator. As his introduction to the "Dark Corner" affirms, the fight could undoubtedly have happened as imagined. What he overheard, after all, was a "Lincoln rehearsal," a preparation for a real encounter; that the story's last paragraph presents his puzzled, almost clinical observation reinforces this possibility, confirming that the threat of dismemberment is not dismissed but postponed. The cries of the dialect characters— "Enough! My eye's out," "Get your owl-eye in agin if you can!"—create images that the pompous language of the narrator can do nothing to dispel. Crushed by the defeat of his expectations, the narrator is reduced to passivity, his superior moral position undercut, his rhetoric deflated. His minute inspection of the battleground, moreover, suggests that he may even at the end vicariously enjoy the closeness of his brush with violence.

> I went to the ground from which he had risen; and there were the prints of his two thumbs, plunged up to the balls in the mellow earth, about the distance of a man's eyes apart; and the ground was broken up, as if two stags had been engaged upon it. (8)

Longstreet laughs at both the savage youth and the anemic cosmopolitan; whether he also laughs at the reader is a moot point. As Brackenridge's Captain Farrago deceives Teague about the treatymaker's interest in his scalp, so too does Longstreet deceive the reader of "Georgia Theatrics" about the reality of this fight. In both fictions, however, the violence transformed into comedy remains in the imagination as a possibility; appearance and reality merge in Longstreet's disturbing final vision of violence that is not violence, the thumb prints of the boy in the soft earth.

Edgar Allan Poe applauded "The Fight" as "a sketch unsurpassed in dramatic vigor" that would "positively make the fortune of any British periodical" because of its "forcible, accurate and original generic delineations of real existences to be found sparsely in Georgia, Mississippi and Louisiana, and very plentifully in our more remote settlements and territories."[17] A detached first-person narrator sets the frontier scene.

> In the younger days of the Republic, there lived in the county of ———, two men, who were admitted on all hands to be the very best men in the county—which, in the Georgia vocabulary, means that they could flog any other two men in the county. Each, through many a hard-fought battle, had acquired the mastery of his own battalion, but they lived on opposite sides of the Court House, and in different battalions: consequently they were but seldom thrown together . . . so that, but for the circumstance which I am about to mention, the question, which had been a thousand times asked "Which is the best man, Billy Stallions, (Stallings,) or Bob Durham?" would probably never have been answered. (53–54)

The slightly inflated rhetoric demonstrates the author's control over the story and its characters, the brief insertion of dialect (corrected parenthetically) a cautious preview of what will follow. Ransy Sniffle is a comtemptible squatter who "never seemed fairly alive except when he was witnessing, fomenting, or talking about a fight. Then, indeed, his deep-sunken grey eyes assumed something of a living fire" (57). Sniffle engineers the fight, embodying Longstreet's worst fears about the kind of men the new country may produce.

As the fight commences, the modulated tones of the narrator are comically broken by the rude cries of the backwoodsmen.

> As he struck the ground, commingled shouts, screams and yells burst from the lower battalion, loud enough to be heard for miles. "Hurra my little hornet!"—"Save him!"—"Feed him!—Give him the Durham physic till his stomach turns!" Billy was no sooner down than Bob was on him, and lending him awful blows about the face and breast. Billy made two efforts to rise by main strength, but failed. "Lord bless you man, don't try to get up!—*Lay* still and take it!—you *bleege* to have it." (62–63)

Their exaggerated oaths of encouragement add fantastic details to the description; yet, as in Hall's "The Backwoodsman," the precise diction of the narrator obtains, shaping the action and defining the limits of involvement: "Billy now turned his face suddenly to the ground, and rose upon his hands and knees. Bob jerked up both his hands and threw him on his face. He again recovered his late position, of which Bob endeavored to deprive him as before; but missing one arm, he failed and Billy rose" (63). The frame closes with a conventional moral injunction, an authorial condemnation of the violence witnessed and recorded on the frontier.

> Thanks to the Christian religion, to schools, colleges, and benevolent associations, such scenes of barbarism and cruelty, as that which I have just been describing, are now of rare occurrence: though they may still be occasionally met with in some of the new counties. Wherever they prevail, they are a disgrace to that community. The peace officers who countenance them, deserve a place in the Penitentiary. (66)

The moral and aesthetic values of the author subdue the frontiersman's; the narrator observes, reports, and evaluates—negatively—the rough country custom. The fight is an aberration, not entirely an amusement but also an occasion for instruction. Whig gentlemen do not bite off each other's ears.

Kenneth S. Lynn explains the function of the frame technique as "a convenient way of keeping . . . first-person narrators outside and above the comic action, thereby drawing a *cordon sanitaire*, so to speak, between the morally irreproachable Gentleman and the tainted life he describes." [18] The frame's flexibility, apparent in the rambling, ponderous introduction and abrupt, staccato conclusion of "The Fight," preserves the violent immediacy of the story intact. It also allows Longstreet time to individualize his characters: Billy Stallions and Bob Durham are not idealized noble savages, but battered men worthy of sympathy; and Ransy Sniffle, the contemptible go-between, gains a reputation that lasts into the twentieth century, where Sniffle is smoothly transposed to Snopes. [19] The brawling and whooping of the backwoodsmen, though contained within the frame, do more than characterize Stallions and Durham unsentimentally; the brutal action and jarring vernacular recreate the turbulence of the historical frontier.

> "Oh, my lark!" cried the east, "has he foxed you? Do you begin to feel him! He's only beginning to fight—He ain't got warm yet."
>
> "Look yonder!" cried the west—"didn't I tell you so! He hit the ground so hard, it jarred his nose off. Now ain't he a pretty man as he stands? He shall have my sister Sall just for his pretty looks. I want to get in the breed of them sort o' men, to drive ugly out of my kin folks."
>
> . . ."Bullets!"—*Hoss*-kicking—Thunder'"—"That'll do for the face—now feel his short ribs, Billy!" (63, 64)

Bullets, wild horses, and thunder symbolize the American landscape of the 1830s. "The Fight," a compressed imaginative rendering of this terrain, captures the vitality of the flush times, embracing momentarily the anarchic forces released in senseless violence. The closing paragraph forms an embarrassing admission of its powers of evocation, the overzealous protest of a voyeur. The tacked-on moral underscores the fragility of the boxlike structure and acknowledges the newly discovered danger of frontier materials—for several reasons their potential is difficult to control. As W. J. Cash points out in *The Mind of the South*, the distinction between southern gentleman and southern roustabout was largely fictitious; both often sprang from identical sources on the frontier, where to every man the tendency to use and approve of violence came naturally.[20] The almost intoxicating effect of the fight on the narrator reveals him less the gentleman than one of the b'hoys; his superiority is torn away as quickly as Billy Stallions's nose. The details of personality and motivation that Longstreet gives the brawlers work against the ostensible containing purpose of the frame, pulling the narrator down to the level of what Poe termed the "horrible and disgusting details of southern barbarity." Like "Georgia Theatrics," "The Fight" expresses the possibility that Americans—Longstreet, his narrator, his reader—are typically Ransy Sniffles, squatters who are secretly thrilled by violence. In this unsettling vision resides the Whig fear of the leveling power of Jacksonian democracy, fear of the frontier's ability to corrupt good men, and fear that each individual hides a secret nature.

"The Horse-Swap" is perhaps the most firmly controlled frontier tale in *Georgia Scenes* and marks a return to the deceptive and ambiguous new country of *Modern Chivalry*. Introduced by a conventional frame-narrator, the traditional frontier pastime—swapping—brings the historical flush times into fictional focus. As both a real and a metaphoric activity, swapping forms an emblem of life in the boom-and-bust days of the border states. Like "The Fight," "The Horse-Swap" reflects these historical conditions in symbolic rituals of identity; their purpose is always to separate reality from deceiving appearances, to decide "which is the best man." The narrator's initial description of the Yellow Blossom from Jasper, however, stresses this contest's potential for comedy, not violence. His colorful language, so unlike the narrative affectations of "Georgia Theatrics," sets a humorous, informal tone well suited to the cavorting Blossom: "he cursed, swore, whooped, screamed, and tossed himself in every attitude which man could assume on horseback" (21). Longstreet assumes that the reader will recognize this descendant of the Yankee Jonathan and Mike Fink. In name, speech, and confidence the Yellow Blossom proclaims himself the archetypal American sharper, while his vernacular boasts form a native refrain that amounts to self-caricature: "I'm the boy . . . perhaps a *leetle*—jist a *leetle* of the best man, at a horse-swap, that ever trod shoe-leather" (21).

Compressing the rambling introduction of "The Fight" into a single brisk paragraph, "The Horse-Swap" begins immediately with a comic threat to the narrator himself: "'Stranger,' said he to me, 'did you ever see the *Yellow* Blossom from Jasper?'" (21). By suggesting that the narrator might become involved with the Blossom, though of course it is Pete Ketch who actually swaps horses, Longstreet blurs ever so slightly the conventional distinction between gentleman frame-narrator and rough frame-character. The Blossom's playful question sets in motion the self-contained and self-completing contest of wits and tongues, an aesthetic ritual as prescribed in form as a medieval joust. Like frontier knights the Yellow Blossom and Pete Ketch enter the lists, each determined to prove that he more skillfully wields the shield of appearance and the lance of reality. The swap swells to near-mythic proportions as the Blossom cries that he can "out-swap any live man, woman or child, that ever walked these hills, or that ever straddled horse flesh since the days of old daddy Adam" (21).

Longstreet transforms his fears—and those of his reader— of the violence and corruption characteristic of the historical frontier into a comic literary dance. As the object of the swap is to lose the worst horse, the tale focuses on the rhetorical strategies used by each biter to convince the other that swapping will give him the best horse. The Yellow Blossom's Bullet is an earless, malformed nag whose tail "exhibited the line of beauty in so many diretions, that it could not fail to hit the most fastidious taste in some of them" (22), while Pete Ketch's Kit appears "a well-formed sorrel of the middle size," though "Bullet had the decided advantage of him in point of intellect" (24).

> "Why, man," said Blossom, "do you bring such a hoss as that to trade for Bullet? Oh, I see you've no notion of trading." (24)

> "Well," said Peter, "I didn't care about trading; but you cut such high shines, that I thought I'd like to back you out, and I've done it. . . ." "Come, old man," said Blossom, "I've been joking with you. I begin to think you do want to trade; therefore, give me five dollars and take Bullet. I'd rather lose ten dollars any time than not make a trade, though I hate to fling away a good hoss." "Well," said Peter, "I'll be as clever as you are. Just put five dollars on Bullet's back, and hand him over; it's a trade."

> Blossom swore again, as roundly as before, that he would not give boot; and, he said, "Bullet wouldn't hold five dollars on his back, no how. But, as I bantered you, if you say an even swap, here's at you."

> "I told you," said Peter, "I'd be as clever as you; therefore, here goes two dollars more, just for trade sake. Give me three dollars, and it's a bargain." (27–28)

The swap concluded, the Yellow Blossom warns Pete Ketch not to hurt Bullet, who, he notes, has a huge sore on his back. "I am, perhaps, a leetle," Blossom laughs, "of the best man at a horse-swap that ever catched a coon" (29). The laugh is turned back on the Blossom, however, as Pete Ketch's son Neddy blurts out that Kit is both deaf and blind. At this point the frame collapses inward, Pete's ironic repetition of the Blossom's boast formally completing the narrative structure: "You are a *leetle* the best man at a horse-swap that I ever got hold of" (30).

The comic shape of the tale moderates the educated writer's exaggerated fears that all Americans in the new country are sharpers, that all swaps or transactions are fraudulent, that one's senses are always untrustworthy, and that the individual will always be fleeced. Longstreet's sketch calls attention to its own fictiveness: the stylized vernacular of the Yellow Blossom, his repeated boasts, the familiar folk and literary motif of "the biter bit," the distance and superiority of the author/narrator from the action of the swap, and the self-contained nature of the swap itself all remind the reader that he is reading a work of the imagination and not a guidebook to the real Southwest. In addition, all that suffers is the self-inflated reputation of the boasting Yellow Blossom, a biter bitten by the unassuming Pete Ketch.

In "The Horse-Swap," Longstreet offers a model for displacing common anxieties about the southwestern flush times. The sharper functions as a literary symbol of the ambiguities of the new country; his aggressiveness, vernacular, and dishonesty form an American frontier type. By using two sharpers, however, Longstreet places a greater distance between the reader and his characters than did Brackenridge in *Modern Chivalry*, and seems to insist that the dishonesty he describes is restricted to an inferior class of American. As the action is thereby contained and held at one remove, the author and reader can condemn the action as representative only of "low" characters while at the same time enjoying the selling of the Blossom. There is no narrative intrusion at the tale's end (as in "Georgia Theatrics" and "The Fight"); Pete Ketch has the last word. In "The Horse-Swap" Longstreet achieves a comic displacement of real anxieties.

In *Georgia Scenes*, Longstreet introduced a new country to a national audience and developed native characters and techniques; in "The Horse-Swap," he immortalized the southwestern sharper, imaginative midwife to the literary convention of the flush-times confidence man.

3 THE EMERGENCE OF THE CONFIDENCE-MAN CONVENTION

> Even on his practical and sordid side, the American might easily have been represented as a victim to illusion. If the Englishman had lived as the American speculator did,—in the future,—the hyperbole of enthusiasm would have seemed less monstrous. "Look at my wealth!" cried the American to his foreign visitor. "See these solid mountains of salt and iron, of lead, copper, silver, and gold! . . . Look at this continent of mine, fairest of created worlds, as she lies turning up to the sun's never-failing caress her broad and exuberant breasts, overflowing with milk for her hundred million children! See how she glows with youth, health, and love!" . . ."Your story is a fraud, and you are a liar and a swindler."
>
> Met in this spirit, the American, half perplexed and half defiant, retaliated by calling his antagonist a fool. . . . For himself he cared little, but his dream was his whole existence. The men who denounced him admitted that they left him in his forest-swamp quaking with fever, but clinging in the delirium of death to the illusions of his dazzled brain. . . . Whether imagination or greed led them to describe more than actually existed, they still saw no more than any inventor or discoverer must have seen in order to give him the energy of success . . . and from them were seldom heard complaints of deception or delusion.
>
> —Henry Adams, *History of the United States* (1889)

In the flush times of the Old Southwest, the wilderness gradually gave way to the geometry of civilization. Writers of the American frontier, pioneers themselves, struggled to impose literary order on a region at once historical and imaginative. "The sole intention of the tales comprised in the following pages," wrote James Hall in *Legends of the West*, "is to convey accurate descriptions of scenery and population of the country in which the author resides. The only merit he claims for them is fidelity."[1] Charles Fenno Hoffman insisted that the "chief merit"of his *Winter in the West* (published in the same year as Longstreet's *Georgia Scenes*) was that his letters were "first and faithful impressions"; "novelty" and "romantic beauty" mark precise descriptions of the frontier, because "there is an ever-salient freshness in the theme of 'The Far West,' which prevents its becoming trite or tiresome."[2] Reports are informed by the perception that the frontier offered incomparable wealth; traveling west from Detroit, Hoffman sees a land of unparalleled opportunity and records original testimony of its bounty.

> What a country this is. Into land like this, which is comparatively undervalued by those seeking to settle on the prairie, a man can run his plough without felling a tree; and, planting a hundred acres, where he would but clear ten in the unsettled districts of New York, raise his twenty-five bushels of wheat to an acre in the very first season. "How is the soil here, sir?" said I to a farmer whose broad fields, though but a year under cultivation, looked as if they had been tilled for ten. "A pretty good gravelly loam of eighteen inches; but I think some of moving off to Kalamazoo, where they have it *four feet deep, and so fat that it will grease your fingers.*" (1:183–84)

The two languages in this passage convey both "romantic beauty" and "novelty": Hoffman celebrates the region in normative terms by means of a rational comparison, while the hyperbolic vernacular of the farmer transforms good land into a vision of fantastically fertile soil. The claims of the farmer serve as a faithful impression of pioneer optimism and western exaggeration.

On the other side of the frontier coin, however, we find not an agricultural wonderland but a menacing terra incognita of fraud, illusion, and deception. Hoffman notes that after being warned of "a gang of counterfeiters and coiners of false money" in the Old Southwest, "the individual who gave the writer this information subsequently palmed a copper dollar upon him" (2:211). Henry Adams, although quick to praise

the confidence of the southwestern frontiersmen, criticized
their substitution of appetite for virtue.

> In the long, unbroken line, pioneers were at work, cutting into
> the forests with the energy of so many beavers, and with no
> more express moral purpose than the beavers they drove
> away.... Greed for wealth, lust for power, yearning for the
> blank void of savage freedom such as Indians and wolves de-
> lighted in,—these were the fires that flamed under the caldron
> of American society.[3]

In the historical and fictional literature describing the flush
times—an imaginative frontier beginning around 1830 and
continuing until the outbreak of the Civil War, and stretching
spatially from Virginia southwest to Alabama, and from Louisiana northward to Missouri—predators appear with more frequency than in earlier American works. Timothy Flint's *Condensed Geography and History of the Western States or the
Mississippi Valley* (1828) provided not only numerous maps,
tables of navigation, and charts of flora and fauna but also
warnings of the methods and location of river robbers and hostile Indians; he enumerates tricks by which unwary travelers
are ambushed and laments the heathen "medicine men" who
stir up their tribes against white settlers. Other accounts confirm that backwoods slyness and cruelty were legendary for
both white and red renegades: James Hall's "Harpe's Head"
(1832) is a novella fictionalizing pirates described in Flint's
History; Charles Fenno Hoffman's *Winter in the West* (1835)
contains prime examples of aboriginal cunning; and Hugh
Henry Brackenridge's *Indian Atrocities* (published in book
form in 1843) catalogs infamous massacres. Speculators in
land, specie, and American votes fall under Flint's censure, as
he outlines an all-too-common path of the pioneer's destruction.

> Lands rose above their value, and speculation in them became
> a raging epidemic. Money, put in circulation by the sale of
> lands, abounded in the country. Town making, steam boat
> building,—in short, every species of speculation, was carried
> to a ruinous excess. Mercantile importations filled the coun-
> try with foreign goods. There were no reasonable foundations
> to the schemes, and no limits to the extravagance of the
> people. To give a more fatal extension and efficacy to the

mania of speculation, banks were multiplied in all the little towns and villages of the West, whose spurious paper, not predicated on banking principles, nor based on capital, answered the turn of speculation, as long as the excitement of confidence lasted. The consequence of all this was, that lands rose to double and triple their natural value, and were bought up by speculators. . . .

New states and territories grew out of this order of things, like the prophet's gourd. . . . A great many forward and plunging young men, whose only qualifications for their great work, were vanity and confidence, composed the legislatures. . . .

Meanwhile, this unnatural state of things could not last long. The tide began to ebb, and things to settle to their natural level. The first indication of this change was, that the banks began to fail, at first as rare occurrences; but these failures soon became so numerous and common, that the paper, except of the banks of Louisiana, Mississippi, and a very few interior banks, became as useless as any other wrapping paper. We have not the data for calculating the amount of loss in the western country, and patience and moderation of feeling would fail us, in contemplating these enormous mischiefs of legislative swindling. An inconceivable quantity of paper perished, not in the hands of the speculators, and those, who had been efficient in generating it; for they foresaw the approaching ruin, and they passed the spurious paper away, before the bubble of confidence, on which it was predicated, burst. It finally rested, and perished in the hands of farmers and mechanics,—the honest and the useful members of the community, who had fairly earned the value of the money. May it be a perpetual warning to the legislatures of the West. . . . A more enormous engine of mischief and dishonesty never was introduced into a community.[4]

Flint's speculators, however, only stole men's goods; another kind of frontier sharper—thought far more dangerous by some—traded in men's souls. In 1834 the *American Protestant Vindicator* warned its readers of godless western lands and men.

It is an ascertained fact, that Jesuits are prowling about all parts of the United States in every possible disguise, expressly to ascertain the most advantageous situations and modes to disseminate popery. A minister of the gospel from Ohio, has informed us, that he discovered one carrying his devices in his congregation; and he says, that the western country swarms with them under the names of puppet show-men, dancing masters, music teachers, pedlars of images and ornaments, barrel organ players, and similar practitioners. . . . Beware of the Jesuits![5]

Fear of religious fanatics seems somehow justified when the case of Joseph C. Dylks is examined. In 1828 he convinced the settlers of Guernsey County, Ohio, that he was himself God Incarnate. Although he failed to perform the miracles he had promised, he insisted that he would proclaim the New Heaven and New Earth for his faithful followers in the forest surrounding Leatherwood Creek. And despite some ungodly behavior in Philadelphia, Dylks's preaching was either so full of conviction or his message so genuinely attractive that members of his congregation insisted as late as 1870 that they had—with their own eyes—beheld Dylks ascend into heaven.[6] Tapping an apparently bottomless well of American innocence, or a deep-seated need to believe (as Adams theorized), charlatans less spiritual than Dylks collected fees for supposed communication with the dead and for demonstrations of animal magnetism and medicinal mesmerism. Dr. David M. Reese rebuked Americans in *Humbugs of New-York* (1838) for encouraging the "popular delusions" of phrenology, homœopathia, and "Ultra-Temperance," and Jereboam O. Beauchamp's 1826 *Confession* suggests that he acted under the guidance of heavenly voices when he killed his fiancée's seducer, Colonel Solomon Sharp, in the sensational "Kentucky Tragedy."[7] Mechanisms ranging from automatic chessmasters to simplified perpetual-motion machines were commonly displayed as wonders of the modern world—even the skeptical Nathaniel and Sophia Hawthorne considered trying mesmerism as a cure for prenuptial headaches.[8]

Wherever men met, at backwood crossroads or in towns, rogues in every form preyed upon the unsuspecting. Davy Crockett, the much-admired frontiersman, himself cozens an inattentive bartender in "A Useful Coonskin" (1834).[9] To pay for repeated rounds of drinks, this hero trades a prize pelt for a bottle of whiskey. Still thirsty but without more barter, Davy spies his original fur beneath the bar, just a short distance from his hand. Stealthily, he manages to reproduce—again and again—the same fur as payment, and merrily toasts each new success with his whiskey-warmed friends. Crockett's manual dexterity is comical, not criminal; the tale's setting in a friendly "doggery," its tone of rugged comradeship, and its action of ritual fellowship make clear that his sleight-of-hand is a humorous feat of skill morally equivalent to hitting a bull's-eye at one hundred yards.

Edgar Allan Poe's "Diddling Considered as One of the Exact Sciences" (1843) also emphasizes the comic aspects of sharping. Americans must be wary of thieves impersonating bill collectors, false newspaper advertisements for "lost" valuables, and dogs trained from birth to swallow welshers' IOU's. Reminiscent of Robert Greene's sixteenth-century pamphlets on cony-catching,[10] Poe's sketch illustrates eleven tricks of urban artists; unlike their predecessors, however, American diddlers work alone. "Were he not a diddler," Poe explains, "he would be a maker of patent rat-traps or an angler for trout."[11] In form and aesthetics Poe echoes De Quincey's "On Murder, Considered as One of the Fine Arts" (1827), claiming for the science an ancestry antedating John Kenney's Jeremy Diddler in "Raising the Wind" (1803).[12] Poe writes:

> The origin of the diddle is referrible to the infancy of the Human Race. Perhaps the first diddler was Adam. At all events, we can trace the science back to a very remote period of antiquity. The moderns, however, have brought it to an perfection never dreamed of by our thick-headed progenitors. (871)

The perfection Poe insists on for the art of swindling confirms that in 1843 he perceived the diddler to be central to American life. In *The Monks of Monk Hall* (1844), George Lippard contends that life in the city is a constant battle with seducers, blackmailers, and fiends. George H. Devol, a literal and perhaps literary sharper, remembers in *Forty Years a Gambler on the Mississippi* (1887) that the flush times were inhabited by only two species of Americans—the diddlers and the diddled. In 1845 E. Z. C. Judson ("Ned Buntline") sought to play a financial game of fast and loose with both categories: he first announced that as a service to his readers his new review, *Ned Buntline's Own*, would print a list of notorious sharpers; in order to capitalize fully on this innovation, however, he then collected a fee from countless rogues to have their names removed from his list. And Jonathan H. Green, the "Reformed Gambler," held that "gaming has attained such an ascendency in our country" because of the "unexampled prosperity" during the era of southwestern expansion.[13]

In these flush times, sharpers, diddlers, gamblers, and thieves assumed new prominence in fictional works. Drawing upon what Jonathan Culler calls the "text" of their culture,[14] writers increasingly created sharpers who expressed and resolved common anxieties about American boom-and-bust society: Poe's "Diddling," for example, gives form to the reader's suspicion that everyone—even a pet dog—is out to rob him. The potential inability to perceive misrepresentation, and the likelihood of deliberate misrepresentation, are both dramatically defined. By focusing on the diddler as artist, however, Poe turns the reader's attention to the intricate aesthetics of diddling and his fears into amused appreciation; he admires the diddler's talents—a combination of "minuteness, interest, perseverance, ingenuity, audacity, *nonchalance*, originality, impertinence, and *grin*" (870)—no longer bothered that these tricks may represent larger clandestine operations in American life, such as the manipulation of land prices by speculators, of import tariffs by northern businessmen, of the value of specie by bankers, or of tax rates by corrupt government officials.

Particularly in the Old Southwest, conditions required of literature more than transcriptions of "first and faithful impressions": the nullification crisis in South Carolina, Nat Turner's slave rebellion, the long and bloody Seminole Wars, and the Panic of 1837 revealed complexities in the South and West that demanded interpretation. The *new country*, the *frontier*, or the *West* seemed to have become inadequate terms for directing the expression of many American authors. As early as 1835, a reviewer of Charles Fenno Hoffman's *Winter in the West* hinted at the limits of fidelity as a satisfactory motive, method, and intention. For "the West," he complained,

> is a vague description of any place in North America. Although there be a distinct meaning in the phrase, well understood by the person using it, yet paradoxical as this is, it points to no locality. Twenty years ago the Alleghany range might,

by most people, be considered in these new countries. Ten
years ago, the Mississippi was the *ne plus ultra* for five-sixth
of Americans. The imaginary line which limited the bounds
of the West, has thus been continually changing.[15]

Without drawing a rigid cause and effect model, I would
suggest that in the 1840s a particular imaginative matrix
emerged from, imposed itself on, and extended earlier conceptions of the new country—the confidence man, who seeks and
wins confidence by deliberate deceit and then abuses that confidence for personal advantage. Writers used the evolving figure of the confidence man to embody a cycle of boom and bust
and to act as a mediating structure between the increasingly
problematic new country and an anxious national audience.
In 1849 the first recorded use of the term *confidence man*
appeared in the *New York Herald*, followed quickly by appearances in the *Knickerbocker*, the *Literary World*, the *Spirit of
the Times*, and even the *National Police Gazette*,[16] testimony
to the era's familiarity with the type and to the appropriateness of the name to disparate audiences. As Jonathan Culler
explains, "The process of developing literary conventions depends on models or operations already current in the social
discourse of the period (in the 'text' of everyday life, of the
'natural attitude,' as well as the discourse of its sciences)."[17]
Frontier fictions of the 1840s in this sense prepared the country to recognize the confidence man as an American convention, for the Southwest humorists peopled the flush times
with shifty characters whose main business it was to trade in
confidence and cash. Foregoing the cities of diddlers and the
wilderness of pioneers, the confidence man inhabits the frontier in between. He illuminates both states, functioning as the
center of an ongoing debate over the merits of nineteenth-
century American society, a stable point of intersection for
conflicting attitudes toward the flush times. The frontier
serves as a backdrop against which the confidence man—and
through him, American society—is seen in bold relief.

Another way to understand this process of literary change
is to envision a vertical model of historical continuity.[18] The
desire to create a native literature led writers in the 1820s and
1830s to insert in American settings inherited conventions
like the prankster with little more than a change of clothes:

the continuity from Brom Bones to Thomas Singularity to Ned Brace is direct or vertical. Longstreet's Yellow Blossom and Ransy Sniffle, however, are new kinds of characters, bound to a particular American locale and sporting symbolically collo- quial American names. They represent a horizontal discontin- uity in our historical model: the horse-swapping Blossom transcends the limitations of the traditional "biter bit" motif, just as Sniffle stands head and shoulders above scores of ne'er- do-wells; each typifies a contemporary experience and serves as a literary nexus for readers uncertain of the southwestern new country. In the 1840s, writers like Johnson Jones Hooper reformed these innovative characters into conventions of fron- tier literature: all at once (or so it seems) Ned Brace's sense of fun, the Yellow Blossom's boasting and swindling, and Ransy Sniffle's insinuating manner emerge in Captain Simon Suggs, the American confidence man par excellence.

Johnson Jones Hooper

Hooper's first literary effort, "Taking the Census in Ala- bama. By a Chicken Man of 1840," appeared in the La Fayette *East Alabamian* in 1843. This humorous reminiscence of mis- adventures in Tallapoosa was immediately applauded by Wil- liam T. Porter, editor of the influential New York weekly *Spirit of the Times: A Chronicle of the Turf, Agriculture, Field Sports, Literature and the Stage.* Introducing "Taking the Census," which the *Spirit* printed in September 1843, Porter outlined for his sixteen thousand subscribers Hooper's literary ancestry: "This Hooper is a clever man, and we must enlist him among the correspondents of the 'Spirit of the Times.' His sketch reminds us forcibly of the late Judge Longstreet's 'Geor- gia Scenes,' and the 'Adventures of Thomas Singularity,' by the late Prof. Nott, of S.C."[19] As Porter implies, "Taking the Cen- sus" is a linear descendant of traditional humorous sketches, an informal description of southwestern oddities: the low dia- lect is a characteristic element of 1830s frontier humor; the punctilious narrator, whose carefully chosen words contrast comically with those of the backwoodsmen, is likewise a con- ventional device. Hooper's comic perspective itself—based on such structural oppositions as those between the country and the city, the community and the stranger, and rebellion and authority—is a well-worn technique, and his deflation of both narrator and vernacular characters echoes Longstreet's methods in "Georgia Theatrics" and "The Horse-Swap."

The main structure of "Taking the Census" consists of humorous confrontations between the "chicken-man" and assorted residents of the Tallapoosa backcountry. In each of these, the narrator's repeated attempts to acquire information are frustrated—by mean dogs, fearful women, and artful circumlocution. A secondary structure emerges, however, which indicates a reorganization of conventional meanings and techniques.

Sol Todd, at first glance a conventional prankster like Longstreet's Ned Brace, lures the unsuspecting census-taker into the bottomless "Buck Hole" of the Tallapoosa River. Unlike Ned Brace, who frustrates Jacques Sancric's attempts at understanding ("The Character of a Native Georgian"), Sol intends more than the chicken-man's amusing embarrassment, for the ducking, we are told, is "but the fulfillment of a threat" (155). The census man represents more than Ned Brace's archetypal foreigner; he is the visible agent of Van Buren, who would personally, the population of Tallapoosa believed, after taking the census levy "a tremendous tax" upon every Alabamian— every man, woman, child, and chicken. To make the chicken-man take a swim in the Buck Hole is therefore to strike out at the personal representative of the federal government. Sol's prank, as opposed to any of Ned's, is motivated by more than a rough sense of fun—it is a political statement. Seen in this light, each encounter in "Taking the Census," although subordinate to a unifying comic structure, is informed by the rough individualism or rebelliousness characteristic of the frontier. Sol Todd and the other vernacular characters are not traditional pranksters playing traditional pranks.

Neither are they playing out the traditional action of the "biter bit." Hooper's "Taking the Census," although containing the ducking of Sol Todd—the prankster pranked—directs attention beyond itself toward a symbolic interpretation of the *duello*, one that suggests new external forces impinging upon the frontier. The 1840 United States Census embodies the intrusion of national political issues into the Southwest and gives particular literary form to the constitutional question of states' rights. The resistance of the vernacular characters to this form of federal regulation not only recalls the nullification crisis but also prefigures the impending Civil War. "Taking the Census" implies no political resolution to the debate, though as a loyal States Rights' Whig Hooper sees to it that the chicken-man's single victory is pyrrhic; rather, the sketch links opposed points of view. In this manner Hooper avoids judging the political issue, insisting instead on the "valueless action" of comedy.[20] Hooper focuses on the narrator's frustration, insulating the reader from the pressures of external problems. By withholding a final resolving action between the narrator and the vernacular characters, he allows the reader to try out each position, to evaluate each without commitment, and, at the tale's end, to retreat to a humorous vision of the whole.

"Taking the Census" reveals the method by which an author like Hooper could condition his audience to accept disturbing new perceptions; he utilizes familiar forms and techniques in order that his readers will be pleased rather than confused by deviations from the expected. The narrator's humorous observations and misadventures form the sketch's conventional main structure, one familiar to contemporary readers of *Georgia Scenes*, and one for which they share a conventional response: laughter. The implications of the confrontations between narrator and characters occupy a secondary position, held in check by equivalent pressures: the narrator, ducked in the Buck Hole by Sol Todd, immediately engineers Sol's own ducking—a balance is maintained.

From "Taking the Census" it is but a short imaginative step to Captain Simon Suggs.[21] The census-taker is, to Hooper's Whig Alabamians, no better than a shifty swindler, the Sixth U.S. Census no more nor less than a cleverly contrived game of theft. Simon Suggs, the "shifty man," is a chicken-man unrestrained by federal forms, a confidence man who at his leisure conducts his own personal census of the American frontier.

Some Adventures of Captain Simon Suggs (1845) borrows its form from nineteenth-century political biographies of prominent men like Andrew Jackson.[22] Written to present potential political candidates to the voters, campaign biogra-

From *Simon Suggs' Adventures* (1881 edition).

phies normally contained information on the office seeker's youth, his mature exploits of honor, his portrait accompanied by a physical description, and a statement of his intentions when elected. Hooper provides Simon Suggs with all of these elements, yet each is informed—or malformed—by the comic perspective of frontier humor. "His whole ethical system," writes Hooper, "lies snugly in his favourite aphorism—'IT IS GOOD TO BE SHIFTY IN A NEW COUNTRY'—which means that it is right and proper that one should live as merrily and as comfortably as possible at the expense of others; and of the practicability of this in particular instances, the Captain's whole life has been a long series of the most convincing illustrations."[23] A portrait by Felix O. Darley (reproduced above) complements a thorough anatomical analysis: the serpentine "lids without lashes," "An ever-present sneer—not all malice, however," and other "facial beauties" (11). "His autograph,—which was only produced unblotted and in orthographical cor-

rectness, after three efforts, 'from a rest,' on the counter of Bill
Griffin's confectionary—we have presented with a view to humor the whim of those who fancy they can read character in
a signature." Pointing out the discrepancy between appearance and reality—and between a conventional form and its
humorous imitation—Hooper states plainly that "all such, we
suspect, would pronounce the Captain *rugged, stubborn, and
austere* in his disposition; whereas in fact, he is *smooth, even-
tempered, and facile*" (10). To complete this parody, the author regrets the lapse of twenty years in Suggs's biography, and
offers only one example from his formative years. It is, however, telling.

In his seventeenth year, Simon is caught playing "seven up"
by his father, the Reverend Jedidiah Suggs. Hooper renders the
hard-shell Baptist preacher, like Simon's Negro friend Bill,
with conventionally exaggerated characteristics, attitudes,
and language.

> "Soho! youngsters!—*you* in the fence corner, and the *crap*
> in the grass; what saith the Scriptur', Simon? 'Go to the ant,
> thou sluggard,' and so forth and so on." (15)

Jedidiah resembles Fielding's Thwackum, a familiar figure of
pompous authority the reader is expected to resent. This conventional response Hooper insures by underscoring Jedidiah's
unbending nature, an even mixture of self-righteous piety and
greed. The reader sympathizes with Simon and desires the
humorous deflation of his humorless dad, who appears to take
more than spiritual enjoyment in disciplining the boys with
canes. Escape, triumph, and laughter are Simon's goals: escape
from punishment, triumph over his environment, and laughter to confirm his success. Simon is symbolically the champion of the individual, the reader's conventional hero of freedom, a truant not entirely unlike a frontier Tom Jones.

Facing a bout of discipline for playing cards with Bill, Simon
boldly proclaims that the punishment will do no good, as he
intends to make his living by gambling. Caught red-handed,
the boy's brashness not only postpones his beating but redi-
rects Jedidiah's thoughts: Simon's impassioned defense of his
card-playing abilities astounds his father and arouses his righteous indignation and pity.

> "Simon! Simon! You poor unlettered fool. Don't you know that all card-players, and chicken-fighters, and horse-racers go to hell? You crack-brained creetur you. And don't you know that them that plays cards always loses their money." (21)

Jedidiah's pulpit logic is no match for Simon's simple question: "Who wins it all then, daddy?" The reader appreciates Jedidiah's embarrassment and savors his fumbling efforts to assert his authority.

> "Shet your mouth, you imperdent, slack-jawed dog. Your daddy's a-tryin' to give you some good advice, and you a-pickin' up his words that way. I knowed a young man once, when I lived in Ogletharp, as went down to Augusty and sold a hundred dollars worth of cotton for his daddy, and some o' them gambollers got him to drinkin', and the *very first* night he was with 'em they got every cent of his money." (21–22)

Jedidiah's advice falls upon ears that are anything but deaf: "I'm as smart as any of 'em, and Bob Smith says them Augusty fellers can't make rent off o' me" (22). Simon's timely invocation of Bob Smith as a higher authority than his father on the perils of city life wounds Jedidiah's pride and arouses his contempt—for Bob Smith.

> "*Bob Smith* says, does he? And who's *Bob Smith*? Much does *Bob Smith* know about Augusty! he's *been thar*, I reckon! Slipped off yerly some mornin', when nobody warn't noticin', and got back afore night! It's *only* a hundred and fifty mile. Oh, yes, *Bob Smith* knows *all* about it! *I* a'n't never been to Augusty—*I* couldn't find the road thar, I reckon—ha! ha. *Bob–Smi–th!* The eternal stink! If he was only to see one o' them fine gentlemen in Augusty, with his fine broad-cloth, and bell-crown hat, and shoe-boots a-shinin' like silver, he'd take to the woods and kill himself a-runnin'. Bob Smith! that's whar all your devilment comes from, Simon." (23)

By a kind of logical sleight-of-hand, Simon confuses his father and severs the link connecting cause (caught gambling) and effect (immediate punishment).

Realizing his advantage, Simon insists that Bob Smith, his gambling tutor, assures him that he cannot be cheated by professional sharpers. "Bob Smith's as good as any body else, I judge; and a heap smarter than some. He showed me how to cut Jack . . . and that's more nor some people can do, if they *have* been to Augusty" (23). Simple Jedidiah, unwilling to ad-

mit his ignorance and to doubt his perceptions, agrees to witness Simon's attempt to cut jack: "If Bob Smith kin do it . . . I
kin too. I don't know it by that name; but if it's book knowledge or plain sense, and Bob kin do it, it's reasonable to s'pose
that old Jed'diah Suggs won't be bothered *bad*" (23–24). It is
the very reasonableness of Simon's explanation that snares
Jedidiah.

> "Well, now the idee is, if you'll take the pack and mix 'em all
> up together, I'll take off a passel from the top, and the bottom
> one of them I take off will be one of the Jacks."
> "Me to mix 'em fust?" said old Jed'diah.
> "Yes."
> "And you not to see but the back of the top one, when you
> go to 'cut,' as you call it?"
> "Jist so, daddy."
> "And the backs all jist as like as kin be?" said the senior
> Suggs, examining the cards.
> "More alike nor cow-peas," said Simon.
> "It can't be done, Simon," observed the old man, with great
> solemnity.
> "Bob Smith kin do it, and so kin I."
> "It's agin nater, Simon; thar a'n't a man in Augusty, nor on
> top of the yeath that kin do it!" (24)

Simon has won his father's confidence, although Jedidiah
knows "that them that plays cards always loses their money."
It is this very distrust of others coupled with an intense faith
in himself that makes the senior Suggs such a willing victim
of the junior's "transaction." For Simon, acutely aware of the
labyrinthine, contradictory impulses of human nature, appeals to the hard-shell preacher's egotistical confidence ("I
know he can't do it, so there's no resk"), his sense of spiritual
office ("I'll jist let him give me all his money, and that'll put
all his wild sportin' notions out of his head"), his plastic morality ("It sartinly *can't* be nothin' but *givin'*, no way it kin be
twisted"), and his greed ("Old Mr. Suggs ascertained the exact
amount of the silver . . . he weighed the pouch of silver in his
hand"). Jedidiah, whose instincts and emotions are now fully
aroused, eagerly responds to a suggestion of the devil and removes all the *"picter"* cards from Simon's deck. Confidently
awaiting the outcome of Simon's cut, Jedidiah is the quintes-
sential victim, the dishonest man who is sure he is about to

outsmart the confidence man. But by "a suspicious working of the wrist of the hand on the cards," Simon defeats his father's expectations, denies the validity of his perceptions, calls into question his powers of reasoning, and presents the jack of hearts for inspection. Astonished—and unwilling to admit his own dishonest manipulations—Jedidiah gives Simon the horse Bunch, a reprise from correction, and agrees with his son's ironic explanation of events.

> "Daddy coun't help it, it was *predestinated*—'whom he hath, he will,' you know;" and the rascal pulled down the under lid of his left eye at his brother. Then addressing his father, he asked, "Warn't it, daddy?"
> "To be sure—to be sure—all fixed aforehand," was old Mr. Suggs' reply.
> "Didn't I tell you so, Ben?" said Simon—"*I* knowed it was all fixed aforehand." (29)

The reader laughs with Simon, for he too understands that fate was fixed. He shares in the triumph of adolescence over sententious authority and delights in the exposure of the preacher's true qualities: avarice, egotism, and an ill-founded self-confidence. Had Jedidiah been a truly honest man, Simon could not have induced him under any circumstances to postpone his "correction" and take part in his "transaction"; Jedidiah reaps exactly as he sows. Hooper's use of the conventional frame technique further enlists the reader's sympathy, as the amused voice of the narrator assures him that this biography of Captain Simon Suggs chronicles the exploits of a humorous fellow worthy of note and that his behavior is completely under rational—narrative—control. It is also difficult to resist a boyish confidence man who wins an impractical horse and his freedom: Simon acts out a common fantasy of adolescent triumph. The confidence man is the youthful new country.

Simon's victory, however, is not without qualification. It is perhaps the result of the needs of frontier authors to reassert their superiority over low characters, or of these authors' awareness that shifty characters symbolize historical threats not completely dismissed by humor, that the confidence man is almost never entirely successful and admirable. His winnings are small, like the unmanageable horse Bunch, and his resolve to "git these here green feller's money" has social implications that are less than amusing. The reader is related, regardless of whether he acknowledges his kinship explicitly, to the confidence man's victim; in the broadest sense, he shares with every man the fate of the "green feller." By anticipating with pleasure Simon's hoodwinking of Jedidiah, the reader recognizes his own predicament and admits his own vulnerability. The same experience that teaches him to expect Jedidiah's victimization also teaches the reader that he too is susceptible to victimization. Although the reader overtly laughs with Simon, the entire episode acts as a kind of multiply refracting mirror in which the reader sees himself as both confidence man and foolish gull. The effect diminishes the confidence man's appeal and reinforces the reader's identification with the narrative voice.

When Simon appears to be the dispenser of poetic justice—Simon surely gives Jedidiah his just reward—his moral posture is vitiated by more than a streak of inhumanity: the malicious glee with which he "very wickedly" drives the mumble-peg deeper into the ground, knowing full well the inevitable consequence for his friend Bill, is bettered by the pipe he fills with gunpowder and leaves for his mother as a reminder of his affection. These are not the poetics of the confidence man, for they require neither confidence nor art—they are the dirty tricks of an irresponsible prankster. Twice Simon deliberately exposes Bill to painful beatings, and Simon's "involuntary sympathy" does little to enhance his appeal; his clear theft of his friend's pennies confirms the fact that the Negro is literally his whipping boy. Simon's often vile behavior clearly separates him from the normative frame-narrator (and author) and shows that the confidence man's ethical system is ultimately self-reflexive rather than social.

The distinction between artistic confidence tricks and blatant dirty tricks is crucial, revealing much more than a historical difference in standards of humor. The confidence man's occasional physical pranks resemble those of Longstreet's Ned Brace; they remind the reader of Simon's ancestry by their conventional form and provide the reader with a conventional model for response. They also invite comparison with confidence art, which implies an inchoate new standard. The confidence man becomes a literary convention precisely at the point that we can distinguish his aesthetic moneymaking schemes from the exploding gimmicks of the traditional prankster. As Hooper notes of Simon Suggs, it is the captain's ingenuity and wit which enable him "to detect the *soft spots* in his fellow . . . to assimilate himself to whatever company he may fall in with," and "which entitle him to the epithet *'Shifty'*" (12, 13). Further, the narrator insists that he will not be guilty of the cheap stunts to which Simon resorts; he can be trusted implicitly—the reader need not fear a similar betrayal of his confidence. As the confidence man triumphs over his victim, so too does the frame narrator triumph over his charismatic character, thereby assuring his audience that the harsh, chaotic world of Simon Suggs is carefully circumscribed. The confidence man's art appears subservient to the narrator's: stuffing his mother's pipe with gunpowder demonstrates Simon's tendency to forgo the rhetorical tools of his profession and seriously qualifies his success. These acts of rough sport signify that although the confidence man is decidedly the master of his frontier world, it is the frame narrator's rhetorical mastery that ultimately shapes and contains it.

Simon's youthful escapade provides a paradigm of expectations and response, its conventional and innovative elements fused through Hooper's overarching perspective of frontier humor. The momentary uneasiness the reader experiences when he recognizes himself in Jedidiah, Bill, Mrs. Suggs, or Simon himself is a defining characteristic of the American confidence man. Like the figure of the fool in Elizabethan drama, the confidence man makes the audience—the reader, not his victim—laugh, but it is laughter always tinged with anxiety: he who laughs at the fool's antics also laughs at himself, for the fool symbolically mirrors the folly to which every man is prone. The tension felt by the audience, common to both confidence man and fool, receives structural reinforcement by their peripheral social status: both function as outsiders, outlaws who simultaneously represent the contradictory human impulses toward society and anarchy. Whether in an English court or the American Southwest, these figures inhabit a symbolic frontier where opposed pressures intersect and intermingle. Thus the fool, lording over his bauble, forms an ambiguous doppelgänger of the king ruling his court, and the confidence man, who abuses frontiersmen, functions as an analogue of those Americans who exploit the frontier.[24] Thus the confidence man embodies and recapitulates the continuous struggle between order and chaos in nineteenth-century America. A child of the frontier, the confidence man embodies its ambiguities; ruled by these ambiguities, he is also defined by the frontier and bound to it. Temporally and spatially, the confidence man symbolizes in a conventional literary form the flush times in the new country.

It is therefore altogether appropriate that Simon Suggs's first mature "operation" is speculation in frontier lands. Hooper carefully initiates the reader in the mysteries of flush times economics, detailing Simon's methods of speculation "without a dollar":

> We admit that there is a seeming incongruity in the idea but have those in whose minds speculation and capital are inseparably connected, ever heard of a process by which lands were sold, deeds executed, and all that sort of thing completely arranged, and all without once troubling the owner of the soil for an opinion even, in regard to the matter? Yet such occurrences were frequent some years since, in this country, and they illustrated *one* mode of speculation requiring little, if any, cash capital. But there were other modes of speculating without money or credit; and Captain Simon Suggs became as familiar with every one of them, as with the way to his own corncrib. As for those branches of the business requiring actual pecuniary outlay, he regarded them as only fit to be pursued by purse-proud clod-heads. Any fool, he reasoned, could speculate if he had money. But to buy, to sell, to make profits, without a cent in one's pocket—this required judgment, discretion, ingenuity—in short, genius! (35)

Simon's genius, undeniably, lies in "that tact, which enables man to detect the *soft spots* in his fellow, and to assimilate himself to whatever company he may fall in with" (12). The confidence man is proud of his ability, a national virtue, to make something out of nothing. Overhearing two speculators discuss a valuable piece of property, Simon, though unable to learn its exact location, formulates an inspired plan to profit from his greatest resource, human nature, and from the confident appearance of knowledge. The shifty man overtakes the speculator, Mr. Jones, and, knowing that one of any fellow's softest spots is his suspicion of others, insinuates that he, Simon Suggs, is also heading to Montgomery to lay claim to Mr. Jones's land. Jones, whose horse has been worn to the bone, allows his fear that Simon is his competition to cloud his reason, and within minutes reveals the coordinates of the property to the confidence man. Certain that Simon—whose horse is fresh—will be able to enter the claim first, Jones, whose blind greed is obvious, agrees to pay Simon $150 not to make the entry, furthermore "convincing" Simon to swap his own fine but tired horse plus $20 for the worthless but well-rested Ball. Using only his genius, Simon makes the speculator pay the price of his profession, for without Jones's desire to make a fast killing and the suspicion that attends such dishonest dealings, the shifty man would have remained the penniless owner of Ball; the victim's own fear and avarice give Simon the opportunity to speculate on him. The confidence man merely confirms (and profits by) Jones's apprehension that the world is filled with men as dishonest as himself.

Simon concludes the episode with a parodic paean to honesty.

> "Now some fellers, after makin' sich a little decent rise would milk the cow dry, by pushin' on to Doublejoy's, startin' a runner the nigh way to Montgomery, by the Augusty ferry, and enterin' that land in somebody else's name before Jones gits thar! But honesty's the best policy. Honesty's the bright spot in *any* man's character!—Fair play's a jewel, but honesty beats it all to pieces! Ah yes, *honesty*, HONESTY'S the stake that Simon Suggs will ALLERS tie to! What's a man without his inteegerty?" (40–41)

The confidence man's mock praise is humorous, for the reader knows that what really stops Simon is that the effort required to register the claim would be tiresome. He is honest only to his nature, which dictates "that one should live as merrily and comfortably as possible at the expense of others" (12). And his insistence on the truth of a traditional aphorism—"honesty's the best policy"—reminds the reader of Suggs's credo: "IT IS GOOD TO BE SHIFTY IN A NEW COUNTRY."

Simon's adventure with Mr. Jones, ending with a parody of conventional wisdom, appropriately introduces the sentimental address with which Hooper's fourth chapter commences.

> READER! didst ever encounter the Tiger?—not the bound-
> ing creature of the woods, with deadly fang and mutilating
> claw, that preys upon blood and muscle—but the stealthier
> and more ferocious animal which ranges amid "the busy
> haunts of men"—which feeds upon coin and banknotes—
> whose spots, more attractive than those of its namesake of the
> forest, dazzle and lure, like the brilliantly varying hues of the
> charmer snake, the more intensely and irresistibly, the longer
> they are looked upon—the thing, in short, of pasteboard and
> ivory, mother-of-pearl and mahogany—The FARO BANK! (42)

Hooper's rhetoric explores new possibilities for the artificial style of much sentimental fiction: the real and fictional worlds intersect, like the animal and mechanical images Hooper employs, and a new synthesis results. It also provides for his audience an immediately recognizable structure of understanding. The conventional address, humorously inflated, forms a familiar literary signpost for the reader and signals to him by its very nature as a set piece that not all traditional values will be inverted or burlesqued in *Simon Suggs*. In addition, Hooper qualifies Simon's activities by devoting much of chapters 4 and 5 to his weakness: the Faro Bank. That Simon has a weakness proves that he is only human, not the Devil Incarnate, and that he is susceptible to other confidence men of greater quickness and skill. The reader reimagines with Hooper the character of Simon Suggs, recalling the truth of Jedidiah's biblical wisdom once so easily dismissed: "Them that plays cards always loses their money" (21). Jedidiah, it seems, may have been right, for "The Tiger" repeatedly makes a poor fool out of Simon.

Hooper's introductory digression, itself a conventional literary device, enforces the reevaluation by the sharp contrast between Simon's obsession and the narrator's normative rhetoric. The narrator's verbal "actions" may be imaginative and energetic, but they will never veer out of control. As in chapter 5, the descriptive digression is reassuring because of its substantiality; the physical details—the "mother-of-pearl and mahogany" Faro Bank, the "huge-lettered advertising cards" of Tuskaloosa—confirm the reader's knowledge of the historical frontier. They also acquaint the green fellow with the operations of gamblers and sharps. And finally, Hooper begins to flesh out the character of one particular confidence man; the

shifty man is defined as an individual, a personality not to be
confused with other types. Unlike Longstreet's Yellow Blossom or Ned Brace, Simon Suggs is the protagonist of fourteen
stories. And as this confidence man becomes a more round
character, there appears a trace of involuntary sympathy in
Hooper's language; Simon's flaw, his "delusion," is lamenta-
ble, a consequence of his fuller personality. In this, Hooper
reveals a new aspect of frontier humor, compassion for the
confidence man, which will be fully developed by Harris, Melville, and Twain. The discovery of Simon's depth, his complexity of character, is Hooper's own, and implies an ambivalence
toward the confidence man and an uncertainty of his identity
as a mere comic device. Appropriately, Simon's next two exploits involve masquerade.

   Simon Suggs is of course itself a form of literary masquerade, the "campaign biography" of an American who is the
antiface of the Leatherstocking ideal, the ironic counterfeit or
mirror image of Cooper's hero. More particularly, Hooper's fiction exemplifies what Henry Nash Smith terms "the nineteenth-century fondness for disguises." [25] Simon Suggs puts on
and takes off identities with less effort than that required to
change hats: at one moment he becomes the representative
from Tallapoosa, only to be transformed in the next into the
heroic hog-driver General Witherspoon. These disguises, provided by acts of mistaken identity, suggest a traditional pattern
of complication; in *Simon Suggs*, however, the conventional
revelations of sentimental and romantic fiction Hooper shares
only with the reader. Simon's victims do not learn his identity
(or their folly) until he has made good his escape. The humor
of each episode depends on concealment rather than on revelation. Finally, the comedy of errors the confidence man perpetuates ends neither in tragedy—as in James Nelson Barker's
"Superstition" (1825)—nor in marriage—as in James Fenimore Cooper's *Pioneers* (1823)—but in an ironic ritual of good-
fellowship. Having been mistaken for the representative from
Tallapoosa by a man desirous of becoming—by the representative's influence—a bank director, Simon good-naturedly accepts a bribe, and with "his new friend travelled the remainder
of the way to Tuskaloosa, in excellent companionship, as it
was reasonable they should. They told their tales, sang their

songs, and drank their liquor like a jovial pair as they were—
the candidate paying all scores wherever they halted" (51).
And after playing the part of General Witherspoon to the tune
of two thousand dollars, Simon entertains the gentlemen of
Tuskaloosa with an oyster supper (on the general's credit) and
a farewell toast.

> "Gentle*men*," said he "I'm devilish glad to see you all, and
> much obleeged to you, besides. You are the finest people I ever
> was amongst, and treat me a d——d sight better than they do
> at home"—which was a fact! "Hows'ever, I'm a poor hand to
> speak, but here's wishing of luck to you all"—and then
> wickedly seeming to blunder in his little speech—"and if I
> forgit you, I'll be d——d if you'll ever forgit me!" (66–67)

The reader, privy to the real import of Simon's speech, agrees
with a smile that they will never forget "General Witherspoon," nor will they soon forget the ease with which they
were manipulated. For Simon has only "to assimilate himself"
to their expectations, parody their fantasies of the general's
liberality, and allow his victims to deceive themselves.

As the legislator from Tallapoosa and as General Witherspoon, Simon acts in "a sublime moral spectacle" with unpleasant social ramifications. Chapter 4 demonstrates that
"there are many reasons why gentlemen of distinction should
at times desire to travel without being known" (49). The confidence man, of course, does not wish to be unmasked; this is
the joke Simon shares with the reader. A dishonest legislator,
as well, desires the protection of secrecy; this joke is on the
reader. The suspicion that all representatives can be bought
impinges upon our amusement, and Hooper's distrust of figures of authority manifests itself both in the confidence man's
ability to assume the identity of a legislator or general and in
the congruence between the practical methods of officials and
con men. Hooper underlines the immorality of heroes and
statesmen by noting that "General Witherspoon" is accepted
in the Tuskaloosa gambling hall by gentlemen, "a large proportion members of the legislature" (55). The unamusing im-
plication is that these crooked fools are actually Representative Men, not the worst America has to offer, like Captain
Simon Suggs, but the best, those to whom the reader has entrusted his faith and his future.

That Hooper employs a central character whose business is dishonesty itself, that Simon Suggs never meets an honest man, and that the reader finds such characters entertaining all suggest a critical impulse to the confidence man's adventures. The new country, which in the 1830s had seemed to offer infinite opportunity, wealth, and security, by 1845 often appeared to have become—again, in the imagination—settlements plagued by necessity, poverty, and uncertainty. The cycle of boom-and-bust, culminating for many pioneers in financial ruin following the Panic of 1837, created anxiety in the Southwest that often appeared as suspicion of those in power who seemed to profit in proportion to the pioneers' loss. The confidence man, who returns to the 1830s in fiction to expose, profit from, and triumph over the speculators, expresses the common fantasy of the disillusioned who, as Timothy Flint noted, watched helplessly as their bubble of confidence burst. Simon Suggs is no frontier guardian angel; he, too, is helplessly tossed about, and though he may float high on the calm surface one day, on the next he must struggle not to go under.

Simon's dealings with Indians, a people who lost everything in the flush times, begin with the conventional *ubi sunt* theme, yet it is modified to accommodate contradictory impulses.

> In those days, an occasion of the sort drew together white man and Indian from all quarters of the "nation"—the one to cheat, the other to be cheated. The agent appointed by the Government to "certify" the sales of Indian lands was always in attendance; so that the scene was generally one of active traffic. The industrious speculator, with his assistant, the wily interpreter, kept unceasingly at work in the business of fraud; and by every species and art of persuasion, sought—and, sooner or later, succeeded—in drawing the untutored children of the forest into their nets. . . .
>
> And where are these speculators NOW?—those lords of the soil!—the men of dollars—the fortune-makers who bought with hundreds what was worth thousands!—they to whom every revolution of the sun brought a reduplication of their wealth! Where are they? (69)

By lamenting the passing of the flush times of rampant speculation Hooper fulfills a comic purpose, for it is amusing to

mourn for confidence men and thieves. Yet his sobering answer to "Where are they, and what are they, now?" defeats the
humorous expectations of the reader.

> They have been smitten by the hand of retributive justice! The
> curse of their victims has fastened upon them, and nine out
> of ten are houseless, outcast, bankrupt! In the flitting of ten
> years, the larger portion have lost money, lands, character,
> every thing! And the few who still retain somewhat of their
> once lordly possessions, mark its steady, unaccountable di-
> minution, and strive vainly to avert their irresistible fate—an
> old age of shame and beggary. They are cursed, all of them—
> blighted, root and trunk and limb! The Creek is avenged! (69–
> 70)

The narrator attempts to have it both ways, affirming first with
one set of values a comedic golden age, and then praising with
a very different set of values that age's destruction. Hooper
suspends the reader between two visions of the 1830s, one a
comic pastoral in which the confidence man is king, and the
other an antipastoral of retribution and wrath. The reader's
confusion may be the result of Hooper's ambivalence toward
the flush times and the confidence man, for the pastoral and
antipastoral illuminate each other by contrast, mutually ex-
clusive images evoking separate responses. The apparently humorous scene of speculation is by narrative fiat transformed
into a court of ultimate justice, the comic perspective so comfortable to the reader becoming suddenly reflective and bitter.
The reader may accept that the Indians have been wronged,
that confidence men deserve their comeuppance, and that
Hooper's sympathy and condemnation are equally genuine;
but what, then, is the proper response to Hooper's Simon
Suggs, who shamelessly speculates in Indian lands? Hooper
appears to intend his literary devices to communicate contradictory attitudes: the Indians lost their ancestral lands to speculators who exploited their innocence; those speculators,
though corrupt, were clever men, and one cannot help but
admire their skill; the passing of both "races" should be
mourned, for the wide-open frontier that gave them life is forever gone; and although some speculators hastened the death
of the frontier through their monomaniacal pursuit of lucre,
there was at least one, Simon Suggs, who was in harmony with

the flush times and who loved the art, laughter, and personal triumph as much as a stack of golden double-eagles.

Hooper clarifies the reader's response to Simon Suggs by directing his attention to a mere criminal, Mr. Eggleston of "the great Columbus Land Company" (71). This fiend has no love for anything save profit. He marries a Creek chief's daughter, Litka, convinces the "Sky Chief" to entrust his lands to himself, sells the lands for three thousand dollars, and thrusts the penniless and homeless old chief and his own very pregnant wife on the mercy of the federal government. Simon Suggs, in sharp contrast, takes from the "Big Widow" only what she in fact offers—and he sees to it that she is paid. Hooper does not allow the reader to question the difference between these two thefts; he asserts the wickedness of Eggleston's and the harmless amusement of Simon's.[26] Bridging these parallel episodes of reprobation and approbation is a humorous interlude of Indian boasting.

> "Coop! coop! hee!" shouts a champion of the Cohomutka-Gartska town. . . . "The Oakfuskee people are all cowards—they run like rabbits! They are liars! They have two tongues! Coop! coop! hee-e-e! the Alligator family is mixed-blooded! they come from the runaway Seminole and the runlet-making Cherokee! The 'Deer' people can beat the Alligator people till they beg for their hides!" (72)

Recalling Colonel Nimrod Wildfire's rhetoric in James Kirke Paulding's *The Lion of the West* (1831), this contest seems a set piece designed to realign the reader's expectations. He laughs at the exaggerations of the Deer and Alligators and, on familiar footing once again, anticipates Simon's future operations without dwelling on their implications.

In chapter 7 Hooper demonstrates that Simon Suggs desires not wealth but power. At Fort Suggs the shifty man wins the confidence and admiration of his frightened pioneer neighbors by assuming the appearance of courage in the face of imminent Indian attack, keeping to himself the knowledge that all the Creeks around the settlement are friendly. The citizens, who expect to be scalped within the hour, vote the cool Simon their leader and insist that he accept the military rank of Captain of "the Tallapoosy Vollantares." Their commission the confidence man assumes with modesty, pride, and pleasure, for he is finally superior to the vagaries of circumstance. He triumphs over the authority earlier represented by his father, legislators, and generals by seizing with his own hands the reins of power. He delights in the direct exercise of military authority and, having no longer to practice the petty subterfuges so much a part of confidence art, publicly court-martials the foolish Widow Haycock. Though Captain Suggs does not overlook this opportunity to fine the widow twenty-five dollars, his enjoyment seems largely the result of his superiority to the community. To command rich widows, merchants, and officials, to be literally above civil law, appears to be the fulfillment of the confidence man's dream: he governs not just pasteboard cards, nor does he rule his victims by impersonating a general—the confidence man is elected captain of the fort because he is Simon Suggs. Though this distinction may at first appear merely a question of semantics, like that between Simon's "Tallapoosy Vollantares" and his "Forty Thieves," it discloses the confidence man apart from the necessity of disguise, releases him from the need to mask his identity. He is free to pursue what activities he prefers, for his manipulation of the settlers' fear of Indians has guaranteed his survival. Rather than "milk the cow dry," as a mere money-grabber like Eggleston might, Captain Suggs enjoys eating, drinking, socializing, playing cards, and—most of all—exercising the privileges of his rank. He is no longer at the mercy of those fickle goddesses, Chance and Luck, but has conquered their frontier domain, consecrating a whiskey barrel— the court-martial's symbolic "drum-head"—to the more appropriate deities Authority and Pleasure. Although master of Fort Suggs, master of his subjects' perceptions, and master of his own fate, Captain Suggs discovers the bounty of his new *Lares* and *Penates* to be limited and temporary.

Captain Simon Suggs's authority does not pass unchallenged. "Yaller-laigs" questions the captain's abilities, makes jokes at his expense, and informs the reader that Suggs has become as jealous of his command as a hard-shell preacher of his pulpit. The confidence man has become "Captain Suggs," an official with a particular social identity, with power over the community he wishes to maintain.

> Suggs . . . remained snug enough at the Fort, subsisting comfortably upon the contributions which he almost daily levied from wagons passing with flour, bacon, and whiskey, from We-

tumpka eastward. In his own energetic language, "he had tuk
his persition, and d——d ef he didn't keep it as long as he had
yeath enough to stand upon!" (111)

Yaller-laigs adds another humorous perspective to the narrative, reminding the reader through his function as a Suggsian
doppelgänger that *Captain* Suggs embodies the authority that
Simon Suggs, the confidence man, hates and distrusts. That
the captain's heckler escapes disciplinary action indicates
Hooper's insistence on the comic values of the confidence
man. It also records a comforting truth: though even the greatest scoundrel may come to power, there will always be enterprising individuals to ambush his flanks and make him smart.
As if aware of the captain's awkward position, Hooper concludes chapter 8 with a revealing aside that merges the perspectives of Yaller-laigs and Captain Suggs: Simon rewards
"Lewtenant Snipes" for honorable service with one of the
Widow Haycock's twenty-five dollars. This division of plunder
relocates *Captain* Suggs in the comic world of the confidence
man, not least of all by Simon's reckoning of the Lewtenant's
percentage. The captain himself, like "Yaller-laigs," does not
take his military status all that seriously; "Lewtenant Snipes,"
in on the joke as surely as the reader, has the privilege of concluding the episode with the confidence man's ritual speech:

> "Capting Suggs . . . I've said it *behind you back*, and I'll say
> it *to you're face*; you're a *gentleman* from the top of your head
> to the end of your big-toe nail! Less go in and liquor; damn
> expenses!" (110)

The confidence man's command over Fort Suggs conveys
more than its ostensible comedic purpose. Hooper deploys
suggestions of real violence throughout these chapters, enlist-
ing historical details when possible to create an undertone of
frontier anxiety. The amusing contest between Alligator and
Deer Indians degenerates into actual hostilities, reinforcing
the narrator's note that in 1836 the Creeks were actually at
war. The survival of Captain Suggs and the "Tallapoosy Vollantares" appears more precarious than comic in light of the
settlers' migration described in chapter 7, for despite the
clearly exaggerated fears of Mrs. Simmons and Mrs. Rollins
(83–84), "several persons, residing in the county of Tallapoosa,

were cruelly murdered by the 'inhuman savages'" (82). The ball game the Volunteers attend turns out to be an Indian trap from which they barely escape. These specters of violence remind the reader that life on the frontier is not all confident fun and confidence games; these festivities, like the earlier boasting contest, culminate in a final image of violence and death. Anticipating the renegades' unsportsmanlike conduct, Captain Suggs and his men steal the Indians' ponies and the ball game's purse. Hooper transforms the "biter bit" motif into an ominous confrontation between red man and white. Cocher-Emartee, chief of the Oakfuskees, pursues the "Vollantares," "foaming and furious."

> He was mounted on a borrowed horse, and now loudly howled forth his demand for the restoration of his gallant bay and the shot-bag of silver; protesting that the whole affair was a joke on his part to try the spunk of the "Vollantares"—that he was "good friends" to the white people, and didn't wish to injure any of them.
>
> "Go to h-ll! you d—d old bandy-shanked redskin!" shouted back Simon; "I know the inemies of my country better'n that!"
>
> Cocher danced, shouted, raved, bellowed, and snorted in his boundless rage! Finally, he urged his pony into the water with the intention of swimming across.
>
> "Kumpny form!" shouted Simon—"blaze away at the d——d old *hostile!*" A volley was fired, and when the smoke cleared away, the pony was seen struggling in the river, but there were no Indians in sight. (116–17)

Hooper has ambushed the reader. The dramatic shift in tone signals a redirection of his attention from the humorous antics of a frustrated Indian to the turbulent waters over a dead chief's body.[27] Although the last short paragraph attempts a return to the comic vision of the cheated confidence man (the state legislature refuses to reimburse Captain Suggs for the loss of his horse), the reader's confidence in the narrative's structure has been shaken; the frontier proves dangerous, even when focused through the humorous lens of the confidence man. Indeed, the episode forces the reader to reconsider the dangers of the confidence man and his flush-times frontier.

Captain Simon Suggs can cause death. Penetrating to this level of seriousness, Hooper reveals—if only for an instant—

a chracteristic ambivalence toward the confidence man:
though clever, amusing, and life affirming, an enthusiastically
anarchic individual, these same qualities threaten not just a
representative Indian but the entire structure of civilization,
its laws, hierarchies, and fundamental order. That the Tallapoosy volunteers kill Cocher-Emartee suggests the wholesale
murder of Indians by whites and strips away the layer of ab-
straction beneath which Americans feared the Noble Savage.
The chief is simply an Indian to be bamboozled and, when he
becomes an obstacle, disposed of by force. His death further
symbolizes the end of an era; Hooper writes no more of Indians, and it seems far from accidental that Simon Suggs's remaining escapades are attempts to accommodate his renegade
frontier style to an increasingly dominant civilization.

Simon Suggs seems up to his old tricks in chapter 10, "The
Captain Attends A Camp-Meeting." Hooper redefines his confidence man, dismissing the implications of the Indian incident by the strategy of omission.

> Captain Suggs found himself as poor at the conclusion of
> the Creek war, as he had been at its commencement. Although
> no "arbitrary," "despotic," "corrupt," and "unprincipled"
> judge had fined him a thousand dollars for his proclamation
> of martial law at Fort Suggs, or the enforcement of its rules in
> the case of Mrs. Haycock; yet somehow—the thing is alike
> inexplicable to him and to us—the money which he had con-
> trived, by various shifts to obtain, melted away and was gone
> forever. To a man like the Captain, of intense domestic affec-
> tions, this state of destitution was most distressing. "He could
> stand it himself—didn't care a d—n for it, no way," he ob-
> served, "but the old woman and the children; *that* both-
> ered him!"
>
> As he sat one day, ruminating upon the unpleasant condi-
> tion of his "financial concerns," Mrs. Suggs informed him that
> "the sugar and coffee was nigh about out," and that there were
> not "a dozen j'ints and middlins, *all put together*, in the
> smokehouse." Suggs bounced up on the instant, exclaiming,
> "D—n it! *somebody* must suffer!" (118)

The reader is directed to a humorous perception of Simon, a
penniless—perhaps hen-pecked—family man who retains
nothing from his days of military glory save his title. The frontier itself has suffered change, visible in the contrast between
the subsistence preaching of the Rev. Jedidiah Suggs and the

affluent evangelicalism of the Rev. Bela Bugg. Their similar
names suggest a similarity of purpose while emphasizing the
difference in their methods as well as Bugg's greater success.
Simon recognizes the threat that the camp meeting poses.

> Amid all this confusion and excitement Suggs stood un-
> moved. He viewed the whole affair as a grand deception—a
> sort of "opposition line" running against his own, and looked
> on with a sort of professional jealousy. (122)

Yet the "grand deception" before his eyes impresses Simon
with its magnitude, its efficiency, and its audaciousness.

> A half-dozen preachers were dispensing the word; the one in
> the pulpit, a meek-faced old man, of great simplicity and be-
> nevolence. . . . The rest were walking to and fro . . . among the
> "mourners"—a host of whom occupied the seat set apart for
> their especial use—or made personal appeals to the mere spec-
> tators. The excitement was intense. Men and women rolled
> about on the ground, or lay sobbing or shouting in promiscu-
> ous heaps. . . .
> "Keep the thing warm!" roared a sensual seeming man, of
> stout mould and florid countenance, who was exhorting
> among a bevy of young women, upon whom he was lavishing
> caresses. "Keep the thing warm, breethring!—come to the
> Lord, honey!" he added, as he vigorously hugged one of the
> damsels he sought to save. (119, 120)

Though Simon admits that "nater will be nater, all the world
over; and I judge ef I was a preacher, I should save the purtiest
souls fust, myself" (123), his tastes are primarily pecuniary.
Hooper himself intrudes in an uncharacteristic footnote, one
that echoes Longstreet's disclaimer in the concluding paragraph of "The Fight," assuring the reader "that the scenes described in this chapter are not now to be witnessed" (122);
both he and Simon are amused by these sensual gymnastics,
yet clearly separate themselves from them. Bela Bugg challenges Simon's professional reputation, and the minister's ca-
resses for this reason do not invite imitation. Simon, like the
new country itself, has matured; he is fifty years old, has a
wife and children, and no longer roams the settlements
cloaked in anonymity. Instead, he wears "his famous old
green-blanket overcoat" (119), and Hooper informs us that at
the camp meeting "great was the rejoicing of the brethren, as
they sang, shouted, and prayed around him—for by this time

it had come to be generally known that the 'convicted' old man was Captain Simon Suggs, the very 'chief of sinners' in all that region" (124). The captain cannot masquerade any more as General Witherspoon; he also cannot afford to lose his reputation—and his livelihood—to the smooth-talking mechanics of Bela Bugg.

Simon trades on the people's knowledge of his identity to make an asset of a liability. He soon has all the brethren admiring the intensity of his conversion, for as Mrs. Dobbs repeatedly testifies, "Glory to my soul . . . it's the sweetest talk I *ever* hearn!" (127). Simon manipulates the congregation like the Devil himself, winning their confidence by confirming their religious visions.[28] The suspicious Bela Bugg, who believes he is using Captain Simon Suggs to attract donations, Suggs in like manner soothes and then betrays. After arousing the brethren's "pride of Purse," encouraging them to "give *accordin'* to their means" (131), Simon offers them the chance—by donating to his cause more than Snooks and Snodgrass—to appear wealthy to their peers. In each case the confidence man turns his knowledge of human nature against his victims, for it is pride, greed, or a stubborn belief in the truth of their perceptions that make them vulnerable.

The sensuality of the camp meeting, the whipping Mrs. Dobbs promises her Negro slave, and the sheer number of preachers fleecing Tallapoosa County suggest that the frontier is not only changing but also shrinking. As it becomes less open, new pressures find expression through the conventional confidence man. The camp-meeting episode questions the function of religion on the frontier; Hooper seems suspicious of a benevolent, patriotic Providence, and even more doubtful and disdainful of the need for socially confirmed personal revelations. The hypocrisy fundamental to the camp meeting is embodied in the fact of slavery and its attendant cruelty, which haunts Mrs. Dobbs's worshipful screams. And the banal aggressiveness of the preachers reflects a decay in confidence art that can be measured qualitatively (they are merely catching cows with lariats) and quantitatively (their tricks are less honorable duels than wholesale roundups). Although the confidence man has not lost his sense of humor—or his ability to amuse—he must work harder to turn a profit, to triumph over the greedy and self-righteous, and to maintain his identity against competition as well as authority. Civilization threatens the flush times and the confidence man as the Oakfuskees never did. In fact, the Oakfuskees first fell victim to the forces that spell ruin for the flush times and the confidence man.

Chapters 11 and 12 present direct threats to the comic vision of the confidence man. Indicted for card-playing, Simon faces a prison cell, an ominous physical symbol of civilization. Brought to trial (an occurrence without precedent in Simon's history), he escapes his fate by a trick requiring no confidence and very little art, but not before the reader perceives an imminent end to the days of boom and bust: when Capt. Simon Suggs requires the services of a lawyer to escape from trouble the flush times have been lost. Hooper's last chapter, "Conclusion—Autographic Letter from Suggs," serves as the confidence man's parting shot at the forces emasculating the frontier. The reader finds Simon in the employ of the "Wetumpky Tradin Kumpiny," a chartered, official-sounding organization that specializes in trading worthless company money. Bela Bugg's religious enterprise pales in comparison to the Wetumpky speculations, as does Simon's own. Mr. Chamberlin commissions Simon Suggs to travel to "Urwinton" to buy slaves with valueless Wetumpky currency; his confederate, Mr. Smith, "jist to *start* the thing" (143), attempts to validate for the other traders the company's specie by selling Simon two slaves for eleven hundred dollars. Although the captain passes to gamblers and innkeepers six hundred dollars of Wetumpky paper, he returns to Chamberlin without Smith's or anyone else's slaves. The confidence man uses those who, like Bela Bugg, thought they were using him, for Simon has sold Smith's slaves for one thousand dollars in proven currency and refuses to tender it to his employers. They learn an expensive lesson, that there is no honor among thieves. They also discover, much to the reader's delight, that Capt. Simon Suggs is by far the shiftiest confidence man in the Old Southwest.

Suggs, however, wins only a border skirmish; the scope of the Wetumpky operation signals the diminution of the individual confidence man's chances of future success, for it anticipates the advance of corporate speculators whose only motive is profit and whose ethic is not comical but criminal. The

wholesale buying and selling of slaves, Chamberlin's method
of acquiring good currency, links these humorless traders to
"the peculiar institution"; though the slave market functions
as a convenient plot device, its appropriateness to Hooper suggests at the least the increasing number of plantations worked
by slaves, while painting a landscape that differs in broad
strokes from his earlier scenes of the frontier. The individual
slowly disappears along with the flush times, to be replaced
by social institutions and civilization. This impression is
strengthened by the epistolary form of the last chapter, which
indicates Simon's awareness of the necessity for accommoda-
tion: changing with the times, he employs pen and ink instead
of his usual gambling "dokkyments," preparing not to fight
the law but to become its agent himself. He seeks, Hooper
notes editorially, "the Sheriffalty of your county. He waxes old.
He needs an office, the emoluments of which shall be suffi-
cient to enable him to relax his intellectual exertions. His
military services; his numerous family; his long residence
among you; his gray hairs—all plead for him! Remember him
at the polls!" (148). Hooper charges the reader to remember
the various "services" Captain Suggs furnished; in his own
words, immortalized at Fort Suggs, the captain served "*fust
his country*, and then his *friends*" (110). If Simon is elected to
serve the law, the law will never be the same. The captain's
hoped-for career anticipates the electoral shenanigans of more
successful literary confidence-men-cum-politicians, including Joseph G. Baldwin's Simon Suggs, Jr. (1853), and Henry
Adams's Senator Silas P. Ratcliffe (1880). It also ironically foreshadows—and determines—another political failure; Hooper
himself was defeated in a race for a House seat in Chambers
County because, he theorized, he was "too d—d knowin'
about Suggs to be honest himself!"[29]

The story of the confidence man as politician, however, does
not rightly belong to Suggs. In the remaining Suggs tales, both
published in 1849,[30] the captain is up to his old tricks again,
not sitting in Congress. "The Muscadine Story" features Simon pursued by Sheriff Ellis of Dadeville, and the shifty man
must ante-up his unpaid hotel bill in "The Widow Rugby's
Husband." As in the final story included in *Simon Suggs*
(1845), "Daddy Biggs' Scrape at Cockerell's Bend," the com-

bined forces of civilization impinge upon the freedom, fun, and identity of the confidence man; Daddy Biggs, a stand-in for Suggs, complains for more than himself: "D—n it boys, it makes me mad to think how them Chatohospa fellows and the town folks do 'trude on we roover people" (194). That Biggs rather than Suggs is the focus and narrator of the last sketch seems the result not so much of Hooper's desire to dissociate himself from Suggs—the 1849 tales belie that—as it is of Hooper's recognition that he had plotted in *Simon Suggs* a completed cycle of rise and fall: Simon Suggs, the conventional confidence man, begins his adventures in the flush times of the early nineteenth century, recapitulates the frantic economics of boom and bust, and, like the frontier, his home and his haven, suffers eclipse by civilization. Although Simon takes a belated crack at romance in "The Muscadine Story," Hooper recognizes the absurdity of revival: the confidence man has, for Hooper, outlived the frontier, the Oakfuskees, and the flush times of the 1830s and witnesses for the reader the onslaught of urban culture. His fast talk reveals—and only temporarily arrests—the advance of "swindlin missheens" like Bela Bugg's camp meeting, incorporated criminals like Chamberlin and Smith, large-scale plantation slavery, bitter regional politics, "cash-only" hotels, threatening jails, persistent sheriffs, and the concomitant decline of individualism and confidence. For Hooper as for Simon Suggs, the flush times were ended; ahead lay not comedy but civil war.

*   *   *

Eleven editions of *Some Adventures of Captain Simon Suggs* were published in as many years, and W. Stanley Hoole writes that at the time of Hooper's death in 1862 "his name, (or, better perhaps, the name of his chief character) was a household word in every section of the United States."[31] The continued popularity of Hooper's creation is proven by the countless reprintings of Suggs's tales in newspapers, unauthorized collections, and anthologies throughout the nineteenth century; the captain even traveled abroad, appearing in William Jerdan's *Yankee Humor, and Uncle Sam's Fun* and Thomas Chandler Haliburton's *Traits of American Humor, by Native Authors* (1852), both published in London. Often cited along with Thorpe, Field, Sol Smith, and others as a founder

of frontier literature (as John S. Robb did in his preface to
Streaks of Squatter Life, 1847), Hooper created in Simon Suggs
a complex character distinct from his predecessors and contemporaries. In 1857 Rufus N. Griswold praised Hooper's
"bold, original and indigenous" sketches,[32] and Henry Watterson more precisely articulated Suggs's uniqueness in *Oddities
in Southern Life and Character* (1882). *Simon Suggs* is, he
wrote,

> a masterpiece. No one who is at all familiar with the provin-
> cial life of the South can fail to recognize the "points" of this
> sharp and vulgar, sunny and venal swash-buckler. As serio-
> comic as Sellers, as grotesque as Shingle, he possesses an orig-
> inality all his own, and never for a moment rises above or falls
> below it. He is a gambler by nature, by habit, by preference, by
> occupation. Without a virtue in the world, except his good
> humor and his self-possession, there is something in his vices,
> his indolence, his swagger, his rogueries, which, in spite of the
> worthlessness of the man and the dishonesty of his practices,
> detains and amuses us. He is a representative character, the
> Sam Slick of the South; only, I should say, the Sam Slick of
> Judge Haliburton is not nearly so true to nature, so graphic, or
> so picturesque.[33]

That Watterson viewed Suggs as not only "original" but also
"representative" suggests the nineteenth-century critic's
understanding of the captain as a new stable form. Simon
Suggs is, in fact, a literary convention that embodies and
shapes perceptions of the American frontier, a device, like the
term *confidence man*, created in the 1840s to express and control anxieties of boom and bust.

Hooper introduces Simon Suggs by means of conventional
literary devices: the episodic structure, the form of a campaign
biography, the narrative frame, the contrast between cultured
narrator and dialect-spouting "low" characters, and the condescending narrative tone are all easily recognized elements
of frontier humor. They structure the reader's response to Simon Suggs, trading upon the reader's familiarity with the
works of Nott, Longstreet, Thompson, and others. Within the
accepted context of frontier humor, Hooper creates a protagonist who redefines the frontier in terms appropriate to the
1840s, clarifying much of the uncertainty of intention present, for example, in Longstreet's "Georgia Theatrics." Hooper

uses conventions from the 1830s to establish continuity: the frontier prankster, Ned Brace, reemerges as the frontier confidence man, taking its form from a synthesis of earlier models—Capt. John Farrago, Davy Crockett, Thomas Singularity, the Yellow Blossom, and Major Jones all join Ned Brace in contributing features to Capt. Simon Suggs. This multiplicity confirms the absence of a conventional figure and action before Hooper's hero, one that he might have merely rechristened and duplicated. A legion of tricksters, biters, shapeshifters, and rogues also crowds the works of Hooper's contemporaries: S. G. Goodrich's dishonest peddler, Philip B. January's rollicking dragoon, Poe's artful diddlers, Sol Smith's tricky steamboatmen, James Hall's wild backwoodsmen, and William Gilmore Simms's reformed gambler testify to the popularity of shifty sharpers, again demonstrating in their diversity the lack of a conventional literary form.[34] If the captain is in fact the conventional confidence man, there should appear following *Simon Suggs* a certain conformity to Hooper's model.

The example of Simon Suggs is visible first of all in the American public's appetite for editions of the captain's adventures. Obviously aware of Hooper's widespread popularity, the editors of the *New Orleans Picayune*, the *Boston Yankee Blade*, the *Cincinnati Great West*, and the *Baltimore Republican and Daily Argus* (to name a few) frequently reprinted Suggs's tales without a sign of embarrassment. The reading public was not alone in its admiration for Hooper; in addition to Griswold and Watterson, William E. Burton included four Suggs tales in his *Cyclopaedia of Wit and Humor* (1858), while James Wood Davidson, in *The Living Writers of the South* (1869), ranked *Simon Suggs* above Longstreet's *Georgia Scenes* because it was more "uniformly humorous." Of even more importance than critics are the fiction writers who applauded *Simon Suggs*. A minimal list would include Thomas A. Burke, John S. Robb, Sol Smith, Joseph M. Field, T. B. Thorpe, Stephen C. Massett, and William T. Porter, who reputedly held up publication of *The Big Bear of Arkansas, and Other Sketches* (1845) in order to include "How Simon Suggs 'Raised Jack.'" Porter also directs us to a clear example of Hooper's influence within *The Big Bear*. In his introduction to "The

Way 'Lige' Shaddock 'Scared Up A Jack,'" he leaves no doubt
as to its origin: "The following sketch was suggested to the
writer—a capital Mississippi correspondent to the 'Spirit of
the Times'—by Hooper's story (previously given in this volume) of 'How Simon Suggs raised Jack!'"[35] A riverboat sharper
bets Lige Shaddock fifty dollars that he can "turn a Jack" at
one try, and, when challenged by Shaddock to perform, tosses
the entire deck of cards face up on the table. The shifty descendant of Simon Suggs, however, observes, "If there is a Jack
in THAT pack, I'll be d—d!" (177). In both title and action, "The
Way 'Lige' Shaddock 'Scared Up A Jack'" pays tribute to Hooper's sketch; though he reverses the roles of Simon and Jedidiah,
the author retains not only the structure of the snap but also
a physical eccentricity of Simon's: "Lige has a way of dropping
one corner of his eye and mouth at the same time—I don't
know how he does it—it's a way he's got—but whenever you
see it, there is *something out*" (176).

Old Tuttle, who appears in Porter's *A Quarter Race in Kentucky and Other Sketches* (1847), also bears Hooper's mark.

> Look at the picture of "Simon Suggs," and you'll see Old T.
> physically; in the *trial* scene you find him intellectually, and
> in the camp-meeting scene, morally. Were it not that Old T.
> never "samples" too much when on business, and fights the
> "*hoss* b'hoys" instead of the "Tiger," I should say they were
> one and the same person.[36]

Even the casual reader must note the resemblance at "Buckeye's" insistence. Old Tuttle's sleight-of-horse, as well, seems
a variation on the confidence man's formula for fleecing Bela
Bugg at the camp meeting, the Creeks at the ball game, and
the slave-trading "Wetumpky Tradin Kumpiny": he wins his
victim's confidence, allows him to think himself the smarter
man, and then reaps the reward of his deception. Old Tuttle
has learned more from Suggs than just how to wink at the
reader.

Polly Peablossom's Wedding (1851), a humorous collection
dedicated to "Johnson J. Hooper, Esq., of Lafayette, Alabama,
(author of Adventures of Simon Suggs,) as a token of respect,"[37] contains several confidence games suggesting a close
reading of the captain's exploits. Thomas A. Burke's "A Losing
Game of Poker" imitates Suggs's method of turning the tables

to turn a profit. Bennett, a gambler, enlists Cole to set up Andy Smith for a stacked deck by pretending to beat Bennett at cards. After winning over one thousand dollars from Bennett, Cole leaves as agreed; he is replaced by the eager Smith, who feels certain that Bennett is a loser. Bennett stacks the deck and cleans out Smith, yet wins only five hundred dollars from his not-so-stupid pigeon. The next day Bennett asks Cole, his decoy, for "a settlement."

> "A settlement! what do you mean? I am not aware that there is anything to settle between you and me."
>
> "Come, come, old hoss, none of your jokes. About that money you won last night; you know well enough what I mean."
>
> "Well, didn't I win it fairly?"
>
> "Why, yes, the playing was fair enough on your part, but you know the cards were stocked, so as to give you the hand you held," said the gambler, who began to feel slightly alarmed at Cole's manner.
>
> "And who stocked them, pray? If you chose to deal me a better hand than you kept yourself, without my asking you to do so, it certainly wasn't my fault."
>
> "I know that," said Bennett, really alarmed at the prospect of losing his money; "Still, it was understood that we were only playing for fun, and I hope you will refund that seventeen hundred, and take half my winnings from Smith."
>
> "I understood the thing, Bennett, in no such way, and shall keep what I won from you, and you are perfectly welcome to *the whole* of what you took from Mr. Smith. Good morning, sir." (48)

Cole springs the "Wetumpky Tradin Kumpiny" reversal quite as neatly as Simon Suggs.

"'Doing' a Sheriff" echoes Hooper's "Muscadine Story," and "War's Yure Hoss?" and "The Thimble Game" recount games of chance not unlike the "soft snap" Simon gets from Jedidiah: in each a confidence man lures the sure but green sucker into an unwise trust in his perceptions. T. W. Lane's "The Thimble Game," moreover, contains a description of "Augusty" that parallels Hooper's in chapter 2 of *Simon Suggs* nearly word for word.

> Augusta was looked upon as Paris and London are now viewed by us. The man who had *never* been there, was a cipher in the community—nothing killed an opinion more surely, nothing

stopped the mouth of "argyment" sooner, than the sneering taunt, "Pshaw! you ha'n't been to *Augusty.*" The atmosphere of this favoured place was supposed to impart knowledge and wisdom to all who breathed it, and the veriest ass was a Solon and an umpire, if he could discourse fluently of the different localities, and various wonders, of *Augusty.* (*Polly Peablossom,* 28–29)

Finally, John S. Robb's confidence man in "'Doing' a Landlord" (in *Streaks of Squatter Life,* 1847) practices the manipulation of appearances Simon put to use in his Indian speculations with the "Big Widow"; the captain's saddlebags and Tom's trunk are both bulging with rocks rather than bullion.

Simon Suggs clearly formed the confidence man exemplum for Hooper's contemporaries. Recognizable in physical appearance, in speech, and in shifty style, Suggs provided a model that proved eminently imitable, variable, and—in a literary, canonical sense—honorable. Once delineated, the narrative and thematic poetics of the confidence man are reimagined and the convention's structural devices are retooled to express new perceptions by succeeding generations of American writers. Baldwin, Harris, Warren, and Melville all demonstrate in their fictions the confidence they had in Hooper's example.

4 FOUR VARIATIONS OF THE CONFIDENCE MAN

There is nothing like the elbow room of
a new country.
—President John Tyler (1843)

The American confidence man abuses the confidence of everyone he meets for personal advantage. Prowling the flush times, he exposes suspicion, dishonesty, naivete, and greed, marking by his success a pattern of faith betrayed that resembles the frontier cycle of boom and bust. Imitators of Captain Simon Suggs sprang up throughout the Old Southwest, some paying explicit homage to Hooper in collections like William T. Porter's *The Big Bear of Arkansas* (1845). The more talented of Hooper's successors varied the humorous convention, investing it with new meaning while retaining the confidence man's mastery of language, his manipulation of appearances, and his exploitation of ambiguities. Sometimes crossing the development of the confidence man with versions of older traditions of the confidence game, authors like Joseph G. Baldwin, George W. Harris, Herman Melville, and Kittrell J. Warren refocused the convention to express distrust of the flush times and to accommodate historical events ranging from the California Gold Rush to the Civil War. The fiction of these writers illustrates four distinct variations of the confidence man, the scope of the convention's historical development, and the proof of Melville's observation that "in new countries, where the wolves are killed off, the foxes increase."[1]

Simon Suggs, Jr., and Ovid Bolus, Esq.

In 1853, Joseph G. Baldwin marks the development of the confidence man as he defines the flush times.

In the fulness of time the new era had set in—the era of the second great experiment of independence: the experiment, namely, of credit without capital, and enterprise without honesty. . . .

97

The old rules of business and the calculations of prudence were alike disregarded, and profligacy, in all the departments of the *crimen falsi,* held riotous carnival. . . . Swindling was raised to the dignity of the fine arts. . . .

Such is a charcoal sketch of the interesting region—now inferior to none in resources, and the character of its population—during the FLUSH TIMES; a period constituting an episode in the commercial history of the world—the reign of humbug, and wholesale insanity, just overthrown in time to save the whole country from ruin. But while it lasted, many of our countrymen came into the South-West in time to get "a benefit."[2]

"Ovid Bolus, Esq., Attorney at Law and Solicitor in Chancery" records the benefits reaped by a confidence man who is a variation of the Suggsian convention, and whose life epitomizes the flush times in the new country.

And what history of that halcyon period, ranging from the year of Grace, 1835, to 1837; that golden era, when shin-plasters were the sole currency; when bank-bills were "as thick as Autumn leaves in Vallambrosa," and credit was a franchise,—what history of those times would be complete, that left out the name of Ovid Bolus? As well write the biography of Prince Hal, and forbear all mention of Falstaff. (1)

In this first paragraph of *Flush Times,* Baldwin introduces a confidence man whose narrative will be more literary than Hooper's, just as Ovid Bolus will be more literate than Simon Suggs. The vulgar ring to *Simon Suggs* becomes the modulated, latinate *Ovid Bolus,* though as the three meanings of *bolus* in the *Oxford English Dictionary* confirm, *bolus* rings false upon inspection: "A medicine of round shape adapted for swallowing, larger than an ordinary pill. (Often used somewhat contemptuously)"; "a small rounded mass of any substance"; "a kind of clay." Like Falstaff, Bolus is a blustering windbag, an "Americanized comic braggart," who, as Walter Blair concludes, traces his ancestry back to *The Frogs.*[3] Baldwin claims a numerous and ancient kinship for Bolus.

Ovid had early possessed the faculty of ubiquity. He had been born in more places than Homer. In an hour's discourse, *he* would, with more than the speed of Ariel, travel at every point of the compass, from Portland to San Antonio, some famous adventure always occurring just as he "rounded to," or while stationary, though he did not remain longer than to see it. (8)

Like Bolus's accounts of his adventures in the United States Senate or the Florida war (8–9), this historical catalogue—ranging from pre-Christian Greece to un-Christian Texas—sets up the confidence man as a mock-heroic figure, a boasting opportunist whose tall tales recapitulate the struggle to civilize the new country.

Baldwin's flush times spawn a confidence man different from Simon Suggs. Simon was the proverbial Ugly Man: "His head is somewhat large, and thinly covered with coarse, silver-white hair, a single lock of which lies close and smooth down the middle of a forehead which is thus divided into a couple of very acute triangles, the base of each of which is an eyebrow. . . . Lids without lashes complete the optical apparatus of Captain Suggs."[4] Ovid, in contrast, is "strikingly handsome."

> There was something in his air and bearing almost princely, certainly quite distinguished. His manners were winning, his address frank, cordial and flowing. He was built after the model and structure of Bolingbroke in his youth, *Americanized* and *Hoosierized* a little by a "raising in," and an adaptation to, the Backwoods. He was fluent but choice of diction, a little sonorous in the structure of his sentences to give effect to a voice like an organ. His countenance was open and engaging, usually sedate of expression, but capable of any modifications at the shortest notice. Add to this his intelligence, shrewdness, tact, humor, and that he was a ready debater and elegant declaimer, and had the gift of bringing out, to the fullest extent, his resources, and you may see that Ovid, in a new country, was a man apt to make no mean impression. (6–7)

Baldwin transforms the Suggsian convention into an almost courtly confidence man—an impression reinforced by repeated allusions to Falstaff—a lawyer who preys not on camp meetings and frontier forts but on the moneyed classes of Boston and Cuba (9–13). The new country has changed, and the confidence man with it, adapting himself with a coat of varnish to towns and cities in the legendary style of P. T. Barnum. Polite manners and white gloves offer the sharper a ready-made disguise.

Ovid Bolus perhaps embodies a greater threat than Simon

Suggs. Bolus's accounts of his amorous escapades may admit embellishment in the exact amount of each girl's fortune, but it seems likely that he left one at the altar with a broken heart (9–10) and a sixteen year old on her plantation with more serious "consequences" (12–13). He repeatedly sells tracts of land he does not own (5), and when he stoops to swindle "poor Ben" (10–11), Bolus collects not the one hundred dollars which gladdened Simon Suggs at the camp meeting but sixteen hundred dollars. Bolus's victims, moreover, seem less deserving of shiftiness than Suggs's, in particular because the scope of his snaps extends beyond Hooper's safely distanced comic frontier to the newly installed drawing rooms of civilization. Baldwin uses his confidence man to expose the pretensions of society in the flush times: Bolus trades on his word of honor repeatedly to gain credit, refuses to marry a Bostonian because of her father's aversion to "Bolus's love for the 'peculiar institution'" (10), and rather than marry the pregnant sixteen year old holds fast to a convenient Protestantism, breaks with the Catholic girl, and offers himself as "a martyr to his Religion" (13).

The conventions that Ovid Bolus exploits for profit, however, reveal implicitly that society in the new country is ripe for picking, a condition Baldwin states explicitly in another sketch.

> The condition of society may be imagined:—vulgarity—ignorance—fussy and arrogant pretension—unmitigated rowdyism—bullying insolence, if they did not rule the hour, *seemed* to wield unchecked dominion. (88–89)

Baldwin's flush-times confidence man in fact earns our admiration by his purely verbal manipulation of appearances.

> Some men are liars from interest; not because they have no regard for truth, but because they have less regard for it than for gain: some are liars from vanity, because they would rather be well thought of by others, than have reason for thinking well of themselves: some are liars from a sort of necessity, which overbears, by the weight of temptation, the sense of virtue: some are enticed away by the allurements of pleasure, or seduced by evil example and education. Bolus was none of these: he belonged to a higher department of the fine arts, and to a higher class of professors of this sort of Belles-Lettres. Bolus was a natural liar, just as some horses are natural pacers,

and some dogs natural setters. What he did in that walk, was from the irresistible promptings of instinct, and a disinterested love of art. His genius and his performance were free from the vulgar alloy of interest or temptation. (2–3)

This is a kind of mock-hagiography, in which Ovid Bolus is satirically enshrined as a higher order of confidence man than those of the Suggsian mold who steal in order to eat. Bolus is an artist of the swindle for whom "the truth was too small" (3), to whom "all ideas were facts" (4), and who "delighted to turn an abstract idea into concrete cash" (5). In this sense he is an ironic doppelgänger to the sketch's narrator, also a maker of aesthetic fictions, from whom Bolus's chicanery elicits only good-humored censure.

> One thing in Ovid I can never forgive. This was his coming it over poor Ben. I don't object to it on the score of the swindle. That was to have been expected. But swindling Ben was degrading the dignity of the art. True, it illustrated the universality of his science, but it lowered it to a beggarly process of mean deception. There was no skill in it. It was little better than crude larceny. A child could have done it; it had as well been done to a child. It was like catching a cow with a lariat, or setting a steel trap for a pet pig. (10–11)

The narrator chides Bolus for exchanging someone else's land for his own profit, a typical confidence-man trick that reaffirms both Bolus's ancestry and his originality. Necessity forces the con man to return to Suggsian basics.

The flush times themselves prove finite: "Bolus, not having confined his art to political matters, sounded, at last, the depths, and explored the limits of popular credulity."

> The denizens of this degenerate age, had not the disinterestedness of Prince Hal, who "cared not how many fed at his cost;" they got tired, at last, of promises to pay. The credit system, common before as pump-water, adhering, like the elective franchise to every voter, began to take the worldly wisdom of Falstaff's mercer, and ask security; and security like something more substantial than plausible promises. In this forlorn condition of the country, returning to its savage state, and abandoning the refinements of ripe Anglo-Saxon civilization for the sordid safety of Mexican or Chinese modes of traffic; deserting the sweet simplicity of its ancient trustfulness and the poetic illusions of Augustus Tomlinson, for the

vulgar saws of poor Richard—Bolus . . . departed from a land
unworthy of his longer sojourn. (18–19)

The confidence man cannot survive in a new country grown
old, or where, following Poor Richard, men no longer bet confidently on dreams. Ovid Bolus must pursue the new country
to "the shadow of the San Saba mountains," trusting that poor
Ben's money will secure him the "repose" he has "earned"
(19). Ultimately, Bolus is no Barnum.

In "Simon Suggs, Jr., Esq.: A Legal Biography," Baldwin uses
Hooper's Captain Simon Suggs as security. He parodies Captain Suggs's mock-heroic campaign biography while trading
on his name to pique interest and insure recognition; "Colonel" Suggs contributes his biography to what he discovers to
be the "vanity" publication of another confidence man, who
for a mere one hundred fifty dollars will perpetuate the name
of Colonel Simon Suggs, Jr., "and establish yours among the
classical names of the American bar" (120). Simon declares he
will "enter a nolly prossy q," but suggests the editor "rite to
the old man!! May be he'd go in with BARNUM!!! May be he'd
like to take TWO chances? He's young—never seen much!!
Lives in a new country!!!" (120–21).

In this variation of the confidence man, Baldwin's explicit
references to Hooper's fiction confirm a line of descent and,
as Susan Kuhlmann notes, serve "as a tribute to the name and
fame of Hooper's creation."[5] Unlike "Buckeye," a writer who
invokes Hooper's Suggs in "Old Tuttle's Last Quarter Race"
(1847), Baldwin ushers Hooper's Suggs into the action of his
sketch, staging a game of "seven up" between the elder Suggs
and young Simon that not only echoes the game between
Suggs and *his* father, Jedidiah, in chapter 2 of *Simon Suggs*, but
also intensifies the humor and the reader's pleasure, for here
in Baldwin both players are consummate sharpers who self-
consciously seem to symbolize the historical development of
the new country.

> Since the game of chess between Mr. Jefferson and the French
> Minister, which lasted three years, perhaps there never has
> been a more closely contested match than that between these
> keen, sagacious and practised sportsmen. It was played with
> all the advantages; all the lights of science were shed upon
> that game. The old gentleman had the advantage of experi-

From *Flush Times* (1853 edition).

ence—the young of genius: it was the old fogy against young
America. For a long time the result was dubious; as if Dame
Fortune was unable or unwilling to decide between her favorites. The game stood at *six and six*, and young Simon had the
deal. Just as the deal commenced, after one of the most brilliant shuffles the senior had ever made, Simon carelessly laid
down his tortoise-shell snuff-box on the table; and the father,
affecting *nonchalance*, and inclining his head towards the box,
in order to peep under as the cards were being dealt, took a
pinch of snuff; the titillating restorative was strongly adulter-
ated with cayenne pepper; the old fogy was compelled to
sneeze; and just as he recovered from the concussion, the first
object that met his eye was a Jack turning in Simon's hand. A
struggle seemed to be going on in the old man's breast between a feeling of pride in his son and a sense of his individual
loss. (129)

The elder Suggs gives Simon his blessing and advises Simon
that he is "wasting his genius in a retail business of 'shy-
keenry'" when nature had designed him for the bar" (130); in

fact, Baldwin notes ironically, "many sagacious men predicted that *the law would yet elevate Simon to a prominent place in the public view"* (130).

Although Simon is never hanged, he is scalped by "a green-looking Georgia sucker" (130–31). The trick brings tears to the elder Suggs's eyes, and it makes Simon realize he must accommodate himself to a new age.

> The losses Simon had met with, and the unpromising prospects of gentlemen who lived on their wits, now that the hard times had set in, produced an awakening influence upon his conscience. He determined to abandon the nomadic life he had led, and to settle himself down to some regular business. He had long felt a call to the law, and he now resolved to "locate," and apply himself to the duties of that learned profession. Simon was not long in deciding upon a location. The spirited manner in which the State of Arkansas had repudiated a public debt of some five hundred thousand dollars gave him a favorable opinion of that people. . . . I shall not attempt to describe the population. It was indescribable. I shall only say that the Indians and half-breeds across the border complained of it mightily. (132–33)

Like Ovid Bolus, Simon searches for a new country because "the hard times had set in." He discovers a ragtag region of corrupt cashiers, domestic squabblers, and penny-ante crooks, a land that bears little resemblance to either Hooper's frontier or the fantastically rich Creation State in T. B. Thorpe's "Big Bear of Arkansas" (1841). Simon's Arkansas parodies tall tales of the new country: cold-blooded bribery takes the place of artful fast talk, forgery succeeds impersonation, and the practice of law rather than its avoidance becomes the confidence man's modus operandi.

> Simon abandoned the favorite pastimes of his youth, and the irregularities of his earlier years. Indeed, he has been heard to declare that any lawyer, fulfilling conscientiously the duties of his profession, will find enough to employ all his resources of art, strategem and dexterity, without resorting to other and more equivocal methods for their exercise. (134)

Simon learns "all the arts and contrivances by which public justice is circumvented" (138) and by "the most insinuating manners" establishes himself at the very center of Arkansas society, tricking a wealthy woman into divorcing her husband and then marrying her himself. From this position he rises quickly to the solicitorship of the state, divorces his now-cumbersome wife for "infidelity," and, taking first the hand and then the lands of a Choctaw chief's daughter, Che-wee-na-tubbe, receives the lucrative appointment of Indian claims agent for the Treasury of the United States.

Simon fulfills the wildest fantasies of Hooper's Captain Suggs, who "waxes old" and "needs an office" (SS, 148). Simon does not, of course, look back, but neither does Baldwin. Once Simon is secure in Arkansas, his mention of the elder Suggs ceases. Wolfgang Iser suggests that literary allusions "'quote' earlier answers . . . answers which no longer constitute a valid meaning for the present work, but which offer a form of orientation by means of which new meaning may perhaps be found."[6] In this sense the disappearance of the elder Suggs can be read as a signal that Hooper's confidence man is changed in Baldwin's fiction to speak to new questions in the 1850s. Baldwin's confidence man threatens an inchoate society rather than rude settlements, and he springs his snaps from within. As a successful lawyer rather than a roving scoundrel he gives form to the fear that all American courts are seats of corruption, while as a claims agent Simon suggests that the government is peopled by men seeking not justice but personal profit.

In these instances, Baldwin echoes the satire of Hugh Henry Brackenridge's *Modern Chivalry* (1792–1815). Brackenridge perceived before Baldwin that new countries encourage and seem to reward shiftiness, especially when shiftiness clothes itself in the style of democratic forms.[7] In "Simon Suggs, Jr.," Baldwin expresses this apprehension that the most dangerous confidence man is often the most successful precisely because he cloaks his deeds in respectable garments. This change from Hooper's confidence man limits the amount of anxiety that is released in laughter; it becomes characteristic of the confidence man in the 1850s to create tensions that are not fully discharged. Hooper's Simon Suggs "waxes old" and harmless; Baldwin's Ovid Bolus travels to Texas, far enough away to be in memory an amusing character; but Baldwin's Simon Suggs,

Jr., locates himself in Washington, the center of American democracy, standing as a reminder that the confidence man's
shiftiness succeeds in the new country.

Sut Lovingood

In the gentlemen's magazines and Tennessee newspapers of
the 1850s, George Washington Harris develops characteristics
of the southwestern confidence man that differ markedly from
Baldwin's. Harris's creation, whose misadventures are collected in the 1867 *Sut Lovingood. Yarns Spun by a "Nat'ral
Born Durn'd Fool,"* shares neither the respectability of Ovid
Bolus nor the success of Simon Suggs, Jr.[8] The flush times have
become the hard times, but what Sut lacks in social graces he
makes up for in "onregenerite pride" (229). And where Baldwin tightened the rhetorical reins of his cultured narrator over
his immoral characters, Harris passes the reins over entirely
to his vernacular character turned narrator, Sut.

In Sut's Tennessee, victimization is the way of all flesh, and
brutality is a means of survival. The world of the *Yarns* is
hostile, a nightmarish landscape in which people, animals,
and even inanimate objects threaten to transform the self into
inhuman things: merely by going to sleep a man can become
a corpse in a coffin ("Frustrating a Funeral"), a simple trip to
town can turn into a near-fatal dance with a crazed bull ("Tau-
rus in Lynchburg Market"), and a new shirt can strip the skin
off a man's back as painfully and professionally as a medieval
instrument of torture ("Sut's New-Fangled Shirt"). Point of
view is important in this unbalanced universe, as Sut explains
in "Sut Lovingood's Daddy, Acting Horse." Sut's father is
chased into a creek by an angry swarm of hornets.

> He kep' up a rite peart dodgin onder, sumtimes afore they hit
> im, and sumtimes arterard, an' the warter wer kivered wif
> drownded ball ho'nets. Tu look at hit frum the top ove the
> bluff, hit wer pow'ful inturestin, an' sorter funny; I wer on the
> bluff myse'f, mine yu. Dad cudent see the funny part from
> whar he wer, but hit seem'd tu be inturestin tu him frum the
> 'tenshun he wer payin tu the bisness ove divin an' cussin. (26)

Humor based on others' physical discomfort is a conventional
southwestern technique for enduring frontier hardships by

making light of them. In "Old Burns's Bull Ride," as Walter
Blair notes, Harris reworks a tale that had been told in print at
least since 1834 by Henry Nott, William Thompson, and others,[9] and Sut retells traditional cruel stories of exploded Yankees, broken-up camp meetings, and snake-bit Irishmen (61,
157, 108). Like the snaps of Simon Suggs, these incidents are
funny to the safely distanced observer and narrator, but in the
Yarns Sut himself must cope with personal threats and inju-
ries.

In "Parson John Bullen's Lizards," first published in 1857,[10]
Sut tangles with a preacher reminiscent of Jedidiah Suggs and
the Reverend Bela Bugg. Like Hooper, Harris uses the popular
narrative-frame technique, yet his reversal of Hooper's emphasis on what Kenneth Lynn has called the "Self-controlled
Gentleman" shatters the reader's expectations of cruel devilry
occurring only within the "cordon sanitaire."[11] The narrative
begins with a reward poster for Sut's hide and is controlled
throughout by vernacular points of view.

AIT ($8) DULLARS REW-ARD
'Tenshun Belevers And Konstables! Ketch 'Im! Ketch 'Im!
This kash wil be pade in korn, ur uther projuce, tu be kolected at ur about nex camp-meetin, *ur tharater*, by eny wun
what ketches him, fur the karkus ove a sartin wun SUT LOV-
INGOOD, dead ur alive, ur ailin, an' safely giv over tu the
purtectin care ove Parson John Bullin, ur lef' well tied, at
Squire Mackjunkins, fur the raisin ove the devil pussonely, an'
permiskusly discumfurtin the wimen very powerful, an'
skeerin ove folks generly a heap, an' bustin up a promisin, big
warm meetin, an' a makin the wickid larf, an' wuf, an' wus,
insultin ove the passun orful.

Test,   JEHU WETHERO.
Sined by me,
JOHN BULLEN, the passun.   (48)

"George," who presents this advertisement to the reader, is
all that remains of the cultured frame-narrator. He is merely
an introductory device, a convenient bridge to help the reader
cross over into the fantastic rhetorical world of the *Yarns*.
George functions as a model of the reader, an amused listener
who, having cut his teeth on Seba Smith's Jack Downing and
James Russell Lowell's Hosea Bigelow, surrenders to Sut's

comic misspellings, outrageous dialect, and grotesque actions.

At a Rattlesnake Springs camp meeting, Sut seeks not money, like Simon Suggs, but love. Sitting

> in a nice shady place convarsin wif a frien' ove mine, intu the huckil berry thickit, jis' duin nuffin tu nobody an' makin no fuss, when, the fust I remembers, I woke up frum a trance what I hed been knocked inter by a four-year old hickory-stick, hilt in the paw ove ole Passun Bullin, durn his alligater hide; an' he wer standin a striddil ove me, a foamin at the mouf, a-chompin his teeth—gesterin wif the hickory club— an' a-preachin tu me so you cud a-hearn him a mile, about a sartin sins gineraly, an' my wickedness pussonely, an' mensunin the name ove my frien' loud enuf to be hearn tu the meetin 'ous. (49–50)

Parson Bullen's artless attack symbolizes Sut's vulnerability to forces beyond his control; unlike Simon Suggs, Sut is not the shifty master of easily manipulated dupes. It is Parson Bullen, rather, who has the upper hand, and who makes Sut and his girlfriend the victims of his petty meanness. In exchange for Sall cooking supper for him, Bullen promises not to tell her mother of Sall's sitting with Sut, but once he has eaten he "went strait an' tole her mam" (51). Like Jedidiah Suggs, Parson Bullen embodies a hypocritical authority that delights in inflicting bodily pain—Sut is beaten and Sall is stropped.

Sut's spirit, however, remains unbruised. Pretending repentance, Sut joins the parson's next camp meeting at Rattlesnake Springs. As Parson Bullen's sermon on "hell-sarpints" reaches a crescendo,

> when he wer a-ravin ontu his tip-toes, an' a-poundin the pulpit wif his fis'—onbenowenst tu enybody, I ontied my bag ove reptiles, put the mouf ove hit onder the bottim ove his britches-laig, an' sot intu pinchin thar tails. Quick es gunpowder they all tuck up his bar laig, makin a nise like squirrils a-climbin a shell-bark hickory. He stop't preachin rite in the middil ove the word "damnation" . . . fetch a vigrus ruff rub whar a hosses tail sprouts: then he's stomp one foot, then tuther, then bof at onst. Then he run his han' atween his waisbun an' his shut an' reach'd way down, an' roun' wif hit; then he spread his big laigs, an' gin his back a good rattlin rub agin the pulpit, like a hog scratches hisself agin a stump, leanin tu

> hit pow'ful, an' twitchin, an' squirmin all over, es ef he'd slept
> in a dorg bed, ur ontu a pisant hill. About this time, one ove
> my lizzards scared an' hurt by all this poundin' an' feelin, an'
> scratchin, popp'd out his head from the passun's shut collar,
> an' his ole brown naik, an' wer a-surveyin the crowd, when ole
> Bullin struck at 'im, jis' too late, fur he'd dodged back agin.
> The hell desarvin ole raskil's speech now cum to 'im, an' sez
> he, "Pray fur me brethren an' sisteren, fur I is a-rastlin wif the
> great inimy rite now!" (53–54)

In battling "the great inimy" Parson Bullen tears off his
clothes, standing before his flock in only "a par ove heavy, low
quarter'd shoes, short wollen socks, an' eel-skin garters tu
keep off the cramp" (56). Stripped of the vestments of his
profession, he vaults—"plum crazy"—over three hundred
watchful "sisteren" screaming "take keer ove yerselves, the
Hell-sarpints *hes got me!*" (56).

What has got Bullen, of course, is Sut's genius, which temporarily forces the parson out of the redemption business.
Sut's trick resembles those of Thomas Singularity or Ned
Brace more than those of Simon Suggs. In Harris's fiction, the
development of the confidence man recrosses older traditions;
having been made a comic butt, Sut assumes the role of
prankster to make Bullen play the fool. Categories of normal
experience break down as Sut switches roles with Bullen by
making his metaphoric religious struggle into a physical, humorous one. Identity is revealed as a precarious substance
when Sut transforms himself from victim to victimizer and
the parson from a man of the spirit into a scratching animal
of naked flesh. At this moment of triumph Sut surely seems
"America's Till Eulenspiegel," as Walter Blair notes,[12] yet Sut's
financial language echoes the rewards of the Suggsian confidence man, suggesting that in Tennessee profits are registered
in different specie: "yere's the way I lifted [Bullen's] note ove
han'"; "I paid him plum up fur hit, an' I means tu keep a payin
him, ontil one ur tuther, ove our toes pints up tu the roots ove
the grass" (51). The new country of the *Yarns* offers reduced
opportunities for a confidence man; Polk County lacks the
cash necessary for gambling, swapping, and confidence art.
Here there are no crops taken to Augusta, and even the parson's eight-dollar reward for Sut's capture is offered "in korn,
ur uther projuce, tu be kolected at ur about nex camp-meetin,

ur tharater" (48). Drinking, dancing, fighting, playing pranks, making love—these are the activities available to Sut, for the unstable community could not afford to support a confidence man, who needs both social conventions to exploit and cash to survive. The country around Rattlesnake Springs is poor on both counts, but its poverty and instability promise other kinds of payment.

Sut sees women as one of Tennessee's most valuable resources. In "Blown Up with Soda" (1857)—a variation of Major Jones's courtship of Mary Stallins[13]—Sicily Burns proves as shiny and hard as a new double-eagle.

> "George, did yu ever see Sicily Burns? Her dad lives at the Rattilsnake Spring, clost ontu the Georgia line."
> "Yes, a very handsome girl."
> "Handsome! that ar word don't kiver the case; hit souns sorter like callin good whiskey strong water, when yu ar ten mile frum a still-hous, hit a rainin, an' yer flask only haf full. She shows among wimen like a sunflower amung dorg fennil, ur a hollyhawk in a patch ove smartweed. Sich a buzzim! Jis' think ove two snow balls wif a strawberry stuck but-ainded intu bof on em. She takes adzactly fifteen inches ove garter clar ove the knot, stans sixteen an' a 'alf hans hi, an' weighs one hundred an' twenty-six in her petticoatail afore brekfus'." (75–76)

George's conventional description, "handsome," Sut perceives as inappropriate; his own language defines her as a precious substance to be admired, measured, and consumed. Sut desires her as Simon Suggs desires to beat "the Tiger," and Sut is similarly blinded by her attractions. She is not, of course, the fulfillment of Sut's fantasies, but a feminine prankster: "'Sutty, luv, I'se got sumthin fur yu, *a new sensashun*'" (80). As he tells George, "'I'd got the idear onder my har that hit wer *lov-powders*, an' I swaller'd the devil red hot from home, a-thinkin that. Luv-powders *frum her*! jis' think ove hit yerse'f solemnly a minit, an' sit still ef yu kin'" (81). The "new sensashun" Sicily gives him is ten doses of soda-powder garnished with nutmeg, a concoction that empties Sut's stomach as readily as the faro bank empties Simon's pockets. Although Simon occasionally plays the fool, an implicit acknowledgement of the confidence man's ancestry, Sut is subjected to repeated bad deals from various sharpers; the Fates themselves seem to have stacked the deck against him, indicative of a disorder in the comic world of the *Yarns* not present in *Simon Suggs*. Simon contends with his devilish father, but the alluring Sicily Burns makes Sut drink "the devil red hot." Unlike Simon's universe, Sut's is populated by other devils who do get the best of him, in large part because everyone is subject to immiment dislocation by impersonal forces, and in small because there are few social conventions adhered to; Sut can manipulate Parson Bullen by feigning repentance, a characteristic sham of the confidence man, but nothing can save him from the parson's hickory stick. And when Sut himself behaves in a conventional manner, as when he plays the obedient lover to Sicily, he sets himself up for victimization.

When Sicily Burns marries the "suckit rider" Clapshaw in "Sicily Burns's Wedding" (1858), she opens the door to Sut's revenge. Sut drives the Burns's bull into their beehives and then into Sicily's wedding reception; the result is sexual revenge and a reassertion of Sut's mastery over the chaotic universe.

> Sicily, she squatted in the cold spring, up tu her years, an' turn'd a milk crock over her head, while she wer a drownin a mess ove bees onder her coats. I went tu her, an' sez I, "Yu hes got anuther new sensashun haint yu?" Sez she—
> "Shet yer mouth, yu cussed fool!"
> Sez I, "Power'ful sarchin feelin bees gins a body, don't they?"
> "Oh, lordy, lordy, Sut, these yere 'bominabil insex is jis' burnin me up!"
> "Gin 'em a mess ove SODY," sez I. (95)

Momentarily satisfied that "her an' him cudent sleep tugether fur ni ontu a week" (96), Sut completes his triumph in "Sut Lovingood's Chest Story."[14] He discovers that although Sicily "never did feel warm tu old Clapshaw" (*HTHT*, 120), she has learned to keep off the chill with Doctor Gus Fabin, a grotesque man "four foot fourteen inches" tall. While spying on the adulterous pair, Sut disturbs their lovemaking and gains his chance: "Ole Gus Fatty" hides in a chest containing two hundred eggs and some lamp black, Sicily "flung on her dress terrectly," and Sut pretends to be too drunk to recognize the obvious. Sicily is glad to fix the "drunk" Sut some dinner, and while she is gone, Fabin asks if "he"—meaning Sut—is gone. Imitating Sicily's voice, Sut, like Hooper's Daddy Biggs at Cockerell's Bend, paints a picture of imminent apocalypse that sets Fabin to praying; his prayers do no good, however, for Sut has tied the chest to Fabin's huge horse, which Sut has carefully prepared to bring on the Day of Doom by smearing luminous fox fire on it and igniting firecrackers round its head. The horse races off, mixing Fabin, eggs, and lamp black into one unholy stew, and as Sut notes, he never laid eyes on

> the chest nor Gus Fatty arter that nite, an I *dont care a durn ef I never do.* Wonder ef Sicily misses much! Ole Clapshaw believes in "witches, an warlocks, an long nebbed things" more than he does in Sicily an his "growin" skeer ov ghostes keeps him at home o' nights. I railly think he's gettin to be a pious man. Poor Sicily, she's warin thin, her eyes am growin bigger, an she hes no roses on her cheeks. She *cant* laugh, an she *wont* cry. Haint hit orful to think ove? (*HTHT*, 125)

Of course to Sut and the reader it is not "orful to think ove," but humorous. As Milton Rickels concludes, when Sicily "binds herself with the institutions, she becomes respectable and has a social place to lose."[15] In as artful a manner, Sut manipulates the adulterous Sheriff Doltin and Mary Mastin in the "Rare Ripe Garden-Seed" trilogy (227–77). He is able to chasten the sheriff, stop Mary's roaming, and drive away the meddlesome Widder McKildrin because they value their social positions and are confident that the authority of the sheriff's title will mask infidelity.

This is not to suggest with critics like Brom Weber that Sut is an agent of morality or cosmic justice;[16] Sut functions more like the soul of anarchy, the traditional fool or the lord of misrule. Sut seeks not justice but freedom and revenge; like Simon Suggs, he is the agent of a comic deity, one who like Simon's satirizes Sut as well. Sut is, as Walter Blair and Hamlin Hill demonstrate, a subversive character whose language, constructed of fantastic details and incongruous images, serves to "camouflage the underlying anarchy."[17] We are amused by Sut's victimization of Clapshaw largely because of Sut's victimization of language; coinages like *suckit rider, insex*, and even the innocent *buzzim* subvert traditionally held values and engage the reader in a rhetorical conspiracy against order. To decipher Sut's dialect is to share Sut's point of view.

That point of view is achieved by the conflation of the confidence man and the fool into a single vernacular narrator. By this stroke of genius, Harris creates a shifty character who, since he has no need of money, is freer than Simon Suggs,[18] and who, since he tells his own story, never suffers defeat. Although the undeniable butt of Sicily Burns's soda-powder trick, Sut triumphs over his humiliation by exaggerating his own ludicrousness. In retelling the story to George, Sut stresses his own foolishness, his own animal and mechanical characteristics, transforming the painful and embarrassing incident into a humorous narrative, his own comic illusion, his triumph.

> Jis' 'bout the time I wer ketchin my breff, I tho't I'd swaller's a thrashin-meersheen in full blast, wif a cuppil ove bull-dorgs, an' they hed sot intu fitin; an' I felt sumthin cumin up my swaller, monstrous like a hi pressur steamboat. I cud hear hit a-snortin, and scizzin. . . . Thar wer a road ove foam frum the hous' tu the hoss two foot wide, an' shoe mouf deep—looked like hit hed been snowin—a-poppin, an' a hissin, an' a-bilin like a tub ove soap-suds wif a red hot mole-board in hit. I gethered a cherry tree lim' es I run, an' I lit a-straddil ove ole Blackey, a-thrashin his hide like the devil beatin tan-bark, an' a-hissin wus nur four thousin mad gangers outen my mouf, eyes, nose, an' years. (81–82)

Even in defeat, Sut wrestles triumph from the incident by embellishing its fantastic details and casting himself as its outrageous star. He not only survives but overcomes his predicament, conquering threats to the self by transforming them into narrative art. His language acts as a distancing medium by which he separates himself and George from the painful event, turning what was humiliating into what is humorous. Like Simon Suggs and Ovid Bolus, Sut Lovingood uses language to master the new country; Sut creates fictions to control disorder and guarantee survival, substituting for one order of reality in which he is the victim another in which he is a comic hero.

From *Sut Lovingood's Yarns* (1867 first edition).

M. Thomas Inge writes that from 1854 to 1869 Sut Loving-
good is "a literary figure living partially in a world of reality
and mostly in a world of his own making, and an ironical and
literal mouthpiece for Harris' political opinions and satirical
attacks."[19] Inge is certainly correct in distinguishing between
Sut's two worlds; in reality, Sut victimizes preachers, sheriffs,
doctors, and all visible representatives of order because they
threaten his individual freedom. Sometimes he succeeds, and
sometimes he is himself pranked or kicked. In either case,
Sut's recreation of the event in bizarre and dislocating language diverts attention from the consequences of these actions: his own pain, seen at this remove, becomes comic, and
his cruelty to others—which can culminate in death—becomes a cause for laughter. When George asks what killed
Mrs. Yardley, Sut replies, "Nuffin, only her heart stop't beatin
'bout losin a nine dimunt quilt. True, she got a skeer'd hoss
tu run over her, but she'd a-got over that ef a quilt hadn't been

mix'd up in the catastrophy" (137). Sut separates common-
sense cause from effect; Mrs. Yardley dies because she cares
too much for quilts.

Sut's victimization of a normative language, though comic,
is itself a threat to the social order, a challenge to conventional
modes of expression, perception, and understanding. A favorite rhetorical device of Sut's—the catalogue—mixes categories of being in a fantastic new order. Sheriff Doltin's wife
appears initially as a traditional symbol of Christian piety, but
Sut's imagery swiftly propels her heavenward in a new incar-
nation.

> She were boney an' pale. A drunk Injun cud a-red a Dutch
> almanac thru her nose, and ther wer a new moon ove indigo
> onder her eyes, away back intu them, fifty foot or so. . . . Her
> wais wer flat, an' the finger cords on her han's wer mos' as
> high, an' look'd es tight, and show'd es clar thru the skin, es
> the strings ove a fiddil. The han' hitself wer white, not like
> snow, but like paint, and the forkid blue veins made hit look
> like a new map ove the lan' ove death. She wer a coughin wif
> her han' on her hart, like she hed no more spittil nur she hed
> tears, an' not much louder nor a crickit chirpin in a flute; yit
> in spite ove all this, a sweet smile kiver'd her feeters. . . . Her
> shoulder blades, as they show'd thru her dress, made me think
> they wer wings a sproutin fur her flight tu that cumfort and
> peace she desarves so well. She's a dealin wif death now. . . .
> *She* is ready, an' *I* raly wish she hed started. (256–57)

Sut's language asserts his mastery of reality, sounding a note
of optimism in an almost claustrophobic, menacing universe. His tales prove that the individual can survive, but only
if he is willing and able to reorder reality—usually by disor-
dering others' perceptions.

In Henry Clay Lewis's "Curious Widow" (1850), three medical students elaborately wrap up an albino Negro cadaver's
face to tempt their curious landlady. They anticipate her cries
of horror as she opens the package, confident that the prank
will teach her a hard lesson. Their expectations of terrible
delight are defeated, however, for she "gazed upon its awfulness in silence as if her eyes were riveted to it forever."[20] After
a moment she laughs, then composes herself and notes scorn-
fully, "I was just *smiling aloud* to think what fools these students made of themselves when they tried to scare me with a

dead nigger's face when I slept with a drunken husband for twenty years" (121). The knowledge she possesses is neither entirely comic nor reassuring; yet she stares into the disturbing face, confronts it, reads it, and finally laughs at it to survive, as she had survived twenty years with her drunken husband. It is this knowledge—of drunken husbands, battered flesh, and all the forces that threaten to anniilate and dehumanize the self—that Sut Lovingood shares with the reader and, in the act of sharing, masters. Sut is like the students who dissect life and discover the need to laugh at the grotesqueries they uncover, yet Sut resembles the landlady as well, who, improbably assaulted, laughs in the face of "awfulness" and thereby claims a desperate triumph. Harris collapses both visions of life into one point of view; as Sut explains, "hit am an orful thing, George, tu be a natral born durn'd fool. Yu'se never 'sperienced hit pussonally, hev yu?" (97).

Even the flexibility of the fool's point of view, however, could not withstand the chaos of the Civil War. Like many of his fellow Southern writers, Harris began to lose confidence in the security and superiority that had allowed him to record the fantastic doings of the Frog Mountain community in tales as temporally separate as "A Snake-Bit Irishman" (1846) and "Blown Up with Soda" (1857). Harris's own sense of order, not a fictitious Sheriff Doltin's, had come under attack. After 1860, as Inge concludes, Sut becomes more and more a vehicle for Harris's fears about the uncertain future of the South, a vindictive spokesman bitterly ridiculing Lincoln, Yankees, and humanity in general.[21] Sut's sense of humor evaporates in the "Travels with Abe" satires (1861), "Sut Lovingood Come to Life" (1866), and "Sut Lovingood on the Puritan Yankee" (1866). In Hoss Lovingood's four-part biography of Sut (1868), Harris parodies Jesse Root Grant's biography of his son, Ulysses S. Grant, and, though Harris's imitation is in spots amusing, the Civil War had dealt Harris's imagination a blow from which neither he nor Sut could hope to recover. In "Sut Lovingood's Allegory" (1868), Sut notes that "we aint as *good* as we wer forty years ago. We am too dam artifichul, interprizin an' *sharp*" (*HTHT*, 312). Anticipating the imaginative methods of Twain and Howells, Sut argues "for the sake ove this an' the nex generashun" (*HTHT*, 316) for a return to a simpler, more traditional way of life like that he portrayed in "The Knob Dance—A Tennessee Frolic" (1846). But in 1869 Harris died, embittered by the Yankee mechanisms of Reconstruction. The past was lost, Harris knew, with the Confederacy; and for Sut Lovingood—an enduring character combining confidence man, prankster, and fool—there would be no recovery.

The Confidence-Man

Herman Melville was not unaware of the conventional form of the confidence man evolving in the literature of the Old Southwest. The popularity and flexibility of the "shifty man" attracted him as they had Johnson J. Hooper, Joseph G. Baldwin, and George W. Harris, while the issue of confidence— how much and what is a "right" confidence?—was central throughout his career. In 1857 the *Boston Evening Transcript* immediately recognized Melville's use of a familiar figure.

> One of our indigenous characters who has long figured in our journals, courts, and cities, is "the Confidence Man;" his doings form one of the staples of villainy, and an element in the romance of roguery. Countless are the dodges attributed to this ubiquitous personage, and his adventures would equal those of Jonathan Wild. It is the fancy of Herman Melville— an author who deals equally well in the material description and the metaphysical insight of human life. He has added by his "Confidence Man" to the number of original subjects—an achievement for the modern *raconteur*, who has to glean in a field so often harvested. The plan and treatment are alike Melvillish; and the story more popularly eliminated [*sic*] than is usual with the author. "The Confidence Man—His Masquerade"—is a taking title.[22]

The reviewer's acknowledgement of the historical and literary ancestors of *The Confidence-Man* anticipates by nearly one hundred years Edward H. Rosenberry's assertions that the novel follows the tradition of frontier humor and that in tracing the evolution of the confidence man from the Old Southwest to the Mississippi, "Ovid Bolus . . . supplies the polish that [Simon] Suggs lacks and narrows the gap between the frontier *picaro* and Melville's metaphysical thimblerigger."[23] Melville does more than simply combine two variations of a frontier convention; he is the first classic American author to call this figure a "confidence man" and to delineate the full range of his literary possibilities. Paradoxically, this treatment at once establishes the confidence man as a literary convention, insures the term *confidence man* a place in American literature, and yet in a sense exhausts the convention's implications by making them explicit. Melville defines, then so thoroughly exposes, the poetics of the confidence man that he bankrupts its potential. In addition, Melville uses the confidence man to illuminate other conventions drawn from humorous, sentimental, and romantic fiction; he pushes stock devices beyond conventional patterns of expectation and response by connecting them with an all-informing shiftiness, suggesting limits to their ability to convey new meanings or to resolve new anxieties. This technique of exaggerating, warping, or inverting conventions, focused through an ambiguous "Anacharsis Cloots congress of all kinds of that multiform pilgrim species, man,"[24] raises the confidence man to a mythic level, on which "material description" gives way to "metaphysical insight," and on which the comic function of the confidence man is wedded to a serious probing of the shaky foundations of American self-congratulation.

The masquerade of *The Confidence-Man* begins on April Fools' Day, a comic device common in the tradition of frontier humor; in George Washington Harris's "Rare Ripe Garden-Seed," Wat Mastin marries the four-and-one-half-months pregnant Mary McKildrin on the first of April. Harris's joke is based on Wat's physical "ticklin sensashuns," and his description of Wat's appearance is earthy: "Wat felt his keepin right warm, so he sot intu bellerin an' pawin up dus . . . an' a-chompin his teef ontil he splotch'd his whiskers wif foam" (*Yarns*, 230–31). Melville's images are culturally exotic, proper introduction for the "advent" of a "stranger" who is not a familiar, duped, good old boy but a mysterious mute: "At sunrise on a first of April, there appeared, suddenly as Manco Capac at the lake Titicaca, a man in cream-colors" (1). This first sentence of *The Confidence-Man* suggests that conventions will be infused with new meaning and sets the stage for the metaphysical tickling to follow.

Melville's setting on board a Mississippi steamboat is also conventional: T. B. Thorpe's "Big Bear of Arkansas" (1841) is perhaps the best-known version of the floating stage used by humorists from Sol Smith to Mark Twain. The "heterogeneous character" of Thorpe's passengers differs from Melville's initial catalogue of American types: Thorpe balances geographical, professional, and moral extremes.

> Here may be seen jostling together the wealthy Southern planter, and the pedler of tin-ware from New England—the Northern merchant, and the Southern jockey—a venerable bishop, and a desperate gambler—the land speculator, and the honest farmer . . . beside a "plentiful sprinkling" of the half-horse and half-alligator species of men, who are peculiar to "old Mississippi," and who appear to gain a livelihood simply by going up and down the river.[25]

Melville's introductory list is one-sided:

> Crowds were gathered about the announcement, and among them certain chevaliers, whose eyes, it was plain, were on the capitals, or, at least, earnestly seeking sight of them from behind intervening coats; but as for their fingers, they were enveloped in some myth; though, during a chance interval, one of these chevaliers somewhat showed his hand in purchasing from another chevalier, ex-officio a peddler of money-belts, one of his popular safe-guards, while another peddler, who was still another versatile chevalier, hawked, in the thick of the throng, the lives of Measan, the bandit of Ohio, Murrel, the pirate of the Mississippi, and the brothers Harpe, the thugs of the Green River country, in Kentucky. (1–2)

The passengers on board the *Fidèle* are a motley assortment dominated by chevaliers, or sharpers; Melville's inventory—like his repetition of the term *chevalier*—creates a vision of the world not unlike the frontier flush times prowled by Hooper's Captain Simon Suggs, a comic universe where dishonesty is the norm.

Although a "stranger" boards a vessel in both "The Big Bear" and *The Confidence-Man*, in appearance and in manner Thorpe's Jim Doggett is the opposite of Melville's man in cream colors. Thorpe's backwoodsman bursts upon the *Invincible* like a tornado: "We were startled most unexpectedly by a loud Indian whoop . . . then was to be heard a loud crowing, which would not have continued to interest us . . . had not the hero of these windy accomplishments stuck his head into the cabin and hallooed out, 'Hurra for the Big Bear of Arkansas!'"

(15). Melville's stranger is a mute who slips silently on board the *Fidèle*, attracting attention not by screaming but by means of "a small slate" and four chalked words: "Charity thinketh no evil" (2). The mute is an eccentric even on board a Mississippi steamer, his biblical injunctions differing radically from Jim Doggett's humorous vernacular whoops and boasts in style and intention, provoking not amused acceptance but hostility: "They made no scruple to jostle him aside; while one, less kind than the rest, or more of a wag, by an unobserved stroke, dexterously flattened down his fleecy hat upon his head" (2). Jim Doggett's "Hurra" identifies him as a conventional type—a "horse," "screamer," or "Big Bear"; the mute's slate, however, marks him as mysterious. The serious "tall tales" that appear on the mute's slate, and the rough treatment he suffers at the hands of the crowd, signal the defeat of expectations for a humorous April Fools' Day cruise. The proximity of another introductory slate, a placard warning Melville's "ship of fools" of "a mysterious impostor," adds one more layer of complexity to the mute: is he a pitiful mute worthy of charity, or is he a confidence man, the protagonist of the novel? Is the crowd right or wrong to dismiss him with a series of shrugs? How is the crowd—and the reader—to evaluate the competing claims of the mute's "Charity" signs and the barber's motto, "No Trust"? What are the bases for confidence and suspicion? And what criteria—moral, religious, practical, aesthetic—are adequate to interpret the mute?

The reader, like the crowd, is trapped in a self-reflexive pattern of advance and retreat, one that the narrative voice mirrors in its qualifying rhetoric replete with antithetical suggestions and self-canceling double negatives. As if to accentuate this involuted motion, Melville begins his fiction again, describing the passengers of the *Fidèle* in conventional terms more akin to Thorpe's:

> Natives of all sorts, and foreigners; men of business and men of pleasure; parlor men and backwoodsmen; farm-hunters and fame-hunters; heiress-hunters, gold-hunters, buffalo-hunters, bee-hunters, happiness-hunters, truth-hunters and still keener hunters after all these hunters. Fine ladies in slippers, and moccasined squaws; Northern speculators and Eastern philosophers; English, Irish, German, Scotch, Danes; Sante Fe traders in striped blankets, and Broadway bucks in

> cravats of cloth of gold; fine-looking Kentucky boatmen, and
> Japanese-looking Mississippi cotton-planters ... jesters and
> mourners, tee-totalers and convivialists, deacons and black-
> legs; hard-shell Baptists and clay-eaters; grinning negroes, and
> Sioux chiefs solemn as high-priests. (6)

Melville suggests Thorpe's balanced pairs and controlled
comic tone, while his emphasis on hunters inverts the characteristic frontier exaggeration of plentiful game. At the head
of Melville's "Anacharis Cloots congress" is Black Guinea,
another "stranger" who at first seems a stock comic Negro
descended from the victim of John Neal's "Yankee Peddler"
(1831). In that story, a fast-talking Yankee tosses his trunk
ashore, where it crushes the foot of a Negro. Neal's Yankee
applies a medicinal "clear grit" to the wound, says a few kind
words, and then calmly demands payment for his "ministra-
tions." "'Why, lor a bressa, massa; massa, so good, he neber
tink o' takin' notin' o' poor nigger, her?'" The Yankee replies
immediately: "'Try me.'"[26] Like Neal's incredulous Negro,
Black Guinea arouses comic expectations. Anticipating
Charles Chesnutt's Uncle Julius, Black Guinea is loquacious,
humorous, and philosophical, a kind of black Jim Doggett who
engages the crowd. The narrator's description of him as a cripple "cut down to the stature of a Newfoundland dog" (7)
underscores that he poses no threat, his meager collection of
pennies and wry conversation labeling him a comfortable object of charity, pity, and curiosity. As the passengers lose interest in him, however, Black Guinea creates a new "game of
charity" which, like the slate of the mute in cream-colors,
arouses disquieting emotions.

> People would have a bout at a strange sort of pitch-penny
> game, the cripple's mouth being at once target and purse, and
> he hailing each expertly-caught copper with a cracked bravura
> from his tambourine. To be the subject of alms-giving is
> trying—and to feel in duty bound to appear cheerfully grateful
> under the trial, must be still more so; but whatever his secret
> emotions, he swallowed them, while still retaining each cop-
> per this side the oesophagus. And nearly always he grinned,
> and only once or twice did he wince, which was when certain
> coins, tossed by more playful almoners, came inconveniently
> nigh to his teeth, an accident whose unwelcomeness was not
> unedged by the circumstance that the pennies thus thrown
> proved buttons. (8)

This "singular temptation at once to *diversion* and charity" (8) reveals the fickleness of the crowd and a new complexity to Black Guinea; the crowd delights in the cripple's self-debasing performance, several "playful" fellows hurting and cheating him deliberately, while Black Guinea's invention of the game and his self-control suggest his subtle understanding of human nature and of the ways in which it can be manipulated. Black Guinea proves more artful than the mute: by creating a second attention-getting "diversion" he rekindles the crowd's waning interest and frees from purses a few additional coppers.

The reader faces a problem of identification and response: if Black Guinea is not a simple comedian but an intelligent unfortunate, is the "game of charity" the passengers play anything but grotesquely demeaning? It reduces both Black Guinea and the crowd to a level far beneath the human, revealing their willingness—even their eagerness—to assume conventional roles that are in fact life-denying. Melville demonstrates that the reader's initial evaluation of Black Guinea is limited, a stock response that results in a reciprocal grotesque transformation dramatized by the crowd's sinister penny-pitching. Throughout the novel, Melville's method is to present conventional models of response to apparently conventional figures and actions, and then to illustrate their inadequacy.

The man with a wooden leg appears at the height of Black Guinea's game of charity, satanically putting into words the vague suspicions of the audience concerning Black Guinea's manipulations. Perhaps because the "playful almoners" know they have mistreated Black Guinea, or because they suddenly feel they have been cheated by him—although even if Guinea is a confidence man they have surely received adequate amusement for their buttons and pennies—or simply because they have found a new "diversion," they begin "to scrutinize the negro curiously" (9). Wooden Leg gives the form of substance to suspicion, but the narrator adds, in a characteristically understated observation, "That these suspicions came from one who himself on a wooden leg went halt . . . did not appear to strike anybody present. That cripples, above all men, should be companionable, or, at least, refrain from picking a fellow-limper to pieces, in short, should have a little sympathy in common misfortune, seemed not to occur to the company" (8–9). The narrator implies that Wooden Leg may have ulterior motives for maligning Black Guinea: bitterness, jealously, or even the fear of beggarly competition. As Wooden Leg discovers, however, once suspicion is unleashed, it bites everyone in range, and he is himself the victim of mistrust and abuse.

Individual passengers come forward to defend and condemn Black Guinea and Wooden Leg, acting out vacillating responses of confidence and suspicion: there is no way for them to determine either the honesty or dishonesty—much less the motivation—of Black Guinea or Wooden Leg. Encountered separately, each unfortunate might elicit sympathy, but together they form a kind of thematic double-negative that casts suspicion on each cripple. Black Guinea is shunned, while Wooden Leg, who is so obviously unpleasant and seems clearly the antagonist, is manhandled by the Methodist minister. However momentarily satisfying, these responses prove nothing: Black Guinea and Wooden Leg remain as mysterious as the mute in cream colors. What becomes clear is the individual human complexity of each apparently conventional character; the Methodist is not strictly a "non-combatant," nor is he entirely charitable. Henry Roberts, the "good merchant" who contributes alms to Black Guinea and the man with the weed, is quick to speculate in the stock of the Black Rapids Coal Company. As the man with the weed notes of Roberts, "'There is sorrow in the world, but goodness too; and goodness that is not greenness, either, no more than sorrow is. Dear good man. Poor beating heart'" (20). This ambiguous analysis is characteristic of *The Confidence-Man*. If Black Guinea is a crippled beggar, Roberts seems charitable to trust him with confidence and money, yet if he is a confidence man, should Roberts deny him charity? Is Guinea perhaps not more unfortunate if he merely masquerades? And who is Roberts to judge, a man full of eagerness to speculate in stocks?

Roberts himself offers the reader oblique assistance; the transfer agent of the Black Rapids Coal Company offers to let him see the company's books.

> "What need to, if already I believe that it is what it is lettered to be?"

"But you had better. It might suggest doubts."
     "Doubts, may be, it might suggest, but not knowledge; for
how, by examining the book, should I think I knew any more
than I now think I do; since, if it be the true book, I think it
.   so already; and since if it be otherwise, then I have never seen
the true one, and don't know what that ought to look like."
(48)

Knowledge cannot be acquired by conventional methods of
analysis; Roberts may be a fool victimized by three confidence
men in quick succession. Melville dramatizes Roberts's uncertainty by extending it to include the reader. The narrator of
Hooper's *Simon Suggs* shares his omniscience with the reader,
making him a comfortable silent partner in Simon's confidence games. In "Ovid Bolus," Baldwin's narrator recounts the
adventures of a consummate liar. The narrator's amused skepticism about Ovid's more extravagant cons marks off two
kinds of fiction, two kinds of confidence games within the
tale: the fabulous lies Ovid tells of deceiving beautiful heir-
esses, and the plain truth of Ovid's conning "poor Ben." The
last story, like those of Simon Suggs, the narrator clearly validates. Melville's genius is in the exploitation of the implications of narrative irony in "Ovid Bolus," denying the reader of
The Confidence-Man a narrative guide who will share with
him ultimate knowledge: Melville's narrator never identifies
a character as the titular "Confidence-Man," nor does any
character include the reader in a celebratory "ho'n." The
reader is led to suspect every character's motives, to doubt
every conventional appearance, to question the authority or
reliability of the narrator, and to mistrust his own complacent
patterns of response.
     The chapter titled "A Charitable Lady" reveals the uncer-
tainties created by Melville's narrative strategy. The Charitable Lady, "a widow just breaking the chrysalis of her mourning" (37), seems at first a stock victim—like Hooper's Widow
Haycock or Harris's Mrs. Doltin—of a conventional confidence man. The man in gray quickly finds loneliness and re-
ligiosity to be the softest spots in her nature.

     "You interest me," said the good lady, in mild surprise.
"Can I in any way befriend you?"
     "No one can befriend me, who has not confidence."

> "But I—I have—at least to that degree—I mean that—"
>
> "Nay, nay, you have none—none at all. Pardon, I see it. No
> confidence. Fool, fond fool that I am to seek it!"
>
> "You are unjust, sir," rejoins the good lady with heightened
> interest. . . . "Believe me, I—yes, yes—I may say—that—
> that—"
>
> "That you have confidence? Prove it. Let me have twenty
> dollars."
>
> "Twenty dollars?"
>
> "There, I told you, madam, you had no confidence."
>
> The lady was, in an extraordinary way, touched. She sat in
> a sort of restless torment, knowing not which way to turn. She
> began twenty different sentences, and left off at the first syl-
> lable of each. At last, in desperation, she hurried out, "Tell
> me, sir, for what you want the twenty dollars?"
>
> "And did I not—" then glancing at her half-mourning, "for
> the widow and the fatherless. I am traveling agent of the
> Widow and Orphan Asylum, recently founded among the
> Seminoles."
>
> "And why did you not tell me your object before?" As not a
> little relieved. "Poor souls—Indians, too—those cruelly-used
> Indians. Here, here; how could I hesitate? I am so sorry it is
> not more." (38)

In her "natural struggle between charity and prudence" (38),
the Charitable Lady chooses to contribute. She seems a fool
betrayed by sentimental values, for that she has been duped is
apparent from the man-in-gray's cause: between 1818 and
1845 the Seminoles engaged in a series of bloody wars with
white settlers, which made widows of many women like the
Charitable Lady. Nevertheless, insofar as there is a narrative
voice in this chapter, it seems to question implicity the motives of the Charitable Lady even as it purports to recom-
mend her.

> At the sofa's further end sits a plump and pleasant person,
> whose aspect seems to hint that, if she have any weak point,
> it must be anything rather than her excellent heart. From her
> twilight dress, neither dawn nor dark, apparently she is a
> widow just breaking the chrysalis of her mourning. A small
> gilt testament is in her hand, which she has just been reading.
> Half-relinquished, she hold the book in reverie, her finger in-
> serted at the xii, of 1st Corinthians, to which chapter possibly
> her attention might have recently been turned. (37)

The extremely qualifying rhetoric here and elsewhere leads us
to suspect her purity; the pleasure she experiences in reading

the passages on charity from her "small gilt testament," which she holds "half-relinquished," and in giving twenty dollars to the man in gray is a kind of pleasure analogous to pitching pennies at Black Guinea—it is self-congratulatory, a sanitary gesture like those of the narrator in "Bartleby the Scrivener" (1853). In addition, her obvious book-dropping to attract the man in gray and the "sparkle" in her eye as he returns it (37) suggest that she is too forward, *apparently . . . a widow*" deserving of sympathy but actually a drawing-room confidence woman who is taken by surprise by the man in gray. The narrative voice is at best equivocal.

Determining the proper criteria for judgment becomes a crucial issue in Pitch's encounters with the Herb-Doctor, the Philosophical Intelligence Office agent, and the Cosmopolitan. These meetings form the novel's structural center and introduce the fast-talking Cosmopolitan, who will dominate its last half. Pitch is a Missouri bachelor full of odds and ends of philosophy, a reasonable man who thinks himself logical, prudent, and perceptive. He welcomes technology and worships truth, fusing the two in a progressive image that excludes sentimentalism: "Truth is like a thrasing-machine; tender sensibilities must keep out of the way" (104). The coughing miser is one whom Pitch thrashes with his rigid machinelike truth.

> "Yarbs, yarbs; natur, natur; you foolish old file you! He diddled you with that hocus-pocus, did he? Yarbs and natur will cure your incurable cough, you think. . . . Because a thing is nat'ral, as you call it, you think it must be good. But who gave you that cough? Was it, or was it not, nature?"
> "Sure, you don't think that natur, Dame Natur, will hurt a body, do you?"
> "Natur is good Queen Bess; but who's responsible for the cholera?"
> "But yarbs, yarbs; yarbs are good?"
> "What's deadly-nightshade? Yarb, ain't it? . . . But who froze to death my teamster on the prairie?" (91–92)

The Herb-Doctor adopts the Devil's oldest ploy—using the truth for his own purposes—to chasten Pitch.

> "Granting that [the miser's] dependence on my medicine is vain, is it kind to deprive him of what, in mere imagination, if nothing more, may help eke out, with hope, his disease? For

you, if you have no confidence, and, thanks to your native health, can get along without it, so far, at least, as trusting in my medicine goes; yet, how cruel an argument to use, with this afflicted one here. Is it not for all the world as if some brawny pugilist, aglow in December, should rush in and put out a hospital-fire, because, forsooth, he feeling no need of artificial heat, the shivering patients shall have none? Put it to your conscience, sir, and you will admit, that, whatever be the nature of this afflicted one's trust, you, in opposing it, evince either an erring head or a heart amiss" (94–95)

As the Missouri bachelor concedes, his own words are "pitiless." The Herb-Doctor, whether healer or sharper, justifies the power of confidence. Truth, he argues, is human, intuitive, individual, moral; truth is therefore relative. Two versions of one truth may exist simultaneously and both be judged "true": to Pitch, herbs may prove superfluous, while to the miser, herbs may prove medicinal.

In like manner, the identity of the Herb-Doctor is itself ambiguously multiple: he seems to do a genuinely good deed for the miser, as he has for the bitter soldier of fortune in chapter 19; however, the reader cannot know for certain either his motives or the results of his Omni-Balsamic Reinvigorator/ Samaritan Pain Dissuader—he may be but a slick snake-oil salesman. As the auburn-haired gentleman muses, after watching the Herb-Doctor apply his own cure to himself, "May he not be knave, fool, and genius all together?" (78). The Herb-Doctor assumes three roles played separately in earlier fiction by the confidence man (knave), his victim (fool), and the narrator (genius). The Southwest humorists' most innovative confidence-man tales are, like Longstreet's "The Horse-Swap," local versions of the universal "biter bit" motif; the author takes care to separate his cultured narrator from the vernacular-speaking sharpers and to identify for our pleasure all the complexities of the snap. Harris comes close to Melville's strategy of conflation, but in the Yarns Sut Lovingood, an uncontrolled gentleman, functions as narrator and guide. In The Confidence-Man, Melville's narrator is an unreliable cicerone to the crowds of hunters and hunted who seek not money, like Simon Suggs, nor vengeful fun, like Sut Lovingood, but who, like the Herb-Doctor, seek to determine the source and the limits of American confidence. The narrative voice in a sense conspires with characters—all of whom seem more or less shifty—not to resolve anxieties concerning appearances but to intensify their metaphysical ambiguities. If Longstreet, Thompson, Hooper, and Baldwin began to evolve a convention of the confidence man by locating the traditional biter in the specific circumstances of the American flush times, thereby demythologizing an archetypal pattern, Melville remythologizes the confidence man, infusing the American convention with universal significance.

Melville's intention and method differ radically from those of his contemporaries. In C. F. Briggs's "Elegant Tom Dillar" (1856), Tom is convinced by the sharp Pete Van Slicer to invest his fortune in Pottawattamy Coal Company stock. The narrator informs the reader of what Tom does not suspect; namely, that Van Slicer is the tool of Ormolu, the auctioneer, who desires to ruin Tom for snubbing his daughter, Fanny.

> Tom was not a spendthrift, nor a gambler; but then he was the merest child in business matters, and had no idea about money transactions beyond drawing his dividends every six months, and contriving to make his income just meet his expenditure. Tom had often wished that his income was larger, for he had long been ambitious of owning a yacht, but was unable to indulge in that costly enjoyment; so, when his young friend, Pete Van Slicer, of the firm of Van Slicer, Son and Co., the great stockbrokers, of Wall Street, one day said to him, as if by accident, "Tom, how would you like to enter into a little speculation, by which you might make a hundred thousand dollars or so?" Tom opened his eyes, and eagerly replied he would like nothing better. . . .
>
> "Trust to me," replied Pete, with a knowing wink, which seemed to Tom so full of sagacity, that he concluded to trust to him, and accordingly gave an order to the firm of Van Slicer, Son and Co., to purchase, for his account, about ten times as many shares of Pottawattamy Coal Stock as he had the means to pay for, Pete undertaking to carry the stock, as he called it, for thirty days, in which time the rise was sure to come.[27]

Briggs's narrator ushers the reader through Tom's inevitable misfortunes, throughout stating clearly the characters' motivations and cueing particular responses; Tom, Ormolu, Pete, and the narrator are conventional figures, typed by their names and deeds, familiar in sentimental, romantic, and confidence-man fiction. The omnisicent narrator details from conception to conclusion the reasons for and the results of the Pottawattamy Coal stock swindle. The only puzzle, Tom's return to riches, is solved quickly and carefully: Tom dons blackface and works in clubs as an "Ethiopian Minstrel" for money. The winking Pete Van Slicer is a kissing cousin of the confidence men in southwestern humor, but the kinship between these shifty operators and Melville's Herb-Doctor, PIO agent, and Cosmopolitan is more distant: Melville's characters form a new breed intended to pose unsettling questions. How can a confidence man be identified? Which character is "The Confidence-Man"? What is the proper response to a literary convention that has been proven inadequate? What are the foundations of American optimism, and are they securely anchored or erected on the quicksands of an illusory new country? By withholding ultimate knowledge, Melville changes the function of the confidence man, withdrawing from the convention its traditional ability to dispel anxieties in laughter while substituting for the bankrupt form the genus *Confidence-Man*, which reveals fundamental contradictions in American character.

Hershel Parker too eagerly crowns Pitch "the most admirable opponent of the Devil's false, delusive optimism."[28] Pitch's proverbial wisdom—"I have confidence in distrust" (93)—is itself a version of "delusive optimism," and Pitch himself appears a parody of the Davy Crockett–Natty Bumppo backwoodsman. Melville suggests that the heroic frontiersman mediating between nature and civilization is in 1857 no longer an adequate symbol of American experience, nor is the frontiersman able to shrug off contradictions by moving away from society to a new country. His limits as a literary convention become as clear as the Suggsian confidence man's. Pitch's forays into philosophical argument succeed only in directing him in circles and in revealing the inadequacy of his nature: "All boys are rascals, and so are all men . . . my name is Pitch; I stick to what I say" (109).

Pitch does not, of course, stick to what he says. Admitting the logic of the Herb-Doctor in the case of the coughing miser, and placing trust in the PIO agent, Pitch momentarily surrenders his mechanistic vision of the future with the three dollars he pays out for a thirty-sixth boy. Trapped in the paranoid's labyrinthine universe and unwilling to accept for any length of time the accuracy of even his own judgments without objective proof, he doubts the truth of both confidence and suspicion. Unable to accept an ambiguous reality, he finally reduces himself to a misanthropic bark: "Hands off!" (113). This rejection of humanity, implicitly underscored by his bachelorhood, qualifies Pitch's appeal; his narrow absolutism can only lead him away from humanity. His isolation warns the reader not to demand certainty where none is to be found—in new countries, in the fictional world of *The Confidence-Man*, in life itself. As the man in gray notes, "The suspicious man kicks himself with his own foot" (25).

A fast talker par excellence, the Cosmopolitan announces his arrival with words "sweet as a seraph's" (113), his outrageous ensemble speaking as loudly as the whoops of Longstreet's Yellow Blossom or Thorpe's Jim Doggett. His appearance bewilders Pitch, who reacts as if Harlequin had just stepped from the stage onto the *Fidèle*. The backwoodsman's attempts to identify the Cosmopolitan produce a series of conventional labels; the parti-colored gentleman seems alternately a "touchan fowl" or chattering actor, "Jeremy Diddler No. 3" or "Mr. Popinjay-of-the-world," in league with "metaphysical scamps," or, finally, "Diogenes in Disguise." Pitch is dissatisfied with each of these names, for the Cosmopolitan resists reduction to a type; though the Cosmopolitan offers to hold Pitch's watch while he dances a hornpipe—an old trick of Elizabethan cony-catchers—the Cosmopolitan walks away from him with the injunction to "get you confidence" (120), an admonition Simon Suggs used only after his pockets were full of his victim's money. Pitch, "the discomfited misanthrope" (120), learns nothing from the Cosmopolitan, remains in ignorance of his identity, and finds himself at last abandoned to his inadequate "confidence in distrust." Melville warns that if the reader follows Pitch's example, he too will gain nothing.

In the second half of *The Confidence-Man* the temptation to identify the Cosmopolitan as the novel's title character increases. Pitch is only the first of many to call him a Jeremy Diddler, and the Cosmopolitan's verbal duels with Charlie

Noble, Mark Winsome, Egbert, and William Cream recall the insinuating strategy of earlier sharpers. As "Quite An Original," the Cosmopolitan "is like a revolving Drummond light, raying away from itself all round it—everything is lit by it, everything starts up to it" (205). Characters approach and attempt to identify the Cosmopolitan; the failures—especially of those who like Pitch believe him a sharper—suggest the manipulations of a master confidence man playing a cosmic confidence game in a new country of metaphysical proportions.

As if to confirm the infusion of new meaning into the confidence-man convention, the narrator addresses the reader directly in chapters 14, 33, and 44. In chapter 14 he bemoans the reader's desire for absolutely consistent characters, who are inevitably unlifelike, partially conceived, stock figures. In chapter 33 he defines the ideal reader, one who wishes "nature unfettered, exhilarated, in effect transformed" (158). Because he hungers for "more reality, than real life itself can show," the ideal reader willingly surrenders to the enchantment of Harlequin, a figure whose conventional form suggests links to an aesthetic universe of infinite possibility: "It is with fiction as with religion: it should present another world, and yet one to which we feel the tie" (158). And in chapter 44 the narrator states that the highest accomplishment is the creation of an "original" character, in which "there is discernible something prevailingly local, or of the age; which circumstance, of itself, would seem to invalidate the claim" (205). To give birth to an original like Hamlet or Don Quixote an author must begin with a conventional—or archetypal—figure, circumstance him in a particular time and place, and yet avoid making him either so intensely local or so realistic as to be merely lifelike. Melville follows this oxymoronic process, recapitulating the history of American literary conventions as he explicates his confidence man by pursuing the new country as a national myth: "Here reigned the dashing and all-fusing spirit of the West, whose type is the Mississippi itself, which, uniting the streams of the most distant and opposite zones, pours them along, helter-skelter, in one cosmopolitan and confident tide" (6). Specifically, Melville makes the flush-times confidence man an archetypal American character, giving him universal rather than merely regional significance, and, in naming him and working through his variations, exhausting the traditional functon of the frontier form.

Charlie Noble, the Cosmopolitan's "boon companion," confirms the Cosmopolitan's originality. Charlie seems a conventional two-bit hustler drawn from the pages of Jonathan H. Green's *Gambling Exposed* (1857), which warns that "when in company, we are too apt to form hasty acquaintances; this frequently, and more especially, occurs with young travellers; and these are the very ones which, above all others, the different classes spoken of [sharpers and confidence men] are constantly on the look-out for."[29] Melville depicts Charlie Noble as a Suggsian confidence man, revealing in the contrast between his inept maneuverings and the Cosmopolitan's consummate artistry the inadequacy of the traditional form. As if to italicize this distinction, the Cosmopolitan rebukes Charlie for his pitiless laughter at "the figure of a pale pauper-boy" (141) and dismisses Charlie as a simple-minded drunk: "Why, Charlie, you are losing your mind. . . . Yes, I think that by all means you had better away, and sleep it off. There—don't apologize—don't explain—go, go—I understand you exactly" (161). The figure Charlie cuts has been, on several levels, exhausted.

Like Charlie Noble, Mark Winsome cannot fathom the Cosmopolitan. In fact, Winsome cannot even identify Charlie as "a Mississippi operator," warning the Cosmopolitan "that he is such, I little doubt, *having had him pointed out to me as such* by one desirous of initiating me into any little novelty of this western region" (168, my emphasis). A bitter parody of a transcendentalist, Winsome applies his "doctrine of labels" without first-hand experience; his calling Charlie a confidence man, and then treating him as such, is irresponsible and reductive, revealing Winsome's limitation of vision and the inadequacy of his philosphical system to explain human experience. Unlike the Cosmopolitan, who packs Charlie off after plumbing his depths, Winsome dismisses Charlie without even testing the water. This is the same method he employs in refusing the Poe-like "crazy beggar" peddling "a rhapsodical tract" (167), whom he labels a scoundrel despite the Cosmopolitan's example of charity. It is also the strategy demonstrated by Winsome's disciple, Egbert, who rejects the Cosmopolitan's entreaties to have confidence in and offer sympathetic assistance to one's friends. Yet in reducing men to labels and human relationships to business transactions, this philosophy fails Winsome's own test of truth: "For any philosophy that, being in operation contradictory to the ways of the world, tends to produce a character at odds with it, such a philosophy must necessarily be but a cheat and a dream" (170). Winsome can use his doctrines to identify neither Charlie, the Cosmopolitan, nor the beggarly poet; his philosophy is merely an intellectual fantasy bearing no relation to the world of men. Like an unindulgent reader of fiction, he refuses to suspend disbelief, expecting the world before him to conform to his rigid preconceptions. As the Cosmopolitan remarks, his system is inhuman, and in comparison makes the games of a confidence man seem genial.

William Cream, the barber of the *Fidèle*, signals the concluding action of the novel. His "gaudy sort of illuminated sign" (3), bearing the legend "No Trust," casts a dim light from chapter 1, where it competes with the mute's small slate. In chapter 42 the barber's emblem is opposed by the Cosmopolitan. The reappearance of the sign points the reader back to the beginning; "No Trust" defines the metaphysical province of the novel within the boundaries of common experience, focusing attention on the oracular barber, an American Everyman, who stands with "'one foot on confidence and the other on suspicion'" (197)—a perfect description of the individual in the new country. The Cosmopolitan suggests that the sign is reductive and untrue, and that for reasonable, intelligent, perceptive men—like William Cream—it is unnecessary and misleading. For in fact the barber does not abide by the letter of his law: "'I don't say, and can't say, and wouldn't say, that I suspect all men; but I *do* say that strangers are not to be trusted, and so,' pointing up to the sign, 'no trust'" (197). His explanation reveals that his motto is neither as simple nor as absolute as it appears; that he knows it is reductive, that he trusts some men while distruting others, marks his own complexity. He is, like Melville, the author of a fiction, a writer who uses what is essentially a convention—the No Trust sign—while recognizing its limitations: it is convenient and familiar, but it does not tell the whole story. The Cosmopolitan suggests that in taking down his sign—his expectations—the barber will free himself to respond to all men on individual terms, to become Melville's ideal reader, one who though not green is not jaded. William Cream, knowing that appearances can be deceiving, that knowledge can only be gained by engaging men, by having confidence, nevertheless cannot willingly restrain his suspicion of the Cosmopolitan's intentions beyond earshot, and rejects ex post facto the Cosmopolitan's written guarantee of good faith.

> Drawing forth his notification from the drawer, he put it back where it belonged; while, as for the agreement, that he tore up; which he felt the more free to do from the impression that in all human probability he would never again see the person who had drawn it. Whether that impression proved well-founded or not, does not appear. (204)

The old man of the final chapter seems at first to avoid kicking himself with his own foot. He is sympathetic to the Cosmopolitan's doubts, and, a careful reader of the Bible, scrutinizes the passages in question and resolves the anxieties they arouse. Willing, intelligent, and human, he seems the "indulgent" reader the narrator mentions as Melville's ideal audience in chapter 33. However, the old man finds himself easily led into suspicion by a "juvenile peddler," who seems the Devil himself when compared to the wrongdoers of advice books like Augustus Ward Loomis's *Learn to Say No; or, The City Apprentice* (1856). The light of the good book cannot dispel the darkness of distrust, and the old man buys a "traveler's patent lock" and a money belt from the youth. A counterfeit detector the boy gives him dramatizes the problem of confidence his suspicions have created; the Cosmopolitan asks if his money is genuine: "'I don't know, I don't know,' returned the old man, perplexed, 'there's so many marks of all sorts to go by, it makes it a kind of uncertain'" (213–14). The old man seems suddenly a parody of Melville's ideal reader, one of many marks who is thrown into confusion by uncertainty and who responds by rejecting and distrusting all things and all men. Only after he gives up the counterfeit detector does he again respond positively to the Cosmopolitan, and again seem like a reader willing to set aside his expectations.

The Cosmopolitan "kindly" leads the old man through the darkening cabin toward the novel's final paragraph, as if he himself were the novel's narrator and the weary old man his reader.

Critics have discovered in the final chapter a vision of the apocalypse, yet surely their accomplishment constitutes a scholarly version of the suspicious man's kick. Melville's method is consistently to create expectations which he then frustrates, leaving both his characters and his reader without the knowledge to evaluate the ultimate results of the ambiguous actions in which they participate. The mute in cream colors seems at once an emblem of Christian purity and a mock-emblem, Black Guinea seems a parody of the docile kneeling slave, the account of Colonel Moredock seems a bitter satire of James Hall's progressive "Indian Hating" (1835), and Pitch seems at last a weary Leatherstocking made uneasy by the midcentury "cosmopolitan and confident tide." The reader should be prepared for the inversion of his expectations, for uncertainty, or perhaps, cued by the title of chapter 45, "The Cosmpolitan Increases in Seriousness," for an intensification of ironic comedy. For as Warwick Wadlington correctly notes, the novel's conclusion "is anti-apocalyptic and counter-teleological."[30] Critics who find proof of the novel's black vision in the ambiguous cries of passengers about the apocalypse and the confidence man have missed Melville's point and are led to use such flimsy evidence as the chamber-pot/life preserver to buoy up their theories. Melville uses these obvious devices as ironic, comic comments on the reader's increasingly serious demands for a conventional conclusion, one in which the author will share with him the omniscient knowledge of his story and characters that the reader desires. Hooper, Baldwin, and even Harris put their shifty characters figuratively to rest in the last paragraphs of their fiction (Sut Lovingood actually goes to sleep), and most popular works of the 1850s—from Maria Cummins's *The Lamplighter* (1854) to Charles Dickens's *Little Dorrit* (1857)—climax in shared moments of resolution. Melville does not suddenly transform the Cosmopolitan into a conventional confidence man, one who winks knowingly at the reader as he manipulates the old man, nor does Melville ultimately identify the confidence man; he uses the reader's familiarity with the comic convention to create "more reality, than real life itself can show," or, more precisely, to produce a more "original" and meaningful fiction than his contemporaries.

Ann Douglas concludes that Melville seizes popular conventions as hostages to force the reader to recognize their shallowness.[31] In *The Confidence-Man* Melville holds many hostages, but focuses his imagination through a central convention, the confidence man, to expose the limitations of conventional patterns of expectation and response. Melville unleashes the duplicity of the confidence man tamed by Hooper, pressing upon the reader a maddening authorial uncertainty and substituting for the self-enclosed humorous snaps of Simon Suggs an unsettling panoply of all human relations as potentially dishonest. In this manner *The Confidence-Man* strips off the veneer of self-congratulatory optimism predominant in American culture in the 1850s. The novel likewise militates against the deadwood structures of contemporary literary practice, demonstrating that conventions have become hypocritical aesthetic solutions to fundamental national problems. Melville attempts to expand their ability to carry new meanings by pushing them beyond their traditional limits; the last sentence of *The Confidence-Man* is deliberately antiformulaic, and in this sense H. Bruce Franklin sees the entire fiction as "a grand *reductio ad absurdum* of the novel form itself."[32] Melville transforms the conventional into the original by defeating the reader's expectations, dramatizing issues that cannot be resolved in easy, superior laughter; a Suggsian confidence man cannot blink the doubts of the American promise of plenty that were manifest in the sectional, economic, and racial tensions soon to erupt in the Civil War. The failure of writers to interpret the war in the 1860s using the confidence man is implicit testimony that Melville has sounded the depths of the convention's meaning; the rediscovery of the confidence man and his flush times during the Gilded Age confirms the accuracy of Melville's ambiguous prophecy: "Something further may follow of his Masquerade."

Billy Fishback, Confederate Straggler

Like George W. Harris, Kittrell J. Warren was a southern writer who supported the Confederacy in the Civil War; unlike Harris, who limited his efforts to satires of Lincoln and

Grant, Warren enlisted as a private in the Eleventh Georgia Volunteers and engaged in real combat. Of his first two literary attempts, *Ups and Downs of Wife Hunting* (1861) is a comic pamphlet for soldiers like himself that admits kinship to William Tappan Thompson's *Major Jones' Courtship*, while the *History of the Eleventh Georgia Vols., Embracing The Muster Rolls, Together with a Special and Succinct Account of the Marches, Engagements, Casualties, Etc.* (1863) is a factual tribute to his comrades in arms. *Life and Public Services of an Army Straggler* (1865) owes its form to Longstreet, Hooper, Baldwin, and Harris, and also to Warren's firsthand combat experiences. Billy Fishback is a Confederate army straggler who roams the no-man's-land of the battle-torn South, a confidence man turned vicious by the war who deserts all causes and denies all human virtues. He has none of Simon Suggs's saving sense of humor, Sut Lovingood's knack for outrageous fun, or Ovid Bolus's abilities and polish. The days of Melville's "one cosmopolitan and confident tide" have been destroyed by the criminal realities of the Civil War; Billy Fishback plays potentially lethal games that mirror the unpredictable chaos of the national conflict. He thus dramatizes a fearfully violent new country.

Billy Fishback and Dick Ellis decide to desert the Confederate army before it engages in battle. By agreement, Ellis steals the major's prized horse, and Fishback, who alerts the major, is sent out to recapture the horse and dispatch the thief. The original plan called for Ellis to wait for Fishback a few miles from the camp, and, sure of no one else pursuing them, the two were to escape together. Fishback, however, requests assistance. Taking advantage of the major's order to "kill the villain" who stole his horse, Fishback sends the obedient Jack Wilcox, who is "armed to the teeth" and unaware of the deserters' pact, on Ellis's trail. As he watches Wilcox ride off, Fishback has "a good laugh over this pleasant and amusing little incident."

> "Dick Ellis aint a guine to pester about tellin nothin. That fool Jack's dun turned him over to the tender mersez uv the carron croze. That's a good joke I've got on Dick, maniged to get his branes shot out thout my tellin a word."[33]

Here the story ends, and the natural conclusion to be drawn from the incident is that Ellis has been killed; that Ellis has by chance not been murdered is revealed forty pages later (87), but this information does nothing to change the reader's horror at Fishback's cold-blooded attempt. This violence is quite different from that in Longstreet's "Georgia Theatrics" or "The Fight" (1835), both of which Warren mentions (30); although Ellis's murder is not in fact accomplished, it is imaginatively accomplished and therefore conveys the discomfort of its execution to the reader.

Warren takes care that no bond of sympathy or humor forms between the reader and the Confederate private: Billy Fishback is no Henry Fleming or Colonel Carter any more than he is Simon Suggs. Fishback is more like Roderick Random, Smollett's eighteenth-century picaro, whom the reader despises with increasing emotion as Random symbolically pistol-whips friends and enemies. Yet unlike Random, who controls the reader's repulsion by telling his own story in the first person, Fishback is introduced within a conventional narrative frame that limits and defines his province.

> I *do wish* I could introduce my hero in a fashionable manner.—yea, verily, I would like to present him sumptuously appareled, reclining gracefully upon a magnificent ottoman,—just resting from the delicious employment of reading (that trans-antropean specimen of splurgey) Macaria. I would have him a grand looking character. Intellect should beam from his lustrous eye, and nobleness peep forth from every lineament of his features. Nature should be in a glorious good humor, smiling graciously upon his first appearance. (5)

The sentimental rhetoric of Warren's narrator contrasts ironically with the "Truth": "With a rather well favored, though remarkably black face, and a stout, robust frame, wrapped in comfortable looking jeans wallowed the immortal William Fishback" (6). The narrator plays with a language unavailable to his "hero," while Fishback's confused admiration of "Captain" Slaughter's oratory marks a limit to his understanding and to the type of role he may assume. To help the illiterate Fishback win the hand of the accomplished and wealthy Miss Callie, Slaughter—for fifty dollars—tells Callie that though Fishback has been courted by the "rich and literary heiress, Miss Julia Evans," Fishback will not be so unprincipled as to marry for money. To do so would be "an imitation of Judas—bartering immortality for a sum of money. We are not the owners of the soul, and have no right to vend it—that eternal element has been entrusted to us as custodians only; a truth which we find beautifully illustrated in the parable of the talents—if we bury it in the cumbrous rubbish of filthy lucre, how fearful will be the ulterior consequences? . . . Bribe the needle to play truant to the pole—train the untrameled wind to blow not 'where it listeth'—teach the thirsty sun-beam to leave undrunk the dews of heaven, but this heart must revolve in its allotted periphery, or cease to move."

Although, so far as we know, our hero was wholly unacquainted with any foreign language, he had caught the gist of the conversation, and now ventured his own sentiments on the subject, in the following laconic style: "I'll be dad blasted ef I hadn't ruther try to set on a dozen rotten eggs twel I hatcht the last one uv 'em, as to marry a umurm jest for her munny, and spect to git along; thar aint narry bit o' use a tryin." (58)

Three languages exist in this passage: the allusive, sentimental oratory of Slaughter; the rough, homely dialect of Fishback; and the normative, controlling rhetoric of the narrator. Fishback's attempt to echo the sentiments of Slaughter and Miss Callie is incongruous, and on this level Warren operates within the tradition of frontier humor; with Warren's narrator, as with Harris's George, the reader shares a superiority to the vernacular characters, though unlike Billy, Sut helps the reader as he helps George to new perceptions.

Language is not Fishback's only limitation; several characters offer successful alternatives to his darkly egotistical vision of the world. Captain John Smith, Fishback's superior, combines the masculine virtues of the explorer with the understanding of a parent. Like Melville's myopic Captain Amaso Delano, Captain John Smith stands for American verities: confidence in mankind, belief in original innocence, and loyalty to boon companions. His desire to think well of Billy Fishback leads him to misperceive his malicious nature, and Billy has no trouble getting Smith drunk.

No sooner were Capt. Smith's eyes closed in the deep sleep of drunkenness than Fishback commenced making an inventory of his pocket-book which was found to contain nine hundred and sixty dollars. Taking out five hundred, he carefully replaced the balance, donned the Captain's uniform and sallied into the street. Arriving in front of Welch's store, he

> suddenly put on a drunken look, pulled his hat over his face,
> and staggered in. "Keep this fur me twell I git sober" said he,
> reaching the pocket-book to a man who stood behind the
> counter.
>   "What name, Captain?" asked the other, as he took the
> book in hand.
>   "John Smith." (36)

It is of course this honest merchant rather than the clever
Fishback who appears to the captain to have lightened his
wallet. Although Smith hugs the real confidence man to his
bosom, Smith's values remain as an antidote to Fishback's.

The narrator himself is robbed by Fishback of a knapsack
containing "a testament, the gift of my beloved Pastor, and
'March's Life of Webster,' presented by Linda the morning I
left home, with a special charge to 'preserve it as I valued her
love'" (42–43). For the most part the narrator provides a model
accessible to the reader; he is a southerner, a soldier, and—
since he is one himself—understands and sympathizes with
Fishback's victims. His intrusions into the text, like his
mock-invective against marriage, assure the reader that Billy's
tricks are at least narratively circumscribed, that a larger order—moral if not entirely comic—will prevail even though he
has been abused. He condemns Fishback's inhuman scavenging, a condemnation symbolized by the narrator's personal
emblems of faith in the satchel, while he also satirizes the
uselessness of extreme sentimentalism in a parody of wifely
chatter: "I want no sugar-lumpshy-plumpshy-sweetness—
pox take all finniken, sickening sugar-lumpshy-plumpshy
sweetness" (80). Most of Warren's readers would have appreciated and identified with this aggressive masculine voice,
neither rotten nor sugary, a voice that in contrast to George
Washington Harris's is full of moral optimism. As if to confirm the values of these normative characters, Fishback's
schemes—like the vicious twists of war they represent—are
hardly ever successful. Mrs. Lane, who believes she has been
widowed, awakens from a dream of her husband to find him
returned to her in the flesh; her horse, which Fishback had
stolen, like Charon escorts her husband home from the land
of the dead. Capt. John Smith ultimately learns of Fishback's
perfidy and renounces him. Fishback cannot even steal his

friend Slaughter's purse: Slaughter anticipates his plan, makes him overconfident by apparently trusting him, and then catches him, literally, in a steel trap in flagrante delicto. Finally, Fishback contracts smallpox by his own attempt at manipulation, endures prison for his crimes, and, after first hearing that it was only his own suspicion that defeated his plans to marry the wealthy Miss Callie, dies.

This is poetic justice with a vengeance. The narrator's direct entreaties to his "most excellent reader," the reordering of the widow's world by the return of her husband, and the convenient end of the exposed Fishback suggest that Warren may be masquerading as a rough frontier humorist while he is in fact pledged to the sentimental values of writers like Mary Noailles Murfree, Thomas Nelson Page, and Joel Chandler Harris. In Warren's *Straggler*, as in mid-nineteenth-century America, two sets of values coexist. Warren attempts a golden mean, humorously exaggerating the "high" culture of J. Rufus Bates, "Captain" Slaughter, and the pretensions of Major Graves, while simultaneously condemning and satirizing the "low" culture of Billy Fishback.

Mrs. Lane, the unassuming widow, functions even more than the occasionally effeminate narrator or the too-trusting Captain Smith as the work's normative center, a woman who though possessing the conventional sentimental tendencies of her sex nevertheless has the strength to continue and the heart to help others, no matter how mean they are or how mean her circumstances. The narrator describes at length Fishback's first meeting with her, "a woman whose husband had been shot on picket a few weeks before":

> The ruin and dilapidation every where apparent, plainly demonstrated the fact that she, a frail and delicate creature, and one whose manner indicated she had been in better circumstances, was compelled, with her own attenuated hands, to perform all the labor done on the premises. To her he applied for rest, rations and lodging for the night. This application she at first refused, by stating that she had already been taxed beyond her ability in feeding soldiers. But he appealed so piteously that her firmness yielded and her sympathies, (there's no plumb-line can fathom the depth of woman's sympathies,) raised the latch and opened the door to our weary and shelterless hero. She told him that while any part remained of

the little that was left to her, she could not send away shivering and hungry, those who were engaged in the service to
which her husband had sacrificed his life. (11)

Mrs. Lane's honesty, accentuated by her initial refusal to take
in one more straggler, seems about to transform a sentimental
episode into a realistic drama; yet, as the parentheses confirm,
Warren is unwilling to close the door on effusions of sentiment. In fact, within two paragraphs Mrs. Lane is sobbing and
groaning over the loss of her husband and her family's inevitable doom. The reader, who at this point believes her husband
to be dead (as he imagines Dick Ellis to have been shot), sympathizes with her and admires her strength, her abilities, and
her confidence. Her tears he forgives, for Mrs. Lane is not a
bloodless martyr from the pages of Sarah Hale's *Godey's
Lady's Book*, but a healthy survivor. What she survives, moreover, is the Civil War, not incarceration by a stern father in her
room. Warren's impulses toward realism, sentiment, and
Southwest humor alternate and intermix.

The Graves family fares none too well at Fishback's hands.
Major Graves and his wife lecture their daughters "on the im-
propriety of encouraging a certain poor suitor, and warmly ad-
vocat[e] the claims of filthy lucre, which they appeared to re-
gard as the only 'one thing needful'" (9). These opportunists
are the traditional targets of Hooper, Baldwin, Harris, and Melville; Warren treats them in the manner of his predecessors,
with Fishback imitating the conventional action of earlier
confidence men. The Graveses' speculative greed, akin to Jedidiah Suggs's, lands them appropriately in the poor house.
Despite the incongruity between Fishback's appearance and
his pose, he convinces them he is a rich Georgia planter by
means of false testimony, forged documents, and Major
Graves's eagerness to believe in his good fortune.

> The Misses Graves were now wholly forgetful of the fact
> that they had ever giggled at the comical chat and gawkish
> manners of our hero. There was nothing gawkish or comical
> about him. *He was such a nice gentleman,—so original and
> unaffected—deported himself in such an artless and indepen-
> dent manner, and might be so appropriately said to draw the
> language in which he conversed, from Nature's pure, un-
> wrought well-spring.* (52)

Their hypocritical change of heart marks the Graves family as fair game for the confidence man's sport. Fishback deflates their pretentions, defeats their aspirations, reduces them to poverty, and brings the reality of the Civil War into their living room: Jack Graves, the major's son, finds himself at the conclusion to the *Straggler* sharing the pest-house with Fishback (96–98). Warren subverts the conventional humor of the confidence man, though his satiric treatment of the Graveses indicates his ability to structure such a world—had he so desired. For the traditional comic order he substitutes lethal disorder, deliberately defeating the reader's expectations. The Civil War, despite the narrative's comic moments, the narrator's syrupy interludes, and Fishback's ultimate failures, is always present; Warren insists that the war maintains its own disorder, over which his own comic, sentimental, and moral vision has only the most tenuous control. This is the "Truth," as he notes, "to which my conscience . . . has rendered me a conquered and loyal subject" (6). The war is a kind of final narrator in *Straggler*, changing the comic to the cruel, the sentimental to the horribly realistic, and redirecting the lives of Warren's characters.

To structure his perceptions of this "Truth" Warren employs devices borrowed from sentimental fiction and frontier humor. The humorists provide the narrative frame, the eccentric vernacular characters, and the detailed action of Fishback's rough adventures. The return of the lover thought dead, the trapping of the fiend in his own trap, and the appropriately agonizing death of the deceiver are traditional sentimental motifs. Warren also uses the picaresque form, supported by humorous stock scenes like the incongruous wedding of Fishback to Miss Callie, and the narrator, digressive and allusive, laces his story with quotations and a full-length parody of Poe's "The Raven" (94–96). Most important is Warren's rendering of the confidence-man convention. Billy Fishback is Simon Suggs impressed into real combat, an Ovid Bolus who cannot escape to Texas, a Cosmopolitan marooned alone, a Sut Lovingood whose soda-powder has been switched to gunpowder.

Fishback's intended victims are not equally deserving of a fleecing. Captain Slaughter, who notes ironically that "I've all pure confidence in your honesty" (73), is a capital comic gull, an enlisted man's Bela Bugg. And in the Graves household, "the character he had established, the confidence he had enjoyed" (91) entitle Fishback to practice his profession. As Captain Smith, Mrs. Lane, and the narrator are victims who seem innocent of greed, pretention, and shiftiness, the reader finds their losses unamusing, while Fishback's methods—artless theft, for the most part—do nothing to engage the imagination. It is as if Warren were retelling Harris's "Snake-Bit Irishman," substituting a live rattlesnake for the harmless intestine. Despite the reprieve these innocents receive, the threat of the rattler remains; Warren's closing vision of the pesthouse containing Fishback, Slaughter, Jack Graves, and the "laborious" poet Delton reveals that the snake's fangs have not been pulled, that these characters have only death before them. The Civil War has soured the confidence man's sense of fun to a vicious practicality and a self-undoing suspicion— like all the other characters, the confidence man falls prey to the war's appetite. As Richard B. Hauck concludes, Fishback is helpless, "caught forever in absurd circles";[34] he seems genuinely lost in labyrinthine lines of advance and retreat, destined to trip over his own feet in his mad rush to escape the war and a disordered new country. Like Jack Graves, who twice appears in time to thwart Fishback's schemes, the war repeatedly materializes when the confidence man least expects it, confusing and immobilizing him.

That Warren consciously varies the literary convention becomes apparent from his allusions to earlier confidence men. J. Rufus Bates, in his biographical sketch of Fishback, refers to Longstreet's "The Fight" and "Georgia Theatrics"; Fishback is a descendant of Ransy Sniffle and the aggressive Georgia youth (30). Fishback's manipulation of appearances is as shifty as Simon Suggs's, as is his studied avoidance of actual combat—except when the odds are forty to one. Warren quotes from chapter 2 of Simon Suggs, noting that an "accident" which befalls Fishback, in the words of Simon Suggs, proves how all was "fixed aforehand" (52). Just before the parody of Poe's "The Raven" (94), the narrator refers to Fishback's friends as his "boon companions," a term like the "fool-killer" Billy cries for (67); both are firmly rooted in the nourishing soil of frontier humor. And Fishback is clearly another proverbial "ugly man."

Warren's fictional response to the Civil War was immediate, and to focus his perceptions he relied on familiar literary forms: the picaresque, the sentimental tale, and the frontier humorist's sketch. The confidence man he creates is a symbol of the "ruin and dilapidation every where" Warren perceives, the new country burned to chthonic ash. The disorder he chronicles is not the vanishing of Hooper's flush times, the dawning of a corrupt "progressive age" heralded by Baldwin, the cruise of a national "ship of fools" Melville satirizes, or the survival of a rough community that Harris celebrates and ultimately despairs of; rather, Warren imaginatively recreates a civilization returned to chaos and embodies this "Truth" in Billy Fishback. It is because Warren wants to believe in a better world that the confidence man must die, an event unique in the history of his American ancestors. Posing as a doctor aboard a crowded train, Fishback diagnoses a soldier's ailment as smallpox so that "Doctor" Fishback may have a seat. The joke, however, is on Fishback, for the soldier gives the "Doctor" not only his rations and his haversack but also his fatal disease.

In modifying the confidence-man convention so radically, Warren created new problems. A humorless shifty man, like Baldwin's Simon Suggs, Jr., requires firm narrative control, a clearly satiric framing rhetoric providing the reader a consistent normative guide. Baldwin's narrator focuses on Simon, demanding that the reader evaluate Simon's actions. Warren's narrator develops Fishback's victims: the Graves family, for example, Warren portrays alternately as hospitable and hypocritical without integrating these characteristics within coherent personalities, a feat Melville accomplishes brilliantly. Warren's loose characterization also confuses the reader's response to Slaughter, who seems both condemnable and commendable; to Mrs. Lane, who seems both pitiful and pitiable; and to Captain Smith, who seems both foolish and good. The narrator himself, like J. Rufus Bates, suffers momentary attacks of effeteness. These abrupt and almost random shifts of allegiance indicate Warren's unsureness of narrative intention and control; to satirize all characters, including the intrusive narrator, unsettles the reader as it frustrates his conventional pattern of response. Unlike Melville, Warren varies his purpose and point of view inconsistently. He may have felt that his new materials required him to modify the conventions he had chosen, or he may have found that the conventions were suddenly beyond his control when used to interpret the Civil War. Warren may also have discovered that his feelings about Billy Fishback and the war were more intense than he had anticipated; the bitterness and cynicism that frequently appear in the narrator's satire seem attributable to attitudes the author has not fully structured in fictional form. Finally, it seems most probable that Warren, a Georgia volunteer attempting to convey his perceptions of the war in 1863–1865, was confused, searching for proper literary vehicles, conventions that would present in recognizable form the anxieties he felt about a country torn apart and no longer "new." His narrative ambivalence, the various languages he employs, and the almost sadistic yet moralistic ending in which he dispatches Billy Fishback suggest the competing and often contradictory pressures under which *Straggler* was written, and are themselves evidence of Warren's doubts and fears. These are, of course, moot points; Billy Fishback, confidence man, embodies—however precariously—the adaptation of the comic convention to express the serious concerns of Civil War. Like the nation itself, the confidence man would need time to recover.

5 THE WAR, MARK TWAIN, AND THE FLUSH-TIMES CONFIDENCE MAN

Art is, after all, the business of our country, and war but a passing incident.

—*North American Review* (July 1862)

Deafness,
Impaired Sight,
Noises in the Head,
and
All Diseases
of
the Eye
and
Ear,
Cured
By D. Von Eisenberg, Oculist and Aurist,
with his newly-invented
Eastachion Explorer,
Atherialearinhalator,
and
Von Eisenberg's Eye Fumigator!

—Advertisement, the New York
Evening Post (19 May 1862)

William Cullen Bryant, praising the Homestead Act of 1862 in the *New York Evening Post*, predicted that "speculators in public lands have now lost their vocation, and [the] right of the people to the free employment of their own property [has been] established. It is one of those victories of peace which are said to be as important as those of war."[1] Moralistic and optimistic, Bryant's language is charged with unintentional irony; the future he envisions—free of conflict and confidence men—is a dream twisted into nightmare by the realities of the Civil War and by the fantastic scandals of the Gilded Age. Less than ten years later, Walt Whitman urges his countrymen to "look our times and lands searchingly in the face, like a physician diagnosing some deep disease."

147

> Never was there, perhaps, more hollowness at heart than at present, and here in the United States. Genuine belief seems to have left us. . . . From deceit in the spirit, the mother of all false deeds, the offspring is already incalculable. . . . The depravity of the business classes of our country is not less than has been supposed, but infinitely greater. . . . The magician's serpent in the fable ate up all the other serpents; and money-making is our magician's serpent, remaining today sole master of the field. The best class we show, is but a mob of fashionably dress'd speculators and vulgarians.[2]

Whitman sheds light on Bryant's hasty reduction of complex social issues to easily legislated morality; speaking the hopes of many in 1862, Bryant reveals a desire to avoid confrontation characteristic of the period's bestselling fiction: the Beadle dime novels and Mary Mapes Dodge's *Hans Brinker and the Silver Skates*, for example, offered escape from reality, posing in their conventional sentimental plots only threats certain to be resolved. The public demanded consolation, confirmation, and—most of all—certainty. Politicians, editors, novelists, and comedians were to provide what the Civil War denied.

Analyzing popular American fiction, Henry Nash Smith concludes, "The passions aroused by the war acted as a forced draft on the development of the confidence and optimism that were so conspicuous in the popular culture of the 1850s. The result was an accelerated coarsening of attitudes."[3] To reassure the population, popular writers polarized good and evil, masking their broadly shared anxieties behind harmless sentimental stereotypes. George W. Bagby, author in the 1850s of the satiric "Mozis Addums" letters, turned to productions like "The Empty Sleeve" during the war.

> Tom, old fellow, I grieve to see
>   That sleeve hanging loose at your side;
> The arm you lost was worth to me
>   Every Yankee that ever died.
> But you don't mind it at all,
>   You swear you've a beautiful stump,
> And laugh at the damnable ball;
>   Tom, I knew you were always a trump![4]

In the remaining stanzas Tom marries his true love and lives a long and uplifting life; fear, pain, and anguish disappear before an only slightly qualified pastoral celebration of continuity in Tom's daughter's marriage. The realities that cannot be ignored are domesticated by simply expressed, emotion-charged "fancies."

The Civil War, which, as Edwin Fussell writes, "destroyed the final vestiges of the American frontier,"[5] destroyed as well the American appetite for fictional characters who represented its ambiguities. The flush times and the confidence man, symbols of anarchic power embodying both humorous and threatening duplicity, were sacrificed on the altar of consolation. At the opposite extreme from Warren's *Army Straggler*, S. Emma E. Edmonds's *Female Spy of the Union Army* (1864) demonstrates how the immoral acts of the confidence man are transformed into heroics. Edmonds's fictionalized narrative of her own exploits celebrates deception, treachery, even murder—when committed for the preservation of the Union. Edmonds condemns as a "wretch" a persistently loyal Virginia woman with whom she exchanges first confidence tricks and then bullets.[6] Edmonds ultimately cures "Her Ladyship" of rebelliousness by the severe application of pistol, harness, and Bible. At no point in *The Female Spy* does the heroine question her own tactics; patriotism, and the need to confirm the righteousness of her cause, license her use of the confidence man's methods.

The confidence man thus becomes either a heroic or a villainous deceiver, his actions judged solely by simplified political and ethical criteria. Ambiguous figures suffer reduction to stereotypes, for in literature, as in life, circumscribed symbols guarantee the comfort that reality denies. The desire for unqualified heroes—one element of the "coarsening of attitudes" Smith notes—manifests itself in the sainthood of Lincoln and the two presidential elections of Grant. Their personal foibles, like those of Jefferson Davis and Robert E. Lee in the South, are forgotten, for in idolizing these leaders the public confirms the values for which so many had fought and died, and by extension images themselves, the rank and file, as local versions of their national heroes. Thomas Wentworth Higginson's *Harvard Memorial Biographies* (1866) and John Esten Cooke's *Wearing of the Gray* (1867) canonize Federal and Confederate martyrs for their "solid conviction and . . . absolute law of conscience";[7] the motivation for these records appears to be at once to cherish the fallen and to comfort the survivors with assurances that a better future has in fact been unambiguously secured.

The confidence man all but disappears from American fiction as the need to idealize intensifies; the strength of this imperative becomes clear by comparing Henry Ward Beecher's *Norwood; or, Village Life in New England,* published serially in 1867 in the *New York Ledger* and in book form in 1868, and John William De Forest's *Miss Ravenel's Conversion from Seccession to Loyalty,* which *Harper's* declined to serialize but printed in a limited edition in 1867. Both chart the course of love redirected by the Civil War, but the immediate success of Beecher's work dwarfs De Forest's. Beecher's manipulation of cardboard stereotypes appeals to a largely female audience that rejects as threatening De Forest's less sentimental portrayal. Readers approved in Beecher's novel the opportunities for moral refreshment and tearful cleansing, which they had also found in Jane G. Austin's *Dora Darling; or, the Daughter of the Regiment* (1865) and Elizabeth Stuart Phelps's popular *The Gates Ajar* (1868). Beecher celebrates a pastoral vision as righteous as it is artificial, a ritual presided over by the personification of October, "a victor, content with his victories, and every where shedding abroad the tokens of his royal complacency."[8] *Norwood* dismisses the vagaries of reality *Miss Ravenel* takes pains to point out, and embraces the future with a confidence foreign to De Forest's novelistic vision. The success of *Norwood* indicates the degree to which Beecher correctly read the desire of the book-buying public to live out their fantasies of an unambiguous moral war, to worship heroes whose feet barely touched the clay, to dismiss the ambivalent figure of the confidence man, and to cherish the unrealized dream of a secure present.[9]

Military men are not the only characters to shoulder aside the confidence man. Jay Cooke, the "financier of the Civil War,"[10] shared in the public adulation awarded to Lincoln and Grant. His rise from humble beginnings parallels the rise of those presidents and, like his wartime activities, confirms one of the essential tenets of American democracy—a lowly clerk may achieve material success and national influence. V. L. Parrington describes the impact of Cooke's career on the popular imagination.

> The greatest salesman that the rising middle class had yet pro-
> duced, a financier who understood the psychology of mass ap-
> peal, a propagandist of truly heroic proportions, he was reck-
> oned no other than a magician by all the lesser money-
> grabbers of the Gilded Age. From nothing he built up a vast
> fortune. Scrupulous in all religious duties, a kind husband, a
> generous friend, benevolent in all worthy charities, simple and
> democratic in his tastes, ardently patriotic, uncreative and un-
> intellectual, he exemplified all the substantial middle-class
> virtues.[11]

As a symbol of middle-class morality and its rewards, Cooke
could not be given enough praise by the American people;
their legislators, as well, awarded Cooke's Northern Pacific
Railway over 47 million acres of public land. Few anticipated
that the brilliant, patriotic, and ever-stable Cooke would be
termed a betrayer and confidence man; the exposure of his
speculations dealt the popular imagination a blow from which
it recovered by embracing transparently heroic fiction.

Although Jay Cooke & Company succumbed to the Crédit
Mobilier scandal and the ensuing panic of 1873, the dream of
repeating Cooke's rise remained imprinted on the American
mind in the novels of Horatio Alger. The moral formula that
perseverance and honesty lead inevitably to wealth forms the
touchstone of the *Ragged Dick* books, an oversimplification
that struck a responsive and reassuring chord in 1867. Drawing upon the sentimental and sensation novel traditions, Alger
creates a youthful, lower-class, morally upright hero; Ragged
Dick acts out the common fantasy of the upwardly mobile,
who triumph imaginatively with him over the perils—moral,
social, and financial—of city life. Confidence men prowl this
world, but they bear little resemblance to the humorous Simon Suggs. They use the methods of Poe's urban diddlers
(1843), yet they do not possess even the redeeming virtue of
the complex comedy of Poe's rascals; they are, quite simply,
sentimental villains, less engaging even than George Lippard's
gothic *Monks of Monk Hall* (1844). As Ragged Dick outwits
them—from Chatham Street swindlers to pocketbook counterfeiters—he validates the optimistic morality of the 1860s:
Good and Evil—despite the historical exemplum of Jay
Cooke—are clearly defined categories of experience, and, even
in Alger's comparatively seamy New York, Good will always
vanquish Evil. It is of no consequence that Ragged Dick uses

shifty tricks; like Edmonds's female spy, he labors in a just cause against wrongdoers and is thereby absolved of guilt. In addition, like Edmonds's rebel spies, Alger's confidence men are neither comic nor sympathetic: they are wretches. As their defeat is preordained by Alger's adherence to the sentimental values of his audience, the threat these confidence men pose is carefully controlled to heighten the pleasure of Ragged Dick's ultimate victory.

The popularity of the Alger books—extending well beyond his death in 1899—sheds more light on the disappearance of the flush-times confidence man; when his ambiguity appears in a new guise, as in Richard B. Kimball's *Undercurrents of Wall Street. A Romance of Business* (1862), it produces only the smallest ripple. Kimball fails to utilize the stereotypes and moral formulas of Alger's fiction, instead picturing upright businessmen as confidence men, questioning the righteousness of the booster morality underlying American commerce in terms anticipating Whitman's. Though Kimball's hero struggles toward enlightenment and the salvation of honesty toward its close, *Undercurrents* could not compete with the complete fulfillment of *Ragged Dick*; Kimball stirred his readers, as the *North American Review* noted,[12] to analyze the difference between "being" and "appearing" and to doubt the ethics of boosterism, while Alger applauded the fantasies of success and wealth his audience half-believed, never letting them for an instant doubt the imminent fulfillment of their dreams.

The optimism and confidence at the heart of American popular culture conspired to affect as well the humor of the 1860s. A comic tradition took shape complementing the sentimental tradition whose motives it reflected: to comfort, to offer escape, and to reaffirm the values of the middle class. The "coarsening of attitudes" Smith puts forth as an explanation for postwar sentimental fiction suggests as well a broad theory to explain the period's domestication of earlier humor: humor that threatened, that pictured unresolved anxieties—the humor of the shifty confidence man, for example—was unacceptable. The aim of the humorist should not be to illustrate a peculiar reality, as it had been in Longstreet's *Georgia Scenes* (1835), but to mask and nullify the often violent peculiarities of reality in a nonthreatening form; reality had perhaps come to seem too clearly a mirror-image of flush-times chaos. The ambiguities, hypocrisies, and anxieties of reality, exploited especially by antebellum Southwest humorists, were ignored or tamed by a new generation of comedic writers. The Civil War, which intensified the sentimental tradition, changed the meaning of American humor, marking as one of its first casualties the *New York Spirit of the Times* (1831–1861). Following the same impulse as the sentimentalists, 1860s humorists diluted the earlier tradition; in all but a few cases, the snaps of Simon Suggs and his confederates seemed played out by 1861.

W. Stanley Hoole concludes that the Civil War disrupted the popular genre of Southwest humor,

> bending and twisting the chain of continuity in a thousand ways and ultimately rendering the "old" writers all but voiceless against the new and noisy "platform" wit of the years that followed. . . . Out of the West and out of the War came a new laughter, a new product, a new era of national literary humor, sponsored mostly by men who were yet unborn when *Simon Suggs* had sprung full-grown onto the American bookstalls.[13]

The Phunny Phellows turn from the regional models and concerns of their predecessors to address a national audience—largely the same one that rejected De Forest and Kimball—that desired entertainment without ambiguity or anxiety, and confidence rather than confidence men.

Representative of these popular literary comedians, Charles Farrar Browne ("Artemus Ward") takes aim at uncontroversial public butts that were fair game on either side of the Mason-Dixon line: sexless Shakers, polygamous Mormons, pretentious lecturers, and "Speeretooul Sircles." Though he borrows from the Southwest humorists the techniques of comic misspellings, burlesque, exaggeration, and tall talk, Ward avoids their extended descriptions of frontier low life, their unsettling portrayal of physical violence, and their characterization of the irresponsible confidence man. The eccentric persona—Artemus Ward—likewise displays little of his literary ancestors' relish for partisan political satire: "I hav no politics. Nary a one. . . . I'm in a far more respectful bisniss nor what pollertics is."[14] In 1862, the year Bryant proclaimed the death of speculation and Kimball published *Undercurrents of Wall Street*, Artemus Ward "interviews" Lincoln and demonstrates his allegiance to Bryant's rhetoric of optimism; Ward saves the president from a horde of office seekers, then advises him to give "the whole country a good, sound administration" (185). The traditional jibe at the spoils system, followed by a correctly spelled, moderate appeal for good government, seems naive in light of the recent battles of Bull Run, but the sentiments are certainly sincere. Avoiding historical events is Ward's plan, and to this end he closes his interview with an again-misspelled solicitation: Lincoln should fill his Cabinet with showmen.

> Showmen is devoid of politics. They hain't got any principles. They know how to cater for the public. They know what the public wants, North & South. Showmen, sir, is honest men. . . . A. Linkin, use the talents which Nature has put into you judishusly and firmly, and all will be well! (185–86)

Artemus Ward intends to create "Fun and Sunshine"; humor should provide diversion from the anxieties of national politics—"It is far better to stay in the Sunshine while we may, inasmuch as the Shadow must of its own accord come only too soon."[15] These words could just as properly introduce the sentimental "leaves" of the still-popular Fanny Fern, or serve as a footnote to Beecher's *Norwood*. When the Shadow can no longer be ignored, however, Beecher transforms the war into an ennobling drama—one that does not threaten since it is subservient to the dictates of the sentimental pattern—while Ward transforms it into a comic prop for his persona. An 1864 lecture is instructive.

> I ought, perhaps, to say something about the war. Perhaps I might as well give you the opinion of a gentleman who resides in the rural districts, and who possesses, in the opinion of many, a massive mind. He has watched the progress and conduct of the war closely, and he said, after having carefully read the editorial articles in all the daily papers about it, and consulted minutely and particularly from day to day, the telegraphic dispatches in regard to it, and subscribed more particularly for the New York Herald and its military maps, and in those lucid maps studying the various bases of operations and movements of our armies in the field, and after organizing a War Club in the little neighborhood where he lived, and ex-

> changing opinions with several of his neighbors in regard to
> the war, and attending the various local meetings that were
> held, and keeping one eye intently fastened on Washington,
> and the other intently fastened on the various State Conven-
> tions held in the different States, as well as the action of dif-
> ferent State Legislatures, and reading carefully the papers pub-
> lished at the capitals of the States, and subscribing for the
> illustrated papers of New York city, and gazing fixedly on the
> various bloody battle scenes—after doing all this he said—
> "he'd be d——d if he knew what he did think about it."[16]

The technique of this passage is to say nothing about the war.
Instead, the audience hears Charles Farrar Browne as Artemus
Ward tell the story of a massive-minded rural's inability to
make any sense at all out of various newspaper accounts of
the Civil War. The war itself is placed at six removes as Ward
directs attention to the befuddled yet earnest rural gentleman's associative, repetitive, eelish rhetoric. No historical details—the names of battles, for instance—are ever mentioned;
rather, Ward substitutes for that threatening reality the harmless disorder of comic confusion. The inability of the bewildered character "to say something about the war" dramatizes
a similar potential confusion in each listener's mind, yet the
persona functions as a comic butt—a fool—for the safe release
of this anxiety in laughter. By insisting on manner rather than
matter, Ward leads the audience to the remote, self-enclosed
comic universe of the lecture that harmlessly collapses inward
upon itself.

   David Ross Locke amused Lincoln and Grant with Petroleum V. Nasby, whose escapes from Federal and Confederate
conscription satirized hypocrites, cowards, and scalawags of
all persuasions. Nasby's nonpartisan evasions of the draft—in
Ohio and Kentucky, by way of Canada and New York—focus
entirely on his absurd theatrical protests while ignoring their
cause.

> Upon a rigid eggsaminashun uf my fizzleckle man, I find it
> wood be wus nor madnis for me to undertake a campane, to-
> wit:—
>   1. I'm bald-headid, and hev bin obliged to wear a wig these
> 22 years.
>   2. I hev dandruff in wat scanty hair still hangs around my
> venerable temples.
>   3. I hev a kronic katarr.

4. I hev lost, sence Stanton's order to draft, the use uf wun
eye entirely, and hev kronic inflammashen in the other.

5. My teeth is all unsound, my palit aint eggsactly rite, and
I hev had bronkeetis 31 yeres last Joon. At present I hev a koff,
the paroxisms uv wich is friteful to behold.[17]

The war appears a backdrop for this rhetorical magician and
escape artist, who first blinks the war and then disappears
himself. Nasby presents himself as a man unwilling to be
suckered into the losing game of conscription, one who substitutes for actual combat the maneuvers of the southwestern
confidence man: disguise, deception, fast talk, and fast feet.
But the Suggsian new country has soured, and Nasby is not
Captain Simon Suggs; as his own narrator, Nasby cannot make
the two-pronged appeal of *Simon Suggs*: Simon creates humor
as he triumphs over even more dishonest hypocrites than himself, and Hooper-as-narrator asserts control in his cultivated
and precise language. Locke narrows Hooper's comic vision to
ensure that each member of his audience, northerner and
southerner, will feel superior to Nasby; Nasby is a watered-
down version of the Suggsian confidence man, one who evokes
only contemptuous laughter. The restricted point of view offers the audience an indirect release of its hostility—toward
the renegade Nasby, who enacts a fantasy of escape, and toward the inescapable reality of historical events. Nasby's
battles with conscription invoke the threat of Civil War, but
offering his escapes as paradigms of experience suggests that
the threat can be reduced, reality avoided, and the demonic
subdued; Nasby also offers amusement to those who go to war,
for they can feel superior to the groveling "low" character who
has no moral fiber, no patriotism, and no manhood. In the
form of the earlier confidence man Nasby provides innocuous
sentimental assurance.

Charles Henry Smith developed the epistolary "Bill Arp" to
create "a side show of the Southern side of the War."[18] As
Nasby turns the war into a game of hide-and-seek, so Bill Arp
transforms the bloody battle of Rome (3 May 1863) into a game
of cards.

> Gen. Forrest had been fighting. . . . But the General was not in
> luck, and had a poor hand, and staked his last dollar. The Yan-
> kess had a *Strait*, which would have taken Forrest and raked
> down the pile, but he looked 'em right in the eye and said "*he*

would see 'em and 4,000 *better."* The Raid looked at him and
he looked at the Raid, and *never blinked.* The Raid trembled
all over in his boots, and gave it up. *The General bluffed 'em,*
and ever since that game was played the little town close by
has been called *"Cedar Bluff."* It was *flush* times in Alabama,
that day, sure. (39, Smith's italics)

By this act of legerdemain—soldiers become dollars in a game
of poker—Arp deflects the attention of his audience; he uses
the familiar language of the flush-times confidence man to
spotlight the comic persona and his rhetorical creation—an
alternative to reality, a sideshow. If in Nasby what remains of
the southwestern confidence-man tradition is his pattern of
rascally escape, in Arp we see only the confidence man's language; this language, however, enacts the shift from threat to
comedy, and, because all that remains of the confidence man
is his language—not his ambiguity—the transformation is
successful, and the horror of battle is nullified.

The novels of Edmonds, Beecher, and Alger contained the
Civil War in a conventional pattern of popular fiction, the
sentimental romance. Arp controls the war by translating its
threats into conventional ludic images reported by an eccentric persona; he reduces reality, offers escape, and thereby pays
tribute to the optimism of the sentimentalists. "The minds of
the people," he wrote in 1866, "needed relaxation from the
momentous and absorbing interests of the war" (5). His comic
misspellings—which he wished "reconstructed"—cue the
reader to the unchallenging nature of his fiction; though critical of President Lincoln, carpetbaggers, and scavenging
troops, Arp's election to the Georgia Senate (150–56) seems to
guarantee a happy ending to his trials, and to the trials of the
South. His wit, though satiric, owes fealty to the sentimental
tradition of moderation and reassurance.

Henry Wheeler Shaw ("Josh Billings") defined humorists
like Arp, Nasby, and Ward in a phrase: "Everybody's Friend."[19]
In Shaw's Josh Billings the influence of prewar southwestern
humor is vestigial, and the displacement characteristic of the
Phunny Phellows seems to reach its final variation. Josh Billings consoles his audience with genial philosophy and general
social satire. As "Billings Lexicon" illustrates, he reduces
complex issues to humorous homilies: "Politicks—The apol-
ogy ov plunder. . . . Bliss—Happiness bileing over and running

down both sides ov the pot. . . . Quack—A doktor whoze science lays in his bill" (462). Corruption, hunger, and fraud are acknowledged only to be dismissed, and the confidence man survives as a blue-plate special: "Hash—A boarding-hous confidence game" (462). And "Anxiety" Billings defines as "Milking a kicking heifer with one hand, and holding her by the tail with the other" (464). The realities of war and reconstruction seem aberrations deliberately forgotten in the haste to improve life's common fare. Alger's *Ragged Dick* and Billings's *Everybody's Friend* are companion pieces (to say nothing of Billings's annual *Farmer's Allminax*), both confident of the average man's improving status, both appealing to an audience hungry for social approval and for emotional security.

Mark Twain

Reflecting on these literary comedians in his *Autobiography* (1906), Samuel Langhorne Clemens ("Mark Twain") criticized their amiability and lack of content, and seems to have had in mind the authors of all species of false optimism.

> Why have they perished? Because they were merely humorists. Humorists of the "mere" sort cannot survive. Humor is only a fragrance, a decoration. Often it is merely an odd trick of speech and of spelling, as in the case of Ward and Billings and Nasby and the "Disbanded Volunteer," and presently the fashion passes and the fame along with it. . . . Humor must not professedly teach and it must not professedly preach, but it must do both if it would live forever. By forever, I mean thirty years. With all its preaching it is not likely to outlive so long as term as that. The very things it preaches about and which are novelties when it preaches about them can cease to be novelties and become commonplaces in thirty years.[20]

Twain is clearly promoting himself at his old cronies' expense, for he himself worked the lecture platform with great facility, took potshots at targets long peppered by Phunny Phellows, and made free use of the comedians' techniques of the comic persona, deadpan delivery, and burlesque. This passage from the *Autobiography* is at once valid criticism, humorous mock-criticism, and the self-questioning musings of Mark Twain. The same strategy informs *The Innocents Abroad* (1869), a travel book that burlesques the banalities of travel books; James M. Cox writes that as the unifying narrative voice is capable of both nostalgia and mock-nostalgia, cynicism and mock-cynicism, "it is often difficult to tell whether Twain is trapped in clichés or simply exploiting them."[21] In *Roughing It* (1872), the curious practices of Mormons, the joys of silver mining, and the evil of desperados come in for satire that smacks of Artemus Ward and his tribe, yet stock figures repeatedly become complex. The outlaw Slade's arraignment for drunkenness recalls George W. Harris's "Contempt of Court— Almost" (in *Sut Lovingood's Yarns*, which Twain had reviewed in 1867), yet Slade's tears, cries, prayers—and hanging—present a problem of interpretation.

> The true desperado is gifted with splendid courage, and yet he will take the most infamous advantage of his enemy; armed and free, he will stand up before a host and fight until he is shot all to pieces, and yet when he is under the gallows and helpless he will cry and plead like a child. . . . I think it is a conundrum worth investigating.[22]

Unlike Artemus Ward's discussion of the Civil War, which is sealed off to be forgotten like an exhausted mine, Twain's investigation of Slade exposes two distinct veins that beg for excavation. Instead of the quick comic capper, however, Twain leaves these two images unresolved in the reader's mind; he is unwilling to solve the conundrum of the desperado. As reality is more complex than a cliché, it cannot be made to vanish when its complexity becomes troubling.

Twain's method is often to bring the conventions of the literary comedians and popular sentimentalists into contact with the earlier tradition of southwestern humor. In chapter 24 of *Roughing It*, he updates Augustus B. Longstreet's "The Horse-Swap" (1835), using the old sketch to explore the new flush times. Longstreet's narrator reports on a duel between frontier confidence men. From his point of view, the result is humorous, for the boasting Yellow Blossom swaps for a horse that is both blind and deaf. The point of view in chapter 24 is not that of Longstreet's simple narrative frame: Twain's narrator is the protagonist, who becomes himself the object of derision because his pretensions to western savvy result in his buying the unrideable genuine Mexican plug. The comic butt, he seems suddenly more like Harris's bamboozled Sut Lovingood than Longstreet's cultured frame-narrator; however, he

retains the rhetorical polish of his ancestor and clearly represents the reader. As the swelling of the narrator is deflated by
the shifty westerner (who has only to encourage the narrator's
illusions to make him a fool), the reader must question his
own preconceptions about the West. In Longstreet's "Horse-
Swap," the superiority of the narrator reaffirms the values and
superiority of the reader over those of the "low" comic characters; in *Roughing It*, Twain suggests that in some cases both
narrator and reader have something to learn. Two ways of
seeing—call them eastern and western—have competed in a
game of bluff, and the eastern greenhorn has lost. Here, as in
the examination of the desperado, what unifies these points
of view is the narrative voice. Having been tricked by the wily
Pete Ketch, the Yellow Blossom has nothing to say; in *Roughing It*, the narrator who recreates the incident is Mark Twain,
who as both protagonist and victim, character and narrator,
has everything to say. Twain is himself proof that the tender-
foot's false assumptions can be corrected—need to be corrected—by the "keen-eyed person" (172). East and West, culture and savvy, and past and present are fused in the voice of
Mark Twain. Twain makes fun of his own "Miss Nancy" illusions, illustrating in his sad attempt to ride the plug that he
did not at the time of its purchase have the skills of the frontier. As he retells the story, however, it is clear that he has
managed to survive by claiming the best from both worlds.

> Now whoever has had the luck to ride a real Mexican plug
> will recognize the animal depicted in this chapter, and hardly
> consider him exaggerated—but the uninitiated will feel justi-
> fied in regarding his portrait as a fancy sketch, perhaps. (177)

These two visions of the genuine Mexican plug distinguish
two kinds of knowledge, and Twain is careful to present both
in qualifying language ("hardly . . . perhaps"); for though the
youthful narrator symbolizes greenness, the plug symbolizes
the frontier's chaotic energy. Like Slade's hanging, it represents the impulse toward violence that Twain as narrator must
first understand and then tame. To accomplish this dual purpose, he turns to the humor of the Old Southwest, modifying
the narrative frame, the action of the horse swap, and the characters who perform the contest.

*   *   *

In *The Gilded Age* (1873), Mark Twain's first novel, traditional devices are again highly visible. The uncertainty that led him to collaborate with Charles Dudley Warner on this full-scale fiction suggests a reason for reliance on conventional models. From the popular novels of sensation and sentiment Twain borrows the plot complications of the adopted orphans and the betrayed maiden, while from Southwest humorists' sketches he draws the credulous Uncle Dan'l and the Suggsian Colonel Sellers. As in *Roughing It*, however, Twain contrasts these modes of perception to achieve a complexity of vision not apparent in the sentimental works of Beecher or the humorous productions of Artemus Ward. Uncle Dan'l's misapprehension of the steamboat as the Lord invokes a stereotype found, for example, in Henry Clay Lewis's "Day of Judgment" (1850). In Lewis's tale, an old Negro at a camp meeting is startled into thoughts of heaven by a band of pranksters who drape themselves in white sheets, set a mule afire, and descend on the meeting.

> White folks riz! De Laud be marsyful! De end of de warld an' de day of judgmen' hab pass and here cums hell rite up de lane! Whoop! I love my Jesus! Master, cum![23]

Twain avoids the contrived situation of the conventional camp meeting terrorized by whites, yet generates humor from Uncle Dan'l's ignorance of technology, his needless terror, and his futile though warmhearted attempt to save the white children.

> Oh, Lord, spah de little chil'en, don't tar de little chil'en away f'm dey frens, jes' let 'em off jes' dis once, and take it out'n de ole niggah. HEAH I IS, LORD, HEAH I IS! De ole niggah's ready, Lord, de old—[24]

The humor in Twain's passage is nostalgic, evoking in Uncle Dan'l's selflessness a persistent myth of the halcyon antebellum South in which slaves desired only to serve their masters; this vein proved pure gold to writers like Thomas Nelson Page and Joel Chandler Harris. Twain plays the scene for its humor, following it with a description of the race between the steamboats *Boreas* and *Amaranth*. Rendered almost entirely in dialogue, the familiar action of the race is cut short by the explosion of the *Amaranth*.

And then there was a booming roar, a thundering crash, and the riddled Amaranth dropped loose from her hold and drifted helplessly away . . . !

As soon as possible the Boreas dropped down to the floating wreck and took off the dead, the wounded, and the unhurt—at least all that could be got at, for the whole forward half of the boat was a shapeless ruin, with the great chimneys lying crossed on top of it, and underneath were a dozen victims imprisoned alive and wailing for help. While men with axes worked with might and main to free these poor fellows, the Boreas's boats went about, picking up stragglers from the river. (38)

The nostalgic image of the past explodes like the *Amaranth* as it touches this realistic reportage: the reader feels the horror of the wreck deeply because of Twain's juxtaposition of narrative modes. After adjusting his expectations, however, the reader is assaulted by a new appeal—to his emotions.

The wreck took fire. . . . It scorched the clothes, it singed the hair of the axemen—it drove them back, foot by foot—inch by inch—they wavered, struck a final blow in the teeth of the enemy, and surrendered. And as they fell back they heard prisoned voices saying:

"Don't leave us! Don't desert us! Don't, don't do it!"

And one poor fellow said:

"I am Henry Worley, striker of the Amaranth! My mother lives in St. Louis. Tell her a lie for a poor devil's sake, please. Say I was killed in an instant and never knew what hurt me—though God knows I've neither scratch nor bruise this moment! It's hard to burn up in a coop like this with the whole wide world so near. Good-bye boys—we've all got to come to it at last, anyway!" (38–39)

In quick succession, a "little wee French midshipman of fourteen" (39) refuses medical aid and the head engineer curses his brother, who had refused to reduce steam, and—calling him his murderer—"tore a ring from his finger, stripping flesh and skin with it, threw it down and fell dead" (40). Twain manipulates the reader with these detailed sensational descriptions; the humorous pastoral scene and the exciting realism of the race intensify the tragedy of the boy's heroics and the engineer's hatred. The chapter concludes with an emotionless summary.

A jury of inquest was impaneled, and after due deliberation and inquiry they returned the inevitable American verdict which has been so familiar to our ears all the days of our lives—"NOBODY TO BLAME." (40)

These alternating modes wrench conflicting responses from the reader: laughter, excitement, tears, and frustration. Twain's Dickensian fillip—"NOBODY TO BLAME"—heightens the episode's pathos and leaves the question of responsibility unresolved. If we trust the "Author's Preface to the London Edition," however, the blame is easily assigned: "In America nearly every man has his dream, his pet scheme, whereby he is to advance himself socially or pecuniarily. It is this all-pervading speculativeness that we have tried to illustrate in 'The Gilded Age'" (473). American boosterism leads steamboatmen to race, for it flourishes at every level of American society—the engineer who refuses to be beaten by the *Boreas* is motivated by the same impulse as Jay Cooke, Ragged Dick, and Simon Suggs. The new-country spirit has resurfaced.

As Twain contrasts the harmless pastoral of Uncle Dan'l with the horrible reality of the *Amaranth*'s explosion, so too does he contrast the innocuous Colonel Sellers with the threatening Senator Dilworthy. Unlike the Phunny Phellows, Twain returns to the flush times of the Old Southwest for inspiration, hoping to discover the reasons for Americans' "all-pervading speculativeness" and for the continuing spirit of frontier optimism. Col. Beriah Sellers combines these attitudes in the conventional literary figure—absent from the 1860s—of the comic confidence man. He enters *The Gilded Age* trumpeting the flush times of the 1840s and 1850s in a letter delivered to "Squire" Hawkins of Obedstown, East Tennessee.

> Come right along to Missouri! Don't wait and worry about a good price but sell out for whatever you can get, and come along, or you might be too late. Throw away your traps, if necessary, and come empty-handed. You'll never regret it. It's the grandest country—the loveliest land—the purest atmosphere—I can't describe it; no pen can do it justice. And it's filling up, every day—people coming from everywhere. I've got the biggest scheme on earth—and I'll take you in; I'll take in every friend I've got that's ever stood by me, for there's enough for all, and to spare. Mum's the word—don't whisper—keep yourself to yourself. You'll see! Come!—rush!—hurry!—don't wait for anything! (21)

Sellers's optimism, energy, confidence, and language echo those of Hooper's Capt. Simon Suggs. Colonel Sellers's ambiguous promise—"I'll take you in; I'll take in every friend I've got"—cues the reader to the presence of the confidence man. Nancy Hawkins, aware of the colonel's resemblance to the captain, nevertheless notes one important difference in their characters; hearing of Colonel Sellers's letter, she reflects.

> I was afraid of it—was afraid of it. Trying to make our fortune in Virginia, Beriah Sellers nearly ruined us—and we had to settle in Kentucky and start over again. Trying to make our fortune in Kentucky he crippled us again and we had to move here. Trying to make our fortune here, he brought us clear down to the ground, nearly. He's an honest soul, and means the very best in the world, but I'm afraid, I'm afraid he's too flighty. He has splendid ideas, and he'll divide his chances with his friends with a free hand, a good generous soul, but something does always seem to always interfere and spoil everything. I never did think he was right well balanced. But I don't blame my husband, for I do think that when that man gets his head full of a new notion, he can out-talk a machine. He'll make anybody believe in that notion that'll listen to him ten minutes—why I do believe he would make a deaf and dumb man believe in it and get beside himself, if you only set him where he could see his eyes talk and watch his hands explain. (19–20)

Although Sellers's schemes to sell slaves, to invent a perpetual motion machine, to process coal oil, and to market "Beriah Sellers Infalliable Imperial Oriental Optic Liniment and Salvation for Sore Eyes" are unsuccessful, Nancy Hawkins recognizes two truths: first, "that fortunes are made nobody knows exactly how, in a new country" (113); and second, that despite his appearance, Colonel Sellers is "an honest soul" (19). Twain reconstructs the Southwest humorists' confidence man and the new country—yet with a difference; Colonel Sellers is a speculative Don Quixote forever tilting his lance at ephemeral windmills while pursuing the American version of fair Dulcinea—wealth—that waits just beyond the border of the frontier. Sellers is a nostalgic character, a confidence man whose snaps are intended to benefit "every friend I've got."

Twain contrasts the humorous Colonel Sellers with the humorless Senator Dilworthy. An unscrupulous political manipulator, Dilworthy traces his ancestry to Baldwin's Simon

Suggs, Jr., and to Alger's confidence men; denying the frontier, he resembles the sentimental villain and marks the passage of the confidence man into contemporary roles. In this respect, *The Gilded Age*, De Forest's *Honest John Vane* (1875) and *Playing the Mischief* (1876), and Henry Adams's *Democracy* (1880) are sibling novels: all explore the corruption and "all-pervading speculativeness" of postwar American society and focus on a confidence man (or woman) who endangers the lives and fortunes of common men. Dilworthy charts a second course of the Southwest humorists' confidence man, seeming to retain all of Simon Jr.'s negative characteristics and to combine them with those of the sentimentalists' villain.

The juxtaposition of Colonel Sellers and Senator Dilworthy heightens our awareness of the threat Dilworthy poses. In language, action, and intention Dilworthy appears a dangerous fraud. He begins a campaign speech in the town of Hawkeye with the familiar words "Fellow citizens."

> It gives me great pleasure to thus meet and mingle with you, to lay aside for a moment the heavy duties of an official and burdensome station, and confer in familiar converse with my friends in your great state. The good opinion of my fellow citizens of all sections is the sweetest solace in all my anxieties. I look forward with longing to the time when I can lay aside the cares of office—["dam sight," shouted a tipsy fellow near the door. Cries of "put him out."]
>
> My friends, do not remove him. Let the misguided man stay. I see that he is a victim of that evil which is swallowing up public virtue and sapping the foundation of society. As I was saying, when I can lay down the cares of public office and retire to the sweets of private life in some such sweet, peaceful, intelligent, wide-awake and patriotic place as Hawkeye (applause). I have traveled much, I have seen all parts of our glorious Union, but I have never seen a lovelier village than yours, or one that has more signs of commercial and industrial and religious prosperity—(more applause). (157)

Dilworthy's inflated political rhetoric pays tribute to the sentimental cult of optimism, ignoring the realities of Hawkeye. He proves false Bryant's prediction that speculators would lose their vocation; by linking patriotism, commerce, and religion with Hawkeye, he exploits the town's desire to think highly of itself, reaping for a small investment of verbal cant a return of hearty applause. Beneath his smooth speech lies a drinker

who trades upon the popular cause of temperance and a religious hypocrite who is descended from Hooper's Bela Bugg and
who prefigures William Dean Howells's fictionalized Joseph
Dylks (*The Leatherwood God*, 1916). A champion of industri-
alism, he can play the frontiersmen for their votes, promoting
for his self-interest the Columbus River Slackwater Navigation Company; though he cares nothing for freed slaves, he
can pose as a moralist by sponsoring the personally profitable
Knobs University bill. His pretentious language—differing
markedly from Sellers's enthusiasms—hides his scorn for the
traditional values he espouses and cloaks his bid for gain beneath a mantle of public interest.

Breaking from the 1860s sentimental and humorous traditions of consolation, Twain revives the flush-times confidence
man of the Old Southwest to illuminate the danger posed by
the contemporary practitioner of confidence art. Sellers and
Dilworthy are of different times, different modes, and their
intersection intensifies the reader's awareness of their characteristics: Colonel Sellers symbolizes the optimism of the
past, the freedom of the frontier, and the confidence of the
common man (however often misplaced) in himself, his countrymen, and the land; Senator Dilworthy embodies the cynicism of the present age, the restrictions of industrialized society, and the failure of American democracy to secure the
new country. These two confidence men, though on parallel
courses, signify two incongruent visions of America. Although repeatedly unsuccessful, Colonel Sellers offers an op-
timism-tempered failure, while Senator Dilworthy's self-
serving cynicism receives only a temporary setback and seems
bound to subvert the principles of American democracy. Unlike Simon Suggs's victims, Senator Dilworthy's—the Hawkins family, Mr. Noble, the American people—are not thieves
and hypocrites; unlike Senator Dilworthy's snaps, those of
Colonel Sellers are victimless. In the contrast between Sellers
and Dilworthy, nostalgic past and cynical present, individu-
alistic West and mechanized East, lies Twain's narrative
method. His satire is modified only at the novel's close and
may represent a concession to the pressures of Charles Dudley
Warner: the reader may catch a glimmer of hope in Colonel
Sellers's ironic determination to join the bar, in Dilworthy's

tumbled house of cards, in the sentimental marriage (and worldly success) of Philip Sterling and Ruth, and even in the death of Laura Hawkins. However, the ending of *The Gilded Age* is tailored to the demands of American "Miss Nancy" culture (from which Twain never entirely freed himself) and seems to indicate the first-novelist's natural fear of the realistic mode and his embrace of sentimental and sensational techniques for security.

*   *   *

Kenneth S. Lynn has demonstrated that Mark Twain was thoroughly schooled in Southwest humor and wise to the wiles of the confidence man.[25] From *Innocents Abroad* (1869) to *Roughing It* (1872) and *The Gilded Age* (1873), Mark Twain tested, deformed, and discredited the literary conventions of popular sentimentalists and literary comedians through narrative juxtaposition with those of southwestern humorists. In *Adventures of Huckleberry Finn* (1884) Twain masterfully engineers collisions of southwest humor, literary or platform comedy, and sentimental, romantic, and realistic fiction to question the contemporary bases of confidence and convention; to accomplish this he reconstructs the antebellum flush times, the source for Twain of cultural contradictions and irreconcilable attitudes which by the 1880s had created what one nineteenth-century analyst termed "American nervousness."[26] Twain uses the confidence man and the issues of confidence he raises to probe the shaky foundations of American optimism, which he perceived to be unfounded, delusional, and ultimately self-destructive. The nostalgic impulse informing the shifty Colonel Sellers in *The Gilded Age* becomes in *Huckleberry Finn* the innocent-seeming critical tool for exposing the violently restrictive cultural attitudes qua stylistic conventions of American society. The southwestern Colonel Sellers and the slick Senator Dilworthy are replaced by characters of greater moral, rhetorical, and behavioral complexity; to Huckleberry Finn all—with the exception of Jim—seem to demand and betray confidence almost randomly, a puzzling amalgamation of conscious confidence men and unconscious hypocrites. Huck subverts this apparent conformity, measuring their inconsistencies from his perspective as a figure marginal to all levels of society.

Huck Finn blends the vernacular language and posture of Southwest humor, the youthful protagonist of the sentimental novelist, and the convention of the good-bad boy popularized by Thomas Bailey Aldrich in *The Story of a Bad Boy* (1870). As the novel's self-deprecating narrator he inspires the reader's trust and emphasizes for him the importance of language; language—in particular diction, syntax, point of view, and tone—defines character, as the author comically warns in an explanatory note on dialect, and is itself a way of perceiving and ordering reality.[27] Huck's description of supper with Widow Douglas, for example, reveals far more than two sets of eating habits.

> The widow rung a bell for supper, and you had to come to time. When you got to the table you couldn't go right to eating, but you had to wait for the widow to tuck down her head and grumble a little over the victuals, though there warn't really anything the matter with them. That is, nothing only everything was cooked by itself. In a barrel of odds and ends it is different; things get mixed up, and the juice kind of swaps around, and the things go better.[28]

Huck stresses two styles of life—the widow's rigid culture and his easy anarchy—in these culinary techniques, tying the reader to the vernacular by silently including him on Huck's side of the table while disarming him with the humorous "barrel of odds and ends" language. In Huck's first-person narration, "things get mixed up . . . and the things go better"; beneath his vernacular is an energy at once comic in its rapid shifts and juxtapositions of styles and eager in its anxiously repetitive attempts to record accurately events the boy doesn't always fully understand.[29] Language serves Huck as a vehicle for apprehending experience, while the language of others serves him as an index to their intentions.

Jim's dialect and superstitions are refined versions of those commonly found in southwestern sketches such as Henry Clay Lewis's "Day of Judgment" (1850);[30] his speculations—in a cow that dies, a bank that "busts," a raft that is stolen—stereotype him within the limitations of a "low" comic character, the bumbling Negro who placidly suffers as the butt of condescending, cruel jokes. Huck learns, however, that Jim's language is deceptive, concealing under a humorous veneer

the complexity of an individual. Huck's own conventional
language has proven inadequate to interpret Jim. After convincing Jim that their separation in the fog was only a dream
(an inversion of the witch-ride prank Tom pulled in chapter
2), Huck is startled by the depth of emotion Jim conveys in
dialect.

> When I got all wore out wid work, en wid de callin' for you,
> en went to sleep, my heart wuz mos' broke bekase you wuz
> los', en I didn' k'yer no mo' what become er me en de raf'. En
> when I wake up en fine you back agin', all safe en soun', de
> tears come en I could a got down on my knees en kiss' yo' foot
> I's so thankful. En all you wuz thinkin' 'bout wuz how you
> could make uv ole Jim wid a lie. Dat truck dah is *trash*; en
> trash is what people is dat puts dirt on de head er dey fren's en
> makes 'em ashamed. (71)

The complexity—and rightness—of Jim's criticism, rendered
in the same style as his superstitions, requires Huck to evaluate him anew, now as a friend, rejecting as inappropriate the
stock figure of Jim as a harmless, humorous, nonhuman slave.
Huck has apparently been confused by the discrepancy between his culturally conditioned expectations of Jim's comic
response and the reality of Jim's sharp pain; in addition, Huck
is taken aback by the contrast between Jim's style of speech
and its substance. Style, an ambiguous word that as Warwick
Wadlington notes assumes through countless repetition
"near-magical properties,"[31] may not be an accurate, immediate indicator of character or motivation but a conventional,
limited mode of expression. Jim's sophisticated manipulation
of the culturally loaded word *trash* strikes Huck with the force
of a slap in the face; as Lionel Trilling contends, at this point
"Huck's one last dim vestige of pride of status, his sense of
position as a white man, wholly vanishes."[32] Jim securely asserts his own superiority to "white trash" folks and their malicious tricks while offering Huck the opportunity to transcend the boundaries of Huck's own limiting stereotype; to
the son of Pap Finn, Jim holds out the offer of concern, companionship, respect, and responsible, reciprocal love.

Huck questions the language of Widow Douglas, Tom Sawyer, Miss Watson, and Pap Finn in a similar fashion, exposing
the "love" each appears to extend as self-serving illusion. Al-

though the widow claims self-righteously that smoking tobacco "was a mean practice and wasn't clean, and I must try
to not do it any more," "she took snuff too; of course that was
all right, because she done it herself" (7–8). Language must be
measured against the actions and values it often hides; the
style of love the widow is willing to give is restrictive and is
based on her self-satisfying design to "sivilize" Huck. Richard
Poirier argues, "It is metaphorically suggested that Tom Sawyer and Widow Douglas are in tacit alliance, and both are indicted by the further suggestion that to be 'respectable' in her
terms is the necessary condition for membership in his gang.
'Respectable' society as represented by the Widow is equivalent to a 'band of robbers.'"[33] Without putting undue pressure
on this assertion, we can agree that both the widow and Tom
insist on remaking Huck, the widow with her Bible and Tom
with his romances. That Huck recognizes identical attempts
to imprison him becomes clear in the language he uses to
reject Tom's tiresome adventures: "It had all the marks of a
Sunday school" (17). David E. E. Sloane widens this conspiracy against Huck to include Miss Watson and Pap Finn, both
of whom desire "to exploit Huck for . . . egotistical satisfaction."[34] Both demand that Huck behave in a proscriptive manner and assure him not of forgiveness and love but of judgment
and punishment for disobedience. Pap's "love" seems at best
a device to keep Huck from acquiring what he perceives to be
a superior style of culture and at worst a ploy to get for himself
Huck's fortune while brutalizing his son physically and emotionally because of his own frustrations. Beneath all these languages lies a threat of violence absent from the relationship
Huck develops with Jim. In abstract terms, Jim alone offers
Huck the chance to rise above conventional limitations to
become a responsible partner in an unconventional relationship based not on upbringing, age, race, or economic class but
solely on mutual trust and respect.

The violence in the widow's style is so implicit that it usually passes without notice, the reader confidently accepting at
face value Huck's conventional assurance that "she never
meant no harm by it" (7). Her hypocrisy over tobacco, however, coupled with her socially condoned intentions, demonstrates how even a good woman can internalize and rationalize

official values that she unconsciously imposes on Huck. Each woman Huck holds up as a paragon of virtue—Widow Douglas, Miss Watson, Mary Jane Wilks, Aunt Sally Phelps—silently supports in broad terms the slave system and propagates it in her efforts to "sivilize" Huck. That readers do not question Huck's adoration illustrates the intention and the success of Twain's narrative point of view: to Huck, their attempts to improve him are in no sense equivalent to enslavement but appear beneficent Franklinian programs to help him achieve a desirable and wholly conventional moral perfection.

Tom's style veils two forms of violence. First, Tom is infected by what Twain tagged in *Life on the Mississippi* (1883) the "Sir Walter Scott Disease."[35] By insisting on the fulfillment of his literary romantic fantasies (especially in the novel's closing chapters), Tom literally threatens life and earns a bullet for his adventuring. Second, and more pernicious, Tom enforces conformity to exclusionary social conventions that dehumanize the individual—Huck, Jim, even Tom himself. In this view Tom is, as Poirier contends, the widow's accomplice.

The danger posed by the discrepancy between language and act is most obvious in the behavior of Pap Finn. Echoing Johnson Jones Hooper's shifty Simon Suggs at a camp meeting (as do the king and the duke), Pap pretends to have seen the light; like Pap, Simon testifies to rebirth and receives congratulation all around.

> "Come up, come up; thar's room for all!" cried brother Bugg, in his evening exhortation. "Come to the 'seat,' and ef you won't pray yourselves, let *me* pray for you!"
> "Yes!" said Simon . . ."it's a game that all can win at! . . . No matter what sort of a hand you've got," added Simon in the fulness of his benevolence; "take stock! Here am *I*, the wickedest and blindest of sinners—has spent my whole life in the sarvice of the devil—has now come in on *narry pair* and won a pile!"[36]

Pap's dramatic performance mimics the pieties of popular reform repeatedly satirized by Southwest humorists.[37]

> "Look at it gentlemen, and ladies all; take ahold of it; shake it. There's a hand that was the hand of a hog; but it ain't so no more; it's the hand of a man that's started in on a new life, and 'll die before he'll go back. You mark them words—don't for-

> get I said them. It's a clean hand now; shake it—don't be
> afeard."
>   So they shook it, one after the other, all around, and cried.
> The judge's wife she kissed it. Then the old man he signed a
> pledge—made his mark. The judge said it was the holiest time
> on record, or something like that. (23)

In the tradition of Simon Suggs and Sut Lovingood, Pap counterfeits the conventional sentimental rhetoric of nineteenth-
century revelation and consolation characteristic of writers
from Mason Locke Weems to Henry Ward Beecher and Elizabeth Stuart Phelps. Just as Jim's low dialect could not long
hide his full nature, so Pap Finn's pretense of repentance
quickly collapses.

> In the night sometime he got powerful thirsty and clumb out
> onto the porch-roof and slid down a stanchion and traded his
> new coat [given him by the credulous reforming judge] for a
> jug of forty-rod, and clumb back again and had a good old time;
> and towards daylight he crawled out again, drunk as a fiddler,
> and rolled off the porch and broke his left arm in two places
> and was most froze to death when somebody found him after
> sun-up. And when they come to look at that spare room, they
> had to take soundings before they could navigate it.
>   The judge he felt kind of sore. He said he reckoned a body
> could reform the ole man with a shot-gun, maybe, but he
> didn't know no other way. (23)

Pap's destruction of the room reveals the violence lurking just
below the surface of his language and prefigures his drunken
antigovernment, anti-Negro tirade which culminates in his
attempt to murder Huck (chapter 6). The conventional piety
and self-serving racist politics Pap mouths suggest that language is not a substitute for violence but a prelude to it; even
the judge's language contains a threat. Words can be used to
hide violent truth. The ease with which the widow, Pap, and
the judge shift styles indicates that language is part of a conventional pose which, like cooking things separately, may be
a device both revealing and concealing values and intentions.
Although Miss Watson preaches to Huck about the horrors of
blasphemy and says "*she* was going to go to the good place"
(8), she betrays Jim's confidence in her: she "awluz said she
wouldn' sell me down to Orleans. . . . Well, one night I creeps
to de do', pooty late, en de do' warn't quite shet, en I hear ole

missus tell de widder she gwyne to sell me down to Orleans, but she didn' want to, but she could git eight hund'd dollars for me, en it 'uz sich a big stack o' money she couldn' resis'" (39). Miss Watson completes the process of rationalization, betrayal, and hypocrisy by attending a camp meeting. At this point in the novel Huck and Jim inhabit a world endangered not by the obvious confidence men of *The Gilded Age* but by an entire society that seems to have assimilated the confidence man's methods and ethics. The threat is all the more frightening because it parades the streets in the guise of respectability.

The discrepancy between language and act is nowhere more apparent than in chapters 17–18 on the Grangerfords and their feud with the Shepherdsons. Their house, which has "so much style" (82), is ruled by the equally impressive Colonel Grangerford: "Col. Grangerford was a gentleman, you see. He was a gentleman all over; and so was his family. . . . He was as kind as he could be—you could feel that, you know, and so you had confidence" (86). Huck misplaces his confidence, for the colonel's impeccable manners, like his emblematic white linen suit, mask the soul of a madman. The Grangerfords appear to have refinement, religion, and respectability, but it is the forms—the style—the family truly cherishes. The religion of this "handsome lot of quality" is little more than a sentimental cult of death, consecrating the irrational feud and hallowing the "spidery" crayon masterpiece of Emmeline as if it were a death-bed self-portrait. Despite the comfort, kindness, and generosity Huck shares in the Grangerford home, the realities of their feud make him sick and reveal to the reader how bankrupt of ultimate moral values is their natural aristocracy. Huck detects an underlying kinship, moreover, between Emmeline's speedy tributes for the dead and Buck's monomaniacal haste to kill a Shepherdson; both illustrate the obsessiveness that has become normal. Emmeline's pictures always give Huck the "fan-tods" in part because they indicate an unhealthy preoccupation with death as an aesthetic, idealized experience.

> Every time a man died, or a woman died, or a child died, she would be on hand with her "tribute" before he was cold. She called them tributes. The neighbors said it was the doctor

first, then Emmeline, then the undertaker—the undertaker
never got in ahead of Emmeline but once, and then she hung
fire on a rhyme for the dead person's name, which was
Whistler. She warn't the same, after that; she never complained, but she kind of pined away and did not live long. (85)

The central place death has assumed during the long years of
the feud has blinded everyone (with the exception of Harney
Shepherdson, who spares Buck and Huck before he elopes
with Sophia Grangerford) to the corrupting influence this
unexamined, obsessive focus has on basically good people.
The highly stylized graveyard portrait of a distraught lover—
"And Art Thou Gone Yes Thou Art Gone Alas"—suggests that
the cultural trappings highly visible in the house's style license the feud's code of violence. Death is either casually dismissed or emotionally applauded. In response to Huck's question "Has anybody been killed this year, Buck?" the boy
replies, "Yes, we got one and they got one" (89). And when
Huck accuses Baldy Shepherdson of cowardice, Buck immediately rallies to his defense: "I reckon he *warn't* a coward.
Not by a blame' sight. There ain't a coward amongst them
Shepherdsons—not a one. And there ain't no cowards
amongst the Grangerfords, either. Why, that old man kep' up
his end in a fight one day, for a half an hour, against three
Grangerfords, and come out winner" (89). Reminiscent of sentimental rationalizations of death common in Civil War fictions such as Beecher's popular *Norwood*, the Grangerfords'
conciliatory program encourages murder though the causes of
the "war" are at best dimly understood by individuals. Violence has become so ingrained in their minds that it domi-
nates their lives, warping their love for the dead Emmeline
and the eloped Sophia. The slaughter at the river, punctuated
by shouts of "Kill Them! Kill Them!," strips away the last
shreds of respectability for the reader and for Huck: "It made
me so sick I most fell out of the tree" (94).

Huck also voices Twain's disgust at the antebellum cult of
sentimentality that linked honor with violence. In *Life on the
Mississippi* he argues that stylistic affectations—castles, false
culture, Sir Walter Scott, and duels—caused the Civil War.
This self-deluding, self-authenticating "Sir Walter Scott disease" made violence a national virtue and, dissociating death

from its context in reality, swept historical (and literary) alternatives aside. Families, individuals, and mobs are encouraged
to prove themselves through rites that are socially sanctioned
forms of murder. Thus the drunken Boggs, a comic figure lifted
from Southwest humor, is honorably gunned down by the aristocratic Colonel Sherburn; honorably, for though Boggs is not
armed, he ignores Colonel Sherburn's gentlemanly warning.
In like manner, the nation ignored warnings of impending war
and accepted the violence of the Colonel Sherburns as heroic.
Boggs, the focus of the delighted crowd, poses an institution-
alized comic threat; Colonel Sherburn, either taking Boggs at
his word or simply bored by him, changes the traditional
comedy of the Old Southwest—the boasting or bluffing contest that is often a substitute for violence[38]—into a sentimental tragedy. To this the crowd reacts by threatening to lynch
Colonel Sherburn, but their threat, like Boggs's, is all bluster.
Twain documents the manner in which sentimental forms of
aristocratic pretension come to dominate the humorous tradition of southwestern humor—kill it, in fact—and the manner in which these idealizations—represented by Colonel
Sherburn—retain their power. Once Sherburn has been recognized as heroic, an epitome of American culture, and has
been awarded a title of public respect ("Colonel"), he has been
given the authority to command respect though he publicly
commits murder. Obeying the very forms the people have chosen to elevate, Colonel Sherburn triumphs over the lynch mob
stylistically.

> The idea of *you* lynching anybody! It's amusing. The idea
> of you thinking you had pluck enough to lynch a *man*! Be-
> cause you're brave enough to tar and feather poor friendless
> cast-out women that come along here, did that make you
> think you had grit enough to lay your hands on a *man*? Why,
> a *man's* safe in the hands of ten thousand of your kind—as
> long as it's day-time and you're not behind him. (117)

Huck doesn't wish to dwell on the implications of Colonel
Sherburn's evaluation of American manhood, for the colonel
seems a cold-blooded killer who successfully defends himself
from the crowd by demonstrating the qualities Americans
most admire—confidence, individualism, and bravery. Categories of experience break down as a comic drunk becomes a

tragic victim and a cowardly murderer seems suddenly a tow-
ering hero. These paradoxical transformations indicate a radical disorder at the center of American culture, one that threatens to wrench Huck from the normative context of referential
language and deed and throw him headfirst into a morally
chaotic world of violent and ambiguous action.

To define this aberrant society Twain turns directly to the
flush-times confidence man. At the center of *Huckleberry
Finn* spring up the king and the duke, a counterforce to the
violent sentimentality promulgated by Colonels Grangerford
and Sherburn. The king and the duke are at first Suggsian
confidence men who recapitulate the entire southwestern humorous tradition; in addition to selling teeth cleaner and running temperance revivals, their repertoire of snaps includes,
according to them, the following:

> "Jour printer, by trade; do a little in patent medicines; the-
> atre-actor—tragedy, you know; take a turn at mesmerism and
> phrenology when there's a chance; teach singing-geography
> school for a change; sling a lecture, sometimes—oh, I do lots
> of things—most anything that comes handy, so it ain't work.
> What's your lay?"
> "I've done considerable in the doctoring way in my time
> [replies the King to the Duke]. Layin' on o' hands is my best
> holt—for cancer, and paralysis, and sich things; and I k'n tell
> a fortune pretty good, when I've got somebody along to find
> out the facts for me. Preachin's my line, too; and workin'
> camp-meetin's; and missionarin' around." (99)

In language, physical appearance, and profession these rogues
recall the confidence men of Hooper, Baldwin, Harris, Melville, and a dozen of their cronies from the *Spirit of the Times*.
Their games are designed to fleece hypocrites, pretenders, and
fools, and as such serve as chastening antidotes to the virulent
poisons of the self-righteous society of murdering heroes. Insinuating themselves with Huck and Jim, they create humorous identities for themselves in a ritual ceremony of mock-
revelation.

> "Gentlemen," says the young man, very solemn, "I will re-
> veal it to you, for I feel I may have confidence in you. By rights
> I am duke!"
> Jim's eyes bugged out when he heard that; and I reckon

From *Adventures of Huckleberry Finn* (first edition).

mine did, too. Then the baldhead says: "No! you can't mean it?"

"Yes. My great-grandfather, eldest son of the Duke of Bridgewater, fled to this country about the end of the last century, to breathe the pure air of freedom; married here, and died, leaving a son, his own father dying about the same time. The second son of the late duke seized the title and estates—the infant real duke was ignored. I am the lineal descendant of that infant—I am the rightful Duke of Bridgewater." (100)

His companion, however, will not be outdone in invention.

"Bilgewater, kin I trust you?" says the old man, still sort of sobbing.

"To the bitter death!" He took the old man by the hand and squeezed it, and says, "The secret of your being: speak!"

"Bilgewater, I am the late Dauphin!"

You bet you Jim and me stared, this time. Then the duke says: "You are what?"

"Yes, my friend, it is too true—your eyes is lookin' at this very moment on the pore disappeared Dauphin, Looy the Seventeen, son of Looy the Sixteen and Marry Antonette." (100–101)

These caricatures parody the convention of concealed royal birth gracing innumerable sentimental fictions and "Wild Western" Beadle novels. Twain sets up and satisfies comic expectations, using the king's rechristening of Bridgewater as "Bilgewater" to deflate the pretensions of both impersonators. And just as Hooper takes a swipe at the airs of real generals and legislators through the masquerades of "Captain" Simon Suggs, so too does Twain burlesque the posturing of real kings and dukes.

Sharing Huck's point of view, the reader recognizes with him "that these liars warn't no kings nor dukes, at all [though they give Huck a moment's pause], but just low-down humbugs and frauds." Huck's instinct, however, is to play along.

> If they wanted us to call them kings and dukes, I hadn't no objections, 'long as it would keep peace in the family; and it warn't no use to tell Jim, so I didn't tell him. If I never learnt nothing else out of pap, I learnt that the best way to get along with his kind of people is to let them have their own way. (102)

Huck characterizes these four as a "family," asserting and extending the complex relationship he has developed with Jim to include two humorous confidence men. They too must be seen as more than mere stereotypes; they are individuals speaking discrete languages, personalities with human emotions and motives. Yet in lumping the king and the duke with Pap in the phrase *his kind of people*, Huck foreshadows a sinister side to these comedians not immediately apparent: the king and the duke are akin to Pap in having the capacity for violence, and they too interpret selfishly the meaning of the word *family*.

There is little evidence of their violence at the Pokeville camp meeting; only the emotions of the congregation are violent.

> You couldn't make out what the preacher said, any more, on account of the shouting and crying. Folks got up, everywheres in the crowd, and worked their way, just by main strength, to the mourners' bench, with the tears running down their faces; and when all the mourners had got up there to the front

benches in a crowd, they sung, and shouted, and flung themselves down on the straw, just crazy and wild. (106)

Critics including Bernard DeVoto and Walter Blair have proven
that Twain's camp meeting owes more than a nod to Hooper's
in style, tone, and action.[39]

> The rest were walking to and fro, (engaged in the other exer-
> cises we have indicated,) among the "mourners"—a host of
> whom occupied the seat set apart for their especial use—or
> made personal appeals to the mere spectators. The excitement
> was intense. Men and women rolled on the ground, or lay sob-
> bing or shouting in promiscuous heaps. More then all, the ne-
> groes sang and screamed and prayed. Several, under the influ-
> ence of what is technically called "the jerks," were plunging
> and pitching about with convulsive energy. (SS, 119–20)

Capt. Simon Suggs and the king exploit the communal desire
for religious ecstasy, which the North American Review
called in 1862 "aesthetic religionism": "It is sought for its
emotions . . . but when emotion is sought for its own sake, it
may become as selfish as the love of money, or the love of
fame. We desire the spiritual luxury, and, if it comes not otherwise, it must be got up."[40] This "sentimental pietism" is
false, a perverse elevation of style over substance suitable for
attack in 1845 (Simon Suggs), in 1862 (the North American
Review), and in 1884 (Huckleberry Finn); it defines one variety of religious experience that continues to haunt the
American mind, manifesting itself in William Dean Howells's
Leatherwood God (1916), Sinclair Lewis's Elmer Gantry
(1927), and Nathanael West's Miss Lonelyhearts (1933) and
The Day of the Locust (1939), to list only a sample from the
early twentieth century.

Mark Twain plays the camp meeting in Hooper's style. The
king's counterfeit of a pious conversion imitates that of Simon
Suggs, though the king's harangue is narrated by Huck while
Simon speaks for himself. The king pretends to be a reformed
pirate of the Indian Ocean while Captain Simon Suggs—
though he pretends to have "got" religion—delights in manipulating the brethren without benefit of masquerade. The reader's enjoyment of the king's snap is limited by the fact that
Twain renders it in the third person; although the congregation may deserve fleecing, Twain wishes the reader to with-

hold complete approval of the king's actions. In other words, Hooper asks the reader to respond directly to Simon Suggs, to triumph with him over the hypocritical congregation and the dangerous Bela Bugg; Twain desires the reader to respond with laughter to the scene, but to maintain enough critical distance from the king to discourage reader-character identification. For this reason the king takes on the self-consciously literary identity of a pirate: he remains at this point a two-dimensional comic character within a larger, conventional, comic structure and does not make the personal demand of empathic approval that Simon Suggs (or Huck Finn) does of the reader. Both confidence men bilk the camp meeting so that they can purportedly begin the good works of the missionary preacher, and as the king concludes (in his one bit of direct discourse), both find the preacher "the truest friend a pirate ever had" (107).

The king and duke's burlesque "Shaksperean Revival!!!" follows the popular tradition of butchered classics[41]: "They laughed all the time, and that made the duke mad; and everybody left, anyway, before the show was over, but one boy which was asleep" (120). The revival, an analogue to the camp meeting, sets the stage for the drunken entrance of Boggs. Twain juxtaposes frontier comedy and frontier violence, suggesting that the inflamed aesthetics of the Arkansas townsfolk encourage Colonel Sherburn to kill Boggs: their "sentimental pietism" casts aside fineness of emotion for intensity of emotion. In the duke's words, "What they wanted was low comedy—and may be something ruther worse than low comedy" (120).

What they get, first of all, is the spectacular murder of Boggs. It is clearly intended to be "worse than low comedy," as is Colonel Sherburn's parallel cowing of the mob. Yet the duke has something different in mind; this town deserves not garbled Shakespeare but his revived revival, "The King's Camelopard or The Royal Nonesuch." The Duke packs the house by printing handbills concluding with the line, "LADIES AND CHILDREN NOT ADMITTED" (120), which the men swallow as a euphemism for *obscene*.[42] They eargerly pay up for three nights, filling the theater as they had filled the street around Boggs, as they had listened to the story of his murder with rapt attention, and as they had rushed to the house of Colonel Sherburn.[43] The duke "said he could size their style"; what they desire is a dehumanizing show.

> And at last when [the duke had] got everybody's expectations up high enough, he rolled up the curtain, and the next minute the king come a-prancing out on all fours, naked; and he was painted all over, ring-streaked-and-striped, all sorts of colors, as splendid as a rainbow. . . . The people most killed themselves laughing; and when the king got done capering, and capered off behind the scenes, they roared and clapped and stormed and haw-hawed till he come back and done it over again; and after that, they made him do it another time. (121)

They are sold in the finest Suggsian tradition. Twain dramatizes a momentary victory of Southwest humor over the cult of emotion and style, which demands that the performance be repeated, like the retelling of Boggs's murder, again and again. In a gesture of poetic justice, the confidence men give the townspeople what they demand. At the Royal Nonesuch, as at the camp meeting, the comic actions of the confidence men offer a corrective to violent sentimentality. In *Simon Suggs* and *Huckleberry Finn* confidence men boil hypocrites in laughter.

Since chapter 19 the novel has been humorously directed by the king and the duke; the heart-wrenching yet conventional sentimental story of Jim's deaf and dumb daughter 'Lisbeth (124–25), however, ushers Huck and Jim into a nightmarish reality. The king and the duke, at first able to exploit the falseness of language and social convention for profit, at last become trapped themselves in the flush-times dream of instant wealth; whereas at the camp meeting or the Royal Nonesuch they had consciously manipulated the forms of society, in the Wilks adventure they succumb to its substance, no longer mimicking but embodying the fantasies of Pap Finn and the violence of Colonel Sherburn. When the king and the duke rationalize selling Jim, they have become part of the culture whose pretensions they had humorously counterfeited. Although they con the naive Wilks girls, Gary Lindberg argues that at this point the king and the duke "must be seen not as peripheral freaks but as stylized exemplars. They help characterize the suckers they exploit, for their methods depend on a massive public willingness to settle for trumpery."[44] Their poor performance, which "was enough to make a body ashamed of the human race" (130), reveals a shift in their function and effect. Confidence art, so important to the comedy of Longstreet's Yellow Blossom, Hooper's Simon Suggs, Baldwin's Ovid Bolus, Harris's Sut Lovingood, and Melville's Confidence Man, is made subservient to what Whitman called the "magician's serpent" of moneymaking; with a wriggle the king and the duke assume the position and the imperative of Baldwin's Simon Suggs, Jr., and Warren's Billy Fishback: "By-and-by the thing dragged through, and everything was sold. Everything but a little old trifling lot in the graveyard. So they'd got to work *that* off—I never see such a girafft as the king was for wanting to swallow *everything*" (153).

The desire to reduce everything to sacks of gold marks the absorption of the king and the duke into the heart of society. In contrast to Simon Suggs, they cease to be marginal characters of the frontier and come to represent instead the direction in which the new country as a whole is headed: all will be assimilated into a modern age of hypocrisy, violence, and greed. Although the gradual souring of the confidence man's humor is present throughout the nineteenth century, the king and the duke cause an especially bad taste to linger: not only is the reader made to sympathize with the victimized Huck, Jim, and the Wilks girls, but the sale of Jim defeats the entire imaginative—and moral—journey of the novel. Even Tom Sawyer, who seems to take up the role of comic confidence man at the end of *Huckleberry Finn*, betrays Huck and Jim to a figurative ride on a rail. Tom obeys the dehumanizing forms of sentimental culture defined by the king and the duke, Pap, Widow Douglas, Miss Watson, the Grangerfords, Colonel Sherburn, and even the good Phelpses. He supports its style, perpetuates its violence, and cherishes its emblem—a totemic bullet. Yet Tom's prank is but a romantic shadow of the southwestern confidence man's art, a betrayal that he attempts to ignore by reversing the traditional Suggsian exchange of cash: "We had Jim out of the chains in no time . . . and Tom give Jim forty dollars for being prisoner" (225).

Mark Twain reimagines the confidence man, a convention representative of the frontier flush times, to reveal the bankruptcy of the twin traditions of sentimental and humorous consolation that inform his contemporary culture. In *Huckleberry Finn* he contrasts southwestern and sentimental fiction, juxtaposing and conflating the confidence man's conscious manipulation of fraudulent social forms with the sentimental character's unconscious acceptance of them as genuine to create a radical new paradigm of American society. The horror at the center of antebellum culture, the cause of the Civil War and the source of the corrupt Gilded Age, is an infinite capacity for confident self-delusion visible in the history of the confidence man; preaching equality, opportunity, and freedom, society enforces submission to its self-serving, self-destructive conventions. Huck Finn recognizes—as the king and the duke (and Tom) do not—that the confidence man is no longer a marginal predator but a national symbol of American culture. Forsaking mastery of the frontier flush times and betraying the heritage of Southwest humor that spawned him, the confidence man stands self-deceived. Twain's variations on the convention suggest that unlike Huck, who can potentially "light out for the Territory," the confidence man loses much of his flexibility and many of his humorous characteristics as he willingly submits—like the new country itself—to Aunt Sally's attempts to "sivilize" him.

Huck Finn should not be seen as yet another confidence man, though as Gary Lindberg notes he "can disengage principle from practice by his dexterity."[45] He does tell lies, assume false identities, and manipulate morality as easily as persimmons. Yet with the exception of the early tricks he plays on Jim in the style of Harris's Sut Lovingood, Huck's deceptions have an implicit consecration of their own. "All of Huck's freely chosen commitments to one face or another of his varied masquerade," writes Daniel Hoffman, "are given with the ultimate end of protecting Jim and himself from the world."[46] Struggling to survive in what Richard Poirier terms "a whole society built on games, tricks, and illusions,"[47] Huck spontaneously adopts when necessary the colors of the enemy—the language of the confidence man. Warwick Wadlington aptly remarks that "the benign, defensive trickster Huck discovers that he cannot pray a lie,"[48] while Richard Boyd Hauck correctly contends that Huck "never develops a conscious knowledge of what lies are for. . . . His beautifully constructed defensive lies succeed in keeping Jim safe, but their success does not help expand Huck's vision."[49] Huck must be seen as distinct from the king and the duke, who acquire from the success of their early tricks the confidence to expand their operations past the breaking point in the Wilks episode. On the raft Jim teaches Huck that the confidence man's grammar of humor masks a language of cruelty and betrayal, and it is this lesson that makes Huck uncomfortable with Tom's romantic charade in the novel's closing chapters. His resistance to Tom's shenanigans, through which Jim must suffer as a literal and figurative "prisoner of style" (208), supports Lionel Trilling's assessment that although Huck may be a skillful liar he never lies to himself.[50] Self-delusion ultimately delimits the convention of the confidence man. The power of Huck's appeal resides in his uncanny ability to transcend literary and cultural stereotypes, even such a protean and practical form as that of the confidence man.

In Twain's later fiction, Hank Morgan is a Franklinian pragmatist whose confident manipulations result in massacre, while the switched infants Pudd'nhead Wilson never satisfactorily sorts out suggest a vision of fate not entirely subject to the confidence man's legerdemain. In the fragments that Albert Bigelow Paine collected and revised as *The Mysterious Stranger* in 1916, the confidence man has become a fantastic being operating in an abstract realm of mythic forces. The confidence man emerges from these pages as Satan, a recombination of the convention with larger traditions. Although Twain himself never finished the manuscripts, Satan's dramatic revelation—that all is "a grotesque and foolish dream"[51]—suggests that to resolve the issues of confidence and convention his fictions raised, Twain was forced to resort to sleight of hand. And as Huck Finn concludes, "I been there before."

6 FROM THE NEW COUNTRY TO THE TWENTIETH CENTURY

> "Can't repeat the past?" he cried
> incredulously. "Why of course you
> can!"
>
> —Jay Gatsby (1925)

In *The Leatherwood God* (1916), William Dean Howells explores the limits of frontier optimism and the capacity for self-delusion exposed by one version of the American confidence man. Joseph C. Dylks, Howells's confidence man, was a historical figure in the drama of the flush times; as such, he formed the perfect focus for the realistic novelist who desired to recreate and appraise the enthusiasms of the formative 1820s. In composing the novel, Howells explicitly used Richard H. Taneyhill's history of Joseph Dylks, an evangelical trickster who in 1828, claiming to be God Almighty, promised to bring down the New Jerusalem in Leatherwood Creek, Ohio. Howells summarized Taneyhill's account in the *Atlantic Monthly* (1871), included the Leatherwood incident in his own *Stories of Ohio* (1897), and closely followed Taneyhill's research in *The Leatherwood God*. Clearly Howells viewed Joseph Dylks as an index to a vanished age.[1]

Richard Taneyhill—an editor, lawyer, and antiquarian—proposes a rational explanation for Dylks's success notable for its common sense and for its applicability as a general law: the Ohio farmers were simply duped.

> Religious impostors have flourished in almost every portion of the historic period. Nor is this remarkable, when we reflect that man, universally, is disposed to give credence to marvelous stories, to put faith in sanctimonious pretensions, and to refer whatever he does not understand to some supernatural agency. These religious cheats have always found ready subjects to impress with their views, however visionary, and to mold into material to promote their ulterior schemes and purposes, however absurd and wicked.
> Such an imposter was Joseph C. Dylks. (7)

As a historian, Taneyhill locates the cause of the Leatherwood incident in nineteenth-century expansionism: the flush times encouraged scoundrels like Dylks to con Americans whose understanding, hope, and faith had been severely tested by conditions in 1820s Ohio. Second- and third-generation settlers had lost the initial driving purpose of their pioneer forefathers and had not yet developed as a community the stabilizing secular comforts of civilization. Their desire for a better world made them easy marks for an evangelical confidence man who promised the ease and splendor of heaven on earth.

Writing of Dylks in the period immediately following the Civil War, Taneyhill represents the Ohio farmers as innocent victims of aggression whose 1828 crisis of faith reflects his own doubts about America in 1870. To him there is nothing amusing in delusion and betrayal, nothing humorous in this historical kinsman of Hooper's Simon Suggs. In fact, despite Dylks's failure to perform promised miracles, despite his trial by the community as an impostor, and despite his flight from Leatherwood to Philadelphia, as late as 1870 Taneyhill interviewed people who firmly believed that Dylks was in truth God Almighty. To Taneyhill—and to Howells—this credulity and naivete typify in microcosm the spirit of the past (and present) new country.

Howells underscores his novel's historical foundation in a "Publisher's Note" (2), but asserts as well his freedom from the historian's strict fidelity to events, reproducing, paraphrasing, or inventing incidents in pursuit of his artistic ends.[2] Distant from both Dylks's 1820s and Taneyhill's 1870s, he apprehends the meaning of the Leatherwood God from several points of view, infusing the Ohio advent with national significance. Through Matthew Braile—the normative "Squire" with whom the fiction's narrative frame opens and closes—Howells analyzes Dylks's appeal from a psychological perspective at once more individual and more universal than the historian's.

> "You see," [Braile] resumed after a moment, "life is hard in a new country, and anybody that promises salvation on easy terms has got a strong hold at the very start. People will accept anything from him. Somewhere, tucked away in us, is the longing to know whether we'll live again, and the hope that we'll live happy. I've got fun out of that fact in a community

where I've had the reputation of an infidel for fifty years; but all along I've felt it in myself. We want to be good, and we want to be safe, even if we are not good; and the first fellow that comes along and tells us to have faith in him, and he'll make it all right, why we have faith in him. That's all." (156–57)

Though no less moral than Taneyhill, Howells is less quick to condemn the impostor, his ready subjects, and the new country, tempering the excited judgments of David Gillespie and the Herd of the Lost—to say nothing of Jane Gillespie and the Little Flock—with Braile's cautious common sense. Early in the novel Howells's tone is in fact less accusatory than nostalgic; like Mark Twain surveying a sleeping town, Howells initially indulges in an almost pastoral impulse.

> Already in the third decade of the nineteenth century, the settlers in the valley of Leatherwood Creek had opened the primeval forest to their fields of corn and tobacco on the fertile slopes and rich bottomlands. . . . The name passed to the settlement, and then it passed to the man who came and went there in mystery and obloquy, and remained lastingly famed in the annals of the region as the Leatherwood God.
>
> At the time he appeared the community had become a centre of influence spiritual as well as material, after a manner unknown to later conditions. It was still housed, for the most part, in the log cabins which the farmers built when they ceased to be pioneers, but in the older clearings, and along the creek a good many frame dwellings stood, and even some of brick. The population, woven of the varied strains from the north, east and south which have mixed to form the Middle Western people, enjoyed an ease of circumstance not so great as to tempt their thoughts from the other world and fix them on this. In their remoteness from the political centres of the young Republic, they seldom spoke of the civic questions stirring the towns of the East; the commercial and industrial problems which vex modern society were unknown to them. Religion was their chief interest and the seriousness which they had inherited from their Presbyterian, Methodist, Lutheran and Moravian ancestry was expressed in their orderly and diligent lives; but in the general prosperity the stringency of their several creeds had so far relaxed that their distinctive public rite had come to express a mutual toleration. (3–4)

In the novel's first two paragraphs Howells recreates an idyllic vision of Leatherwood, Ohio, in 1828; it is an imaginative vision still powerful in 1916, a symbolic landscape evoking a lost Golden Age characterized by recently won "ease of circumstance" and "general prosperity." To Howells, Leatherwood typifies both the initial material success of nineteenth-century pioneers and the persistent frontier spirit of mutability and yearning. The juxtaposition in narrative sequence and style of Matthew Braile's domestic satisfaction and the "curious doin's" at the camp meeting, for example, illustrates the breadth of Leatherwood's "mutual toleration," which blankets the "infidel" and the faithful, the intellectual and the unsophisticated, in "general prosperity." Abel Reverdy's account to Braile emphasizes stylistically disparate responses to post-frontier conditions; the energies of the people, no longer necessary to tame the wilderness, find an outlet in revivalism.

> "Yes, sir . . . he had 'em goin' lively, about midnight, now I tell you: whoopun' and yellun', and rippun' and stavun', and fallun' down with the jerks, and pullun' and haulun' at the sinners, to git 'em up to the mourners' bench, and hurrahun' over 'em, as fast as they was knocked down and drug out. . . . They had eight camp-fires goun' instead o' four, on top of the highest stageun's yit, so the whole place was lit up as bright as day. . . . 'What shall we pray for?' and just then there come a kind of snort, and a big voice shouted out, 'Salvation!' and then there come another snort,—*Hooff!*—like there was a scared horse got loose right in there among the people; and some of 'em jumped up from their seats, and tumbled over the benches, and some of 'em bounced off, and fell into fits, and the women screeched and fainted, thick as flies. . . .
>
> "What was it? A man! A stranger that nobody seen before, and nobody suspicioned was there till they hearn him give that kind of a snort. . . . He was in his bare head, and he had a suit of long, glossy, jet-black hair hengun' down back of his ears clean to his shoulders. . . . He was dressed in the slickest kind of black broad-cloth, with a long frock-coat, and a white cravat. He had on a ruffled shirt, and a tall beaver hat, the color of the fur, and a pair of these here high boots, with his breeches strapped down under 'em." (7–8)

Side by side with the narrator's image of pastoral (albeit progressive) tranquility, Braile's scornful "Hoonch," Dylks's horselike "Hooff," Abel's low vernacular, and the emotionalism of evangelical revelation express harmlessly channeled, eccentric points of view. The cavorting, jerking, and bellowing of the camp meeting, rendered by Abel and undercut by Braile, harken back to the rough sketches of Southwest humor, while

Dylks's first appearance as a slick mysterious stranger con-
jures up visions of traditional confidence men like Longstreet's Yellow Blossom, Melville's Cosmopolitan, and Twain's
king and duke. Howells blends literary and historical elements to recreate the flush times.

The community's intensity of emotion—released in the
camp meeting and visible, though repressed, in the Brailes'
grief over their son's death—makes them susceptible to manipulation. Dylks's preaching at the temple dramatizes their
vulnerability to a confidence man who appeals to their hunger
for salvation.

> He gave out a passage of scripture, as a sort of text, but he did
> not keep to it; he followed with other passages, and his dis-
> course was a rehearsal of these rather than a sermon. His
> memory in them was unerring; women who knew their Bibles
> by heart, sighed their satisfaction in his perfectness; they did
> not care for the relevance or irrelevance of the passages; all
> was scripture, all was the one inseparable Word of God, dread-
> ful, blissful, divine, promising heaven, threatening hell.
> Groans began to go up from the people held in the strong
> witchery of the man's voice. They did not know whether he
> spoke long or not. (21)

The uncritical ones emotionally approve Dylks's stylistic
"perfectness" without examining its intention; their ecstasy
of faith denies the validity of all but self-fulfilling visionary
claims. Isolated from the rest of the community by their desire
for immediate consolation, they lose the ability to discriminate rationally between sincere religious faith and fanatical
frenzy, surrendering volition to the confidence man's "strong
witchery." Matthew Braile ridicules his neighbors' excesses
and trances, while Dylks's slick Bible-quoting act and Abel
Reverdy's wide-eyed account of the "curious doin's" implicitly criticize those who would mistake this confidence game
for the humorous tricks of Simon Suggs or Sut Lovingood.
Initially presented in comic terms, Dylks is suddenly characterized by his symbolic apposition with a bat (19), while his
evil nature is fully disclosed in his conversation with David
Gillespie.

> "Listen here, Joseph Dylks! I know what you're after here be-
> cause you always was: other people's money. I've got some

money; I've got three hundred dollars saved up since I paid off
the mortgage. If you'll take it and go"—
       "Three hundred dollars! No, no! Keep your money, old
man. . . . I work my work. . . . I come from God."
       Gillespie looked at him as he paced back and forth. "If I
didn't know you for the common scoundrel that married my
sister against my will, and lived on her money till it was gone,
and then left her and let her believe he was dead, I might believe you *did* come from God—or the Devil, you—you turkey
cock, you—stallion!" (26–27)

Having previously taken advantage of Nancy Gillespie, Dylks
seems suddenly to combine the most threatening aspects of
two conventional literary types—the confidence man and the
sentimental villain. As Howells portrays him, Dylks is at once
a smooth-talking betrayer, an animal shouting his horselike
"Hooff," and an avatar of the Arch-Deceiver himself. He succeeds, Howells's narrator concludes, because

in that day of remoteness from any greater world the people of
the backwoods longed to feel themselves near the greatest
World of all, and well within the radius of its mysteries. They
talked mostly of these when they met together, and in the
solitude of their fields they dwelt upon them; on their weekdays and workdays they turned over the threats and promises
of the Sabbath and expected a light or a voice from on high
which should burst their darkness and silence. (41)

This constant hunger for earthly proof of a providential design, a natural response to the uncertainties of backwoods life,
leaves the people of Leatherwood open to exploitation. Peter
Hingston, a wealthy widower, finds comfort in his new role as
a saint; the brothers and sisters of Dylks's Little Flock discover
new joy in the belief that they will never die; even Matthew
Braile, who calls the Leatherwood God a "rascal," admits a
similar yearning, keeps a coon given him by a boy who reminds him of his dead son, and wields his irony like a club
against the inevitable. Using a repetitive, highly allusive language, Dylks tempts the community by appealing to the longing for ultimate certainty, offering an everlasting life of luxu-
rious ease, all the rewards of heaven with none of its sacrifices;
all this he pledges to "the faithful," beguiling the Little Flock
into a corrupt, a self-centered false hope and a violent, self-
righteous faith: "They accepted the differences which parted

husband, wife, parent and child, and set strife between brothers and neighbors as proof of his divine authority to bring a sword; they knew by the hate and dissension which followed from his claim that it was of supernatural force" (52). The threat of this confidence man is greater by far than that posed by his literary kinsmen, for he appeals to the most natural and best impulses of good people in such a gradual fashion, inflaming their hopes and fears, that his ascension from teacher to prophet to God Almighty seems reasonable. Why not expect a new covenant in a new country? Why not a nineteenth-century revelation in the Promised Land? Why not the New Jerusalem in Leatherwood, Ohio?

Dylks rhetorically fulfills the implicit American dream of rebirth without death and wealth without work, yet at the novel's structural center he attempts empirically to convince the community of his divinity by publicly performing a miracle. From his apparent failure to create a seamless raiment, *The Leatherwood God* pivots to conclusion: Jim Redfield tears out a patch of Dylks's hair, proving that his "prophecies of doom to those who should lay hands upon him had been falsified" (97). Jane Gillespie—representative of many believers—is wooed from her confidence in Dylks by this evidence that his claims are merely rhetorical, inflated to the level of unassailable truths by her own religious and sexual desire. Having lost his aura of supernatural authority, the confidence man is arraigned before and acquitted by Matthew Braile, the justice of the peace, and, in a continuing parody of Christ's trials, Dylks escapes to wander in the wilderness.

Howells's omniscient narrator records Dylks's thoughts to expose the confidence man's fraudulence to the reader.

> The place where the hair had been torn from his head burned like fire; it burned like the wound of a man whom he had once heard tell how it felt to be scalped by an Indian . . . and Dylks pitied himself that it should be so with him, and cursed himself for his unguarded boast that any one who touched a hair of his head should perish. He promised that if God would show him a little mercy, and send a raven with something for him to eat, something warm, or send him a cup of coffee, somehow, or even a raw egg, he would go forth before the people, get up in the Temple amidst his believers and declare himself a false prophet and a false god. (109)

Dylks's similar confessions of confusion to Nancy Gillespie (110–14) and Matthew Braile (116–21) emphasize his impotence; as Haskell Springer points out, this narrative technique of repetition "purges . . . even the slightest suggestion of supernatural agency in connection with Dylks."[3] The failure of the Leatherwood God to live up to his promotion, however revealing of his confidence game to the reader, has less effect upon the Little Flock, who as Dylks admits would rather martyr him than renounce their consoling new faith (114, 116–17). This obsession is quite different from the passion for money, revenge, or sport characteristic of the gulls of conventional literary con men: to his victims, Capt. Simon Suggs swears, "I'll be d——d if you'll forget me," implying an ironic, belated revelation of his snaps; although Howells adumbrates the conventional appearance of Dylks's pose—one that places him in the company of Simon Suggs, the Cosmopolitan, Sut Lovingood, and the king and duke—Howells stresses, as does Taneyhill, that the survivors of the Little Flock as late as 1870 persist in mistaking Dylks's empty rhetoric for divine truth. This blindness is a permanent affliction and seems especially horrifying because self-inflicted; they ante up their faith and lose not dollars or pride but (in conventional Christian terms) the hope of ever discovering divine truth.

The members of the Little Flock are not the only ones who are self-deceived. Howells explores the confidence man's inner drama, concerned equally with his psychology and the mechanics of his game, and reveals that Dylks is himself cut off from other men and from God; he confesses his shaky confidence in his divinity to Matthew Braile, yet as the squire makes clear, this confidence man cannot even claim the distinction of originality.

> "Why, you poor devil, you're not in any unusual fix. It must have been so with all the impostors in the world, from Mahomet up and down! . . . That's the way it's always gone: first the liar tells his lie, and some of the fools believe it, and proselyte the other fools, and when there are enough of them, their faith begins to work on the liar's own unbelief, till he takes his lie for the truth. . . . Why, you poor bag of shorts!" he said, "I could almost feel sorry for you, in spite of the mischief you've made. Why, *you* oughtn't to be sent to the penitentiary, or even lynched. *You* ought to be put amongst the county idiots in the poorhouse." (118–19)

Braile's recognition that the Leatherwood God deserves pity marks a new variation of the American confidence man as a literary convention; Dylks is the victim of the very forces he employs to win and betray the confidence of others. Although Mark Twain suggested this characteristic of the con man in Huck Finn's sympathy for the tarred and feathered king and duke (a punishment considered for Dylks), it is Howells who expounds upon his pathetic self-delusion; unlike Colonel Sellers and Captain Suggs, Joseph Dylks has no comic resilience.

Howells surveys the development of nineteenth-century America using the historical confidence man, Joseph C. Dylks, to focus his fictional examination of the progressive dangers of frontier self-reliance, millenarianism, evangelicism, and sentimental piety. In *The Leatherwood God* he charts a growing awareness that the confidence man's drama is not comedy but tragedy: Dylks begins as a snorting, Southwest humorist's sharper; becomes a smooth-talking, serious threat to the social order; suffers exposure and is variously hated, pitied, and still believed; and, taking his confidence game "Over the Mountains," survives his death-by-drowning to become a local legend. These four stages may serve as an abbreviated history of the confidence-man convention, sketching not only what Howells calls the "psychological evolution" of Joseph Dylks but also the evolution of the convention's form and function in nineteenth-century American fiction. In addition, these stages act as a condensed review of nineteenth-century frontier history. What is striking is that they form a consistent pattern of confidence given, confidence betrayed, and confidence nonetheless reaffirmed. Howells locates his novel in the 1820s, grounds it in historical events, because he perceives that period to be fundamental to an understanding of American optimism. The flush times gave rise to an intense individual and collective faith in the opportunities of the new country. The New Eden appeared in 1828 to be immediately and personally realizable because the frontier wilderness was rapidly giving way to farms, because a democratic society had been successfully established, and because it seemed that nothing was beyond the abilities of the American determined to achieve his dream.

Yet Howells also perceived—as Taneyhill perceived in 1870—that the nineteenth century was a period of betrayal, during which many Americans chose slavery over democracy, sectionalism over nationalism, materialism over millenari- anism, and illusion over reality. To Howells this created a pat- tern of betrayal repeated again and again in the nineteenth century. It is to Howells's credit that he understood this be- trayal to be self-inflicted and insidiously tenacious: Joseph Dylks and the people of Leatherwood betray themselves, be- tray their dream, and nevertheless insist on the reality of their vision. Howells suggests that this insistence is the root of American optimism and that the myth of the realized—or realizable—American Eden, like that of Joseph Dylks, is still potent and dangerous in 1916. Its power Howells locates in the historical and imaginative development of the new country; its danger lies in its tendency to seduce Americans from an often hard reality to a comfortable, self-righteous, self- congratulatory illusion.

The ultimate proof of the persistence of American opti- mism may be found in the conclusion of *The Leatherwood God*. For although Matthew Braile notes the burned, aban- doned temple (155), the closed hotel (152), and the decimating fever (158), symbols of Leatherwood's religious, social, and physical decay, Howells bows to the dictates of nineteenth- century sentimentalism, concluding his novel with the opti- mistic assertions that Joey Dylks-Billings has grown up to be the "best man" in Leatherwood, that Jim Redfield and Jane Gillespie are blessed with children, that the Reverdys, like the Brailes, survive with their good humor and love intact, and that the confidence man is ultimately a curious—but none- theless harmless—"superstition" (159). In fact, despite How- ells's recognition that the confidence man is a symptom of diseased American optimism, he chooses narratively to deny it, asserting lamely a belief in the power of domestic virtues, in the myths that every reasonable American can discover the truth and that the destiny of America is determined by provi- dential design. Calling *The Leatherwood God* a "romance," a contemporary review in the *Boston Evening Transcript* states wryly that it "sets all [Howells's] pet theories to naught, and it proves how impossible it is for any man, no matter how strong he may be in the faith, to practice always what he preaches."[4] Or it may be that Howells adheres to a larger pattern of American history characteristic of 1828, 1870, and 1916, a persistent assertion of faith in the confident new country; for as the novel reveals the historical dangers of delusion, it also insists on both literary and cultural optimism.

Epilogue

The American confidence man is a product of the 1840s, the boom-and-bust flush times, and the ambiguous and shifty new country. In less than one hundred years the confidence man appears on the southwestern frontier, rises to prominence as a symbol of the new country, becomes aligned with the archetypal trickster, falls victim to the Civil War, reappears amid the boosterism of the Gilded Age, and disappears into the twentieth century.

The popularity of confidence-man fiction, of the term as a name for historical criminals, and of P. T. Barnum's soft sells suggests a fundamental American habit of mind. The interaction between popular literature and popular culture in the nineteenth century engendered the corresponding literary and cultural conventions known as the *confidence man* to express a basic perception of the new country. Simon Suggs and P. T. Barnum both exploit the hunger for confidence in the self and the suspicion of duplicity in others. The form itself, the conventional nature of the confidence man, offers a familiar model of response: the reader of *Simon Suggs* knows that the tales are fictions, self-contained snaps of foolish and greedy men; he laughs at their greed, their blindness, and Simon's skillful manipulations, enjoying from a safe distance his own feelings of superiority. The viewer of the Feejee Mermaid likewise willingly enters the familiar structure of the curio museum to savor his knowledge of Barnum's artistic manipulation of the gullible. The formal limits of each as a fiction make the potentially disturbing encounter with a confidence man safely amusing.[5] The threat to the self is only a mock-threat; like the dangers suffered by heroes and heroines of sentimental fiction, the threat merely heightens the reader's or viewer's pleasure, for the form assures him from the start that all will end well.

Evert A. Duyckinck quotes with approval in 1849 a description of a historical confidence man in the *Merchants' Ledger* that discovers a reassuring optimism in duplicity.

> That one poor swindler, like the one under arrest, should have been able to drive so considerable a trade on an appeal to so simple a quality as the confidence of man in man, shows that all virtue and humanity of nature is not entirely extinct in the nineteenth century. It is a good thing, and speaks well for human nature, that, at this late day, in spite of all the hardening of civilization and all the warning of newspapers, men *can be swindled.*[6]

To name a particular kind of criminal a confidence man is enough; the confidence man as a cultural convention seems fixed, a term that purports to explain but does not explore specific forms of dishonesty. As a cultural convention it retains even today an assumed meaning that licenses the use of the term *confidence man* to describe, delimit, and dismiss discrete species of historical and fictional tricksters. As a literary convention, however, the confidence man leads a more focused life, the newly imagined tensions producing the need for further speculation and new fictions. Whether the predisposition of Americans toward confidence men is a result of the Puritan distrust of appearances and habit of introspective analysis or a natural response to the scope and scale of the new country itself, the confidence man must be recognized as a coherent literary expression of conflicting, deeply felt, nineteenth-century attitudes.

The twentieth century marks an end to the confidence man as a distinct literary convention. Inextricably tied to the new country, the confidence man vanishes along with this imaginative frontier. The exact date of these disappearances is of course impossible to determine with confidence, but one is tempted to speculate. The completion of the four geological and geographical United States surveys of the West, 1867–1879, certainly had the power to transform the unknown into the familiar, just as the defeats of chiefs Crazy Horse and Sitting Bull in 1876 symbolically opened the West for safe settlement. 1876 further offers itself as the United States Centennial, an obvious benchmark for the numerically minded. The last great land rush occurred in Oklahoma in 1889, which gains credence as an apt date in light of the bulletin issued by the superintendent of the census for 1890: "Up to and including 1880 the country had a frontier of settlement, but at present the unsettled area has been so broken into by isolated bodies of settlement that there can hardly be said to be a frontier line. In the discussion of its extent, its westward movement, etc., it can not, therefore, any longer have a place in the census reports."[7] The year 1893 marks not only the opening of the Chicago World's Columbian Exposition and the beginning of a national panic but also Frederick Jackson Turner's delivery of his famous analysis, "The Significance of the Frontier in American History," to the American Historical Association. Turner's concluding statement speaks for itself.

> Since the days when the fleet of Columbus sailed into the waters of the New World, America has been another name for opportunity, and the people of the United States have taken their tone from the incessant expansion which has not only been open but has even been forced upon them. . . . For a moment, at the frontier, the bonds of custom are broken and unrestraint is triumphant. There is not *tabula rasa* . . . and yet, in spite of environment, and in spite of custom, each frontier did indeed furnish a new field of opportunity, a gate of escape from the bondage of the past; and freshness, and confidence. . . . And now, four centuries from the discovery of America, at the end of a hundred years of life under the Constitution, the frontier has gone, and with its going has closed the first period of American history.[8]

The 1920 census revealed that for the first time in history the urban population exceeded the rural population, while the stock market crash of 1929 surely put an end to many dreams. The Spanish-American War (1898–1899) proclaimed the entrance of the United States into global politics, and in retrospect sharply contrasts with the disillusioning world wars of the twentieth century. The years 1917 and 1941 record major passages in the death of American innocence.

The twentieth century registers the death of both the new country and the confidence man. Some of the best American fiction is peopled by tenuous survivors inhabiting an anti-Eden of unconfidence. Hemingway's Nick Adams returns to the American West, himself a battered archetype, only to discover that the new country, Nature itself, has been charred, corrupted, its redemptive powers radically reduced. The resilience characteristic of the new country, the confidence man, and the nineteenth century has disappeared, the regenerative American humor has been replaced by the unconscious security of habit, and the sense of limitless personal possibility celebrated by Turner has been constrained by the impersonal forces Henry Adams perceived as early as 1904.[9] Confidence—in America as new country or in the self—seems in short supply. When a recognizable confidence man appears, such as Pat Stamper in William Faulkner's *The Hamlet* (1940), he functions as a nostalgic device signaling the end of the new country, of humorous horse swaps, and of a coherently ordered nineteenth-century world, and the advent of modern America, of humorless business deals, and of an increasingly disordered twentieth century. Snopesism makes explicit the implications of shiftiness adumbrated in Brackenridge's Kickapoo impostor, in Hooper's Bela Bugg, and in Twain's Senator Dilworthy; to quote Brackenridge, "These things are now reduced to a system."[10] Flem Snopes and his clan form a vast, nearly faceless, emotionless machine that dispassionately victimizes everyone in Frenchman's Bend. The point of view is external to Flem, for Faulkner perceives this confidence man as an indecipherable mystery symbolic of cosmic chaos. In a new country rapidly becoming a shadow of its former size and power, cut up and sold and forgotten, the psychological maneuvers of a shifty operator recede from prominence, replaced by the drama of his normative victims. Flem appears less a conscious confidence man than a tool or emblem of the impersonal forces that are systematically destroying the new country.

F. Scott Fitzgerald reveals another modern version of the confidence man in *The Great Gatsby* (1925), a dealer in liquor and fixes who creates a new identity out of whole cloth. Yet Jay Gatsby is tied—as few nineteenth-century confidence men are—to numerous partners and business associates; as Poe noted in 1843 of a diddler, "Should he ever be tempted into magnificent speculation, he then, at once, loses his distinctive features, and becomes what we term 'financier.'"[11] Gatsby is in Poe's terms related more to Theodore Dreiser's Cowperwood, Drouet, and Sister Carrie, and suggests the impossibility of confident, successful, humorous snaps in twentieth-century America. Furthermore, Gatsby is, like Dreiser's characters, like Sinclair Lewis's Elmer Gantry, like Nathanael West's Miss Lonelyhearts and so many modern manipulators, a victim of his own unrealizable visions—visions that are essentially those of a vanished new country. Gatsby and his compatriots come to be pathetic figures like Howells's Joseph Dylks, self-deluded and self-betrayed, or seem to be pitiful victims betrayed by a vision of the new country that retains only the power to delude rather than to fulfill. Fitzgerald's Nick Carraway identifies Gatsby's betrayal with the land itself and with the process of historical change.

> And as the moon rose higher the inessential houses began to melt away until gradually I became aware of the old island here that flowered once for Dutch sailors' eyes—a fresh, green breast of the new world. Its vanished trees, the trees that had made way for Gatsby's house, had once pandered in whispers to the last and greatest of all human dreams; for a transitory enchanted moment man must have held his breath in the presence of this continent, compelled into an aesthetic contemplation he neither understood nor desired, face to face for the last time in history with something commensurate to his capacity for wonder.[12]

The point of view, which is initially external to Gatsby's psychology, becomes internal and aligns itself with Gatsby's vision in unconscious empathy. Nick sees the new country as Gatsby saw it, as the Dutch sailors saw it, an icon promising fulfillment of "all human dreams." As Leo Marx contends, "Here, for the first time, Nick locates the origin of that strange compound of sentiment and criminal aggressiveness in Gatsby. . . . It also represents the curious state of the modern American consciousness. It reveals that Gatsby's uncommon 'gift for hope' was born in that transitory, enchanted moment when Europeans first came into the presence of the 'fresh, green breast of the new world.'"[13] Nick—and the reader—discovers that the new country continues into the modern world only as a nostalgic motive force. Gatsby has become the victim not of a positive or ambiguous new country (as had been the case in much nineteenth-century fiction), but of a negative, pandering new country, which in Fitzgerald's deliberately historical context seems to have been all along the predator or confidence man in a cosmic game with man. At the moment

Gatsby freely places confidence in his dream, he loses control over his fate and consigns himself to betrayal and death.

In "Sincerity and Authenticity" Lionel Trilling proposes that "the hypocrite-villain, the conscious dissembler, has become marginal, even alien, to the modern imagination of the moral life."[14] Susan Kuhlmann maintains that the twentieth-century individual "is pointedly denied the full and reliable knowledge of life that is the *sine qua non* of the confidence man."[15] Although shifty characters are no strangers to modern American fiction, Trilling and Kuhlmann are correct in arguing that these manipulators share little of the form and function of conventional nineteenth-century confidence men. When twentieth-century versions of the confidence man appear (for other than nostalgic or purely historical purposes), they usually don one of three often-overlapping guises: They may be secondary characters whose main function is to reveal the helplessness and alienation of the protagonist as victim.[16] Alternately, they may appear as self-deluded manipulators who fall prey either to the social forms they initially juggle or to their unfounded confidence in their control over their own destinies.[17] Last, shifty characters may act as symbols of the forces of universal disorder, victimization, and betrayal that seem representative of the modern age.[18]

Each appearance reveals the reduced status of the confidence man as a distinct, central literary convention. To function as successful protagonist the confidence man requires not only knowledge, as Kuhlmann contends, but also a society fluid enough to penetrate and yet stable enough to evince shared ideals, normative values, and predictable social roles. Captain Simon Suggs can masquerade as General Witherspoon because he can anticipate and imitate how a general would act in a society that reveres pig-driving military men. One of the ironies of the nineteenth-century new country is that though it encouraged individuals to create new identities, as Henry Adams noted, "individuals were important chiefly as types."[19] The relevant characteristic of types is their function as conventional labels of identity; though convenient to social intercourse, these labels are masks of individual identity and can be assumed or dropped for positive or negative, social or antisocial purposes: like Simon Suggs, Mark Twain's king and duke sail under various false colors and succeed because the broad outlines of types are easy to imitate. Huck Finn, likewise, can become George Jackson, and Jim can be disguised as a sick Arab; the reader may see one pair of impostors as positive and one as negative, yet Twain insists that both pairs draw their ability to masquerade and the naturalness of masquerade from the same source: a society in flux that categorizes individuals as types. Given this state of affairs, American society in *Huckleberry Finn* opens itself to fraud and defrauds individuals of identity.

In much twentieth-century American fiction, the norm is often the bizarre or the abnormal, and individuals do not appear to fit conventional preconceptions of behavior and motivation. The modern norm seems suddenly to have become the world at war, as in Joseph Heller's *Catch-22* (1961), Kurt Vonnegut's *Slaughterhouse-Five* (1969), and Thomas Pynchon's *Gravity's Rainbow* (1973); or, the world seems to be an absurd theater in which identity itself is nearly impossible to maintain, as in William Gaddis's *The Recognitions* (1955), Thomas Pynchon's *V.* (1963), or Gilbert Sorrentino's *Mulligan Stew* (1979). These norms, like the categories into which modern confidence men fall, are not discrete but overlapping and interpenetrating, as evidenced by such works as Norman Mailer's *The Naked and the Dead* (1948) and Ralph Ellison's *Invisible Man* (1952). The fictional worlds created by twentieth-century American writers differ markedly in several respects from those nineteenth-century worlds of Hooper, Melville, and Twain from which they appear to evolve. First, Hooper's *Simon Suggs* is a closed, comic world that consciously and precisely limits the reader's involvement by positioning him outside the action and distancing him by language from direct involvement. Modern fictions insist that their worlds, governed by their norms, are at the least open to the reader's world; the function of history in *V.* is to suggest a correlation between that fictional world and the reader's, thereby mounting a substantial noncomic threat to the reader. In one sense the reader's point of view is assimilated into the fiction, becomes internal rather than external. Or, the fictional world appears so authentic in detail and event that the reader mistakes it for reality, or begins to suspect that his previous conceptions of reality are not as true as this fictional rendering; or perhaps the reader finds in this fiction an order and coherence (albeit traditional disorder) he instinctively craves and finds missing from his own. The absurd, the bizarre, and the abnormal begin to seem the norm in the wake of World Wars I and II, the Holocaust, Hiroshima and Nagasaki, and wars that are not wars. At this point we have entered what R. W. B. Lewis calls the apocalyptic era, "Days of Wrath and Laughter";[20] the reader senses that reality is becoming fictional, that his world may have already been transformed into the world of *V.*

Identity in the twentieth century is no longer, as it was in the nineteenth century, the stable, demonstrable bastion of individual consciousness. As Max F. Schulz concludes, "In the twentieth century the self as definable entity has vanished in the ironic acceptance of a world without metaphysical center, one fragmented into multiple realities."[21] In Pynchon's *V.* Benny Profane wants desperately to conform to a comic type, the schlemiel, to give himself a sense of identity; Herbert Stencil has only the blurred traces of identity bequeathed him by his father, Sidney; V. herself appears the identityless embodiment of the inhuman; Pig Bodine repeatedly breaks the obvious stereotype through charitable deeds of friendship or by discussing Sartre's notion that modern man impersonates identity; and even nineteenth-century myths and fictions lose some of their integrity as Pynchon burlesques Davy Crockett's superhuman feats (Profane pissing out the sun) and Ahab's quest for Moby-Dick (Profane's hunt of albino alligators in New York sewers). Authentic, original, individual action has vanished. Allbee, the doppelgänger to the protagonist in Saul Bellow's *The Victim* (1947), sums up the modern view: "The day of succeeding by your own efforts is past. Now it's all blind movement, vast movement, and the individual is shuttled back and forth."[22]

As modern fictional characters confront a norm that has no respect for individual identity and that threatens to destroy the self altogether, the confidence man as a convention loses his particular advantage and recedes from prominence. The confidence man, who prides himself on an intimate knowledge of human nature in general and on his acute awareness of individuals and types in particular, cannot adapt to an absurd, disordered, impersonal modern world; to operate effectively himself—and to serve as a useful fictional device—he requires confidence in social forms, confidence in his perception and imitation of specific types of individuals, and confidence in others' recognition of the individual roles he counterfeits. Even if collective reality in the Gilded Age came to seem a systematic confidence game, as Gary Lindberg argues,[23] in the nineteenth century there were still discoverable, consistent rules by which individuals could play or refuse to play: this is the state of affairs, after all, on board Melville's *Fidèle*. If a character is baffled by or suspects the Cosmopolitan, he can retreat and disengage himself from that emblem of temporary ambiguity. But when identity, motives, and behavior are apparently random, without predictable order or discoverable purpose, when as in Barth's *End of the Road* Jacob Horner has lost faith in the Cartesian technique of self-authentication, our best writers then envision the individual not as a confidence man but as his victim, a tenuously surviving heir to what Richard B. Hauck terms "A Heritage of Corpses."[24] Without control over his own destiny and without the confidence necessary to manipulate others, the victim-as-Everyman suffers the universal kick of a cosmic foot. At best, the victim may be Pynchon's Oedipa Maas, awaiting revelation of order, disorder, or cabal at the end of *The Crying of Lot 49* (1966), or Thomas Berger's Reinhart, searching for an integration of identity as he stumbles through the rubble of Western civilization in *Crazy in Berlin* (1958); at worst, he is Mailer's initiated, disillusioned DJ in *Why Are We in Vietnam?* (1967), or West's Lemuel Pitkin, betrayed, dismembered, and destroyed while seeking the American Dream in *A Cool Million* (1936). As Ihab Hassan concludes, the individual has become "The Victim with a Thousand Faces":

> The World, in our time, seems to have either vanished or become a rigid and intractable mass. The anarchy of nihilism and the terror of statism delimit the extremes between which there seem to be no viable mean. Mediation between Self and World appears no longer possible—there is only surrender or recoil.[25]

In contrast to nineteenth-century fictions, which may reward surrender with riches or alternately punish surrender with a coat of tar-and-feathers, twentieth-century fictions most often equate surrender with death. Laughter—and there is undeniably much laughter—is no longer a pleasurable response to incongruity or shiftiness shared by writer, reader, and character, but has become the near-hysterical response of writer, reader, and character to a perception of their common fate as butts of a humorless joke. The reader is forced to recognize an all-too-accurate image of himself in Pynchon's SHROUD or in the maddened victims of "Dr. Know-All Pierce-All" in West's *Day of the Locust*. Recoiling in shock, the reader joins West's Tod Hackett in laughing and noisemaking, an admission that he is trapped like Poe's victims in a nightmare of individual disintegration, the victim of a modern humor not of profit but of loss.

This shift completes the formal possibilities of the confidence man as a literary convention; to envision the victim as fictional protagonist marks a return to the broad picaresque tradition of *Don Quixote, Roderick Random, Arthur Mervyn,* and *Modern Chivalry*. The American confidence man appears and disappears in the nineteenth century. Yet he will always profit from fast talk, delight in flush times, and insist on confidence in a shifty country that for him—and for us as we read—continually becomes new.

APPENDIX

The Confidence Man in Nineteenth-Century America

Below are given some nineteenth-century avatars of the confidence man, including related texts, tracts, events, and commentaries.

1801 – Sarah Wood, *Dorval; or, the Speculator.*

1803 – The character "Jeremy Diddler" appears in John Kenney's English farce, "Raising the Wind."

1805 – *The Gamesters; or, Ruins of Innocence. An Original Novel Founded in Truth.* By Caroline Matilda Warren.

1808 – Mason Locke Weems, *Life of George Washington With Curious Anecdotes, Equally Honourable to Himself and Exemplary to His Young Countrymen,* "6th edition" (contains the fanciful story of the cherry tree).

1809 – "A Miserable Prejudice—Yankee Tricks," in the *Port Folio* (December), by Matthew Carey.

1812 – Mason Locke Weems, *God's Revenge Against Gambling, Exemplified in the Miserable Lives and Untimely Deaths of Persons of Both Sexes, Who Had Sacrificed their Health, Wealth, and Honor at Gambling Tables,* 2d ed.

1815 – Hugh Henry Brackenridge, *Modern Chivalry* (first collected ed., 4 vols.)

1818 – Mason Locke Weems, *The Drunkard's Looking Glass* (contains the "Awful History of Young Dred Drake"), "6th edition."

1819 – Washington Irving, "The Legend of Sleepy Hollow."

1824 – James Nelson Barker, the tragedy "Superstition."

1826 – The *Confession* of Jereboam O. Beauchamp, an account of "the Kentucky Tragedy." (See Charles Fenno Hoffman, *A Winter in the West* (1835), 2:332–43.)

1828 – The advent of Joseph C. Dylks in Leatherwood, Ohio. (See Richard H. Taneyhill, *The Leatherwood God (1869–1870) in Two Versions,* and William Dean Howells, *The Leatherwood God* (1916)).

1829 – James Kirk Paulding, "The Yankee Roué."

1830 – Seba Smith begins the "Jack Downing" letters in the *Portland Courier.*

1831 – John Neal, "The Yankee Peddler."

1832 – James Hall, "Harpe's Head" and "The Seventh Son."

1833 – Augustus Baldwin Longstreet begins publishing several "Georgia Scenes" in the *State Rights Sentinel.*

— Seba Smith, *The Life and Writings of Major Jack Downing of Downingville, Away Down East in the State of Maine.*

1834 – Asa Green, *The Perils of Pearl Street; including a Taste of the Dangers of Wall Street, by a Late Merchant.*
     – Exhibition of Maezael's automatons in New York.
     – *Narrative of the Life of David Crockett of the State of Tennessee, Written by Himself.*
     – Henry Junius Nott, "Thomas Singularity" and "The Counterfeiters."
     – *American Protestant Vindicator* warns of Jesuit missionaries masquerading as puppeteers and showmen (24 December).
1835 – Augustus Baldwin Longstreet, *Georgia Scenes, Characters, Incidents, &c., in the First Half Century of the Republic.*
     – Moon Hoax. In the New York *Sun* Richard Adams Locke reported the discovery of men and animals on the moon by Sir John Herschel.
1837 – Robert Montgomery Bird, *Nick of the Woods, or the Jibbenainosay.*
     – Thomas Chandler Haliburton, *The Clockmaker; or, the Sayings and Doings of Samuel Slick.*
1838 – *Humbugs of New-York: Being a Remonstrance Against Popular Delusion; Whether in Science, Philosophy, or Religion. By David Meredith Reese, M.D.*
1839 – George Pope Morris, *The Little Frenchman and His Water Lots.*
1841 – Samuel G. Goodrich, "The Peddler."
1842 – P. T. Barnum, the Feejee Mermaid hoax.
1843 – Edgar Allan Poe, "Diddling Considered As One Of The Exact Sciences."
     – William Tappan Thompson, *Major Jones's Courtship.*
1844 – Charles Dickens, *The Life and Adventures of Martin Chuzzlewit.*
     – Johnson Jones Hooper begins Simon Suggs tales in *East Alabamian.*
     – George Lippard, *The Monks of Monk Hall.*
1845 – Johnson Jones Hooper, *Some Adventures of Captain Simon Suggs, Late of the Tallapoosa Volunteers.*
     – E. Z. C. Judson begins publishing *Ned Buntline's Own.*
     – William T. Porter, editor, *The Big Bear of Arkansas and Other Sketches* (including tales by Hooper, Robb, Smith, etc.).
     – William Gilmore Simms, "The Last Wager, or the Gamester of the Mississippi."
1846 – John S. Robb, *Streaks from Squatter Life, and Far-West Scenes . . . by "Solitaire."*
1847 – Joseph M. Field, *The Drama in Pokerville.*
     – William T. Porter, editor, *A Quarter Race in Kentucky, and Other Sketches* (including tales by Harris, Lewis, January, etc.).

- John S. Robb, "'Doing' a Sheriff."
1849 – The Gold Rush begins.
     – The term *confidence man* appears in articles in the *New York Herald* (8 July) and the *Literary World* (18 August).
1850 – Henry Clay Lewis ("Madison Tensas"), *The Louisiana Swamp Doctor.*
1851 – Thomas A. Burke, *Polly Peablossom's Wedding* (including tales by Hooper, Robb, Lane, etc.).
1853 – Joseph Glover Baldwin, *Flush Times of Alabama and Mississippi.*
1854 – George Washington Harris begins publishing Sut Lovingood tales in William T. Porter's *Spirit of the Times.*
1855 – P. T. Barnum, *The Life of P. T. Barnum.*
1856 – C. F. Briggs, "Elegant Tom Dillar."
     – Augustus W. Loomis, *Learn to Say No; or, the City Apprentice.*
1857 – *Gambling Exposed. A Full Exposition of All the Various Arts, Mysteries, and Miseries of Gambling. By the "Reformed Gambler,"* Jonathan H. Green.
     – Herman Melville, *The Confidence-Man: His Masquerade.*
1858 – William E. Burton, *The Cyclopaedia of Wit and Humor.* 2 vols.
1862 – Richard B. Kimball, *Undercurrents of Wall Street. A Romance of Business.*
1864 – S. Emma E. Edmonds, *The Female Spy of the Union Army.*
     – Richard M. Johnston, *Georgia Sketches.*
1865 – Kittrell J. Warren, *Life and Public Services of an Army Straggler.*
1867 – Horatio Alger, *Ragged Dick.*
     – Henry Ward Beecher, *Norwood; or, Village Life in New-England.*
     – George Washington Harris, *Sut Lovingood's Yarns* (collected ed.).
1871 – Henry Clay Lewis, *The Swamp Doctor's Adventures in the South-West,* and John S. Robb, *Streaks of Squatter Life, and Far-West Scenes* (republished in one volume by T. B. Peterson).
     – Walt Whitman, *Democratic Vistas.*
1872 – The Great Diamond Hoax.
1873 – Samuel Langhorne Clemens and Charles Dudley Warner, *The Gilded Age: A Tale of To-Day.*
1875 – Henry Brooks Adams, *Democracy: An American Novel.*
     – Joel Chandler Harris, *Uncle Remus, His Songs and His Sayings.*
1882 – Henry Watterson, editor, *Oddities of Southern Life and Character* (including selections from *Georgia Scenes, Simon Suggs, Flush Times,* etc.).

1884,– Samuel Langhorne Clemens, *Adventures of Huckleberry*
1885   *Finn*.
1887 – George H. Devol, *Forty Years a Gambler on the Mississippi*.
1899 – Charles Chesnutt, *The Conjure Woman*.

NOTES

Chapter 1: The New Country

1. *New York Literary World*, 18 August 1849, 133. For a complete discussion of the confidence man's appearances in 1849, see Johannes Dietrich Bergmann, "The Original Confidence Man."

2. Review of Herman Melville's *The Confidence-Man: His Masquerade*, *Boston Evening Transcript*, 10 April 1857.

3. Herman Melville, *The Confidence-Man: His Masquerade*, ed. Hershel Parker, p. 28.

4. William C. Spengemann, *The Adventurous Muse: The Poetics of American Fiction, 1789–1900*, p. 6.

5. See Howard Mumford Jones, *O Strange New World—American Culture: The Formative Years*, pp. 7–8.

6. Wayne Franklin, *Discoverers, Explorers, Settlers: The Diligent Writers of Early America*, p. 191.

7. Quoted in ibid., p. 101. On promotion literature see ibid., pp. 87–103, and Jones, *O Strange New World*, pp. 179–93.

8. William Bradford, *Of Plymouth Plantation: 1620–1647*, ed. Samuel Eliot Morison, p. 76. Subsequent references will be to this edition and will be cited parenthetically in the text as *OPP*.

9. Cotton Mather, *Magnalia Christi Americana: or, the Ecclesiastical History of New England*, pp. 537–51. Subsequent references will be to this edition and will be cited parenthetically in the text as *MCA*.

10. *Original Narratives of Early American History: Winthrop's Journal, "History of New England," 1630–1649*, ed. James Kendall Hosmer, 2:315–18.

11. *The Journal and Major Essays of John Woolman*, ed. Phillips P. Moulton, p. 53.

12. Quoted in Franklin, *Discoverers*, p. 55.

13. Quoted in Merle Curti, *Human Nature in American Thought: A History*, p. 26.

14. Quoted in ibid., pp. 28–29.

15. See Jones, *O Strange New World*, pp. 157–58.

16. See especially Milton M. Klein, "Corruption in Colonial America"; and Gary Lindberg, *The Confidence Man in American Literature*, pp. 117–18.

17. Benjamin Franklin, *The Autobiography of Benjamin Franklin*, ed. Leonard W. Larabee et al., pp. 167–68.

18. Richard B. Hauck, *A Cheerful Nihilism: Confidence and the Absurd in American Humorous Fiction*, pp. 64–65. See also Melville's characterization of Franklin as shifty in *Israel Potter* (1854–1855).

19. Daniel Hoffman, *Form and Fable in American Fiction*, p. 36. See the fine discussion of many American tricksters in chapter 3, "The American Hero: His Masquerade."

20. Constance Rourke, *American Humor: A Study of the National Character*, pp. 12–13. I am indebted throughout to this excellent study, especially to chapters 1 and 2.

21. Michel Guillaume St. Jean de Crèvecoeur, *called* J. Hector St. John de Crèvecoeur, *Letters from an American Farmer*, p. 43.

22. See Gary Wills's stimulating analyses throughout *Inventing America: Jefferson's Declaration of Independence*.

23. Daniel J. Boorstin, *The Americans: The National Experience*, p. 1.

24. Michael Kammen, *A Season of Youth: The American Revolution and the Historical Imagination*, p. 34. This rigorous, challenging work has obviously been of great use to me in Chapter 1.

25. See Hoffman, *Form and Fable*, pp. 93–96.

26. Henry Nash Smith, *Virgin Land: The American West as Symbol and Myth*, p. 19.

27. Crèvecoeur, *Letters*, p. 46ff.

28. Quoted in Smith, *Virgin Land*, pp. 42–43.

29. Edwin Fussell, *Frontier: American Literature and the American West*, p. 4.

30. See Ray Allen Billington, *America's Frontier Heritage*, p. 25.

31. On the myth of the "Great American Desert," see Smith, *Virgin Land*, chapter 16.

32. See Crèvecoeur, *Letters*, pp. 54–55.

33. Quoted in Lindberg, *Confidence Man*, p. 118.

34. Quoted in ibid., p. 94.

35. James Fenimore Cooper, *The Prairie: A Tale*, in *The Works of James Fenimore Cooper*, 5:1–3, 445–46. See also Crèvecoeur, *Letters*, pp. 46–56; the disparaging comments of Byrd and Woodmason quoted in Curti, *Human Nature*, pp. 34, 36; Flint's remarks in Lindberg, *Confidence Man*, p. 118; and Tocqueville's attack in Kammen, *Season of Youth*, pp. 3–4. "Harpe's Head," by James Hall, can be found in his *Legends of the West* (1832, 1853).

36. On the frontier as place and process see Billington, *America's Frontier Heritage*, p. 25 and passim; on the frontier as location and direction see Fussell, *Frontier*, p. 4.

37. Quoted in Boorstin, *The National Experience*, p. 239.

38. Quoted in Billington, *America's Frontier Heritage*, p. 59.

39. Quoted in ibid., p. 59.

40. Boorstin, *The National Experience*, p. 219.

41. Morris's story is collected in William E. Burton, ed., *Cyclopaedia of Wit and Humor*, pp. 152–54.

42. The important section of Kirkland's *Western Clearings* is reprinted in ibid., pp. 273–77.

43. Quoted in Boorstin, *The National Experience*, p. 162.

44. Quoted in Kammen, *Season of Youth*, pp. 3–4.

45. Quoted in Billington, *America's Frontier Heritage*, p. 27.

46. For a fine analysis of George Washington and Davy Crockett as paradoxical American symbols see Boorstin, *The National Experience*, pp. 327–56.

47. Ibid., p. 332.

48. Johnson Jones Hooper, *Some Adventures of Captain Simon Suggs, Late of the Tallapoosy Volunteers . . .* , p. 12.

49. Gary Lindberg kindly shared with me in 1977 a chapter outline of *The Confidence Man in American Literature*, from which I profited both consciously and unconsciously; most of my own work had been completed by the time his book reached me, thereby saving me from the temptation to modify my argument. Another fortunate late arrival was Karen Halttunen's *Confidence Men and Painted Women: A Study of Middle-Class Culture in America, 1830–1870*, especially chapters 1, 2, and the epilogue. See also Susan Kuhlmann, *Knave, Fool, and Genius: The Confidence Man As He Ap-

pears in Nineteenth-Century American Fiction; Richard B. Hauck, *A Cheerful Nihilism: Confidence and the Absurd in American Humorous Fiction*; Warwick Wadlington, *The Confidence Game in American Literature*; and John G. Blair, *The Confidence Man in Modern Fiction: A Rogue's Gallery with Six Portraits*. For other useful treatments of confidence men, confidence games, and related shifty figures, see Constance Rourke, *American Humor: A Study of National Character*; Kenneth S. Lynn, *Mark Twain and Southwestern Humor*; Victor M. Hoar, "The Confidence Man in American Literature"; Jesse Bier, *The Rise and Fall of American Humor*; and Walter Blair and Hamlin Hill, *America's Humor: From Poor Richard to Doonesbury*.

50. Hugh Henry Brackenridge, *Modern Chivalry*, ed. Claude M. Newlin, p. 502.

51. Quoted in Neil Harris, *Humbug: The Art of P. T. Barnum*, p. 54.

52. Quoted in ibid., pp. 55–56.

53. Ibid., pp. 230–31.

54. Quoted in ibid., pp. 70–71.

55. Ibid., p. 78.

56. Blair and Hill, *America's Humor*, pp. 50–52.

57. P. T. Barnum, *The Life of P. T. Barnum, Written by Himself*, p. 355.

58. Quoted in Harris, *Humbug*, p. 217.

59. Kuhlmann, *Knave, Fool, and Genius*, pp. 123–29.

60. Johan Huizinga, *Homo Ludens: A Study of the Play Element in Culture*, p. 10 and passim.

61. Ibid., pp. 10–11.

62. Melville, *The Confidence-Man*, p. 158.

Chapter 2: The Early Tradition of Confidence Games

1. See Wendy Martin, "The Rogue and the Rational Man: Hugh Henry Brackenridge's Study of a Con Man in *Modern Chivalry*."

2. Hugh Henry Brackenridge, *Modern Chivalry*, ed. Claude M. Newlin, p. 11. Subsequent references will be to this edition and will be cited parenthetically in the text.

3. See ibid., p. 3: "I shall consider language only, not in the least regarding the matter of the work."

4. *Pittsburgh Literary Examiner and Western Monthly Review*, June 1839.

5. William H. Gardiner, unsigned review of *The Spy* by James Fenimore Cooper.

6. "The Yankee Roué" is collected in Paulding's *Tales of the Good Woman. By a Doubtful Gentleman*.

7. Alexis de Tocqueville, *Democracy in America*, trans. Henry Reeve, ed. Henry Steele Commager, p. 279.

8. Gardiner, review of *The Spy*, pp. 257–58.

9. Roy Harvey Pearce, *Savagism and Civilization*, pp. 199–200. Both "The Indian Wife" and "The Frontier House" are collected in *The Legendary*, ed. N. P. Willis; "The Backwoodsman" appears in Hall's *Legends of the West*. See also the persuasive study by Richard Slotkin, *Regeneration Through Violence: The Mythology of the American Frontier, 1600–1860*.

10. Andrew Lang, as quoted in Walter Blair, *Native American Humor*, p. 70.

11. *A Dictionary of Americanisms on Historical Principles*, ed. Mitford M. Mathews (Chicago: University of Chicago Press, 1951), attributes the first use of the phrase, "half man, half horse, and half alligator," to Washington Irving,

History of New York: "It is for similar reasons that the back-woodmen of Kentucky are styled half man, half horse, and half alligator by the settlers on the Mississippi, and held accordingly in great respect and abhorrence."

12. Tocqueville, *Democracy in America*, pp. 281–82.

13. Henry Adams, *History of the United States of America During the First Administration of Thomas Jefferson*, 1:54.

14. William T. Porter, as quoted in Norris W. Yates, *William T. Porter and the "Spirit of the Times,"* p. 18.

15. Blair, *Native American Humor*, p. 91.

16. Augustus Baldwin Longstreet, *Georgia Scenes, Characters, Incidents, &c., in the First Half Century of the Republic*, pp. 30–31. Subsequent references will be to the first edition and will be cited parenthetically in the text.

17. Edgar Allan Poe, review of *Georgia Scenes*.

18. Kenneth S. Lynn, *Mark Twain and Southwestern Humor*, p. 64.

19. Faulkner's Flem Snopes, Kittrell Warren's Billy Fishback (1865), and "Lige" Shaddock (appearing in Porter's *The Big Bear of Arkansas and Other Tales*, 1845) are only a sample of Ransy Sniffle's offspring who acknowledge explicitly their progenitor.

20. W. J. Cash, *The Mind of the South*, pp. 14–58, especially p. 26.

Chapter 3: The Emergence of the Confidence-Man

1. James Hall, *Legends of the West*, p. 5.

2. Charles Fenno Hoffman, *A Winter in the West*, vol. 1, preface, n. p. Subsequent references will be to this edition and will be cited parenthetically in the text.

3. Henry Adams, *History of the United States of America During the First Administration of Thomas Jefferson*, pp. 177–78. Subsequent references will be to this edition and will be cited parenthetically in the text.

4. Timothy Flint, *A Condensed Geography and History of the Western States or the Mississippi Valley*, pp. 449–50.

5. Quoted by Hershel Parker in his edition of Herman Melville's *The Confidence-Man: His Masquerade*, p. 79, n. 2.

6. For a full account of Joseph C. Dylks, see Richard H. Taneyhill, ed., *The Leatherwood God (1869–1870) in Two Versions*; and William Dean Howells's novel *The Leatherwood God*.

7. See David Meredith Reese, M.D., *Humbugs of New-York*; and Robert D. Bamberg, ed., *The Confession of Jereboam O. Beauchamp*.

8. Sophia's sister, Elizabeth, had translated a laudatory French essay on Mesmer, and Sophia's dentist, Dr. Fiske—who shared her father's practice—regularly treated his patients with hypnotism. Hawthorne, however, came to distrust the "magnetic miracles" and implored Sophia "to take no part in them. I am unwilling that a power should be exercised on thee, of which we know neither the origin nor the consequence, and the phenomena of which seem rather calculated to bewilder us, than to teach us any truths about the present or future state of being . . . it seems to me that the sacredness of an individual is violated by it" (letter, Nathaniel Hawthorne to Sophia Peabody, 18 October 1841). See also Hawthorne's *The House of the Seven Gables* (1851), especially chapter 13 and *The Blithedale Romance* (1852), chapter 23. Following Hawthorne's advice, Sophia did not allow herself to be hypnotized; nonetheless, her headaches ceased almost immediately after she married. For a critical survey of mesmerism in this period, see Taylor Stoehr, "Hawthorne and Mesmerism," *Huntington Library Quarterly*, 33 (1969), 33–60.

9. Crockett's "Useful Coonskin" is available in David Crockett, *A Narrative of the Life of David Crockett, of the State of Tennessee.*

10. See Gamini Salgado, ed., *Cony-Catchers and Bawdy Baskets: An Anthology of Elizabethan Low Life* for Robert Greene's essays.

11. Edgar Allan Poe, "Diddling Considered as One of the Exact Sciences," in *Collected Works of Edgar Allan Poe*, 3 vols., ed. Thomas Ollive Mabbott, 3:870. Subsequent references will be to this edition and will be cited parenthetically in the text.

12. Jeremy Diddler appears in John Kenney's *Raising the Wind* (1803), collected first in Elizabeth Inchbald's *A Collection of Farces* (1815) and, more accessibly, in Michael R. Booth, ed., *English Plays of the 19th Century* (London: Oxford Univ. Press, 1969–1973), 4: Farces.

13. See George Lippard, *The Monks of Monk Hall*, ed. Leslie A. Fiedler, and George H. Devol, *Forty Years a Gambler on the Mississippi*. For an extremely readable book on Ned Buntline's long career, see Jay Monaghan, *The Great Rascal: The Life and Adventures of Ned Buntline*. The paragraph's last quotation is from *Gambling Exposed. A Full Exposition of All the Various Arts, Mysteries, and Miseries of Gambling. By the "Reformed Gambler," Jonathan H. Green*, p. 64.

14. Jonathan Culler, "Literary History, Allegory, and Semiology," p. 262.

15. Anonymous review in the *American Quarterly Review* 17 (1835): 178–79.

16. For a thorough and excellent discussion of the first appearances of the term *confidence man* in print, see Johannes Dietrich Bergmann, "The Original Confidence Man."

17. Culler, "Literary History," p. 262.

18. For this flexible model of literary continuity and change I am indebted to Wolfgang Iser, "The Reality of Fiction: A Functionalist Approach to Literature."

19. *Spirit of the Times* 13 (9 September 1843): 326. For more information on the relationship between Hooper and Porter, see Norris W. Yates, *William T. Porter and the "Spirit of the Times,"* chapter 2; and W. Stanley Hoole, *Alias Simon Suggs: The Life and Times of Johnson Jones Hooper.*

20. The phrase *valueless action* of comedy I have borrowed from a very different context in Elder Olson, *The Theory of Comedy*, p. 36.

21. Hooper's second sketch for the *East Alabamian*, "Our Hunt Last Week," Porter borrowed in 1843 for the *Spirit of the Times*. Like "Taking the Census," this humorous piece was well received; the *Spirit* even reprinted excerpts from it, retitled "The Biters Bit," in July 1844. Editors of such geographically diverse publications as the *Nashville Daily Gazette*, the *New Orleans Picayune*, and the *Boston Yankee Clipper* reprinted Hooper's sketches from the *Spirit*, and Hooper suddenly found himself with a national reputation.

22. See Robert Hopkins, "Simon Suggs: A Burlesque Campaign Biography." Hopkins argues that Hooper directly parodies specific biographies of Andrew Jackson, deriding Old Hickory's military and political achievements.

23. Johnson Jones Hooper, *Some Adventures of Captain Simon Suggs, Late of the Tallapoosy Volunteers*, p. 12. All future references to Hooper's work, unless otherwise indicated, will be from the first edition and will be cited parenthetically in the text.

24. See William Willeford, *The Fool and His Scepter: A Study in Clowns and Jesters and Their Audience*, for an excellent discussion of the fool's role.

25. Henry Nash Smith, *Virgin Land*, pp. 92–94.

26. Although the reader may find it hard to believe that Simon has a wife and children (chapter 11), he never betrays a woman for profit like Eggleston. Simon also mourns the simplicity of the Indians (74), yet argues that if someone is going to take them, why shouldn't he?

27. Whether Cocher-Emartee is actually killed is irrelevant; the Tallapoosy Vollantares intended their volley to kill the chief.

28. Like the Devil, Simon must have his little jokes; for example, he thoroughly enjoys befuddling the congregation as he parodies their pretentions to divine revelation.

"And then," continued Suggs, "I wanted to git off, but they hilt me, and bimeby I felt so missuble, I had to yonder"—pointing to the mourners' seat—"and when I lay down thar it got wuss and wuss, and 'peared like somethin' was a-mashin' down on my back—"

"That was his load o' sin," said one of the brethren—"never mind, it'll tumble off presently, see ef it don't!" and he shook his head professionally and knowingly.

"And it kept a-gittin heavier and heavier, ontwell it looked like it might be a four year old steer, or a big pine log, or somethin' of that sort—"

"Glory to my soul," shouted Mrs. Dobbs, "it's the sweetest talk I *ever* hearn! You Sukey! aint you got John yit? never mind, my lady, I'll settle wi' you!" Sukey quailed before the finger which her mistress shook at her.

"And arter awhile," Suggs went on, "'peared like I fell into a trance, like, and I seed—"

"Now we'll get the good on it!" cried one of the sanctified.

"And I seed the biggest, longest, rip-roarenest, blackest, scaliest—" Captain Suggs paused, wiped his brow, and ejaculated "Ah, L-o-r-d!" so as to give full time for curiosity to become impatience to know what he saw.

"*Sarpent!* warn't it?" asked one of the preachers.

"No, not a sarpent," replied Suggs, blowing his nose.

"Do tell us *what* it war, soul alive!—whar *is* John?" asked Mrs. Dobbs.

"Allegator!" said the Captain.

"Allegator!" repeated every woman present, and screamed for very life. (126–27)

29. Quoted by Hoole, *Alias Simon Suggs*, p. 66. In 1861 Hooper was more successful, and was elected secretary of the Southern Congress, soon to become the Provisional Congress of the Confederate States of America. Hooper lost even this job, however, when two houses were formed of the Congress.

30. "The Muscadine Story; The Unwritten Chapter in the Biography of Captain Suggs" first appeared in the *Spirit of the Times* 19 (24 March 1849): 55. When Hooper became the editor of the *Chambers County Tribune* in September 1849, he contributed to that paper the last Suggs sketch, "The Widow Rugby's Husband; A Story of Suggs."

31. Hoole, *Alias Simon Suggs*, p. 176.

32. Rufus W. Griswold, *The Prose Writers of America*, p. 546. Griswold directs his praise to Longstreet, Thompson, Thorpe, and Morgan Neville (who wrote of Mike Fink) (p. 37).

33. Henry Watterson, *Oddities in Southern Life and Character*, p. 39.

34. These examples, typical of frontier humor, are chosen more or less at random: S. G. Goodrich ("Peter Parley"), "The Peddler" (1841); Philip B. January ("The Man in the Swamp"), "A Rollicking Dragoon Officer" (1843); Poe,

"Diddling Considered as One of the Exact Sciences" (1843); Sol Smith, "A Bully Boat and a Brag Captain" (1845); James Hall, "Peter Featherton" (1845); and William Gilmore Simms, "The Last Wager, or The Gamester of the Mississippi" (1845). For a wider contemporary sampling, see Griswold, *Prose Writers* (1857); William E. Burton, *Cyclopaedia of Wit and Humor* (1858); and James Wood Davidson, *The Living Writers of the South* (1869).

35. William T. Porter, ed., *The Big Bear of Arkansas and Other Sketches*, p. 175. All references to tales appearing in *The Big Bear* will be to this edition and will be cited parenthetically in the text.

36. "Old Tuttle's Last Quarter Race," by "Buckeye," in William T. Porter, ed., *A Quarter Race in Kentucky and Other Sketches*, p. 118. All references to tales appearing in *A Quarter Race* will be to this edition and will be cited parenthetically in the text.

37. Thomas A. Burke, *Polly Peablossom's Wedding and Other Tales*, p. 5. Burke also included Hooper's "Shifting the Responsibility" in this volume (143–45). The tales referred to are Burke's own "A Losing Game of Poker" (44–48) and "'Doing' A Sheriff" (98–101); "War's Yure Hoss?" by "a Missourian" (41–43); and Lane's "The Thimble Game" (28–40).

Chapter 4: Four Variations of the Confidence Man

1. Herman Melville, *The Confidence-Man: His Masquerade*, ed. Hershel Parker, p. 2.

2. Joseph Glover Baldwin, *Flush Times of Alabama and Mississippi. A Series of Sketches*, pp. 81, 85, 91. Subsequent references will be to this first edition of *Flush Times* and will be cited parenthetically in the text.

3. Walter Blair, "Americanized Comic Braggarts," p. 335.

4. Johnson Jones Hooper, *Some Adventures of Captain Simon Suggs*, pp. 10–11. Subsequent references will be to this first edition of *Simon Suggs* and will be cited parenthetically in the text.

5. Susan Kuhlmann, *Knave, Fool, and Genius: The Confidence Man As He Appears in Nineteenth-Century American Fiction*, p. 30.

6. Wolfgang Iser, "The Reality of Fiction: A Functionalist Approach to Literature," p. 30.

7. See Brackenridge's satire of democratic treatymakers among Kickapoo "Indians," in *Modern Chivalry*, pp. 55–62.

8. George Washington Harris. *Sut Lovingood. Yarns Spun by a "Nat'ral Born Durn'd Fool.["] Warped and Wove for Public Wear*, p. vii. Subsequent references unless otherwise noted will be to sketches revised by Harris and collected in this edition of the *Yarns* and will be cited parenthetically in the text.

9. Walter Blair, *Mark Twain and Huck Finn*, pp. 242–43.

10. Milton Rickels includes a fine bibliography listing the first known publication date of Harris's fictions in *George Washington Harris*, pp. 145–47, which I have followed throughout this chapter.

11. Kenneth S. Lynn, *Mark Twain and Southwestern Humor*, p. 64.

12. Walter Blair, *Native American Humor (1800–1900)*, p. 101.

13. Rickels, in *George Washington Harris*, p. 30, notes Harris's debt to Thompson; the name *Stallins* may have been lifted from Longstreet's "The Fight."

14. "Sut Lovingood's Chest Story" can be found in M. Thomas Inge's excellent edition of Harris's previously uncollected works, *High Times and Hard Times: Sketches and Tales by George Washington Harris*. Subsequent

references to this edition will be cited in the text using the abbreviation *HTHT*.

15. Rickels, *George Washington Harris*, p. 53.

16. See Brom Weber's introduction to *Sut Lovingood*, pp. ix–xxix.

17. Walter Blair and Hamlin Hill, *America's Humor: From Poor Richard to Doonesbury*, p. 216.

18. Rickels, *George Washington Harris*, p. 103.

19. Inge, *High Times*, p. 106.

20. The most available edition of Lewis's fiction is John Q. Anderson, *Louisiana Swamp Doctor: The Life and Writings of Henry Clay Lewis*. All references to "The Curious Widow" are from this collection and will be cited parenthetically in the text.

21. Inge, *High Times*, p. 106; see pp. 222–31 for an analysis of Harris's satires. See also Donald Day, "The Political Satires of George Washington Harris," *Tennessee Historical Quarterly* 4 (December 1945): 320–38, for a broader interpretation of Harris's political inclinations.

22. *Boston Evening Transcript*, 10 April 1857.

23. Edward H. Rosenberry, *Melville and the Comic Spirit*, p. 175.

24. Herman Melville, *The Confidence-Man: His Masquerade*, ed. Hershel Parker, p. 6. Subsequent references will be to this edition and will be cited parenthetically in the text.

25. Thomas Bangs Thorpe, "The Big Bear of Arkansas," in William T. Porter, ed., *The Big Bear of Arkansas and Other Sketches, Illustrative of Characters and Incidents in the South and South-West*, p. 14. Subsequent references to "The Big Bear" will be from this collection and will be cited parenthetically in the text.

26. John Neal, "The Yankee Peddler," in William E. Burton, ed., *The Cyclopaedia of Wit and Humor*, pp. 78–79.

27. C. F. Briggs, "Elegant Tom Dillar," in ibid., pp. 423–24. Melville's stories of Charlemont and China Aster, as well, seem to be parodies of conventional sentimental sketches like those of Briggs and his confreres; for a wider selection of contemporary fiction, see Rufus Wilmot Griswold, *The Prose Writers of America*.

28. *The Confidence-Man*, ed. Parker, p. 133, note 3.

29. Jonathan H. Green, *Gambling Exposed*, p. 106.

30. Warwick Wadlington, *The Confidence Game in American Literature*, p. 165.

31. Ann Douglas, *The Feminization of American Culture*, chapter 9, "Herman Melville and the Revolt Against the Reader," pp. 289–326, especially pp. 299–302, 314–20.

32. H. Bruce Franklin, *The Wake of the Gods: Melville's Mythology*, p. 153.

33. Floyd C. Watkins, ed., *Life and Public Services of an Army Straggler. By Kittrell J. Warren*, p. 46. Subsequent references will be to this edition and will be cited parenthetically in the text.

34. Richard B. Hauck, *A Cheerful Nihilism: Confidence and the Absurd in American Humorous Fiction*, p. 69. Hauck is one of the few modern critics to notice Warren's *Straggler*; though I am unwilling to see Fishback as a prototypical "absurd" antihero, Hauck's reading is perceptive and stimulating.

Chapter 5: *The War, Mark Twain, and the Flush Times*

1. William Cullen Bryant, "Free Homesteads," p. 89.

2. Walt Whitman, "Democratic Vistas," in Floyd Stovall, ed., *Walt Whitman: Prose Works 1892*, Vol. II, pp. 369–70.

3. Henry Nash Smith, "The Scribbling Women and the Cosmic Success Story," p. 60. See also his *Democracy and the Novel: Popular Resistance to Classic American Writers*, especially pp. 3–15, 56–74.

4. George W. Bagby, "The Empty Sleeve" (stanza 1), rpt. in James Wood Davidson, *The Living Writers of the South*, p. 28.

5. Edwin Fussell, *Frontier: American Literature and the American West*, p. 301.

6. S. Emma E. Edmonds, *The Female Spy of the Union Army*, especially pp. 82–97.

7. Thomas Wentworth Higginson, Introduction to *Harvard Memorial Biographies*, p. v. Cooke echoes these characteristic sentiments almost word for word.

8. Henry Ward Beecher, *Norwood; or, Village Life in New England*, p. 541.

9. Henry Nash Smith, in *Democracy and the Novel*, 57–58, notes that the *New York Ledger* had a circulation of three hundred thousand and that the book rights to *Norwood* were bought for thirty thousand dollars.

10. See E. P. Oberholtzer, *Jay Cooke, Financier of the Civil War*.

11. Vernon Louis Parrington, *Main Currents in American Thought*, 3:42.

12. "Moral Types of Mankind," unsigned review of *Undercurrents of Wall Street: A Romance of Business*.

13. W. Stanley Hoole, *Alias Simon Suggs: The Life and Times of Johnson Jones Hooper*, p. 177.

14. Charles Farrar Browne, *Artemus Ward: His Book*, pp. 176–79. Unless otherwise noted, subsequent references will be to this edition and will be cited parenthetically in the text.

15. Charles Farrar Browne, "Vale," *Cleveland Daily Plain Dealer*, 10 November 1860, p. 3.

16. Reprinted in Edgar M. Branch, "'The Babes in the Wood': Artemus Ward's 'Double Health' to Mark Twain," pp. 965–66.

17. In Walter Blair, *Native American Humor (1800–1900)*, p. 410.

18. Charles Henry Smith, *Bill Arp, So Called. A Side Show of the Southern Side of the War*, pp. 5–6. Subsequent references will be to this edition and will be cited parenthetically in the text.

19. Henry Wheeler Shaw, *Everybody's Friend, or; Josh Billing's Encyclopedia and Proverbial Philosophy of Wit and Humor*, p. iii. Subsequent references will be to this edition and will be cited parenthetically in the text.

20. Samuel Langhorne Clemens, *The Autobiography of Mark Twain*, ed. Charles Neider, p. 273.

21. James M. Cox, "*A Connecticut Yankee in King Arthur's Court*: The Machinery of Self-Preservation," p. 95.

22. Samuel Langhorne Clemens, *Roughing It*, pp. 103–4. Subsequent references will be to this edition and will be cited parenthetically in the text.

23. Henry Clay Lewis, "The Day of Judgment," in John Q. Anderson, *Louisiana Swamp Doctor: The Life and Writings of Henry Clay Lewis*, p. 106.

24. Samuel Langhorne Clemens and Charles Dudley Warner, *The Gilded Age: A Tale of Today*, ed. Bryant Morey French, p. 28. Subsequent references will be to this edition and will be cited parenthetically in the text.

25. Kenneth S. Lynn, *Mark Twain and Southwest Humor*, especially chapter 6. See also Constance Rourke, *American Humor*; Bernard DeVoto, *Mark Twain's America*; and Walter Blair, *Mark Twain and Huck Finn*.

26. George Miller Beard, *American Nervousness: Its Causes and Conse-

quences. In Beard's view Americans were the victims of rapid urbanization and technological advances.

27. See James M. Cox, *Mark Twain: The Fate of Humor*, p. 160.

28. Samuel Langhorne Clemens, *Adventures of Huckleberry Finn*, ed. Sculley Bradley, Richmond Croom Beatty, and E. Hudson Long, p. 7. All references will be to this modern edition and will be cited parenthetically in the text.

29. See Richard Bridgman, *The Colloquial Style in America*, pp. 119–30.

30. Henry Clay Lewis's "Day of Judgment" can be located in John Q. Anderson, *Louisiana Swamp Doctor: The Life and Writings of Henry Clay Lewis*.

31. Warwick Wadlington, *The Confidence Game in American Literature*, p. 247.

32. Lionel Trilling, "Huckleberry Finn," in *The Liberal Imagination: Essays on Literature and Society*, p. 107. See also Wadlington's fine analysis of social hierarchy in *Confidence Game*, pp. 261–262.

33. Richard Poirier, *A World Elsewhere: The Place of Style in American Literature*, p. 182.

34. David E. E. Sloane, *Mark Twain as a Literary Comedian*, pp. 135, 141.

35. Samuel Langhorne Clemens, *Life on the Mississippi*, chapter 46, "Castles and Culture," and chapter 38, "The House Beautiful." See also Walter Blair's discussion in *Mark Twain and Huck Finn*, pp. 285–99.

36. Johnson Jones Hooper, *Some Adventures of Captain Simon Suggs*, p. 129. Subsequent references will be to this edition and will be cited parenthetically in the text using the abbreviation *SS*.

37. In addition to Hooper's "The Captain Attends A Camp-Meeting" and Lewis's "Day of Judgment," the most memorable sketch is George Washington Harris's "Parson John Bullen's Lizards" in *Sut Lovingood's Yarns*.

38. See Walter Blair, "Americanized Comic Braggarts."

39. DeVoto, *Mark Twain's America*, p. 255, and Blair, *Mark Twain and Huck Finn*, pp. 279–84. I disagree with Kenneth Lynn's conclusion that "in Hooper's story, the Confidence Man is a symbol of the age; in Chapter XX of *Huckleberry Finn*, he is a freak" (*Mark Twain and Southwest Humor*, p. 225).

40. "Moral Types of Mankind," p. 123.

41. For historical ancestors of the king and the duke, see Oscar G. Brockett, *History of the Theatre*, p. 498, and David Grimsted, *Melodrama Unveiled: American Theater and Culture 1800–1850*, pp. 48–49. Other useful treatments of Shakespeare and frontier theater include Ray Allen Billington, *America's Frontier Heritage*, pp. 85–87, and William G. B. Carson, *The Theatre on the Frontier: The Early Years of the St. Louis Stage*, especially pp. 246–306.

42. Walter Blair traces the possible evolution of this incident in *Mark Twain and Huck Finn*, pp. 316–21. An oral version of the episode that makes its obscene character obvious is reported by Wallace Graves, "Mark Twain's 'Burning Shame.'"

43. An excellent discussion of the people of Bricksville and their entertainments is found in Gary Lindberg, *The Confidence Man in American Literature*, p. 194.

44. Ibid., p. 195.

45. Ibid., p. 197.

46. Daniel Hoffman, *Form and Fable in American Fiction*, p. 345.

47. Poirier, *World Elsewhere*, p. 185. See also Lindberg, *Confidence Man*, p. 197.

48. Wadlington, *Confidence Game*, p. 252.

49. Hauck, *A Cheerful Nihilism*, pp. 148, 150.

50. Trilling, *Liberal Imagination*, p. 101.

51. William M. Gibson, ed., *Mark Twain's Mysterious Stranger Manuscripts*, p. 405.

Chapter 6: From the New Country to the Twentieth Century

1. Richard H. Taneyhill, *The Leatherwood God (1869–1870) in Two Versions*; and William Dean Howells, *The Leatherwood God*, intro. Eugene Pattison. Subsequent references will be to these editions and will be cited parenthetically in the text.

2. For fine discussions of Howells's use of Taneyhill's accounts see Eugene H. Pattison, "From History to Realism: Howells Composes *The Leatherwood God*," and his Introduction to the Indiana University Press edition of *The Leatherwood God*, pp. xvii–xxiii.

3. Haskell S. Springer, "*The Leatherwood God*: From Narrative to Novel," p. 196.

4. E[dgett] E[dwin] F[rancis], "Mr. Howells's Vigorous Romanticism/The Great Apostle of Realism Writes a Romantic Story of Events in His Native Ohio," 2:8.

5. Barnum seems to have had no illusions about the Feejee Mermaid; it was an oddity and hence a moneymaker. See *The Life of P. T. Barnum, Written by Himself*, pp. 230–42, especially p. 235: "Assuming, what is no doubt true, that the mermaid was manufactured, it was a most remarkable specimen of ingenuity and untiring patience." Some people, of course, may have expected and perceived a "real" wonder of the world; in either case, the museum offered a safe environment in which to view the curiosity.

6. *New York Literary World*, 18 August 1849, p. 133.

7. Quoted by Frederick Jackson Turner in *The Frontier in American History*, p. 1.

8. Ibid., pp. 37–38.

9. See *The Education of Henry Adams*, especially chapter 34, "A Law of Acceleration."

10. Hugh Henry Brackenridge, *Modern Chivalry*, ed. Claude M. Newlin, p. 57.

11. Edgar Allan Poe, "Diddling Considered As One of the Exact Sciences," in *Collected Works of Edgar Allan Poe*, ed. Thomas Ollive Mabbott, 3:870.

12. F. Scott Fitzgerald, *The Great Gatsby*, p. 182.

13. Leo Marx, *The Machine in the Garden: Technology and the Pastoral Ideal in America*, p. 360.

14. Quoted in John Blair, *The Confidence Man in Modern Fiction: A Rogue's Gallery with Six Portraits*, p. 131.

15. Susan Kuhlmann, *Knave, Fool, and Genius: The Confidence Man As He Appears in Nineteenth-Century American Fiction*, pp. 128–29.

16. A representative selection might include Nathanael West's Shrike (*Miss Lonelyhearts*, 1933), Ralph Ellison's Rinehart (*Invisible Man*, 1952), Joseph Heller's Milo Minderbinder (*Catch-22*, 1961), Saul Bellow's Dr. Tamkin (*Seize the Day*, 1956), John Barth's Doctor (*End of the Road*, 1961), and Flannery O'Connor's Hoover Shoats (*Wise Blood*, 1952).

17. William Dean Howells's Joseph Dylks heads this list, which is made up of such diverse figures as F. Scott Fitzgerald's Jay Gatz (*The Great Gatsby*,

1925), Sinclair Lewis's Elmer Gantry (*Elmer Gantry*, 1925), Nathanael West's Lemuel Pitkin (*A Cool Million*, 1934), Flannery O'Connor's Haze Motes (*Wise Blood*, 1952), Norman Mailer's Rojack (*An American Dream*, 1965), and William Gaddis's JR (*JR*, 1975).

18. Into this category fall William Faulkner's Flem Snopes (*The Hamlet*, 1940), Thomas Pynchon's V. (*V.*, 1963), the protagonist of Jerzy Kosinski's *Steps* (1968), and Robert Stone's Antheil (*Dog Soldiers*, 1974).

19. Henry Brooks Adams, *History of the United States During the First Administration of Thomas Jefferson*, 9:222.

20. R. W. B. Lewis, "Days of Wrath and Laughter," in his *Trials of the Word*, pp. 184–236.

21. Max F. Schulz, *Black Humor Fiction of the Sixties*, p. 52.

22. Saul Bellow, *The Victim*, p. 70.

23. Gary Lindberg, *The Confidence Man in American Literature*, pp. 203–208. See also Karen Halttunen, *Confidence Man and Painted Woman: A Study of Middle-Class Culture in America, 1830–1870*, p. 210: "In the success mythology of twentieth-century corporate America, the confidence man has been effectively welcomed into the mainstream of American middle-class culture."

24. Richard B. Hauck, *A Cheerful Nihilism: Confidence and the Absurd in American Humorous Fiction*, pp. 237–45.

25. Ihab Hassan, *Radical Innocence: Studies in the Contemporary American Novel*, p. 327.

BIBLIOGRAPHY

Adams, Henry Brooks. *Democracy: An American Novel.* New York: Airmont, 1968.
———. *The Education of Henry Adams: An Autobiography.* Boston and New York: Houghton Mifflin Co., 1918.
———. *History of the United States During the First Administration of Thomas Jefferson.* 9 vols. New York: Charles Scribner's Sons, 1889.
Albanese, Catherine L. *Sons of the Fathers: The Civil Religion of the American Revolution.* Philadelphia: Temple University Press, 1976.
Alger, Horatio, Jr. *Ragged Dick and Mark, the Match Boy.* New York: Collier, 1962.
Anderson, John Q. *Louisiana Swamp Doctor: The Life and Writings of Henry Clay Lewis.* Baton Rouge: Louisiana State University Press, 1962.
Baldwin, Joseph Glover. *Flush Times of Alabama and Mississippi.* New York: D. Appleton & Co., 1853.
Bamberg, Robert D., ed. *The Confession of Jereboam Beauchamp.* Philadelphia: University of Pennsylvania Press, 1966.
Bank, Stanley, ed. *American Romanticism: A Shape for Fiction.* New York: G. P. Putnam's Sons, 1969.
Barker, James Nelson. "Superstition." *Representative American Plays: From 1767 to the Present.* Ed. Arthur Hobson Quinn. New York: Appleton-Century-Crofts, 1953.
Barnum, P. T. *The Life of P. T. Barnum, Written by Himself.* New York: Redfield, 1855.
Bartlett, Irving H. *The American Mind in the Mid-Nineteenth Century.* London: Routledge & Kegan Paul, 1968.
Beard, George Miller. *American Nervousness: Its Causes and Consequences.* New York: Putnam, 1881.
Beecher, Henry Ward. *Norwood; or, Village Life in New England.* New York: Charles Scribner & Company, 1868.
Bellow, Saul. *Seize the Day.* New York: Viking, 1956.
———. *The Victim.* New York: Vanguard, 1947.
Bergmann, Johannes Dietrich. "The Original Confidence Man." *American Quarterly* 21 (1969): 561–77.
Berthoff, Warner. *The Example of Melville.* New York: W. W. Norton, 1962.
———. *The Ferment of Realism: American Literature, 1884–1919.* New York: Free Press, 1965.
Bier, Jesse. *The Rise and Fall of American Humor.* New York: Holt, Rinehart and Winston, 1968.
Billington, Ray Allen. *America's Frontier Heritage.* New York: Holt, Rinehart and Winston, 1966.

——. *The Westward Movement in the United States.* Princeton, N.J.: D. Van Nostrand, 1959.

Blair, John G. *The Confidence Man in Modern Fiction: A Rogue's Gallery with Six Portraits.* New York: Barnes & Noble, 1979.

Blair, Walter. "Americanized Comic Braggarts." *Critical Inquiry* 4 (1977): 331–49.

——. *Mark Twain and Huck Finn.* Berkeley: University of California Press, 1960.

——. *Native American Humor (1800–1900).* New York: American Book Co., 1937.

Blair, Walter, and Hill, Hamlin. *America's Humor: From Poor Richard to Doonesbury.* New York: Oxford University Press, 1978.

Blair, Walter, and Meine, Franklin J. *Mike Fink: King of Mississippi Keelboatmen.* 1933; rpt. Westport, Connecticut: Greenport, 1971.

Bonner, T. D. *The Life and Adventures of James P. Beckwourth, Mountaineer, Scout, Pioneer, and Chief of the Crow Nation of Indians; Written from his own Dictation by T. D. Bonner.* Williamstown, Mass.: Corner House, 1977.

Boorstin, Daniel J. *The Americans: The Democratic Experience.* New York: Random House, 1973.

——. *The Americans: The National Experience.* New York: Random House, 1965.

Booth, Michael R., ed. *English Plays of the Nineteenth Century.* London: Oxford University Press, 1969–1973.

Botkin, B. A. *A Treasury of Mississippi River Folklore.* New York: Crown, 1955.

Boudinot, Elias. *Journey to Boston in 1809.* Ed. Milton Halsey Thomas. Princeton, N.J.: Princeton University Library, 1955.

Brackenridge, Hugh Henry. *Indian Atrocities (1782, 1843).* Cincinnati: U. P. Jones, 1867.

——. *Modern Chivalry.* Ed. Claude M. Newlin. New York: American Book Co., 1937.

Bradford, William. *Of Plymouth Plantation: 1620–1647.* Ed. Samuel Eliot Morrison. New York: Alfred A. Knopf, 1966.

Branch, Edgar M. "'The Babes in the Wood': Artemus Ward's 'Double Health' to Mark Twain." *Publications of the Modern Language Association* 93 (1978): 955–72.

Bridgeman, Richard. *The Colloquial Style in America.* New York: Oxford University Press, 1966.

Brockett, Oscar G. *History of the Theatre.* Boston: Allyn and Bacon, 1968.

Brodhead, Richard H. *Hawthorne, Melville, and the Novel.* Chicago: University of Chicago Press, 1976.

Browne, Charles Farrar. *Artemus Ward: His Book.* New York: Carleton, 1862.

——. "Vale." *Cleveland Daily Plain Dealer.* 10 November 1860, p. 3.

Bryant, William Cullen. "Free Homesteads" (unsigned article). *New York Evening Post,* 7 May 1862, p. 89.

Burke, Thomas A. *Polly Peablossom's Wedding and Other Tales.* Philadelphia: T. B. Peterson and Brothers, 1851.

Burton, William E., ed. *Cyclopaedia of Wit and Humor; Containing Choice and Characteristic Selections from the Writings of the Most Eminent Humorists of America, Ireland, Scotland, and England.* 2 vols. New York: D. Appleton and Co., 1858, 1866.

Carson, William G. B. *The Theatre on the Frontier: The Early Years of the St. Louis Stage.* New York: Benjamin Blom, 1965.

Cash, W. J. *The Mind of the South.* New York: Alfred A. Knopf, 1941.

Cawelti, John G. *Adventure, Mystery, and Romance: Formula Stories as Art and Popular Culture.* Chicago: University of Chicago Press, 1976.

Clemens, Samuel Langhorne. *Adventures of Huckleberry Finn.* Ed. Sculley Bradley, Richmond Croom Beatty, and E. Hudson Long. New York: W. W. Norton, 1961, 1962.

———. *The Autobiography of Mark Twain.* Ed. Charles Neider. New York: Harper & Brothers, 1959.

———. *The Gilded Age: A Tale of To-Day.* Ed. Bryant Morey French. Indianapolis and New York: Bobbs-Merrill, 1972.

———. *The Innocents Abroad: or, The New Pilgrims Progress.* New York: New American Library, 1966.

———. *Life on the Mississippi.* Boston: Osgood, 1883.

———. *Roughing It.* Berkeley: University of California Press, 1972.

Cohen, Hennig, and Dillingham, William B., eds. *Humor of the Old Southwest.* Boston: Houghton Mifflin, 1964.

Cohen, Ralph. "Historical Knowledge and Literary Understanding." *Papers in Language and Literature* 14 (1978): 227–48.

Comstock, Anthony. *Frauds Exposed; or, How the People Are Deceived and Robbed, and Youth Corrupted.* Montclair, N.J.: Patterson Smith, 1969.

Conrad, Peter. *Imagining America.* New York: Oxford University Press, 1980.

Cooper, James Fenimore. *The Prairie: A Tale.* In *The Works of James Fenimore Cooper* ("Mohawk Edition"). 32 vols. New York & London: G. P. Putnam's Sons/The Knickerbocker Press, 1912.

Cox, James M. "A Connecticut Yankee in King Arthur's Court: The Machinery of Self-Preservation." *Yale Review* 50 (1960): 89–102.

———. *Mark Twain: The Fate of Humor.* Princeton, N.J.: Princeton University Press, 1966.

Crèvecoeur, J. Hector St. John de. *Letters from an American Farmer.* New York: E. P. Dutton, 1912.

Crockett, David. *A Narrative of the Life of David Crockett, of the State of Tennessee.* Philadelphia: E. L. Carey and A. Hart, 1834.

Culler, Jonathan. "Literary History, Allegory, and Semiology." *New Literary History* 7 (1976): 259–70.

———. *Structuralist Poetics: Structuralism, Linguistics and the Study of Literature.* Ithaca, N.Y.: Cornell University Press, 1975.

Curti, Merle. *Human Nature in American Thought: A History.* Madison: University of Wisconsin Press, 1980.

Davidson, James Wood. *The Living Writers of the South.* New York: Carleton, 1869.

Day, Donald. "The Political Satires of George Washington Harris." *Tennessee Historical Quarterly* 4 (1945): 320–38.

De Forest, John William. *Miss Ravenel's Conversion from Seccession to Loyalty.* San Francisco: Rinehart, 1955.

Devol, George H. *Forty Years a Gambler on the Mississippi.* Cincinnati: Devol & Haines, 1887.

DeVoto, Bernard. *Mark Twain's America.* Boston: Little, Brown and Company, 1932.

Dickey, Dallas C. *Seargent S. Prentiss: Whig Orator of the Old South.* Baton Rouge: Louisiana State University Press, 1945.

Douglas, Ann. *The Feminization of American Culture.* New York: Alfred A. Knopf, 1977.

Edmonds, S. Emma E. *The Female Spy of the Union Army . . . .* Boston: De Wolfe, Fiske and Co., 1864.

Ellison, Ralph. *Invisible Man.* New York: Random House, 1952.

Faulkner, William. *The Hamlet.* New York: Random House, 1940.

Feidelson, Charles, Jr. *Symbolism and American Literature.* Chicago: University of Chicago Press, 1953.

Fiedler, Leslie A. *Love and Death in the American Novel.* New York: Criterion, 1960.

Fisher, Marvin. *Going Under: Melville's Short Fiction and the American 1850s.* Baton Rouge: Louisiana State University Press, 1977.

Fitzgerald, F. Scott. *The Great Gatsby.* New York: Charles Scribner's Sons, 1925.

Flint, Timothy. *A Condensed Geography and History of the Western States or the Mississippi Valley.* Ed. Bernard Rosenthal. 2 vols. 1828; rpt. Gainesville, Florida: Scholars' Facsimiles and Reprints, 1970.

F[rancis], E[dgett] E[dwin]. "Mr. Howell's Vigorous Romanticism/ The Great Apostle of Realism Writes a Romantic Story of Events in His Native Ohio." *Boston Evening Transcript,* 1 November 1916, 2:8.

Franklin, Benjamin. *The Autobiography of Benjamin Franklin.* Ed. Leonard W. Labaree et al. New Haven: Yale University Press, 1964.

Franklin, H. Bruce. *The Wake of the Gods: Melville's Mythology.* Stanford, Cal.: Stanford University Press, 1963.

Franklin, Wayne. *Discoverers, Explorers, Settlers: The Diligent Writers of Early America.* Chicago: University of Chicago Press, 1979.

Frederickson, George M. *The Inner Civil War: Northern Intellectuals and the Crisis of the Union.* New York: Harper and Row, 1965.

Frye, Northrop. *Anatomy of Criticism.* Princeton, N.J.: Princeton University Press, 1957.

————. *The Educated Imagination.* Bloomington: Indiana University Press, 1964.

Fussell, Edwin S. *Frontier: American Literature and the American West.* Princeton, N.J.: Princeton University Press, 1965.

Gaddis, William. *JR.* New York: Alfred A. Knopf, 1975.

————. *The Recognitions.* New York: Alfred A. Knopf, 1955.

Gardiner, William H. Unsigned review of *The Spy* by James Fenimore Cooper. *North American Review* 6, no. 1 (July 1822): 250–82.

Gibson, William M., ed. *Mark Twain's Mysterious Stranger Manuscripts.* Berkeley and Los Angeles: University of California Press, 1969.

Graves, Wallace. "Mark Twain's 'Burning Shame.'" *Nineteenth-Century Fiction* 23 (1968): 93–98.

Green, Jonathan H. *Gambling Exposed. A Full Exposition of All the Various Arts, Mysteries, and Miseries of Gambling. By the "Reformed Gambler."* Philadelphia: T. B. Peterson, 1857.

Greene, Asa. *The Perils of Pearl Street.* New York: Betts & Anstice, and Peter Hill, 1834.

Grimsted, David. *Melodrama Unveiled: American Theater and Culture 1800–1850.* Chicago: University of Chicago Press, 1968.

Griswold, Rufus W. *The Prose Writers of America.* 4th ed. rev. Philadelphia: Parry & McMillan, 1857.

Hall, James. *Legends of the West.* 1832; author's rev. ed. New York: G. P. Putnam & Co., 1853.

————. *Sketches of History, Life, and Manners, in the West.* Philadelphia: Harrison Hall, 1835.

Halttunen, Karen. *Confidence Men and Painted Women: A Study of Middle-Class Culture in America, 1830–1870.* New Haven: Yale University Press, 1982.

Hargrave, Catherine Perry. *A History of Playing Cards: and a Bibliography of Cards and Gaming.* New York: Dover, 1966.

Harris, George Washington. *Sut Lovingood, Yarns Spun by a "Nat'ual Born Durn'd Fool." Warped and Wove for Public Wear.* New York: Dick & Fitzgerald, 1867.

————. *Sut Lovingood.* Ed. Brom Weber. New York: Grove Press, 1954.

Harris, Neil. *Humbug: The Art of P. T. Barnum.* Boston: Little, Brown, 1973.

Hassan, Ihab. *Radical Innocence: Studies in the Contemporary American Novel.* Princeton, N.J.: Princeton University Press, 1961.

Hauck, Richard B. *A Cheerful Nihilism: Confidence and the Absurd in American Humorous Fiction.* Bloomington: Indiana University Press, 1971.

————. "The Literary Content of the New York *Spirit of the Times,* 1831–1856." Ph.D. diss., University of Illinois, 1965.

Hemingway, Ernest. *In Our Time.* New York: Boni & Liveright, 1925.

Higginson, Thomas Wentworth. *Harvard Memorial Biographies.* Sever & Francis: Cambridge, 1866.

Hoar, Victor M. "The Confidence Man in American Literature." Ph.D. diss., University of Illinois, 1965.

Hoffman, Charles Fenno. *A Winter in the West. By a New-Yorker.* 2 vols. New York: Harper & Brothers, 1835.

Hoffman, Daniel. *Form and Fable in American Fiction.* New York: Oxford University Press, 1961.

Hoole, W. Stanley. *Alias Simon Suggs: The Life and Times of Johnson Jones Hooper.* University: University of Alabama Press, 1952.

Hooper, Johnson Jones. *Some Adventures of Captain Simon Suggs, Late of the Tallapoosy Volunteers; Together with "Taking the Census," and Other Alabama Sketches. By a Country Editor. With a Portrait from Life, and Other Illustrations, by Darley.* Philadelphia: Carey & Hart, 1845, 1846, 1848.

————. *Some Adventures of Capt. Simon Suggs.* Upper Saddle River, N.J.: Literature House/Gregg Press, 1970.

Hopkins, Robert. "Simon Suggs: A Burlesque Campaign Biography." *American Quarterly* 15 (1963): 459–63.

Hosmer, James Kendall. *Original Narratives of Early American History: Winthrop's Journal, "History of New England," 1630–1649.* 2 vols. New York: Charles Scribner's Sons, 1908.

Howells, William Dean. *The Leatherwood God.* New York: Century, 1916.

————. *The Leatherwood God.* Intro. Eugene Pattison. Bloomington: Indiana University Press, 1976.

Hoyle's Games: Containing the Rules for Playing Fashionable Games. Revised from the last London edition. Philadelphia: J. B. Lippincott, 1857.

Hudson, Frederic. *Journalism in the United States from 1690 to 1872.* 1873; rpt. New York: Harper & Row, 1969.

Huizinga, Johan. *Homo Ludens: A Study of the Play Element in Culture.* Boston: Beacon, 1955.

Hunt, Freeman. *Worth and Wealth: A Collection of Maxims, Morals and Miscellanies for Merchants and Men of Business.* New York: Stringer & Towsend, 1856.

Inge, M. Thomas, ed. *The Frontier Humorists.* Hamden, Conn.: Archon Books, 1975.

————. *High Times and Hard Times: Sketches and Tales by George Washington Harris.* Nashville, Tenn.: Vanderbilt University Press, 1967.

Irving, Washington. *The Work of Washington Irving.* 15 vols. New York: G. P. Putnam, 1848–1851.

Iser, Wolfgang. *The Implied Reader: Patterns of Communication in Prose Fiction from Bunyan to Beckett.* Baltimore: Johns Hopkins University Press, 1974.

————. "The Reality of Fiction: A Functionalist Approach to Literature." *New Literary History* (1975): 7–38.

Jameson, Frederic. "Magical Narratives: Romance as Genre." *New Literary History* 7 (1975): 135–64.

Jefferson, Thomas. *The Papers of Thomas Jefferson.* Ed. Julian P. Boyd. vol. 1, 1760–1776. Princeton, N.J.: Princeton University Press, 1950.

Jones, Howard Mumford. *The Age of Energy: Varieties of American Experience 1865–1915.* New York: Viking, 1971.

———. *O Strange New World—American Culture: The Formative Years.* New York: Viking, 1964.

Kammen, Michael. *A Season of Youth: The American Revolution and the Historical Imagination.* New York: Alfred A. Knopf, 1978.

Kimball, Richard B. *Undercurrents of Wall Street. A Romance of Business. By the author of "St. Leger," etc.* New York: G. P. Putnam, 1862.

Klein, Milton M. "Corruption in Colonial America." *South Atlantic Quarterly* 78 (1979): 57–72.

Knight, Sarah Kemble. *The Journal of Madam Knight.* Intro. George Parker Winship. New York: Peter Smith, 1935.

Kuhlmann, Susan. *Knave, Fool, and Genius: The Confidence Man As He Appears in Nineteenth-Century American Fiction.* Chapel Hill: University of North Carolina Press, 1973.

Leslie, Eliza. *The American Girl's Book.* New York: C. S. Francis and Co., 1857.

Levenson, J. C. *The Mind and Art of Henry Adams.* Stanford, Cal.: Stanford University Press, 1957.

Levin, David. *In Defense of Historical Literature: Essays on American History, Autobiography, Drama, and Fiction.* New York: Hill & Wang, 1967.

Levin, Harry, ed. *Perspectives of Criticism.* Cambridge: Harvard University Press, 1950.

Lewis, David K. *Convention: A Philosophical Study.* Cambridge: Harvard University Press, 1969.

Lewis, R. W. B. *The American Adam.* Chicago: University of Chicago Press, 1953.

———. *Trials of the Word.* New Haven: Yale University Press, 1965.

Lindberg, Gary. *The Confidence Man in American Literature.* New York: Oxford University Press, 1982.

Lippard, George. *The Monks of Monk Hall.* Ed. Leslie A. Fiedler. New York: Odyssey, 1970.

Longstreet, Augustus Baldwin. *Georgia Scenes, Characters, Incidents, &c., in the First Half Century of the Republic.* Augusta, Georgia: Printed at the S. R. Sentinel Office, 1835.

———. *Master William Mitten.* Macon, Ga.: Burke, Boykin & Co., 1864.

Loomis, Augustus Ward. *Learn to Say No: or, The City Apprentice.* Philadelphia: Presbyterian Board of Publication, 1856.

Lowes, John Livingston. *Convention and Revolt in Poetry.* Boston: Houghton Mifflin, 1919.

Lynn, Kenneth S. *Mark Twain and Southwestern Humor*. Boston: Little, Brown, 1959.

Lynn, Kenneth S., ed. *The Comic Tradition in America: An Anthology of American Humor*. New York: W. W. Norton, 1958.

Mailer, Norman. *An American Dream*. New York: Dial, 1964, 1965.

———. *Why Are We in Vietnam?* New York: G. P. Putnam's Sons, 1967.

Martin, Terence. *The Instructed Vision: Scottish Common Sense Philosophy and the Origins of American Fiction*. Bloomington: Indiana University Press, 1961.

Martin, Wendy. "The Rogue and the Rational Man: Hugh Henry Brackenridge's Study of a Con Man in *Modern Chivalry*." *Early American Literature* 8 (Fall 1973): 179–92.

Marx, Leo. *The Machine in the Garden: Technology and the Pastoral Ideal in America*. London, New York: Oxford University Press, 1964.

Mather, Cotton. *Magnalia Christi Americana; or, The Ecclesiastical History of New England*. New York: Russell & Russell, 1967.

Mathews, Mitford M., ed. *A Dictionary of Americanisms on Historical Principles*. Chicago: University of Chicago Press, 1951.

Maurer, David W. *The American Confidence Man*. Springfield, Illinois: Charles C. Thomas, 1974.

May, John R. *Toward A New Earth: Apocalypse in the American Novel*. Notre Dame: University of Notre Dame, 1972.

McElderry, B. R., Jr., ed. *Georgia Scenes*. By A. B. Longstreet. New York: Sagamore Press, 1957.

Melville, Herman. *The Confidence-Man: His Masquerade*. Ed. Hershel Parker. New York: W. W. Norton, 1971.

Meyer, D. H. *The Instructed Conscience: The Shaping of the American National Ethic*. Philadelphia: University of Pennsylvania Press, 1972.

Monaghan, Jay. *The Great Rascal: The Life and Adventures of Ned Buntline*. New York: Bonanza, 1951.

Mott, Frank Luther. *A History of American Magazines 1741–1850*. New York and London: D. Appleton, 1930.

Neider, Charles, ed. *The Adventures of Colonel Sellers*. By Mark Twain (Samuel L. Clemens). London: Chatto & Windus, 1966.

Noble, David W. *The Eternal Adam and the New World Garden*. New York: Grosset & Dunlap, 1968.

Nott, Henry Junius. *Novellettes of a Traveller; or, Odds and Ends from the Knapsack of Thomas Singularity, Journeyman Printer*. 2 vols. New York: Harper & Brothers, 1834.

Oberholtzer, E. P. *Jay Cooke, Financier of the Civil War*. Philadelphia: G. W. Jacobs & Co., 1907.

Olson, Elder. *The Theory of Comedy*. Bloomington: Indiana University Press, 1968, 1975.

Parrington, Vernon Louis. *Main Currents in American Thought*. New York: Harcourt, Brace, and Company, 1927, 1930.

Parton, Sarah Payson ("Fanny Fern"). *Fern Leaves from Fanny's Port-Folio*. Auburn: Derby and Miller, 1853.

Pattee, Fred Lewis. *The Development of the American Short Story: An Historical Survey*. New York: Harper & Brothers, 1923.

———. *The Feminine Fifties*. New York: D. Appleton-Century Co., 1940.

Pattison, Eugene H. "From History to Realism: Howells Composes *The Leatherwood God*." *The Old Northwest* 4 (1978): 195–218.

Paulding, James Kirke. *Tales of the Good Woman. By a Doubtful Gentleman*. New York: G. & C. & H. Carvill, 1829.

Pearce, Roy Harvey. "Note on Method in the History of Ideas." *Journal of the History of Ideas* 9 (1948): 372–79.

———. *Savagism and Civilization: A Study of the Indian and the American Mind*. Baltimore: Johns Hopkins University Press, 1965.

Poe, Edgar Allan. *Collected Works of Edgar Allan Poe*. 3 vols. Ed. Thomas Ollive Mabbott. Cambridge, Mass.: Belknap Press, 1978.

———. Review of *Georgia Scenes*. *Southern Literary Messenger* 2 (March 1836): 287–92.

Poirier, Richard. *A World Elsewhere: The Place of Style in American Literature*. New York: Oxford University Press, 1966.

Porte, Joel. *The Romance in America*. Middletown, Conn.: Wesleyan University Press, 1969.

Porter, William T., ed. *The Big Bear of Arkansas and Other Sketches*. Philadelphia: T. B. Peterson, 1845.

———. *A Quarter Race in Kentucky and Other Sketches*. Philadelphia: Carey and Hart, 1847.

Pynchon, Thomas. *The Crying of Lot 49*. Philadelphia: Lippincott, 1966.

———. *Gravity's Rainbow*. New York: Viking, 1973.

———. *V*. Philadelphia: Lippincott, 1963.

Reese, David Meredith, M.D. *Humbugs of New-York: Being a Remonstrance Against Popular Delusion; Whether in Science, Philosophy, or Religion*. New York: John S. Taylor, 1838.

Rickels, Milton. *George Washington Harris*. New York: Twayne, 1965.

Robb, John S. *Streaks of Squatter Life, and Far-West Scenes*. Ed. John Francis McDermott. Gainesville, Fla.: Scholars' Facsimiles and Reprints, 1962.

Rogers, Franklin R. *Mark Twain's Burlesque Patterns: As Seen in the Novels and Narratives 1855–1885*. Dallas: Southern Methodist University Press, 1960.

Rosenberry, Edward H. *Melville and the Comic Spirit*. Cambridge: Harvard University Press, 1955.

Rossiter, Clinton. *The American Quest: 1790–1860*. New York: Harcourt Brace Jovanovich, 1971.

Rourke, Constance. *American Humor: A Study of the National Character*. New York: Harcourt, Brace, 1931.

Rubin, Louis, Jr., ed. *The Comic Imagination in America*. New

Brunswick, N.J.: Rutgers University Press, 1973.

Salgado, Gamini, ed. *Cony-Catchers and Bawdy Baskets: An Anthology of Elizabethan Low Life.* Middlesex, Eng.: Penguin, 1972.

Schulz, Max F. *Black Humor Fiction of the Sixties.* Athens: Ohio University Press, 1973.

Shaw, Henry Wheeler. *Everybody's Friend, or: Josh Billing's Encyclopedia and Proverbial Philosophy of Wit and Humor.* Hartford, Conn.: American Publishing Co., 1874.

Siegel, Adrienne. "When Cities Were Fun: The Image of the American City in Popular Books, 1840–1870." *Journal of Popular Culture* 9 (1975): 573–82.

Slatoff, Walter J. *With Respect to Readers: Dimensions of Literary Response.* Ithaca, N.Y.: Cornell University Press, 1970.

Sloane, David E. E. *Mark Twain as a Literary Comedian.* Baton Rouge: Louisiana State University Press, 1979.

Slotkin, Richard. *Regeneration Through Violence: The Mythology of the American Frontier, 1600–1860.* Middletown, Conn.: Wesleyan University Press, 1973.

Smith, Charles Henry. *Bill Arp, So Called. A Side Show of the Southern Side of the War.* New York: Metropolitan Record Office, 1866.

Smith, Henry Nash. *Democracy and the Novel: Popular Resistance to Classic American Writers.* New York: Oxford University Press, 1978.

———. "The Scribbling Women and the Cosmic Success Story." *Critical Inquiry* 1 (1974): 47–70.

———. *Virgin Land: The American West as Symbol and Myth.* Cambridge: Harvard University Press, 1950. Rpt. 1970.

Spengemann, William C. *The Adventurous Muse: The Poetics of American Fiction, 1789–1900.* New Haven: Yale University Press, 1977.

Springer, Haskell S. "*The Leatherwood God*: From Narrative to Novel." *Ohio History* 74 (1965): 191–202.

Stewart, David, and Mickunas, Algis. *Exploring Phenomenology: A Guide to the Field and Its Literature.* Chicago: American Library Association, 1974.

Stock, Brian. "Literary Discourse and the Social Historian." *New Literary History* 8 (1977): 183–94.

Stoehr, Taylor. "Hawthorne and Mesmerism." *Huntington Library Quarterly* 33 (1969): 33–60.

Stoker, Bram. *Famous Impostors.* New York: Sturgis and Walton Company, 1910.

Stone, Robert. *Dog Soldiers: A Novel.* Boston: Houghton Mifflin, 1974.

Stowell, Marion Barber. *Early American Almanacs: The Colonial Weekday Bible.* New York: Burt Franklin, 1977.

Taneyhill, Richard H. *The Leatherwood God (1869–1870) in Two Versions.* Gainesville, Fla.: Scholars' Facsimiles and Reprints, 1966.

Thompson, William Tappan. *Major Jones' Chronicles of Pineville*. Philadelphia: T. B. Peterson and Brothers, 1846.

———. *Major Jones' Courtship*. Philadelphia: Carery & Hart, 1844.

———. *Major Jones' Scenes in Georgia*. Philadelphia: T. B. Peterson and Brothers, 1858.

Tocqueville, Alexis de. *Democracy in America*. Trans. Henry Reeve; ed. and intro. Henry Steele Commager. New York: Oxford University Press, 1947.

———. *Democracy in America*. Trans. Henry Reeve. 2 vols. London: Saunders and Otley, 1838.

Trilling, Lionel. "Huckleberry Finn." In *The Liberal Imagination: Essays on Literature and Society*. Garden City, N.Y.: Doubleday, 1953.

Turner, Frederick Jackson. *The Frontier in American History*. New York: Holt, Rinehart and Winston, 1962.

———. *The Rise of the New West, 1819–1829*. New York: Collier, 1962.

Twain, Mark (Samuel L. Clemens), and Warner, Charles Dudley. *The Gilded Age: A Tale of To-Day*. Ed. Bryant Morey French. Indianapolis and New York: Bobbs-Merrill, 1972.

Tyler, Royall. *The Contrast*. In Arthur Hobson Quinn. *Representative American Plays from 1767 to the Present*. New York: Appleton-Century-Crofts, 1953.

Unsigned review of *Undercurrents of Wall Streert: A Romance of Business*. North American Review, 95, no. 196 (July 1862), 119.

Von Steinwehr, A. *The Centennial Gazetteer of the United States*. Philadelphia, Cincinnati, Chicago, St. Louis: J. C. McCurdy & Co., 1876.

Wadlington, Warwick. *The Confidence Game in American Literature*. Princeton, N.J.: Princeton University Press, 1975.

Watkins, Floyd C., ed. *Life and Public Services of an Army Straggler*. By Kittrell J. Warren. Athens: University of Georgia Press, 1961.

Watterson, Henry. *Oddities in Southern Life and Character*. Boston: Houghton, Mifflin, 1883.

Weber, Brom. ed. *Sut Lovingood*, by New York: Grove, 1954.

Webster, Noah, Preface to *An American Dictionary of the English Language*. New York: S. Converse, 1828.

Weems, Mason Locke. *God's Revenge Against Gambling. Exemplified in the miserable lives and untimely deaths of a number of persons of both sexes, who had sacrificed their Health, Wealth, and Honor at Gambling Tables*. 2d ed. Philadelphia: printed for the author by Lydia R. Bailey, 1812.

Wellman, Manly Wade, ed. *Adventures of Captain Simon Suggs, Late of the Tallapoosa Volunteers*. By Johnson Jones Hooper. Chapel Hill: University of North Carolina Press, 1969.

Welsford, Enid. *The Fool: His Social and Literary History*. New York: Farrar & Rinehart, 1936.

West, Nathanael. *Collected Works*. New York: Farrar, Straus and Cudahy, 1957.

White, Hayden. "The Problem of Change in Literary History." *New Literary History* 7 (1975): 97–112.

Whitman, Walt. *Walt Whitman: Prose Works 1892.* Ed. Floyd Stovall. New York: New York University Press, 1964.

Willeford, William. *The Fool and His Scepter: A Study in Clowns and Jesters and Their Audience.* Evanston, Ill.: Northwestern University Press, 1969.

Willis, N. P., ed. *The Legendary.* 2 vols. Boston: Samuel Goodrich, 1828.

Wills, Gary. *Inventing America: Jefferson's Declaration of Independence.* New York: Doubleday, 1978.

Wirt, William. *The Letters of the British Spy.* Intro. Richard Beale Davis. Chapel Hill: University of North Carolina Press, 1970.

Woolman, John. *The Journal and Major Essays of John Woolman.* Ed. Phillips P. Moulton. New York: Oxford University Press, 1971.

Yates, Norris W. *William T. Porter and the "Spirit of the Times."* Baton Rouge: Louisiana State University Press, 1957.

Ziolkowski, Theodore. *Disenchanted Images: A Literary Iconography.* Princeton, N.J.: Princeton University Press, 1977.

INDEX

Adams, Henry: *Democracy*, 90, 165; *Education of Henry Adams, The*, 198; *History of the United States*, 43, 59, 200

Aldrich, Thomas Bailey, *The Story of a Bad Boy*, 168

Alger, Horatio, 151–52, 157, 158, 163, 165

American Protestant Vindicator, 60–61

"Artemus Ward." *See* Charles Farrar Browne

Arthur Mervyn, 204

Atlantic Monthly, 185

Austin, Jane G., *Dora Darling*, 150

Bagby, George W., 148

Baldwin, Joseph Glover: 117, 128, 135, 142, 145, 176; *Flush Times of Alabama and Mississippi*, 97–106; "new country," 14–15; "Ovid Bolus," 23, 98–102, 113, 117, 124, 182; "Simon Suggs, Jr.," 90, 102–6, 145, 164–65, 182

Barker, James Nelson, 78

Barlow, Joel, 37

Barnum, P. T., 23–28, 99, 102, 195

Barth, John, 22, 203

Bartram, William, 4

Beadle Dime Novels, 148, 178

Beauchamp, Jereboam O., 61

Beecher, Henry Ward, *Norwood*, 150, 154, 157, 172, 174

Bela Bugg, 86–89, 166, 198

Bellow, Saul, 202

Berger, Thomas, 203

Bergson, Henri, 8

Big Bear of Arkansas, 91, 93, 97

"Big Bear of Arkansas," 104, 118–21, 130

"Bill Arp." *See* Smith, Charles Henry

Billington, Ray Allen, "new country," 13, 15

Blair, John, 22–23

Blair, Walter, 25, 44, 98, 107, 109, 112, 179

Boone, Daniel, 11, 44

Boorstin, Daniel, 8–9, 15, 19

Boston Evening Transcript, 117, 194; review of *The Confidence-Man*, 117

Brace, Ned, 45–46, 65, 109

Brackenridge, Hugh Henry: *Indian Atrocities*, 59; *Modern Chivalry*, 7, 11–12, 23, 29–37, 50, 53, 56, 105, 198, 204; "new country," 13, 14–15

Bradford, William, *Of Plymouth Plantation*, 3–4, 5–6, 7–8, 33

Briggs, C. F., 128–29

Brom Bones, 11, 38, 46, 65

Brown, Charles Brockden, 37, 204

Browne, Charles Farrar ("Artemus Ward"), 153–55, 159

Bryant, William Cullen, 12–13, 147–48, 153–54, 165

Bumppo, Natty, 14, 18, 44

Burke, Thomas A., 93, 94–95

Burton, William E., *Cyclopaedia of Wit and Humor*, 93

Byrd, William, *History of the Dividing Line*, 5

Camp-meeting, 86–89, 107–10, 171–73, 178–80, 188–89

Cash, W. J., 53

Child, Lydia M., "Indian Wife," 41

Civil War, 67, 116, 136–37, 137–46, 147–50, 152–58, 174

Clemens, Samuel Langhorne ("Mark Twain"): *Adventures of Huckleberry Finn*, 167–84; *Autobiography*, 158; *Connecticut Yankee in King Arthur's Court, A*, 184; *Gilded Age, The*, 161–67, 173; *Innocents Abroad*, 158; *Life on the Mississippi*, 171, 174; *Mysterious Stranger, The*, 184; *Pudd'nhead Wilson*, 184; *Roughing It*, 159–60

Collinson, Peter, 4

Colonel Sellers, 163–67

Confidence man, definitions of, 1, 17–28, 64, 73–74, 149, 193, 197–98

Contrast, The, 7, 45–46

Cooke, Ebenezer, 5

Cooke, Jay, 150–57, 163
Cooke, John Esten, 149–50
Cooper, James Fenimore, 12, 14, 38, 39, 78
Cotton, John, 4
"Counterfeiters, The," 39–40
Crane, Ichabod, 10–11, 38, 49–50
Crédit Mobilier, 151
Crevecoeur, J. Hector St. John de, 8, 12, 13–14
Crockett, Davy, 7, 18–19, 42–44, 49, 61–62, 93, 202
Culler, Jonathan, 63
Cummins, Maria, The Lamplighter, 135
Cyclopaedia of Wit and Humor, 93

Davidson, James Wood, 93
De Forest, John William: Honest John Vane, 165; Miss Ravenel's Conversion, 150; Playing the Mischief, 165
De Quincey, Thomas, 62
Devol, George H., 62
DeVoto, Bernard, 179
Dickens, Charles, 25, 135
Diddler, Jeremy, 62, 130–31
Dodge, Mary Mapes, Hans Brinker and the Silver Skates, 148
"'Doing' a Landlord," 96
"'Doing' a Sheriff," 95–96
Don Quixote, 30, 204
Douglas, Ann, 136
Drake, Daniel, 14–15
Dreiser, Theodore, 198–99
Duyckinck, Evert A., 195–96
Dylks, Joseph C., 61, 166, 185–95

East Alabamian, 65
Edmonds, S. Emma E., Female Spy of the Union Army, 149, 152, 157
"Elegant Tom Dillar," 128–29
Ellison, Ralph, 201
Emerson, Ralph Waldo, 22, 23
Evening Post (New York), 147

Farrago, Captain John, 29–37
Faulkner, William, 198
Featherton, Pete, 7, 42
Female Spy of the Union Army, 149, 152, 157
Field, Joseph M., 91–93
Fitzgerald, F. Scott, 198–200

Flem Snopes, 198
Flint, Timothy, Condensed Geography and History of the Western States, 14, 59–60
Flush Times of Alabama and Mississippi, 97–106
Forty Years a Gambler, 62
Frame technique, 45, 51–52, 72, 107, 138
Franklin, Benjamin: Almanac, 7; Autobiography, 5–8, 22, 32–34
Franklin, H. Bruce, 136
Franklin, Wayne, 2–3
Freeman, Thomas, 13
Fremont, Colonel, 27
Freneau, Philip, 11–12, 37
Frontier, 12, 36, 44, 57, 64, 86, 88
Fussell, Edwin, 12, 15, 149

Gaddis, William, 201
Gantry, Elmer, 22
Gardiner, William H., 39, 40–41, 43
God's Revenge Against Gambling, 39, 172
Goodrich, S. G., 93
Grangerford and Sheperdson Feud, 173–74
Green, Jonathan H., 63, 132
Greene, Robert, 62
Griswold, Rufus N., 92, 93
Guyot, Arnold, 12

Hale, Sarah J.: "Frontier House," 41, 211; Godey's Lady's Book, 142
Haliburton, Thomas Chandler: Sam Slick, 7; Traits of American Humor, 91
Hall, James: Legends of the West, 14, 58, 59, 93, 135; "The Backwoodsman," 41, 51–52, 93; "Harpe's Head," 59; "Indian Hating," 135
Hans Brinker and the Silver Skates, 148
Harris, George Washington: Sut Lovingood's Yarns, 78, 106–17, 117, 127, 135, 136–37, 140, 142, 144, 145, 159, 176, 182, 183; "Blown Up With Soda," 110–11; Civil War, 116; "new country," 14–15, 109; "Parson John Bullen's Lizards," 107–9; "Rare Ripe Garden-Seed," 115, 118; "Sicily

Burns's Wedding," 111; "Sut Lov-
ingood's Chest Story," 111–13
Harris, Joel Chandler, 141, 161,
Harris, Neil, 24, 25
Harrison, William Henry, 38
Harvard Memorial Biographies,
149–50
Hassan, Ihab, 203
Hauck, Richard B., 6–7, 22, 183–84,
203
Hawthorne, Nathaniel, 22, 61, 212n
Hawthorne, Sophia, 61, 212n
Heller, Joseph, 201
Hemingway, Ernest, 197
Hemphill, Minister, 5–6, 34
Higginson, Thomas Wentworth, 149
Hill, Hamlin, 25, 112
Hoffman, Charles Fenno, *Winter in
the West*, 58, 59, 63
Hoffman, Daniel, 7, 183
Homestead Act of 1862, 147
Hoole, W. Stanley, 91, 153
Hooper, Johnson Jones: 65–96;
*Some Adventures of Captain Si-
mon Suggs*, 20–28, 67–96, 98,
102–5, 119–24, 126, 136, 176–79,
180, 181, 182, 186, 200; "The
Muscadine Story," 90–91; "new
country," 14, 72, 76, 87; "Taking
the Census," 65–67; "The Widow
Rugby's Husband," 90–91
Howells, William Dean: *The Leath-
erwood God*, 166, 179, 185–95;
"new country," 15, 186, 193; *Sto-
ries of Ohio*, 185
Huckleberry Finn, 167–84
Humbugs of New York, 61
Humbugs of the World, The, 27
Huizinga, Johan, 27

Ichabod Crane, 10–11, 38, 49
Indians, 2, 5, 14, 17, 19, 21, 31, 38,
39, 40, 59, 63, 80–81, 84
Inge, M. Thomas, 114, 116
Irving, Washington: Deitrich Knickerbocker, *History of New York*,
10–11; "Legend of Sleepy Hollow," 10–12, 38; "Rip Van Winkle," 10–12, 38
Iser, Wolfgang, 105

Jack Downing, 7, 107
Jackson, Andrew, 38

January, Philip B., 93
Jerdan, William, 91
Jim Doggett, 118–21, 130
Jones, Richard, 14
"Josh Billings." *See* Shaw, Henry
Wheeler
Judson, E. Z. C. ("Ned Buntline"),
62

Kammen, Michael, 9
Keaine, Robert, 4
Keith, Governor, 6
Kennedy, John Pendleton, 37
Kenney, John, 62
"Kentucky Tragedy," 61
Kimball, Richard B., 152, 154
King and the Duke, 176–84
Kirkland, Caroline, 14; *A New
Home*, 16; *Western Clearings*, 16
Kuhlmann, Susan, 22, 27, 102, 200

Lamplighter, The, 135
Lane, T. W., 95
Lang, Andrew, 42
Learn to Say No, 134
Leatherstocking, 18–19, 78, 135
Leatherwood God, The. See How-
ells, William Dean; and Dylks, Jo-
seph C.
Legends of the West. See Hall, James
Lewis, Henry Clay: "The Curious
Widow," 115; "The Day of Judge-
ment," 161, 168
Lewis, Sinclair, 179, 199
Life of Washington, 9
Lindberg, Gary, 22, 181, 183, 203
Lion of the West, The, 82
Lippard, George, *The Monks of
Monk Hall*, 62, 151
Literary World (New York), 1
"Little Frenchman and His Water
Lots, The," 16
Locke, David Ross ("Petroleum V.
Nasby"), 155–56
Long, Major Stephen H., 13
Longstreet, Augustus Baldwin:
Georgia Scenes, 44–56, 65, 67,
152–53, 159; "The Character of a
Native Georgian," 45–46; "The
Fight," 50–53, 54, 56, 138; "Geor-
gia Theatrics," 47–50, 54, 56, 66,
138; "The Horse-Swap," 53–56,
127–28; Ned Brace, 46, 65, 66, 73,

78, 93; "new country," 45; Ransy
Sniffle, 51–53, 65; Yellow Blos-
som, 53–56, 65, 78, 127–28, 130,
182, 189
Loomis, Augustus Ward, 134
"Losing Game of Poker, A," 94
Lowell, James Russell, 107
Lyford, John, 3–4, 7
Lynn, Kenneth S., 52, 107, 167

Madame Merle, 22
Mailer, Norman, 201, 203
Major Jones, 93
Marx, Leo, 199
Massett, Stephen C., 93
Mather, Cotton, 4, 6–7, 10, 34
Melville, Herman: "Bartleby the
Scrivener," 126; "Benito Cereno,"
139; The Confidence-Man, 78,
117–36, 137, 143, 145, 176, 189,
192–93, 201, 203
Merchants' Ledger, 196
Mike Fink, 54
Modern Chivalry. See Brackenridge,
Hugh Henry
Morris, George P., 16
Morton, Thomas, 5, 8, 33
Murfree, Mary Noailles, 141

Native American literature, 12, 37,
38–39
Neal, John, 7, 121
Ned Brace. See Longstreet, Augus-
tus Baldwin
Ned Buntline's Own, 62
"New country," 8–17, 34, 45, 97, 99,
109, 129, 130, 131, 137, 144, 164,
180, 182, 186, 193, 198
New Orleans Picayune, 93
New York Evening Post, 147
New York Ledger, 150
New York Literary World, 1
Nimrod Wildfire, 82
North American Review, 39, 152,
179
Norwood, 150, 154, 157, 172, 174
Nott, Henry Junius: 39, 65, 92, 107;
Novelettes of a Traveller, 40

Oddities of Southern Life, 92
Old Northwest, 13, 15
Old Southwest, 13, 15, 20, 58, 63

"Old Tuttle's Last Quarter Race,"
102
Oral tales, 42–44
"Ovid Bolus." See Baldwin, James
Glover

Page, Thomas Nelson, 141, 161
Panics, 17, 21, 37, 63, 80, 151, 197
Parker, Hershel, 129
Parrington, V. L., 150
Pastorius, Francis Daniel, 5
Paulding, James Kirke, 2, 39, 82
Penn, William, 3
Pete Ketch, 54–56
"Petroleum V. Nasby." See Locke,
David Ross
Phelps, Elizabeth Stuart, The Gates
Ajar, 150, 172
Phunny Phellows, 153–58
Pierce, Jack, 43
Pike, Zebulon Montgomery, 13
Pioneers, The, 78
Pittsburgh Literary Examiner and
Western Monthly Review, 36
Poe, Edgar Allan: 12, 204; "Did-
dling," 62–63, 93, 198; review of
Longstreet's Georgia Scenes, 50,
53; "The Raven," 143
Poirier, Richard, 170, 171, 183
Polly Peablossom's Wedding, 94–95
Porter, William T.: editor, The Big
Bear of Arkansas, 93, 97; editor, A
Quarter Race in Kentucky, 94;
editor, The Spirit of the Times
(New York), 44, 65, 153, 176
Pynchon, Thomas: The Crying of
Lot 49, 203; Gravity's Rainbow,
201; V., 201, 202, 204

Raising the Wind, 62
Ragged Dick, 151, 152, 158, 163,
165
Ratcliffe, Senator, 90
Red Book, 37
Reese, Dr. David M., 61
Republican and Daily Argus, 93
Richardson, Albert D., 16
Rickles, Milton, 112
Robb, John S., 92, 93, 96
Robinson, John, 5
Roderick Random, 138, 204
Rosenberry, Edward H., 117
Rourke, Constance, 8

Sam Slick, 7
Sancric, Jacques, 66
Scott, Sir Walter, 38; "Sir Walter Scott Disease," 171, 174
Senator Dilworthy, 163–67
Shaw, Henry Wheeler ("Josh Billings"), 157–58
Simms, William Gilmore, 93
Slavery, 21, 63, 90
Sloane, David E. E., 170
Smith, Captain John, 5, 8, 22, 33
Smith, Charles Henry ("Bill Arp"), 156–57
Smith, Henry Nash, 11, 78, 148, 149
Smith, John Rawson, 15
Smith, Seba, 7, 107
Smith, Sol, 91–92, 93
Smollett, Tobias, 138
Sniffle, Ransy. See Longstreet, Augustus Baldwin
Snopes, 52, 198
Sol Todd, 66
Sorrentino, Gilbert, 201
Southwestern humor, 22, 23, 64, 153, 161, 167, 171
Spectator, 30, 37, 46
Spengemann, William C., 2
Spirit of the Times, 44, 65, 153, 176
Spy, The, 39
Streaks of Squatter Life, 92, 96
Suggs, Simon. See Hooper, Johnson Jones
Suggs, Simon, Jr. See Baldwin, Joseph Glover
Sut Lovingood. See Harris, George Washington
"Swamp Fox," 9

Taneyhill, Richard H., 185–86, 192, 193
Tassel, Katrina Van, 10
Teague O'Regan, 31, 33
"The Thimble Game," 95
Thomas Singularity, 40, 41, 46, 65, 93, 109
Thompson, William Tappan, 92, 107, 128
Thomson, James, 49–50
Thoreau, Henry David, 22
Thorpe, Thomas Bangs, "The Big Bear of Arkansas," 92, 118–21, 130
Timothy Flint, 80

Tocqueville, Alexis de, 14, 16, 40, 43
Tom Thumb, 27
Trilling, Lionel, 169, 184, 200
Turner, Frederick Jackson, 197, 198
Twain, Mark. See Clemens, Samuel Langhorne
Tyler, Royall, 7, 45

Undercurrents of Wall Street, 152, 154

Van Buren, Martin, 66
Vonnegut, Kurt, 201

Wadlington, Warwick, 22, 135, 169, 183
Warren, Kittrell J.: History of the Eleventh Georgia Volunteers, 137; Life and Public Services of an Army Straggler, 137–45, 182; Ups and Downs of Wife Hunting, 137
Washington, George, 9, 11, 18, 24, 27
Watterson, Henry, 92, 93
Wearing of the Gray, The, 149
Weber, Brom, 112
Weems, Mason Locke, 9, 39, 172
West, 12, 58
West, Nathanael: A Cool Million, 203; The Day of the Locust, 179, 201; Miss Lonelyhearts, 179, 199
Westervelt, 22
White, Abiram, 14
Whitman, Walt, 148, 182
Willis, N. P., 26
Wills, Gary, 8
Winter in the West, 58, 59, 63
Winthrop, John, 4
Wirt, William, 9
"Wolves in Sheeps' Cloathing," 6, 34
Woodmason, Charles, 14
Woolman, John, 4

Yankee, 7, 9, 22, 54, 121
Yankee, The, 121
Yankee Blade, 93
Yankee Humor, and Uncle Sam's Fun, 91
"Yankee Peddler, The," 121
"Yankee Roué, The," 39
Yellow Blossom. See Longstreet, Augustus Baldwin

Shadows
on the Coast
of Maine

An Antique Print Mystery

Lea Wait

SCRIBNER

New York London Toronto Sydney Singapore

🕯

SCRIBNER
1230 Avenue of the Americas
New York, NY 10020

For information regarding special discounts for bulk purchases,
please contact Simon & Schuster Special Sales at 1-800-456-6798
or business@simonandschuster.com

Designed by Colin Joh
Text set in Sabon

Manufactured in the United States of America

1 3 5 7 9 10 8 6 4 2

Library of Congress Cataloging-in-Publication Data

Wait, Lea.
Shadows on the coast of Maine: an antique print mystery/Lea Wait.
p. cm.
1. Women detectives—Maine—Fiction. 2. Prints—Collectors and
collecting—Fiction. 3. Antiques dealers—Fiction. 4. Maine—Fiction.
I. Title.

PS3623.A42S535 2003
813'.6—dc21
2003042535

ISBN 0-7432-2554-6

MYS
Wait

For Bob, who brought joy back into my life.

And for Susanne Kirk, caring and exacting editor, who believed in me and in Maggie.

The summer I was five I woke in the night and saw a great white owl perched in the moonlight on the post of the bed I shared with Sally and Eliza. The house was new then, in 1774, and Grandma Brewer had opened our shutters for the river breezes. Even in Maine there are stifling July days.

I can still see that owl looking down at me as I lay naked under my shift. Just looking. I stared at it until it raised its wings and flew out and over the Madoc River.

I told no one, because I knew it was a sign meant only for me.

Now changes are coming to this house, which has been mine for so long. Mine by right of pride and heritage, and because no one else wanted it and I kept the roof in repair and the bats from the chimney. Despite those years, soon the house will be moved to the mainland, and although my cousin says I am welcome to stay, I know I am not.

But parts of me will go with this house, and one part will be these words. I pray they will bring rest to me, and to the house, and to everything within it. Now, and in years too distant to see, there must be an end to the evil I have brought to this place.

The dark is coming on. The cows need tending. The living must always be tended before the dead. There will be time for words later.

Chapter 1

The District of Maine, *map of pre-1820 Maine (when it was still a part of Massachusetts) by Philadelphia engraver John G. Warnicke, c. 1812. Hand-colored lines marking county boundaries of that time. Horizontal fold mark. 11 x 15.25 inches. Price: $260.*

"Please, Maggie, you have to come to Maine a day early. I need you. Drew has to fly back to New York overnight and I don't want to be alone. Not in this house."

Maggie Summer kept hearing Amy's words as she gave her excuses to Gussie White. She'd been staying on Cape Cod with her friend Gussie while she displayed her nineteenth-century prints at an antiques show. She'd been looking forward to an extra day of relaxing on the beach, but Amy's call was too strange to ignore.

"Amy is the most realistic, straightforward, organized person I have ever known," she explained to Gussie as she

3

tightened the tops on her shampoo and conditioner bottles before packing them. "In high school, before she got her driver's license she took an auto mechanics course. In college her term papers were always done early, her dorm bed was made, and when she said she wanted to go to homecoming with Joe Smith, that's what happened. She's the last person in the world to be nervous about staying alone. That's why I have to go."

Gussie had given her a hug and nodded. "If you're worried, then I am too, Maggie. You go. Let me know how everything is once you're settled in."

That had been five hours ago. Maggie took another swig of diet cola. She'd forgotten just how far midcoast Maine was from the Cape. Thank goodness she was finally off the Maine Turnpike and heading up Route 1. She glanced at the directions she'd taped on the van dashboard. Madoc shouldn't be far now.

She hadn't seen Amy in a couple of years, not since Amy's wedding to Drew Douglas. It had been an elegant affair at the Short Hills Country Club in New Jersey, with Amy's mother and stepfather looking stylish and proud. And rich, Maggie thought to herself. Maggie had gotten by with scholarships and loans at the state college, but Amy had never explained why, with her family's money and her top grades, she hadn't gone to a private college or university. Maybe even Ivy League. "Montclair State is close to home" was all she'd say, as she crossed off the next item on her day's "to do" list. Amy's daily list started with "healthy breakfast" and went on from there.

Rooming together had sometimes been frustrating for both of them, Maggie remembered. But she had always known whom she could borrow deodorant from, and who would have an extra box of typing paper the night before a report was due. Amy was reliable. And she put up with Maggie's bed not always being made, and Maggie's casual social life. Amy would never go out for pizza without scheduling it ahead of time. Never.

When Amy had called in May, Maggie had been glad to chat, as always. She had sat down in amazement when she learned Amy was not calling from her condo in New York City near the ad agency where she worked and uptown from Drew's office on Wall Street, but from a small town in Maine.

"You have to come and visit. It's a wonderful house, Maggie. Built in 1774, on a hill with a great view of the river. You'll love it. And you can give me advice on historic preservation. You know about these things. And, of course, I'll be needing a lot of antique prints for these old walls, so be sure to bring some from your inventory."

Maggie's time was her own. She wasn't teaching summer courses at the college this year; all she had planned was doing several antiques shows. Since her husband Michael's death last winter, she had been restless. Besides, Maine was a great place to find new inventory to add to her business, Shadows. Shadows of past worlds; shadows to share with the present. Maggie loved her print business's name. She loved her life, even if it was a lonely one just now.

Amy was right; she couldn't say no to a trip to Maine to see an old friend.

So here she was, driving her faded blue van up the coast through postcard-pretty towns full of two-story, white houses, art galleries, gift shops, and BEST LOBSTER ROLLS HERE signs. Many of the antiques shops looked inviting. But not today. She would stay a week or two; there would be time later.

Amy's house stood on a hill, rising above the road and a

line of pines close to the Madoc River. Maggie drove around the curve in the road that made up two borders to the property, then made a sharp left turn into the driveway. She parked near the ell that joined the barn and the house in true New England fashion. She didn't need to see the pickup truck already parked next to Amy's Volvo wagon or the ladders leading up to the roof to know that the old house needed work. A lot of work. The roof was probably only the beginning.

"Maggie!" Amy came running from what must be the kitchen door. "I'm so glad you're here!"

"What's happening? Why the emergency?" Amy looked as always—short blonde hair in place, fitted designer jeans, and a NEW YORK CITY navy T-shirt. The only unusual part of her attire was a wide, white bandage circling her left arm. "Are you hurt?"

"I'm fine, now that you're here. I'll tell you all the gory details and you can tell me I am absolutely crazy after you get settled in and I open a bottle of wine."

"Speaking of wine . . ." Maggie reached behind the faded red Metropolitan Museum canvas bag that served as her travel pocketbook and pulled out two bottles of a good Australian chardonnay. "I can never resist those New Hampshire wine prices." Despite her bandaged arm Amy managed to balance the bottles while Maggie picked up her duffel bag. "It's a beautiful site, Amy. No wonder you love it. I can hardly wait to see the house."

"Tour coming right up." Amy seemed more relaxed than she had sounded on the phone that morning. But Maggie noticed that Amy didn't look directly at her and was chattering more than normal. As they started toward the house, several old wooden shingles tumbled from the roof and fell directly in front of them. "Giles! There are people down here!"

Maggie could now see a big man and a teenaged boy balancing on the roof of the ell, holding hammers. "Sorry, Mrs. Douglas. They slipped again."

Amy shuddered. "Well, be more careful." She turned to Maggie as they entered the house. "Giles and his son Brian are doing the roof, and I hope they'll have time to help with some other work. Depends on how many calls Johnny Brent's construction company gets this summer."

Maggie looked around in delight. The kitchen was large, full of light, and lined with high cabinets. Storage space! The appliances were 1930s vintage, and the walls could use paint, but the possibilities were limitless.

"Crystal, this is my college roommate, Maggie." The attractive blonde teenager who was washing dishes smiled at them. "I'm hoping she will be staying with us a couple of weeks."

"Nice to meet you." The girl wore tight jeans and a short, bright pink tank top.

"And since I'll have company, you can go for the day after you finish the dishes. I'll be fine."

Crystal nodded. "If it's okay, I'll stay till Brian is finished. He said he'd give me a ride home."

"No problem." Amy turned back to Maggie. "Just wait until you see the rest of the house! After apartment living for fifteen years, I'm loving the space. There's a small room just off the kitchen; I'm turning it into my study. I'm not sure yet what I'll do there—maybe take up oil painting—or learn to quilt—but it will be all mine!" The small room was indeed cozy. It was almost filled by an executive-office-sized wooden desk covered with piles of papers and a floor-to-ceiling bookcase half-filled with books.

"Looks as though you've already got at least one project going."

"I've been checking the town archives for information on this house. I'm curious about who lived here before us."

"This must have been the birth and death room," said Maggie. "They were usually small rooms, easily heated, and close to the kitchen for warmth and accessibility."

"I knew you'd be able to figure this place out. Just wait until you see the view from the living room!"

The house was just as Maggie had imagined it: a classic New England home with a central hall, fireplaces in most of the rooms, and four bedrooms on the second floor. A space that might have been for storage at some time had been made into a bathroom, and there was electricity, but otherwise the house looked as it must have a hundred or more years ago. The faded wallpaper still hanging on the cracked clamshell-plaster walls was definitely late nineteenth century. Possibly earlier.

"Drew is using one of the bedrooms as his study," Amy explained as Maggie touched the crumbling black-and-white-speckled plaster and wondered how complicated it would be to repair. "And this is our guest room, all yours for as long as you can stay." Maggie hoped the cracks in the buckling ceiling didn't indicate problems of immediate concern. Amy had found a bright modern brass bed and covered it with a quilt. The quilt was no doubt made in China, but it was patchwork. The room was bright and cheerful despite the crumbling plaster.

Amy and Drew's bedroom was the most finished of the rooms Maggie had seen, with new yellow paint and small-sprigged floral wallpaper that made it cozy and welcoming. And the four twelve-paneled windows had the same wonderful view of the Madoc River as the living room below.

"And this"—Amy smiled, opening the door to the fourth bedroom—"is for the future." The room was a perfect Saks

Fifth Avenue display nursery. A white crib topped by a lace canopy stood in the center of the room. In one corner an upholstered, navy blue rocking chair waited, next to a bookcase filled with picture books. Floor-to-ceiling shelves held an assortment of stuffed animals and toys near a newly built closet. Of course. A house of this age would not have been built with closets.

"You didn't tell me! Congratulations!" Maggie grabbed Amy and gave her a hug. "Oh, how wonderful! I have to tell you, I'm a little envious!"

"Not yet," Amy said, as she closed the door and walked into the hall. "No congratulations yet. But we have plans. You unpack your clothes and then let's break out some of that wine."

Plans? Amy would not be drinking wine if there was a chance she was pregnant. Maybe they were adopting. But why hadn't she said so?

By the time Maggie had unpacked her clothes and hung them in a pine wardrobe, she found Amy sitting on the front porch overlooking the river. Amy poured the wine into red bohemian glasses and offered a plate of wheat crackers and Brie.

"Mmmm." Maggie settled into the green-and-white-striped cushions on the Adirondack chair and looked around. "I'm set. You may have to move me after a while, this is so comfortable." She sipped her wine and then turned toward Amy. "So what is happening? Why did you call this morning?"

Amy hesitated. "I don't know, Maggie. That's the problem. Or one of them. Nothing seems to be turning out quite the way I planned."

Maggie remembered Amy's lists and plans in their college days.

"Like?"

As Amy poured more wine, Maggie noticed Amy's finger-nails were carefully polished in creamy pink, but badly chipped. The Amy she knew would have touched up those nails immediately. Although it would be crazy to try to keep nails polished neatly while working on an old house.

"This place has so much potential. We fell in love with it the first time we saw it, and the price was right. The owner was leaving the country and wanted to sell quickly. But—I know this is all going to sound very strange, Maggie. And not like me at all. But right after we moved in, I felt something was wrong. And the woman next door, Shirley Steele, who is also the hairdresser in Waymouth, told us there have always been stories about this house."

"Stories?" Maggie's wine was slightly dry, just as she liked it, and she couldn't imagine any stories that would make this house less lovely. "You mean you have ghosts? What fun!"

"Sometimes at night I swear I can hear a baby crying. But it stops almost as soon as I notice it. And one night Drew and I both saw shadows that looked like a woman in a long dress, moving across the moonlight on our wall."

"A house that has been home to as many people as this one has, over so many years, must be filled with memories," Maggie answered. "And it's so different from your apartment in the city, or from Short Hills, that you're probably just very conscious of everything. Plus"—she paused for a moment—"it's so quiet here! You can hear the birds. Those are chickadees, aren't they?" She listened again. "And I think mourning doves."

"And we can hear every car that goes by, and every lob-sterman who checks his traps on the river at five in the morning. Yes; you're right. At first we thought maybe our imaginations were just filling the silences. But that's not all."

"What else?"

"There are the accidents." Amy looked down at her arm. "This one happened yesterday. I opened one of the windows, to try to wash the outside. Most of the windows are the old blown-glass kind, with bubbles in it. We don't want to replace any that aren't broken. But suddenly the glass shattered, and I jumped a little, and the window came down on my arm. It took an hour in the emergency room to take out all the little pieces of glass and stop the bleeding. My arm is pretty badly bruised."

"A nasty accident," said Maggie. "But it's an old house. Things do happen. It looks as though no one has done anything to maintain it recently. The ceilings in a couple of rooms look pretty precarious. But that isn't ghosts. It's just part of fixing up an old house." Maggie tried to sound knowledgeable. Several friends had restored Victorian homes near hers in New Jersey, but she couldn't begin to imagine the time and money they'd spent. She usually got involved only when the owners had reached the point of decorating and wanted authentic Victorian prints to match their furnishings. One couple had hung Currier & Ives prints in every room of their house. Maggie was happy to have them as customers, but she preferred a more eclectic look for her own home.

"It's not the only accident," Amy continued. "There are the shingles that keep falling off the roof. You saw some today."

"But the roofer, Giles? He said he was sorry. He must have dropped them."

"He always apologizes. But they fall even when he's not here. Even when we know he has checked and assured us they're not loose. And the lights flicker at strange moments. And there are noises in the pipes."

All just part of owning an old home, Maggie thought.

"And then there was the fire."

"Fire?" Maggie sat up straighter.

"Thank goodness we had installed smoke detectors as soon as we moved in, so we knew, even though it started in the middle of the night. It was in one of the empty rooms in the ell. I called the local volunteer fire department, but luckily we had two fire extinguishers in the kitchen. Drew was able to put out most of the fire before anyone got here. A fireman told me we were lucky; a house this age can go up quickly."

"What started the fire?"

Amy shook her head. "That's one of the scary parts. There was no wiring involved, and no one had even been in that room recently. We had cleaned it out and left it empty. We thought we'd eventually use it for storage. We're working on the main house before we get to the ell. There's no heat there, no gas lines, no materials to catch fire. In fact, one of the walls in that room is brick."

"Strange."

"The firemen thought so too. One of them asked Drew if we knew anyone in the area who would want to make trouble. Of course, we just got here. We haven't been here long enough to make many friends, and certainly not long enough to make any enemies." Amy smiled weakly at Maggie. "After that we started getting weird hang-up calls. The phone would ring, we'd answer, and whoever was on the other end would hang up immediately."

"Heavy breathing?"

"Nothing. No background noise; no voices. Some days we'd get a dozen calls. The ones in the middle of the night really freaked me out. Last night I was having trouble sleeping; my arm was throbbing, and it was hard to get comfortable. I had finally gotten to sleep at two-thirty when one of those calls woke us. And then after the call we both heard the baby crying. Drew hadn't heard it before; he thought I'd been dreaming. We looked everywhere; we don't know where the sound comes from. It lasts about thirty seconds. One night I timed it by the minute hand on our clock. It's a horrible sound. Almost an echo. As though the baby was crying a long time ago, and we're just hearing it now." Amy took more than a sip of her wine. "I'm sure you think I'm crazy. But I couldn't sleep after that, and I couldn't face being in the house alone tonight. Drew had to fly to the city to talk to one of his old clients. The guy wanted his old financial adviser, and Drew's company was glad to pay to keep the man happy. Drew will be back tomorrow. That's why I called you."

"It does sound awful," Maggie said. "But I assumed you were just here for the summer. Has Drew left the brokerage house?"

"Didn't I tell you? We both left our jobs. We decided a less stressful lifestyle would be best for us, and for our children. Someday," Amy added quickly. "Drew is thinking about teaching, and maybe I'll write the great American novel."

"Whew. You've taken on some major lifestyle changes." Amy had always loved the city; the pace, the excitement, the theaters, the clubs.

"And the changes will work. I'm sure they will. I've planned it all out. But something, or someone, is making the transition harder than we imagined." Amy took another gulp of wine. "I was the one who suggested this move; Drew was always reluctant. Expenses are higher than we thought they'd be, and with the strange noises, and the fire, and the telephone calls . . . Drew's been drinking a bit more than he should and is beginning to talk about going back. That's one reason he stayed over in New York tonight. I'm sure he could have flown down, had his meeting, and come back today. But he's meeting some friends for dinner."

"He'll probably have a wonderful time, miss you terribly, and be home tomorrow. And tonight I'll be here to help cope with telephone calls and crying in the night. Have you called the telephone company about the mysterious calls?"

"The lines out here are old; we can't get caller ID. And the caller never hangs on long enough for them to trace anything."

Maggie poured herself another glass of wine. She was glad Drew would return tomorrow. There must be more to this story than Amy was sharing. Maybe Drew would have more answers.

The phone rang.

Maggie and Amy looked at each other. One of them would have to answer it.

Chapter 2

―――❦―――

A New England Home, *hand-colored lithograph pub-lished by Currier & Ives, c. 1850. Elegant white colonial home on hill, surrounded by tall trees; horse-drawn car-riage and children in drive in front; barn and animals to right, bottom of hill. 8 x 12.8 inches (small folio). Price: $375.*

The phone call had been from Drew, checking to see that Amy was all right. There were no more telephone calls that night, and although Amy seemed more relaxed by the next morning, Maggie was still concerned. Ghosts? A baby's cry in the night? Perhaps Amy's imagination was merely work-ing overtime. Shingles falling off the roof and the window's shattering could be put in the "challenges of living in old houses" column. But the fire and the telephone calls should be investigated.

"I've been meaning to have my hair trimmed. Did you say

your neighbor had a salon?" Maggie put down the *Portland Press Herald* as Amy debated her agenda for the day. Amy had also said the neighbor knew this house's history.

"Shirley Steele. Her salon is Cut 'n' Curl, across the river in Waymouth. She's not bad. Everyone goes there."

"I think I'll give her a call. You sound as though you have some things to do. And then, if you don't mind, I see that tomorrow there's an auction at a place called Walter English Auctions, and the preview is open today. I'd like to check it out." Maggie paused. "I know someone who may also be visiting near here, but we missed calls before I left for the Cape, and I'm not sure about the exact dates he'll be in Maine. Sometime while I'm here I should call him."

"'Him'?" Amy looked up. "Who?"

"Will Brewer, an antiques dealer from Buffalo. I met him when we were both doing the Rensselaer County Antiques Fair in May." Maggie hesitated. It probably wasn't the right time to mention the two dealers who had been murdered at that show. "In July, Will and I met in New York to see a museum exhibit. He's nice." She held the paper up so Amy couldn't see the faint blush she couldn't control.

"'Nice'? Maggie, *nice* is for maiden aunts. I assume this man is a possibility? You're a widow now, and you're still young. Keep your options open!"

"He has an aunt in Waymouth, and thought he'd be in Maine in August. I have her number; maybe I'll call in a couple of days."

"If you don't, I'll remind you. For sure. In the meantime, have your hair done and get prettied up. This morning I'm going to talk with Giles about his progress on the roof, and then I need to get some groceries. Drew should be home by early afternoon, and I wouldn't want to cause a crisis by being out of his favorite brand of chocolate milk. Or vodka." Amy went back to her list, then looked up. "If you go to the auction preview, would you keep an eye out for a pine corner cupboard for the living room? I'd like one that is late eighteenth or early nineteenth century, the same period as the house."

"Does the living room have corner beams?"

"Yes. So the cupboard would have to have a straight back or a corner cut out. Not fit directly into the corner the way later ones sometimes do."

"I'll look, and if I see any possibilities, I'll report back so you can check them out for yourself. Depending on what's in the sale, I might or might not go to the auction tomorrow, if that's okay with you?"

"You're on vacation! Whatever you want to do is fine with me. Are you looking for anything in particular?"

"I could always use some more copies of *Harper's Weekly*, especially from the early 1870s. Eighteen seventy-three is the most valued year for print dealers because Winslow Homer's Gloucester Series was printed then. And I could use some good Curriers, or any pre-1850s books with hand-colored botanical or zoological prints. My inventory is low on astronomy and astrology just now. And sometimes I'll buy a drawing or painting, or even a dramatic early-twentieth-century print or lithograph, or some folk art. Something that catches my eye and that I think might catch a customer's. It's hard to predict. So many prints were produced and hand-colored in such small editions that there are few records of them, and even a dealer may only find them once."

"I'd like to look through your portfolios. I'll need some prints for these walls. Maybe fruit, for the kitchen, or butterflies. It's hard to say until I decide exactly what our color scheme will be."

"Better to wait then. But looking at the prints could give you ideas too. I'd love to show you some of my things. And they're right out in the van. No problem."

"Another day, then. Definitely. When Drew is here. I think he'd find them fascinating, especially since this house has reawakened his undergraduate interest in American history."

"'Prints are a keyhole to the past.' That's a Maggie Summer quote, from my Introduction to American Civilization course. I use a lot of prints to illustrate the way America saw itself, especially in the mid– and late nineteenth century."

Amy looked down at her list again. "Is there anything special you'd like me to get at the store?"

"As long as you have diet cola, I'll be set."

Amy made another note. "Will do. If only all of life were that simple!"

Cut 'n' Curl was easy to find, just off the main street (conveniently called Main Street).

Shirley Steele was a middle-aged blonde whose pink hairdresser's smock stretched across her ample front. "So, are you visiting in Waymouth?" she asked as she tied a gray plastic coverall around Maggie's neck and tucked in a towel to prevent leakage. "How much of this do you want off?"

Maggie resisted the urge to jump out of the chair before Shirley picked up her shears. "Just even it out and take off the split ends. Maybe an inch."

Shirley backed up and looked at Maggie's hip-length, wavy brown hair critically. "Short hair's more the style now, you know. Most people stopped wearing it this long in the sixties." She picked up a few strands. "But you've got good, thick hair; you can carry it off."

"Thank you."

Shampooed, conditioned, and seated in front of a mirror,

Maggie tried to focus on the conversation and not watch Shirley circling her chair and assessing. "I'm visiting an old friend, Amy Douglas. She recommended you."

Shirley grew at least an inch. "Amy's such a friendly woman. She and Drew—that's her husband, but you already know that—moved in next door to me a couple of months ago."

"It's an interesting house. Amy mentioned it has a history."

"Like any house over two hundred years old."

"Do you think there could be ghosts there?" How much more direct could she be?

"Has Amy seen one?" Shirley knelt unsteadily to reach the ends of Maggie's hair.

"Not exactly. I just wondered, since the house is so old."

Shirley focused on a strand of hair and then snipped. And snipped again. "I'll tell you what I told Amy. What everyone knows. For the last hundred years only unmarried women have lived in that house. No men. Until Amy's husband, of course."

"Interesting." Maggie covered her naked left hand. Michael's death in a car accident last December had not erased his infidelities, and she did not feel that wearing her wedding ring or playing the bereaved widow accurately reflected her current status. Or state of mind.

"Of course, there were men living in the house in the nineteenth century. Sea captains, mostly. Most of them outlived at least a couple of wives."

How cheering. "Then there are no ghosts?"

"Never heard of a murder there, or a suicide. Folks say ghosts stay with a house after an unsettling death. Of course, Charlotte did once tell me—Charlotte Leary lived there until she died last year—a natural death, she was eighty-two—she did tell me the house creaked and moaned a lot, and sometimes the wind cried in the chimney. Does in our house too.

Nor'easters come right across the river and up the hill and hit those two houses." Shirley snipped again. Maggie wished she could see her back and monitor what Shirley was cutting. "Charlotte was a dear woman; very active in the church. Can't think of any reason a ghost would bother her."

So ghosts only bothered certain people. Say, nonchurch-goers?

The tiny woman sitting in the chair next to Maggie's, her blueing hair standing straight up with coloring formula, was clearly taking in the conversation. "Shirley, tell the woman what she's wanting to hear. Can't do much harm now. Those New York folks bought the house right and proper and they've got a right to know what they've got themselves in for."

Maggie tried to look at the elderly woman, but couldn't move her head while Shirley was measuring her hair. "Do you know the house I'm talking about?"

"The old Brewer house has been there as long as any, and a lot of people who live here have roots there. A few folks . . ." The woman paused. "A few folks were a bit peeved that it was sold out of the family. But that wasn't anything to do with you, or your friends. That's family business."

Shirley's scissors snipped loudly and rapidly several times.

"So does the house have ghosts, then?" Maggie asked.

"Some say it does. But Shirley's told you straight. No murders or suicides anyone can remember, and there's folks here should know. I'm the oldest now, I'd wager, but I can't think of any violence done in that house outside the usual family squabbles and a couple of women died in childbirth. But that used to be pretty common. Captain Eben Brewer, back in the fifties"—Maggie realized the woman meant the 1850s—"he lost three wives in birthing. Couldn't hardly find a fourth to marry, but my grandmother, Becca Giles, she said, 'Three's a charm; no point in looking to the past,' and she married him and had seven children and outlived the captain."

"So there are ghosts?" Maggie tried to get back to the point before it was totally lost in memories.

"Some say there's a woman who walks the halls. A woman with a baby. Haven't heard the story in years, though. I don't think Charlotte paid the two of them any heed."

Maggie shivered slightly. Maybe Amy wasn't crazy. "Maybe the ghost is one of those women who died in childbirth."

"Could be. Might be. That's as good a guess as any. But you tell your friend that those ghosts ain't never bothered no one. That woman and her baby, they're quiet spirits. Some woman over to Brunswick I heared had some force in her house that knocked pictures off the wall and dishes off her cabinet shelves. Brewer house ghosts are civilized. Never bothered no one."

"Nettie, that's nonsense. Ghosts can't be civilized. It's against their nature." Shirley stood up and surveyed the ring of dark brown hair now surrounding Maggie's chair.

"Some are the kind to bother folks, and some are not. Brewer ghosts ain't the meddlin' sort."

Shirley looked at the older woman. "Those ghosts wouldn't bother kinfolk, I believe. But these people from New York ain't kinfolk. They're from away. Ghosts might be uncomfortable living with them."

Nettie looked directly back at Shirley. "Well now, Shirley, I'd say those ghosts should just calm down and accept what has to be accepted. Lizzie made her decision. Nothing to be done about it now."

"Who's Lizzie?" asked Maggie. Why did she have the feeling a couple of different conversations were taking place at the same time?

"Lizzie Colby. She's the one sold the house to your friends." Shirley took out the hand dryer and started blow-drying Maggie's not-quite-as-long-as-it-had-been hair. With the noise of the dryer no further conversation was possible.

Her hair had survived the trim. Actually, not a bad job, Maggie thought as she looked in the mirror. And both Shirley Steele and this other woman had agreed there might be ghosts in the house. Maybe Amy wasn't crazy. Or, maybe everyone was. With that many women dying in childbirth it made sense for the ghosts to be a woman and a baby.

Maggie shook her newly trimmed hair a bit as she headed to the auction gallery. Had she just rationally justified the existence of two ghosts? She had been in Maine for less than a day. No wonder people whose families had lived here for generations seemed able to coexist comfortably with the spirits of the past.

The auction preview was crowded. August was not the best time of year to look for bargains at a Maine auction. Usually auctiongoers were dealers, collectors, or individuals furnishing a home. The more dealers the better, since collectors would pay high prices for particular items to complete collections, as would someone looking for the perfect bureau for their guest room. Dealers wouldn't usually bid over 50 percent of retail, since they would have to price the item so they could make a profit. Auctions were basic hunting grounds for antiques dealers.

But this crowd of preview lookers was heavily laced with vacationers. The plaid shorts, dramatically manicured nails, and T-shirts emblazoned with puffins, lobsters, and moose were dead giveaways. An elderly man to her left was leaning on a wooden cane covered by stickers that told the world he had visited YELLOWSTONE, DISNEY WORLD, GRAND CANYON, and ACADIA.

Maggie looked briefly at two aisles of pine and cherry furniture and at three small tapestries hanging on the wall in back of the furniture. No corner cupboards of any kind, and she wasn't interested in the vintage chandelier or milk-glass light fixture hanging from a beam overhead. Oak Victorian furniture was in a corner and included a nice ornately carved pump organ labeled "From First Congregational Church." Interesting, but not for her. Maggie paused at three glass showcases filled with estate jewelry. Sometimes she splurged and bought something for herself; at auctions pieces of jewelry might sell at a small percentage of appraised value. Her favorite sapphire and pearl ring had come from an auction like this one.

Today none of the jewelry held her attention, and she wasn't interested in silver or glass or majolica. There were several cartons of books on a side table that she would check out, and one wall of framed items. So far she hadn't seen any reason to sign up for a bidding number.

The first carton of books was full of mid–twentieth-century bestsellers. Nothing she wanted to read, and certainly nothing for her business. The second carton held some of the same, but also included five late-nineteenth-century illustrated children's books.

She pulled each out and looked at it critically. The Kate Greenaway had been much loved and much scribbled in; only three of the plates could be removed and sold as prints. The Aunt Louisa book was beautiful, and the lithographs were in excellent condition, but there were paragraphs in the middle of the artwork so they wouldn't frame well. If the story hadn't been consecutive, so illustrations were on the reverse of others, some pages could have been have framed as a nice series grouping. But this book would best be kept intact and sold to a book collector. Gussie might be interested; her shop featured dolls and toys, but she carried a few beautifully lithographed children's picture books. This one would retail between $100 and $200. That meant a dealer might pay $50 or $60 for it. Maggie made a mental note and went on. One early-twentieth-century Volland nursery rhyme book with torn pages. No. One linen book. No. One book of animal stories that included four usable lithographs: one pig, one goat, one pony, and one dog. The dog would definitely sell, and probably the pony. The other pictures were nice, but would be slow sellers. If she were to bid on this box, she'd be bidding on perhaps seven prints, plus the Aunt Louisa she might be able to resell. If the carton went for $60 or less, she quickly decided, it would be worth the effort. But she wouldn't pay more, and she wouldn't go to the auction just for that carton. One more carton to check. Maggie waited a moment as the man ahead of her finished his perusal. At least one early atlas, Maggie could see over his shoulder. She wondered if it included any astronomy prints. Sometimes early atlases included maps of the heavens.

"Maggie Summer!" The voice was close, and the hand on her shoulder was gentle and familiar. Maggie spun around quickly, smiling at the face sporting a soft graying blond beard and a grin.

"Will Brewer!"

"Why didn't you call? You never told me exactly when you'd be in Maine!"

"I just got here late yesterday afternoon." Why did she always feel like smiling when she saw Will? She had only known him a short time but she felt as though they were old friends.

"And, of course, the first thing you did was go to an auction preview!" Will grinned. "What else would a dealer do? Certainly not call a friend." He looked around. "Is the college roommate you're staying with here?"

They stepped away from the tables to leave room for other people checking out the lots.

"No; she had some errands to do, so I just took off." Thank goodness she had stopped at Cut 'n' Curl on the way. "How long have you been here?"

"In Waymouth, about ten days; at the preview, about six minutes. My aunt is quite elderly now, and every year she saves up an assortment of small jobs for me. I've already reglued four chairs, replaced two cracked windowpanes, found a small leak by the chimney and retarred and reshingled that part of the roof, made several trips to the dump, and pruned a dozen rosebushes. I spent most of yesterday unsticking windows."

"You're a handy man to have around. Do you charge by the hour?"

"I've been visiting Aunt Nettie each summer since I was little; Maine is a great place to vacation, and Nettie became a 'summer mother' to me. She's ninety now, and still living alone. We both look forward to my visits."

"And to a little buying for the business?"

"In this case, mixing pleasure with pleasure. Not to speak of running into an attractive print dealer."

Maggie's cheeks blushed even more. "Seen anything here worth coming back for tomorrow? I'm not enthused so far. But I haven't checked everything out yet."

"I haven't either. The preview ad listed several fireplace sets and a box of tools, so I'll know after I find them." Will specialized in early fireplace and kitchen equipment, and tools. "That shouldn't take more than another fifteen minutes. There's a great place for totally evil fried clams and scallops down the road. Would you be free for lunch?"

"I'd love that."

Maggie hummed to herself as Will went on his way and

she looked through the last lot of books. The atlas didn't include any astronomy prints, and only about a dozen maps quickly salable to her customers. The others were of Europe and Asia, not fast sellers, and states in the Far West. She only did shows in Pennsylvania, New York, New Jersey, Connecticut, and Massachusetts. She had just about given up hope of finding any treasures when, underneath two leather-bound family Bibles—sadly, valuable only to the families whose records they contained, and who must have discarded them—she found a volume that had once been leather-bound and complete. She recognized it immediately, scanned through it quickly, and put it back under the Bibles. She was definitely going to attend this auction tomorrow.

It was half of an 1832 edition of Alexander Wilson's *American Ornithology*, printed in Edinburgh. Although it was a breaker, a book whose binding was broken or missing and therefore of limited value to a book dealer, the half that was still there contained eighteen of Wilson's hand-colored, steel-engraved American birds. More people today recognized the name John James Audubon, but Audubon had come after Wilson and, in fact, was said to have based some of his drawings on Wilson's studies. An Audubon portfolio was way over Maggie's budget. She'd seen in *Maine Antique Digest* that a complete Bien 1859 edition of his *Birds of America* had sold for over $300,000 at a recent auction. Of course, Mark Catesby had been the first artist to record the birds of America, in the early eighteenth century. But his prints were even beyond Audubon's in price, if, indeed, anyone was ever lucky enough to find any. Wilson had been next, almost a hundred years later, a weaver and peddler who met naturalist William Bartram in 1802 and started drawing birds. His first volume was published in 1808, twenty years before Audubon's. More people were discovering Wilson's work every year. These were his small folio prints, but she could easily price them at $80 to $100 each, depending on their subject. The auction gallery's staff must not have recognized the book, since it was stuck in a lot with books of considerably lower value.

Maggie smiled to herself and checked out the wall of framed prints. One primitive watercolor of an egret was interesting. The Currier & Ives the auction gallery had advertised in the paper was a repro, she saw at once. It was a large folio, about fourteen by twenty inches, and she knew without checking that *Winter Morning in the Country* had only been printed in a small folio. It might be an early reprint, but it definitely was not an original.

The registration desk where she and Will had agreed to meet was over in one corner. Maggie pulled out her resale tax information and went over to set up an account and get a bidding number.

Within half an hour she and Will had settled themselves in the blue, plastic-covered seats of a booth in a singularly unimpressive-looking restaurant filled with the wonderful smells of fried seafood.

"I started coming here when I was about twelve," Will said, smiling. "Maine's version of fast food."

"I noticed most of the cars in the parking lot had Maine license plates."

"This place is open year-round. Fried haddock, fried scallops, fried clams, fried chicken, fried potatoes, and fried onion rings. Plus the requisite lobster or crabmeat rolls. Clearly a restaurant valuing taste over concerns about cholesterol. Although a couple of years ago they did add a salad to the menu."

"And I noticed peanut butter sandwiches and vegetarian vegetable soup on the list."

"Something for everyone."

Their seafood platters arrived quickly, along with a diet cola for Maggie, an iced tea for Will, and a dish of coleslaw to divide. They both dug in and it was several minutes before Maggie raised her head and grinned. "I haven't had fried clams this good in years. Not even on Cape Cod."

"Of course not. These are the best. Trust a man with Maine roots who has summered here for more years than I care to divulge." Will's eyes reflected the blue of his shirt.

"Then your family originally came from Maine?"

"My father's family did. Maine sea captains back into the mid-1700s. My grandfather was born here; Aunt Nettie is his sister. But the family was hit hard by the Great War."

"We're talking World War One?"

"That's the one. Nettie's husband was killed, as was my great-uncle William, who was very close to my grandfather. My grandfather survived, but couldn't face the empty place at the dinner table. He moved to Buffalo and got a job in the hydroelectric plant at Niagara Falls. Met a local girl, married, and stayed in Buffalo. He named his one child, my father, after his brother. I'm named after both of them. They're all gone now, but Nettie tells me at least once a year how proud she is there's still a William Brewer in the family."

"Nettie. That's an unusual name." Maggie suddenly thought of the blueing woman at the beauty shop.

"It's really Jeannette, but she's always been 'Nettie.'"

"Is Aunt Nettie a tiny little woman, with white hair?"

"And enough gumption and sass for the whole town. That's her. How did you know?"

"I think I met her this morning at the beauty salon."

"It's Thursday morning . . . it must be Cut 'n' Curl." Will grinned. "She's been having her hair done there once a week for years. What she doesn't hear at church she picks up there. Did you get an earful?"

"Actually, yes. I was asking about the house my friends bought. She was talking about possible ghosts there."

Will paused between bites. "Your friends didn't buy Charlotte's house by any chance?"

"Charlotte. That name sounds familiar. But your aunt also said something about a 'Lizzie,' I think."

"I should have guessed it! Your friends are the ones who bought our family home. Why do outsiders come in and think they can just buy anything!"

Maggie frowned. "The house was for sale. They bought it. I don't understand."

Will sighed. "I'm only an out-of-state member of the family. I wasn't involved. But I sure heard about it. The family felt strongly that the house shouldn't have been put on the market at all. It's been in the Brewer family since it was built in the late 1700s."

"Whoa, Will. Amy and Drew bought a house. That's all. And they're going to fix it up. Whoever lived there before, Charlotte, may have been from the right family, but she clearly hadn't done a lot of work on that house in fifty years. And I don't think her name was Brewer. I would have remembered that, since it's your name."

"Charlotte's mother was my great-aunt Sarah, Nettie's only sister. Sarah married Silas Leary, so Charlotte's last name wasn't Brewer. But that doesn't mean she wasn't part of the family. There are Brewers living all around here who don't have the Brewer name. Cousin Charlotte lived in that house all her life."

"And then?"

"Everyone thought she would leave it to Shirley, her niece. You met Shirley at Cut 'n' Curl. Shirley took care of Charlotte at the end and didn't have a house of her own after her husband headed north to fish in Alaska and didn't take her with him."

Maggie shook her head. "That's far too much family for me to keep straight. And I thought Shirley lived in the house next door to Amy and Drew."

"She does. She and her twins, Sorrel and Sage, moved in with her brother Tom after her husband left. It was convenient for her to help Charlotte, and everyone just expected the house would be hers someday. I'm sure Tom thought her moving in was temporary. For the last hundred years or so the house has always been owned by an unmarried woman in the family. Traditions are strong in Maine."

"So what happened?"

"Charlotte must have decided Shirley didn't qualify, since she had once been married. She left the house to Lizzie, Shirley's older sister, who worked at the town office. The will came as a surprise to everyone. No one had ever paid much attention to Lizzie. She was quiet, about fifty, never married, and owned a small house in Waymouth."

"And?"

"Lizzie didn't tell anyone what she was going to do. It's a great family scandal. Last spring, right after the estate was settled, she advertised the house in *The New York Times*— not even in a Maine newspaper!—and sold both that house and her own before anyone in the family knew what she was doing. You'll love this part. Lizzie took the money from both houses, flew to New Zealand, and married a sheepherder she'd been writing to on the Internet."

Maggie grinned and raised her fist in solidarity. "Right on for Lizzie! But let me guess: Shirley hasn't been too happy about all of this."

"To put it mildly. The only person less happy is Tom, who had hoped to have his quiet bachelor's hideout back. I got here a couple of weeks ago and have heard the whole story from at least seven people. The town has been buzzing, as they say."

"It all sounds pretty silly to me. I'm sorry Shirley didn't get her house, but Lizzie got her heart's desire, and Amy and Drew love their home. Except for a few problems they seem to be having with it."

"Leaking gutters and roof?"

"Fires and phone calls. And a couple of ghosts."

Will put down his fork.

Chapter 3

News from the War, *wood engraving by Winslow Homer published in* Harper's Weekly, *June 14, 1862. Sketches illustrating ways people got information about the Civil War: woman receiving letter, sailors and army staff reading dispatches, boys racing to "the newspaper train," wounded veteran telling news "from Richmond"; and one of Homer's few self-portraits, of a man sketching soldiers, captioned "our special artist," the title given Homer by* Harper's Weekly. *20.25 x 13.25 inches. Price: $325.*

A new, bright red Jeep—perhaps Drew's—was in the driveway when Maggie got back after lunch. The truck next to it, plus the hammering, meant the roofing was still in progress. The young roofer—Brian, she remembered—waved from the peak of the ell, and she smiled and waved back. The sky and water were both dark blue, sunflowers were blooming in the field beyond the lawn, she and Will would meet at the auction tomorrow, and she felt happily full of Maine seafood. Amy must still be grocery shopping.

She knocked on the screen door by the kitchen, but no one answered, so she walked in. Dishes were draining, newly polished silver flatware and kitchen knives were drying on a towel, and a blueberry pie was cooling. Amy, or maybe that girl who helped her, Crystal, had been at work. As always, Amy's kitchen, even this kitchen that could definitely use at least a coat of paint, was immaculate. Maggie noted a box of disposable gloves by the sink. Typical Amy.

She'd get the mystery she was reading and perhaps a light sweater for river breezes and settle on the porch until Amy got home. Perhaps Drew was in his study.

As Maggie walked up the front staircase toward her room, she became increasingly conscious that she was not alone in the house. And the sounds she was hearing were not ghostlike. They were coming from the master bedroom. Amy must have left her car somewhere, because the sounds were definitely not conversational. Maggie walked as lightly as she could. This did not sound like a good time to make her presence known. She had to walk past the bedroom door on the way to her room, and the door was only partially closed. She took a deep breath, smiled to herself, and started to tiptoe by.

Even with her eyes averted, she couldn't miss the discarded shorts and bra in the doorway.

Amy had been wearing jeans that morning.

Maggie flushed red, but she couldn't stop herself from glancing through the doorway as she passed.

She hadn't seen Amy's husband since their wedding, but

the slender build and the slightly tousled black hair were definitely Drew's. Equally certain, that was not Amy on the bed with Drew. That was Crystal.

Maggie cursed the pine floor that creaked, but she got to her room and closed the door as quickly as she could. They had probably been too occupied to hear her.

She sank down onto the bed. Poor Amy! Here she was, coping with ghosts and annoying phone calls, and planning a family with that bastard, who was taking advantage of a girl barely old enough to legally consent. And in Amy's own bedroom!

Had Michael done the same thing? The thought consumed her with anger. Maggie's husband had other women, but she had never imagined that betrayal could be so flagrant. Were all men pigs? Selfish idiots? What if she just walked back there, flung open the door, and denounced them both?

And then what?

She paced the room, not caring if her footsteps were heard all over the house. Did Amy know? Had this happened before? Should she tell Amy? How could she *not* tell Amy? How could she face Drew after what she'd seen?

Part of her wanted to throw her clothes into her suitcase and leave. Let Amy cope with her own ghosts. Forget the auction, forget Will. Just get out of here.

But how would she explain leaving so suddenly? Maggie's fingernails ground into the palms of her hands as she walked up and down, her thoughts swirling.

She was startled when there was a light tap on her door and she realized she'd been pacing over half an hour.

"Maggie? Are you resting?"

Maggie took a deep breath. Stay calm. Being upset wouldn't help Amy. "Come in, Amy."

"I just got home and saw your car, so I was sure you were here. How was the auction preview? And your lunch? I got the message you left on the machine. What fun that you ran into your friend!"

Had Amy seen what was going on? How could she not have? How could she be so calm? "Not a spectacular auction, although there are a couple of lots I might bid on. I asked them to reserve a seat for me for tomorrow morning. No corner cabinets of any sort, though."

"Just my luck. But keep looking for the cabinet when you're antiquing. You never know where there might be one."

"They're not that unusual. I'm sure you'll find one you like somewhere." Should she say anything? How could Amy have missed what was happening?

Amy sat on the other side of the bed. "And how was your friend?"

"He's fine. He's been here a couple of weeks." Should she tell Amy all she had learned about this house at the beauty salon and from Will? Now none of it seemed very important. "His great-aunt lives in Waymouth, and he's doing some repairs for her. He used to teach woodworking at a school near Buffalo, before he went into the antiques business full-time."

"He's a competitor of yours, then."

"No. My prints are a long way from the fireplace equipment and early kitchen tools he specializes in. No competition there. In fact, we're going to meet at the auction tomorrow."

"Then you must invite him for dinner tomorrow night! And his aunt too. I'd love to meet him, and the more people Drew and I know locally, the faster we'll feel we belong here."

Would an invitation to dinner at the old family home be considered friendly, or infuriating? "I'll ask Will tomorrow at the auction. I don't know if he has any plans."

"No problem either way. We'll just barbecue, and make sure we have extra steaks."

Maggie and Amy looked at each other in strained silence. Amy broke it. "I'm going down to my study to pay a couple of bills. You're probably tired. You had a long trip yesterday, we were up late chatting, and you've been out today. Rest a little, and then come down to the porch when you're ready for some afternoon libations. Take your time." Amy got up.

Was she telling Maggie to stay in her room? "It's such a beautiful day, I thought I might take a walk."

"Why not wait until a little later, and I'll join you. I just have to handle a few things. It won't take more than thirty minutes or so." The door clicked as Amy closed it.

What was going on? Why did Amy want her to stay in her room? Maggie walked to the window, feeling less like lying down than she had all day. Her room faced the back of the house, away from the river. She could see the roof of the ell. Giles and Brian Leary must have finished for the day. They were gone.

It was a beautiful day, but Maggie sensed a large, dark cloud over the house.

She decided to lie down after all.

Chapter 4

———

The Fore and Aft Sails of a Twenty-Gun Ship, *copper engraving by D. Steel, London, September 1, 1794. Detailed rendering of ship at sea, with identifying notations on sails. One small fox mark in sky. 7.5 x 10 inches. Price: $225.*

Forty minutes later Maggie gently opened her door. There was no sign of Drew or Crystal, and Amy was happily sorting papers in her study.

"Thank goodness you've come to rescue me!" Amy dropped the pile she was holding.

"Can I be rude and ask what you're looking at?" Maggie peeked over at the desk. The papers Amy had put down appeared to be covered with pictures of children.

"We'll talk and walk," Amy answered, as they headed out the door. "Isn't this day wonderful?" She took a deep breath. "We're far enough upriver so you can't always taste the salt in the air, but today the wind must be from the ocean."

There was definitely a salt smell in the breeze. "A perfect Maine day," Maggie agreed. An August day at home in New Jersey would no doubt have been sweltering: high temperatures, high humidity, tempers flaring, cars overheating, mosquitoes buzzing. Here all was cool and peaceful. No wonder people moved to Maine.

"I can hardly wait for our first winter here," said Amy. "Locals say we won't get as much snow on the coast as most people imagine, and the tourists all go home, leaving lots of parking spaces and peace."

Wasn't Amy complaining about the quiet just last night? "You can probably see even more of the river when the leaves are off the trees." Contrary to what many people imagined, there were lots of trees in Maine that were not evergreens. "But those temperatures will be pretty low, I've heard."

"I'm not worried. We have central heating. People have lived in this house all year round since the eighteenth century; there's no reason Drew and I can't too. And we'll have a woodstove by then, and bottled water, in case we can't get out for a couple of days, or lose power for a while. There were some bad ice storms here a few years ago." Amy pointed at some birches that were still bent over. "You can tell which ones were damaged. Some have never recovered."

They walked down by the river on the road below the ninety-degree turn. Two people in a red kayak paddled by and waved. Farther out on the river a small motorboat sped toward Waymouth. Only a few cars passed them. "This road dead-ends about three miles down the peninsula," Amy explained. "We have about five acres but most of it goes back from the road. Shirley and her girls and her brother live up there." She pointed at a yellow Victorian house with rust-colored trim up on the hill, parallel with hers. "Our neighbor in the other direction is too far away to see, but Shirley and Tom's lights are clear through the trees, which is nice. There's even a rough stone path between the two houses."

"My friend Will is some sort of cousin to Shirley and her brother. He told me Shirley helped take care of the woman who lived in your house last."

"Charlotte Leary. I know. Shirley told me. Charlotte was her aunt. Everyone up here seems related to everyone else. Giles and Brian, who are doing the roofing, have the last name Leary too. I guess that's one of the charms of these old Maine communities."

If charms included people angry because you'd bought their family home.

"And who is Crystal, that girl I saw in the kitchen yesterday?" Maggie looked determinedly out at the river so her face wouldn't give away any emotions.

"Crystal and her mother, Rachel, live in a small house on the other side of our property, up on the next road. Rachel works at the library. I met her when I started doing research about the history of our house. Crystal was looking for a summer job, so I suggested she come and help Drew and me. There was so much unpacking and sorting to do when we first got here."

Ah. That's what Crystal was doing. Helping. So why didn't that make total sense? Maggie changed the subject.

"What have you found out about the house?"

"Lots of great stuff! It was built in 1772, but then it burned down and had to be built again, in 1774. And it was built on an island." Amy walked ahead a little and pointed across the river. "That point, over there? It's really the tip of an island. Our house was built there, and then moved to the mainland in the 1830s sometime. I can't pin down the date."

"Moved? How could such a big house be moved?"

"The records say twenty yoke of oxen pulled it across the Madoc River, which was frozen that year, and up the hill to where it stands now. It was set as a channel marker for ships turning at the north eastern end of the island toward Waymouth harbor. The ell and barn were built at the new location."

"Wow. What a job." Maggie looked up at the hill and then across the river. "So the river freezes in winter?"

"Not for maybe a hundred years. Global warming, I guess. But I found references to boats iced in for the winter back in the late eighteenth and early nineteenth centuries. We don't think about weather changing that much, but it must have."

"James Fenimore Cooper wrote in *Satanstoe,* which is set in eighteenth-century Albany, that young couples would race sleighs on the Hudson. No one is trying that now!"

"For sure. Anyway, the house must have been empty for a while in the early nineteenth century; I couldn't find any records for that period. Then it was owned by several captains. At least one sailed ships to the Far East. I'm sure there is more in the Waymouth Courthouse Archives, but I haven't gotten to them yet."

"Change of topic. Amy, I have to ask! Are you and Drew adopting a baby? I saw the nursery, of course, and those pictures of children on your desk." Maggie hesitated. "If that question is out of line, say so. But I'll admit I've thought about adoption myself, and I'd love to know more."

"You? Adoption? Maggie, you'd make a great mom! You don't have to be married to adopt now. And there are so many children who need homes."

"So what are you and Drew doing?"

"It's a long story. Both Drew and I really, really want to be parents. Drew was adopted himself. He was left on the steps of St. Patrick's Cathedral when he was a baby. His adoptive parents are wonderful people, but Drew has always wanted to have someone in his life who was biologically related to him. His two brothers were also adopted, but they don't feel that way. They're just fine with who they are, and with the little they know of their history. But Drew has always wanted what he calls a 'real' family."

"Did he try to find his biological family?"

"For years. It wasn't just a matter of records being sealed. There were no records. He knows the date he was found at the cathedral, and how he was assigned a birth date, and even why he was given the name Andrew. The name came from an alphabetical list of names at the New York Foundling Hospital, where he lived until he was adopted when he was six months old. But there's no way he can locate a mother who couldn't be found forty-two years ago. That's why it's so important to Drew that he have a child of his own."

Maggie nodded. "I've never thought what it must be like never to know anyone biologically related to you. You'd have curiosity, if nothing else. To know whether someone else's eyes looked like yours." Involuntarily she thought of Will's eyes, and flushed a little.

"At first Drew and I thought it would just take time for me to get pregnant. I did everything I'd heard of from protein diets to taking my temperature every morning to find the right time of month, to convincing Drew to give up his Jockey shorts. You don't know what we tried!"

And Maggie really didn't want to know.

"Nothing worked. And we're getting older. I tried to get Drew to think about adoption; that's why we have all those pictures in my office. I got on the mailing list for every domestic and international agency I could find, and they keep sending me pictures of 'waiting children.' Drew doesn't even want to look, but I keep thinking maybe I'll see a face that looks like Drew's, and that he'll change his mind and decide adoption is all right."

"He doesn't believe in adoption?"

"He believes it's a good thing. He loves his adoptive parents. He just wants at least one child that is 'really his.' After that, he says maybe we could adopt. But time is passing."

Amy was the same age as Maggie. Thirty-eight. "And you tried all the infertility treatments?"

"Some of them." Amy hesitated. "It's my fault, Maggie. When I was in high school, I got pregnant. Believe me, it was not my fault. But I couldn't have a baby. Not at fifteen."

"You had an abortion."

Amy's voice dropped. "My stepfather arranged it. It was supposed to be clean and easy. Only it wasn't." She paused. "I was all right in a few days. But my fertility doctor told me the abortion created scar tissue, which is probably one reason I'm having a problem getting pregnant. Plus, of course, being over thirty-five doesn't help."

Maggie felt old and wrinkled just listening to her. This was a side of Amy she had never guessed at. The young Amy had made a mistake. The Amy she knew had always been in control.

"How did Drew react when you told him?"

Amy walked a few steps before answering. "I couldn't tell him, Maggie. How could I tell someone whose mother had chosen to have him even if she couldn't take care of him that I had chosen to kill my baby? He would never forgive me. He's not dealing well with my not getting pregnant. Telling him I'd had an abortion that prevented my conceiving could end our marriage." She hesitated. "Sometimes I think the only reason he married me was to have a child." Amy walked a few steps toward the river and then turned around. "I'd do anything to make this marriage work, Maggie. If Drew knew it was my fault we haven't had children, if he thought I couldn't conceive, he would divorce me."

"Oh, Amy, you can't believe that," said Maggie, but then she remembered the scene in the bedroom. And the baby's room just down the hall. "What about the nursery? It's so perfect!"

"Drew bought the crib for me as a wedding present, and then the other things we bought because we really thought it was just a matter of time until I got pregnant. Oh, Maggie, I don't know what will happen if we don't have a baby!"

"Have you been to a doctor in Maine yet?"

"I went last week. Of course she wants all my medical records transferred from New York before she can make any recommendations. She just suggested all the same things everyone suggests and mentioned several times how fertility begins to decrease at age thirty."

"You can't give up hope, Amy. Someone I work with was told she could never have children. She and her husband adopted two cute little boys from Korea. Then she got pregnant and had a little girl!"

"People keep telling me stories like that. Maybe that's one reason I wanted us to apply to adopt. But we're getting too old even to apply for an infant. So many people want to adopt healthy babies that agencies are really selective. They don't want parents over forty. We'd have to adopt a baby with a medical problem, or an older child, or a child from overseas."

"My friend's Korean sons are terrific."

"I'm sure. But that isn't what Drew is looking for, and I'm

not sure I could handle having children who didn't look like us. And I've read information on dozens of children. Most of the older ones have emotional problems of some sort."

"But their major problem is not having someone to love them."

"I'm just not ready for all of that. I want a perfect baby who looks like Drew, and maybe even like me, to go in that canopied crib."

Maggie tried not to hear the growing hysteria in Amy's voice. "Why don't we turn around and head for home and a glass of wine? I'm glad you told me, Amy. I understand what it is to want to be a mother." And, suddenly, Maggie did understand. As they headed back, she found herself wondering about all those children in the pictures on Amy's desk. Children no one wanted. Children who might not fit perfectly into a white, canopied crib. She shivered, wrapped in her own thoughts.

Chapter 5

———ⵑ———

The Mirror Carp: Cyprinus carpio, *lithograph, dark
green background; brown fish with gold markings.
From oil painting by American artist John Petrie, of a
"specimen—weight 1½ pounds—caught and painted at
the New York State Hatchery, Mumford, New York."
From 1895 limited-edition portfolio* The Fishes of North
America That Are Captured on Hook and Line, *by
William C. Harris, editor of* The American Angler.
11.5 x 18.5-inches. Price: $160.

Drew had already opened the wine by the time they got back
to the house. At least that's what Maggie thought until she
realized he was filling his goblet with vodka instead of white
wine. And he had clearly been doing so for a while. He was
more dressed than when she had last seen him; he was wearing a pair of pressed jeans and a dark gray polo shirt. And
his black hair was not as tousled.

"I finally get to see the mysterious guest!" Drew's hug was encompassing, although he didn't put down his glass. Maggie felt a chill of liquid seeping through her T-shirt down her back. "Amy says you've been here since yesterday."

"You were away last night and I guess I missed you today." Maggie turned and poured herself some red wine. She didn't want her glass to get mixed up with Drew's, although it didn't seem likely he'd put his down anytime soon.

"So how's the antiques business? Outperforming the stock market these days?"

"It's doing all right. No business is doing what it was in the nineties. But investing in any limited commodity is never a bad idea, and that's what antiques are."

"True. Before you leave, Amy and I want to take a look at some of your prints. Do you have many from 1774? That's when this house was built."

"I have a few from that period, but not many, and they'd be European. Even American artists had most of their engraving done in Europe until the middle of the nineteenth century. Printing techniques and equipment were much more sophisticated abroad. Paintings and folk arts like embroidery were more common in America than prints until Currier and Ives proved prints could be commercially successful. I do have some wonderful American engravings and lithographs from 1850 on. And a few from before. I'd be happy to show you."

"Since we're now Mainers, I suppose we should be buying Winslow Homers, or one of the Wyeths. Or—who is that man who did wood engravings and paintings on Monhegan, Amy?"

"You're thinking of Rockwell Kent." Amy turned to Maggie. "We saw an exhibit of his at the Metropolitan Museum last winter. Very powerful."

Maggie nodded. "I have quite a few Winslow Homer

wood engravings, and some N. C. Wyeths. Andrew and Jamie Wyeth are too recent for my business, although I certainly admire their work."

"We'll look at them soon. Winslow Homer sounds good. He did some Civil War stuff too, didn't he?" Drew poured himself some more vodka.

"Quite a few. He was the 'special artist' for *Harper's Weekly* during the Civil War, although there were also a half dozen other artists reporting with their pencils from the battlefront. He and Thomas Nast are the best known today. I have some Nasts too."

"I've always found the Civil War period fascinating. Did Amy tell you I majored in American history in college?"

"She mentioned that you were a history buff." She had also mentioned Drew had been drinking too much recently.

"I'm thinking of teaching up here in Maine. They need teachers everywhere, and I suppose I could pass a test or take courses or whatever it takes to get certified here."

"That would be a major change of profession for you." Maggie couldn't imagine this former stockbroker in charge of a group of children. Especially after the interaction she'd seen him having with one teenager a couple of hours ago.

Amy rose. "I think we need to get dinner started. I'm going to put some chicken breasts and potatoes in the oven. Drew, I told Maggie that tomorrow we'd have a barbecue. She has a friend who is visiting in Waymouth, and I thought it would be fun to invite him over."

"Do you need help, Amy?" Amy's arm was still bandaged. In fact, Maggie noticed a little blood seeping through the gauze.

"I'll be fine. Crystal fixed everything earlier so all I have to do is put it in the oven. You relax and keep Drew company." Amy left the porch.

"So your friend is vacationing Down East too, Maggie."

"He has an aunt in Waymouth. He's also an antiques dealer; we're going to an auction tomorrow morning."

"That's nice." Drew pulled his chair closer to Maggie's. "While you were on your walk, did Amy tell you all our family secrets?"

Maggie hoped Amy's trip to the kitchen would be a quick one.

"All about the crying baby and the ghost woman?" Drew added.

Thank goodness it was those secrets he was talking about. "Yes, she told me. The telephone calls sound awful. And the fire must have been frightening."

"It's all nonsense. The fire was just an accident. And everyone gets some wrong numbers. Amy is a little high-strung."

"I never thought of her that way."

"Well, think, then. She gets uptight when everything doesn't go her way."

Amy had always wanted life to be controllable, Maggie agreed silently. And a lot of aspects of Amy's life right now were not under control. That was becoming clearer every hour.

Drew topped off his glass.

In the distance, Maggie heard the telephone. She hoped it wasn't one of those hang-up calls. Amy had enough to deal with tonight.

Amy was in the doorway. "Drew, do you know when Crystal left this afternoon? Her mother is calling. Crystal hasn't gotten home yet."

"I don't know when she left. A while ago. Plenty of time to walk home. Or maybe that Leary boy gave her a ride."

"But you don't know for sure when she left."

"Hell, I don't keep track of all the help. Tell her mother to relax. She's a teenager. She'll be home when she's ready to get there."

"She must not be with Brian Leary. Her mother says she had a date with him tonight, and he's there at her house now, waiting for her."

"I don't know anything."

"Rachel seems very upset. Maggie, would you mind taking another walk? I'd like to follow the path Crystal takes from our house to hers and make sure she didn't fall or something."

"A good idea," Maggie agreed. Crystal might just be lollygagging, but it was strange that she would be this late. Could something have happened to her?

Chapter 6

In the Bath, *one in a series of French steel engravings illustrating the 1838 memoirs of Casanova (1725–1798), an Italian adventurer who traveled throughout Europe as a preacher, alchemist, gambler, violin player, and spy. His memoirs tell of his rogueries and amours. Some engravings in this series are overtly sexual or scatological. This one depicts an unwilling woman, undressed except for her cap, being forced into an early-nineteenth-century bathing tub by a fully dressed man. 3 x 4.25 inches. Price: $50.*

Amy and Maggie headed past the ell and barn and driveway and small garden, across the lawn, and into a field. At first, Maggie couldn't see any path. There certainly wasn't a path by suburban standards, but in places the tall grasses and golden-rod had been stepped on, breaking some of their thick stems.

"This is our land," Amy said, turning her head toward

Maggie as they pushed their way through the waist-high grasses. "Used to be hayed, I'm told. We may get a small tractor and turn part of it into lawn next year." The field was a couple of acres of difficult walking. Two crows screamed their indignation at the women invading their territory.

"Are you sure this is how Crystal gets home? Why doesn't she take the road?"

"There are no direct roads from her house to ours. Cutting through the fields and woods leads her straight home. Crystal!" Amy's voice was loud.

As the crow flies, Maggie thought. But—crows could fly. Maybe Crystal was light enough that her footsteps didn't always break down the grasses. They crossed a damp section of ground, perhaps over an underground spring, and Maggie brushed aside a thick milkweed stem. An orange-and-black monarch butterfly fluttered away.

"I've been this way a few times," said Amy. "Just to see our land. The borders of our property are pretty narrow. In the eighteenth century, when most of the property lines were drawn, lots by the river often were narrow and deep, so as many people as possible could have water access. There was no bridge across the Madoc to Waymouth then. Everyone had a boat. Most lots go back, as ours does, almost to the next road, which is Egret Point, where Rachel and Crystal live, on another little peninsula. Their house isn't near the water, but houses on the end of their point are."

Emerging from the field, they entered a smaller area of woods. "Crystal? Can you hear me?" Amy called. They stood and listened, but there was no answer.

"This feels as it must have when Native Americans lived here," Maggie said quietly. The only sound was their footsteps crunching on the fallen pine needles and mosses and some gulls crying high above them.

"There haven't been many Indians here since the early eighteenth century. The early settlers and the Abenakis weren't the greatest of friends. After the French and Indian Wars the Abenakis who were left went north or west, leaving this section of the shoreline to the whites." Amy stopped and looked around, as she had several times before. "There's no sign of Crystal. I thought she might have fallen, or was walking very slowly, and we'd catch up with her. Let's hope she's already safe at home."

"Does she walk back and forth every day?"

"She works five days a week, but not always the same days, depending on when I need her to help me. Sometimes Brian or Giles drive her home in their truck."

"I take it Brian is her boyfriend."

"Could be. They spend a lot of time together. But Crystal has ambition. She doesn't want to settle in Madoc, the way her mother did. She wants to see the world."

"She looks pretty young to be making major decisions about her future." Maggie couldn't get the picture of Drew and Crystal out of her head. "How old is she?"

"Eighteen. Old enough to know what she wants and do something about it." Amy stepped over a fallen branch that was blocking the way.

"When I was eighteen, all I knew was I had to finish high school and go to college somewhere. Everything else seemed very far in the future."

"I don't think Crystal is the college type. She's thinking of becoming a model. She's been borrowing my copies of *Vanity Fair* and *New York*."

"She is pretty," Maggie had to agree. "But aren't most models almost emaciated? And taller." Crystal was only about five feet four inches and parts of her were definitely not emaciated.

Amy shrugged. "Maybe. That she'll have to find out on her own. She's just thinking about different possibilities now." She stepped over a large rock in the path and moved another branch out of their way. "I've been trying to give her some mentoring advice. Teenaged girls never listen to their mothers anyway. She's very impressed that Drew and I are from New York."

Maggie pointed ahead. "Is that her home?"

Just beyond the end of the tree line was a small, brown-shingled cottage, perhaps a third the size of Amy's house, nestled comfortably between the woods to its rear and a small lawn and garden of pink and mauve and white and purple delphiniums. A police vehicle and a car were parked in front, just on the other side of a large winter-ready woodpile.

"Let's hope she's home safely by now," said Maggie, as they approached the back door. A plump, brown-haired woman opened it.

"Did you see any sign of her, Amy?"

"Not one. She still hasn't called or come home?"

"Brian took his truck and is out checking the roads and some of their friends' homes." They entered the small kitchen, where a big man in navy trousers and a blue shirt was seated at the table. "Have you met Owen Colby? He's a neighbor, and he works in the sheriff's office." Owen Colby rose and offered a strong hand to Amy and Maggie.

"I understand Crystal's been working for you this summer, Mrs. Douglas."

"Yes. Most weekdays, and sometimes on the weekend. She's been helping us get unpacked and settled in."

"And she was over at your place today."

"She washed up the dishes and cleaned out a cabinet in the kitchen while I was grocery shopping. She made a pie with the last of the blueberries too."

"Crystal's a real good cook," her mother added. "She's always liked to bake."

"When did you last see her, Mrs. Douglas?"

"I was out doing errands most of the day. So was Maggie. When I got home, about three o'clock, she was finishing up. I told her she could leave after she'd put the groceries away, and I went into my study to do some work. When I came out forty minutes later, she was gone. I assumed she'd gone home."

"And your husband doesn't know exactly when she left either."

"No. He was in his study, upstairs. Or on the front porch. Not near the kitchen, where Crystal was working."

Maggie ground her nails into the palms of her hands, hoping desperately Owen Colby wouldn't ask her where *she* had last seen Crystal. But he didn't.

"Well, Rachel, I can't help but think Crystal will turn up soon enough. She's at an age where they just take off sometimes. Think being independent means not telling anyone where they're going." Deputy Colby put away his notebook.

"But can't I file a missing person's report or something?" Rachel Porter was obviously distressed. "She has crazy ideas, sometimes, about taking off to live in New York." Maggie noted Rachel did not look at Amy when she said that. "Or being a model. Maybe she's hitchhiking south."

"Has she mentioned any plans to travel?"

"Not right out. But her room is full of brochures about New York."

"Rachel, you keep in touch. We can't file a missing person's report on her until tomorrow afternoon, but I'll let the state police know she's gone missing, and if they see anyone meeting her description, they'll pick her up. If you hear from her, now, you let me know. I'll talk to some folks in town.

Chances are someone has seen her. Or she may have just taken a long way home to think. She could walk in the door at any moment."

Maggie and Amy followed the deputy out the door, and he indicated they could sit in the back of his car. Not the best way to be seen by your neighbors, Maggie thought, but here in Madoc probably the whole town would know within an hour just what was happening.

Most likely Crystal would be home by then. Maggie hoped so. But she feared nothing would be that simple. How could a teenaged girl have disappeared during such a short country walk?

Chapter 7

———✦———

Carrying the Flag, Good Housekeeping *cover, July 1931, by Jessie Willcox Smith (1863–1935). Young boy, perhaps age six, waving an American flag. Smith was a well-known Philadelphia illustrator, the only woman who studied with Thomas Eakins, and then with N. C. Wyeth and Maxfield Parrish under Howard Pyle. She specialized in paintings of children. 8.5 x 10 inches. Price: $60.*

Later that night Maggie sat in bed, looking through a pile of the "waiting children" pictures Amy had given her. Children not only from all over the United States, but from China, Thailand, Korea, Colombia, Russia, Peru . . . the number of faces and stories was overwhelming, and Maggie felt torn in too many directions to give them the attention they deserved. All these children needed a home. Deserved a home. And Amy and Drew had a perfect white nursery waiting for a baby who for some reason couldn't be any one of these children. Did that make sense? Did anything in this house, or in Amy and Drew's marriage, make sense? Maggie had been in Maine for just a little over a day, and she felt like Alice in Wonderland, in a strange universe with different rules.

Amy had the marriage and the house she wanted. But those things weren't enough. She wanted a child. A child for Drew. As Maggie thought back, she didn't remember Amy's focusing strongly on wanting a child for herself. The child was required to meet Drew's needs. Maggie shuddered. What a heavy responsibility both Amy and Drew were already putting on that poor unborn child's head.

How had her parents felt before they had children? Maggie wished she could pick up the telephone and ask her mother. "Mom, how did you know when it was the right time to have children? How did you know focusing your life on them would give your own life more meaning?"

It had been almost ten years since their car had crashed, but Maggie found herself wiping a tear away. It always happened like this. She wouldn't think about her parents for days, but then, suddenly, she needed them, and the realization that they were gone would hit her all over again.

Did her brother Joe ever think of them that way? She doubted it. She and Joe had never been close; he was twelve years older than she was, and he always seemed to have interests other than a little sister or parents. He'd left home as soon as he graduated from high school and, after that, called only once or twice a year. He'd worked in Wyoming, in Chicago, in Seattle. Ten years ago he'd been working in Florida. Her parents had been on their way to visit him when a car going in the other direction had veered into their station wagon. Joe had come to the funeral, but Maggie had only gotten a couple of Christmas cards from him since then. Last she'd heard, he was in Arizona.

She looked down at the pile of pictures. She had two extra bedrooms in her house. She had no ghosts. And she would love to have a child to take to the circus and to read stories with. To share Christmas and the first day of school with. Was love enough? Did these children really want a family, or would they be like Joe and escape the confines of people who loved them as soon as they could? She shook her head. She couldn't think about those things now. She needed to think about what was going on in this house.

This house that came with a heritage that was more than a history, in a community that seemed very accepting of the possibility of ghosts. There was certainly a strange undercurrent in the family who had owned the house. But even if some of them were sorry it had been sold, the sale couldn't be undone. Amy and Drew were here. Unless . . . she shook her head again. If Amy and Drew had problems, and it was clear they did, then the problems between them had started long before they'd bought this house.

And Amy didn't even seem to know about Crystal's relationship with Drew! Was she so naive? Didn't she care? Was she one of those wives who would tolerate anything to keep her husband? Or did she not want to know?

Maggie turned off the light and punched her pillow several times.

Amy had always known what she wanted, and she had never let anyone push her around. What had changed?

Maggie closed her eyes and tried to sleep. She had an auction to attend tomorrow. She was meeting Will there. She turned over abruptly. What was Will really like? She hardly knew him! For all she knew he had a woman in every city he visited. He could be at some Maine pub right now, romancing some waitress.

She punched the pillow again. Why was life so complicated? Why couldn't everyone just be honest with everyone else? How could men do this to women?

She drifted into a restless sleep, seeing photos of unwanted children turning in front of her eyes. Hundreds of children without love. Without families. Their eyes followed her accusingly. What could she do? It wasn't her fault that their parents were gone. The children started crying, at first just a few tears, but then louder, and louder. Maggie sleepily pulled the pillow over her ears. She couldn't stand the crying. Then her door opened, and the light switched on. Amy was standing there in a long white nightgown. "Maggie! Don't you hear? It's the baby!"

Maggie's fuzzy mind groped for logic as she sat up, half in dream and half in Amy's guest bedroom. She thought she had heard a child crying. But now it had stopped.

"You heard it too! You had to! You did hear it!" Amy took quick steps over to the bed. "Maggie, I'm not crazy! There was a baby crying in this house!"

Maggie reached over as Amy sat down and buried her head in Maggie's shoulder.

"I heard it, Amy. I did. It was a baby. A baby crying so your heart would break."

Chapter 8

⁓

Niagara Falls (from the top of the ladder on the American side). *Hand-colored steel engraving by J. C. Bentley for W. H. Bartlett showing the Falls and several elegantly dressed people observing them; 1839. Bartlett's engravings were some of the best and earliest depictions of American scenes. Published in London and hand-colored after publication. 7.25 x 5.5 inches. Price: $75.*

The Walter English Auction House was full by nine the next morning, although the auction wouldn't start until ten. Maggie wove her way between people who were making the most of the last preview hour until she reached the two chairs she and Will had reserved. Pieces of masking tape marked places for BREWER and SUMMER next to each other. She put her bottle of Poland Spring water and a navy cardigan sweater on her seat. With this number of auctiongoers there would be a lot of people standing. Better to reinforce the reserved seat with a message that said, "Don't sit here! This seat taken!" The same game was being played throughout the room; chairs were covered by jackets, newspapers, books, cups of coffee, and on the chair in front of Maggie's, a piece of needlework in progress. Like animals marking their territory, she thought. Her sweater would tell Will that she was somewhere in the crowd. Luckily she had registered and picked up her bidding number yesterday. The line for that table was out the door. She headed toward the woman who was frantically collating and stapling extras copies of the auction catalog. Catalogs were good references during the auction, and afterward, if you noted the prices items sold for. She pulled out her $3 and waited for the woman to turn around with another several copies. When the woman did turn, she and Maggie looked at each other in surprise.

"Rachel! What are you doing here? Did Crystal get home last night?"

Rachel took Maggie's $3 and handed her a catalog. "No. I left the lights on and sat up all night waiting. She didn't even call. She's never been out all night before. Not without calling."

"I'm so sorry. Maybe today you'll hear from her."

"Johnny promised Walter I'd help out this morning, and I couldn't stand just pacing the floor and doing nothing, so I came. I'm going to the sheriff's office as soon as the auction starts to see if now they can officially list her as missing. This isn't like Crystal."

"Hey, hurry up there. People are waiting for catalogs!" called an impatient voice behind Maggie.

"If Amy or I can help," Maggie said, looking into Rachel's brimming eyes, as she moved away, "call. Really."

Rachel smiled weakly as she turned to her next customer.

Crystal's mother was not coping well. But, then, why

should she? If only that girl would come home! Did she feel guilty about yesterday afternoon? Did she sense that she and Drew had been seen? There was certainly no hint that what was happening in Amy's bedroom was not consensual, but who knew what an eighteen-year-old girl would think. Maggie felt very old; as though she had been born eighteen centuries ago. And she didn't think she had ever been the kind of eighteen Crystal was now. She thought of all the young women she had taught over the years. For some reason, Crystal seemed different.

Maggie shook her head slightly and focused on the scene at hand. There was nothing she could do about Crystal here. She decided to take a closer look at the tapestries she had passed by the day before.

She maneuvered her way through the crowd and checked them out, then confirmed the lot numbers she had noted yesterday for the boxes of books she had hopes of buying and circled them in her catalog. She also circled the number of the egret watercolor. Good; all the numbers she was interested in were under three hundred. There were six hundred lots in this auction, and she didn't want to spend a full day sitting on a hard folding chair inside a country auction house. Especially with a missing girl on her mind. She had hardly met Crystal; she had certainly not been impressed with her behavior. But Crystal was eighteen and she was missing. Maybe she and Amy could think of or do something that would help.

She glanced over at where Rachel was working. Being a mother was not easy.

Will put a cup of coffee on his seat as she approached. "Good morning, print lady! How was your evening?"

Maggie grimaced. "Memorable. We can talk later. Do you have to check anything out before the auction starts?"

"I want to take another look at one set of brass andirons. I looked them up last night and there should be a maker's mark if they are what I think they are." He spoke quietly, as did most dealers at auctions, for the same reason Maggie was holding her catalog close to her body so no one could see the circled lots she planned to bid on. No one wanted to advertise their particular interests before the bidding. It might encourage—or discourage—others if they knew what specific dealers thought was worth bidding on.

Maggie sat, turned over her auction catalog, and opened her bottle of Poland Spring. Water was fine, and this was Maine, but she would rather have diet cola.

"Dear," interrupted an older woman on her right. "Have you ever been to an auction before?"

"Yes," replied Maggie. "A few." A few hundred, at least.

"This is my very first," said the woman in the blue dress with matching pocketbook. The friend next to her nodded. "We've been watching *Antiques Roadshow* on the TV, and we wanted to see what it was all about."

"Have you registered, so you can bid?"

"Is that how you get those cards with numbers on them?" The woman pointed at Maggie's bidding card.

"Yes. You can get them over at the registration desk. You can't bid without one."

"Then I guess we'd better register." The woman rose and squeezed her way past Maggie. "I'll be right back, Flora. We don't want to miss anything."

"Are there always so many people here?" asked Flora. "And so many—sorts—of people."

"It all depends on what's in the auction, and on the time of year," Maggie answered. "A Maine auction in August is bound to attract a lot of people."

"Oh, yes. You know, I was afraid we weren't quite dressed

up enough for an auction. I've seen auctions in movies. Everyone looks very elegant. But Sophia said we didn't have to dress that way for a morning auction, and I see there are even people here in shorts!"

Maggie smiled to herself. Heavens. The woman would probably have worn her tiara for an evening auction. Of course, auctions were like any other events: they varied considerably. Those attending a farm auction on a Saturday night in Maine would probably not dress in precisely the same way as would those in New York at Parke-Bernet. Although the basic procedures were the same. She hoped these two ladies wouldn't ask her to explain every term used during the day.

Will returned and sank down, opening the top on his coffee. "I'm interested in three lots. And one more, if it goes low enough. You?"

"About the same. How fast does this auctioneer go?"

"He's one of the faster ones. About one hundred lots an hour."

Maggie nodded. Thank goodness. Some auctioneers took forever and only got through perhaps fifty lots an hour. Again, of course, a gallery like Sotheby's wouldn't even be in the same ballpark when it came to speed. Elegance and big dollars were expected to take time. It was part of the show. "I'd like to be out of here by one."

"Your highest lot number?"

"Two sixty-six."

Will nodded. "It'll be close, but I think you'll make it. I have one item higher than that. We'll see how the prices go in any case. It looks like a liquid crowd."

They both looked around. It definitely felt like a tourist crowd with money. The question was, would they spend it here or bore easily and take their wallets off to an antiques show or gift shop? Lots at the end of the auction would no doubt bring less money than those in the first couple of hundred numbers, as this crowd inevitably moved on to other amusements.

"Lunch again today?"

"I don't think so, Will. But Amy and Drew would like you and your aunt Nettie to come for a barbecue tonight if you can."

Will hesitated just a moment too long and then shrugged his shoulders. "Why not? It will give the old girl more to talk about."

"Will she feel awkward, visiting a house that was once in her family?"

"Oh, she'll love that part. She'll report back exactly what they're doing wrong with it." He hesitated again and then grinned self-consciously. "I was thinking of what she'd say about you. She's been trying to match me up with women ever since my wife died eight years ago. And here's a pretty lady just arriving out of nowhere."

"If it would be too embarrassing . . ."

"Hell, no. The more I think about it, the more fun it will be." He reached over and squeezed Maggie's hand. "I'd like you to meet Aunt Nettie officially. And I think she'll like you."

Maggie smiled, but then gently removed her hand. She liked Will. She wanted to trust him. But the memories of Drew and Crystal were still too clear.

"Will, you don't happen to know a Crystal Porter?"

"Sure. Rachel's daughter. She must be ten or twelve by now."

"Try eighteen." Did everyone in Maine know everyone else?

"Where did you run into her?"

Why did a direct question feel so filled with implications?

"She's been helping Amy and Drew around the house this summer. But yesterday afternoon she didn't come home. Her mother is really worried about her."

Will glanced quickly over at the table where Rachel was still stapling and selling auction programs. His voice lowered. "So she takes after her mother, eh? I guess I haven't kept up-to-date with that part of the family."

"The family? You mean they're related to you too?"

"Pretty distantly. I couldn't figure it out without a diagram. Rachel and I share the same great-grandmother or something like that."

"And Rachel has a past."

"Pretty far distant. About eighteen years, I'd say, if Crystal is that old now."

"And Crystal's father?"

"As I recall at the time there were a number of candidates for that honor, but Rachel just shut her mouth and raised Crystal alone. She got pregnant just after she graduated from high school."

"And she never married?"

"Don't think so." Will lowered his voice even further. "Although rumor has it she's been spending time the last couple of years with Johnny Brent."

Johnny Brent. "I've seen his name on the roofers' truck at Amy's house."

"He has a good-sized construction company now, maybe a dozen trucks and crews. Not new homes, for the most part. He specializes in fixing up older homes, adding rooms, replacing roofs, doing interior work. That sort of thing."

The crowd parted as a tall, burly man strode to the front of the room and stood at the lectern. He banged on it with a worn mahogany gavel as people found their seats. "Good morning. I'm Walter English, and welcome to this morning's auction. Be sure to read the terms and conditions of the sale on your bidding card. A twelve percent buyer's premium will be added to the total of all purchases, with a two percent discount for cash or check. We reserve the right to hold your purchases until the check clears. Sales tax will be added unless you have a valid resale number on file with us prior to the sale. You must be registered and have a number to bid. I'll tell you what I know about any item coming up, but if you haven't looked it over before the sale, I suggest you don't bid on it. Everything is sold as is, where is. All sales are final. Small items will be brought to your seat. Empty cartons and newspapers are in the corner for you to use in packing. Larger items will be put outside the door. As soon as I say 'Sold!' the item is yours. You are responsible for making sure it is safe, and that it is paid for and removed from this property. In that order. If there are no bids commensurate with the value of an item, I reserve the right to pass it. If an item is passed, it will not come up again in this sale. My assistant"—he waved at a woman sitting at a table to his left—"will be placing absentee bids." He took a breath and looked around the room. "Are there any questions?"

Silence.

"The first item up for bid today is this fine maple sideboard. Been refinished, and brass hardware on the drawers has been replaced. Excellent condition, though, all of it. Who'll start the bidding at three hundred dollars? Two hundred dollars? One hundred dollars? All over the house. Who'll give me one-fifty!"

There was no time to talk. Even the two women sitting next to Maggie seemed transfixed as they watched the wide assortment of goods come to the block. A set of tools, maybe twenty years old. A Victorian oak footstool with a modern needlework cover. A copy of the Mona Lisa in charcoal. A box of Christmas decorations from the 1930s. An oil painting of Boothbay Harbor signed by somebody no one had heard of. A wooden carton filled with glass apothecary bottles. A carton of chipped silver overlay glass from the 1920s. A gold watch. A cherry sideboard. Four boxes of well-used kitchen pots and pans.

Maggie smiled to herself. When people out of the trade thought of "estate auctions," they seldom realized that meant *everything* in the estate, including the old paint cans in the basement, should the owner or auctioneer think anyone would value their labels. A true estate auction meant everything in the estate had either gone into the Dumpster or into the auction house.

Will bought a set of iron fireplace implements with owls on the handles. Maggie decided not to bid on the box holding the children's books when it went for more than $60. Flora was delighted to purchase a shoebox full of costume jewelry for $35. "For my grandchildren to play with!" she whispered to Maggie with excitement, as a dealer two rows back sighed in exasperation. Maybe he'd hoped to buy the box and sell the jewelry piece by piece on eBay.

Will stopped bidding on a box of tools when it went over $200. And Maggie delightedly bid $70 for the box of old Bibles and the Wilson birds and won it. The egret she liked was too popular; a well-dressed tourist bid it up to $400, which was way over its retail value. He seemed pleased, and Maggie shrugged. That would have been an extra for her and certainly wasn't worth that price. She had the carton she came for. It had been a good auction.

"I'm going to sign out," she whispered to Will. "See you at about five this afternoon?"

"I'll be there, with Aunt Nettie. Enjoy the afternoon!"

It took just a few minutes to turn in her bidding number and pay the $70 plus $7 buyer's premium for the carton of books. No sales tax for a dealer. Another auctiongoer held the door for Maggie as she carried the heavy carton of leather-bound books to her van. She put it on the front seat. The cargo section of the van was filled with prints. She'd have to repack before she headed back to Jersey.

What a beautiful afternoon! She glanced at her watch. Just a little past one o'clock. She'd check in with Amy, and maybe they could drive down to Pemaquid Point to see the breakers. She'd been on the coast of Maine two days now and hadn't even seen the ocean.

Chapter 9

‒‒‒◇‒‒‒

August in the Country—The Seashore. *Wood engraving
by Winslow Homer, published in* Harper's Weekly
*August 27, 1859. Beach scene with many (fully dressed)
people enjoying the sunshine. Includes man trying
(unsuccessfully) to scare ladies by waving a lobster
at them, and a boy whose finger has been caught
by a crab. An early Homer, less dramatic than his later
work, but already showing his sense of humor and
ability to depict people's faces and elaborate fashions.
13.75 x 9.12 inches. Price: $325.*

"How was the auction?" Amy was settled comfortably on a
porch lounge chair overlooking the river, a glass of iced tea in
her hand. "Before you tell me, there's a plate of sandwiches in
the refrigerator. And take some iced tea or diet cola."

"Have you already eaten?" Maggie suddenly realized a
sandwich was just what she needed.

"I was hungry, so I ate early. But you and Drew weren't home, so I just kept creating. Take what you'd like."

Maggie found a plate and chose half an egg salad sandwich and half a tuna. They looked so good she added half a ham sandwich too. Amy had made enough sandwiches for the neighborhood. And diet cola was definitely Maggie's drink of choice. She was back on the porch with her plate in less than three minutes.

"Now, how was the auction?"

"Crowded. Noisy. Things went a bit higher than I would have liked. But I got the carton I was hoping for at a good price."

"Congratulations! I told you Maine was a wonderful place! And how is your friend Will?"

Maggie finished chewing her bite of tuna salad sandwich first. "This is delicious. You added sweet pickles?"

"And a few chopped olives."

"Nice touch. Will's fine. I left him there. He was waiting for another lot or two to come up. But I didn't want to miss this beautiful Maine afternoon."

"Did you invite him for dinner?"

"He and his aunt Nettie. I said 'barbecue at five,' and he promised to come. I did tell you they're from the original family to own this house, right?"

"You told me. But that's true of half the state of Maine, it seems. The only difference is that Will's last name really is Brewer."

"Where's Drew?"

"He took off somewhere with Tom Colby, Shirley's brother, from next door. I think Tom said something about checking out a cemetery."

"A cemetery?"

"Tom's on the board of the Madoc Historical Society, and

one of their projects is recording the names in all the old family graveyards and restoring the headstones. He teaches history at Waymouth High and is a Civil War reenactor. Drew is a Civil War buff too, so they especially like locating the resting places of Civil War veterans. They clean off the mosses and put up small flags and so forth."

"Sounds like a good thing to do."

"It keeps them busy. Drew said he'd stop for steaks on the way home. If he forgets, we have some in the freezer."

"I'm not worried." Maggie put down her plate. It was embarrassing how fast those three half sandwiches had disappeared. "And I'm certainly not hungry now. Have you heard anything more about Crystal?"

"Nothing. I'm sure she's just staying with a girlfriend. Maybe she had an argument with her mother. Teenaged girls do."

"I saw Rachel at the auction this morning, and she still seemed pretty upset."

"Rachel was at the auction?"

"She was putting auction catalogs together and selling them. She said something about 'Johnny' asking her to help."

"'Johnny'? Oh, probably Johnny Brent. He owns the construction company Giles and Brian Leary work for. Rachel and Johnny are pretty close."

"But how would that explain her being at Walter English's auction?"

Amy frowned a bit. "I'm not sure. I heard something about Walter English and Johnny Brent doing something together." She threw up her hands. "Or maybe they're just friends. Everyone up here seems to know everyone else."

That was for sure.

Maggie took a last drink of diet cola.

"It's such a beautiful afternoon I thought maybe we could drive down to Pemaquid Point for an hour or so. I was there years ago, when Michael and I vacationed in Maine." Maggie stopped for a moment, remembering the good times. "It was such a beautiful spot. Do you have time?"

"Sounds like a great idea." Amy looked at her watch. "The roofing guys won't need us. It's a little past two. We can easily be back in a couple of hours to turn on the grill if Drew isn't home by then. And he should be. It would be good for me to get out of the house for the afternoon too."

"I left a sweater in my car. Do I need anything else?"

"Nothing. But the sweater is a good idea. Sea breezes can be cool on an August afternoon."

"Last night I started looking at some of those pictures of the children needing homes. Do you have any books on adoption I could borrow while I'm here?"

"Stacks of them. Just check in my study while I run upstairs to get a sweater. Take whatever seems interesting. I'll write a note to let Drew know where we've gone."

Amy's study was neat and orderly. The bookshelves were divided between books on Maine history and books on children. As always, Amy was organized. One entire shelf on baby and toddler care, authors alphabetized. One shelf on infertility and pregnancy. The adoption books were down lower. She pulled out one on "open adoption." What was that? And *Adopting the Older Child,* and *Today's Options in Adoption.* The bottom shelf was stacked with copies of *Adoption Today* magazine, and another pile of what appeared to be booklets and brochures from adoption agencies. She'd look more carefully tomorrow. She had enough for now. Maggie stepped back and stumbled against Amy's wastebasket. She reached to push it farther under the desk.

She couldn't help noticing a box pushed loosely underneath an assortment of what looked like junk mail. An empty home pregnancy kit.

Maggie winced. Amy would have said something, she was sure, if it had been positive. But she clearly was still trying. It would definitely be good for her to get out of the house for the afternoon.

The shelves of gray and black rocks leading into the crashing surf at Pemaquid Point were as dramatic as Maggie had remembered, although she hadn't remembered the three tour buses full of Texans who were also climbing on the rocks and admiring the view.

Maine was beautiful, with or without people in Stetson hats. She and Amy didn't talk much as they relaxed and enjoyed the ocean view, the lobster boats, the herring gulls, and rafts of eider ducks. Neither of them mentioned Drew's drinking or pregnancy tests or crying ghosts in the night. We've been friends for a long time, Maggie thought. Amy's going through some difficult days. I'm glad I'm here.

A little girl, perhaps six years old, tentatively walked on the rocks not far away, holding tightly to her mother's hand. The two stopped and bent down to look into a tide pool. There were so many wonders for a child to discover.

Maggie stretched and felt the warm sun all through her body. She hadn't needed her sweater after all.

The peace didn't last long. Five vehicles were already in Amy's driveway when they pulled in. Maggie had left her van there. The Brent Construction truck meant Giles and Brian Leary were still working on the roof. Drew's Jeep was easy to identify. An old Ford truck was parked next to it. But, most dramatically, a police car with its radio left on was next to the Ford. And then an ambulance pulled in behind them.

A man in uniform walked quickly out from the kitchen door.

Maggie felt as though she were in a time warp: the uniform was that of a Civil War soldier.

The ambulance driver called out, "Where?"

"Field in back of the barn," replied the Union soldier.

"Drew?" Amy paled, as a woman from the ambulance ran past her and around the barn. "What's happened to Drew?"

"It's not Drew," said the soldier, coming up and touching her shoulder. "Drew is fine. He's in back of the barn with Giles and Brian."

"Then?"

"It's Crystal Porter. Brian Leary found her over in the grasses behind your barn. Drew and I had just pulled in when Brian came running, and Drew called 911."

"What happened? How is she?" Maggie and Amy both started running toward the barn.

"No need to run," the soldier called after them. "She looks pretty dead."

Chapter 10

The Lobsterman (Hauling in a Light Fog). *N. C. Wyeth illustration for Kenneth Roberts's* Trending into Maine, *1938. Lobsterman in traditional wooden dory, checking a lobster trap in a rough sea. Gulls follow dory in the fog. Wyeth and Roberts were close friends, and both had homes in Maine. 5.5 x 7 inches. Price: $75.*

Brian Leary stood on the border of the field, his face as pale as the faded white paint on the barn. His father was next to him. Perhaps twenty feet out in the high grasses that separated the Douglas home from the one where Shirley and Tom lived, Maggie could see a policeman and the woman from the ambulance. They were talking quietly, but no one seemed to be taking any sort of action. Not a good sign.

Amy suddenly burst into tears and sat on a large rock that looked as though it had been part of a stone wall many years before. Maggie walked up to the Learys. "The man in the uniform said you'd found her, Brian."

"Dad and I were up on the roof, working on that corner of the ell." He gestured somewhere above where they stood. "I noticed half a dozen crows making a racket over there. When I came down for more shingles, I went over to see. I thought maybe a dog or cat had been injured. It wasn't a dog or cat." Brian turned suddenly and ran a few steps back toward the edge of the field. He bent over and vomited.

"Brian and Crystal were friends," his father said quietly, as though an explanation were needed. "And she was so young."

Maggie nodded. Drew was sitting next to Amy, rocking her gently in his arms. The soldier came up to Maggie.

"I don't believe we've met," he said, extending his hand. "Drew says you're an old friend of Amy's. I'm glad you're here."

"Thank you," said Maggie. "And you are?" His uniform certainly looked authentic.

"Tom Colby. I live next door." He pointed in the general direction of the house just visible on the other side of the high grasses. The high grasses where Crystal lay.

"You're Shirley's brother." Maggie suddenly connected. "The Civil War reenactor."

"Yes."

"You had me a for a moment. Are you with the Twentieth Maine?"

"No, ma'am." Even under the circumstances Tom straightened up and smiled slightly. "I'm with Company D of Berdan's Second Regiment."

"A sharpshooter."

His eyes opened in amazement. "Almost no one knows about Berdan's Second anymore. Are you a Civil War buff?"

"No; just an antiques dealer and American civilization professor. Tom, you were here with Drew when Brian discovered Amy. What happened?"

"I don't rightly know. Drew and I had just pulled in. We went to work on some local graveyards this afternoon. We had been to one of them before, and I had done some research and verified that three of the men buried there had fought in Maine regiments."

"In the Civil War."

He nodded. "When I find that, I usually try to have a quiet ceremony for them, after I clean off the grave and record the information for anyone seeking relatives. I put a small flag near their stone to honor them. When I can, I like to wear my uniform. Seems fitting."

"So then you and Drew came back here."

"I'd left my truck around the other side of the barn; we'd taken his Jeep. As we pulled into the driveway, Brian came tearing around the side of the barn. We figured out pretty fast we needed help. I stayed with Brian until Giles came down from the roof, and Drew called 911. I was just calling my sister to say I'd be home a little late. The police got here just before you and Amy did."

"Did you see Crystal?"

"I didn't touch her or nothing. I did go to see if what the boy said was true."

"And?"

"She was dead, sure enough. I'd say for some time. A body in a field attracts all sorts of—"

"That's all right, Tom," Maggie stopped him. "I believe you. But how did she die? And why was she over there?" Maggie looked at the area. They were in back of the Douglas barn. Farther down to her left she saw an open stone path. "Is that the path to your house?"

"Sure is. Been there for a hundred years, most likely. This was the old Brewer home, you know, and Captain Eben's cousin built the house I own about 1870. That's when the path was first laid. Shirley and I kept it clear. She used to come over each day to check on Charlotte. Until last winter, of course."

When Charlotte had died. But Crystal wasn't anywhere near that path. Nor was she near the much less formal path Amy and Maggie had followed yesterday between the Douglas home and the Porters'. The path to Tom and Shirley's house went north, paralleling the river. The path they had followed yesterday had led east, across the field beyond the barn. Crystal's body lay somewhere in between.

"How?"

Tom shook his head. "Couldn't tell right off. I didn't touch her. Didn't want to. She could have fallen, I guess. The field is pretty uneven out there. Hard to tell what happened. As I said, the creatures hadn't left her alone."

Maggie shuddered. She didn't want to think about the condition of Crystal's young body, which she had seen alive and full of life just yesterday. The policeman was on his cell phone. The whole scene suddenly reminded her horribly of the antiques fair last Memorial Day. The fair where there had been two murders. The fair where she had met Will.

Will. Will was invited for dinner, with his elderly aunt. This was no time for visits.

"Tom, I'm going to make a phone call. I'll be right back." She stopped briefly to tell Amy and Drew what she was doing. Neither paid attention to her. Their minds were far removed from an evening barbecue.

In the house she dialed the number in her wallet and let it ring ten times. No answer. Darn. And no answering machine, either. She couldn't even leave a message.

As she walked back outside, a Maine State Trooper's car pulled in. Reinforcements. Within minutes crime scene tape was circling a large section of the field, and pictures were being taken. The ambulance was pulling out. It was clear the services of its crew were not needed.

All was quiet. Everyone stood in groups as though waiting for a daguerreotypist to capture them. Brian and Giles Leary. Amy and Drew. The Union soldier. And Maggie. The deputy who had arrived first and the two state troopers he had called were out in the field, carefully checking the ground. No one else was allowed near. Finally one of the state troopers came toward them.

"Nothing much more we can do here, folks. The girl's dead. You all know that. We don't know why, so we're securing the site. I've called for someone in the medical examiner's office to come and take a look, then remove her body. They'll probably take her to Augusta to take a look at her." He hesitated and turned toward Brian. "You found her. You know who she is?"

"Crystal Porter," he said softly. "We go to high school together. We were friends. Good friends."

"That the girl went missing last night?"

"She lives with her mother, up on Egret Point. Over there." Brian pointed. "Her mom was real worried about her."

The trooper's voice was soft. "We'll be sending someone to tell her mother. And your name is?"

"Brian Leary."

"Age?"

"Eighteen."

"And how did you happen to find her, Brian?"

"My dad and I were doing some roof work for the Douglases. Up there." He pointed at the ell. "The crows were making a fuss down in the field. I went over to see why. And I saw her."

If possible, Brian got even paler.

"Did you touch her body, Brian?"

"No! I yelled, and ran back to get my dad. To get help. I found Mr. Douglas and Mr. Colby. They were just getting in. Mr. Douglas called the police."

"And when did you last see Crystal Porter alive?"

"Yesterday, around noon, I guess. She was in the kitchen fixing some things for Mrs. Douglas when I went down to get a glass of water."

"Did you talk with her?"

"Not much. We were going over to Brunswick to see a movie last night with a couple of the other kids, and I told her I'd pick her up around six o'clock. She said she was finishing up pretty soon and would be going home. She'd see me at six."

"You didn't have any arguments, or disagreements?"

"No, sir!"

"And did she see you at six?"

"She didn't come home. I was there at six. She hadn't called or anything. I drove around looking for her all evening, and called all our friends, but no one had heard from her or seen her."

"Did you see her leave here?"

Brian looked at his father. "Dad and I were working on the back part of the ell roof, like we were today. Crystal would have gone out the back door and walked across the lawn and field on the other side. If I'd stood up or something, then I might have seen her. But I don't remember doing that. And we did leave earlier than usual yesterday. We needed more roofing paper."

"What about you, Mr. Leary?"

Giles shook his head. "I don't remember seeing her leave either. People did come and go—Mr. and Mrs. Douglas, and Mrs. Douglas's friend, here—so I heard cars. But I don't remember seeing or hearing Crystal. But, of course, I wasn't paying special attention. She was here most afternoons."

"How about you folks?" He looked at the rest of them. "Mrs. Douglas? Mr. Douglas? What time did Crystal leave here yesterday?"

Amy shook her head. "She was here until at least three o'clock. I told her she could go after she'd finished cleaning out a cabinet in the kitchen. I was in my study, and I didn't watch her. I'd say she left shortly after that."

"Mr. Douglas?"

"I was upstairs. I don't know when she left. Crystal's hours were Amy's business."

"Did you happen to notice, Ms. . . . ?"

"Maggie Summer. I'm visiting the Douglases. I was resting at about three, upstairs in the guest room. I didn't hear or see anything." Maggie crossed her fingers that the detective wouldn't ask her when she'd seen Crystal before that. But he didn't. She needed to talk to Amy before this situation got more complicated. She wouldn't lie to the police.

"Thank you all," the detective said. A man and a woman walked around the corner of the barn and he raised his hand toward them. "That's the medical examiner's team. I need to work with them. I'll be in touch with all of you." He hesitated. "At this point it's too early to tell what happened to Crystal Porter. Do any of you know whether she was involved with drugs or alcohol?"

Silence.

Amy said, "I never noticed anything, Detective. And she worked here most weekdays this summer."

"Brian?"

Brian glanced at his father in embarrassment. "I've seen her have a beer, sometimes. A lot of the kids do it. But I've never seen her take anything else."

"Okay. If any of you remember something that might be helpful, you call me." He handed out his cards. Detective Nicholas Strait. "I'll probably be back to talk with all of you as soon as we know what questions need to be asked." He looked at Brian. "I'll talk to the girl's mother." He went over to the two newcomers and started pointing toward the field.

"Why don't you two pack up your gear and go home," Drew said to Giles and Brian. "It's getting late anyway."

"I have to go too," said Tom. "I promised I'd get dinner started for Shirley and be there when the bus brings the kids home from day camp. Thanks for the help at the cemetery, Drew."

Brian and Giles began picking up the tools that had been left on the ground, and the rest of them went toward the front of the house.

Will Brewer and Great-Aunt Nettie were just pulling in.

"Oh, Lord," said Amy. "We have dinner guests."

Chapter 11

───⁓───

Untitled fashion plate from Gentleman's Magazine, *April 1852. Hand-colored steel engraving of elegant man and woman in outdoor afternoon attire with two small children, one dressed in the popular tartan plaid of the period. 7 x 9 inches. Price: $70.*

Maggie was the first to reach the car. "Will, I tried to call you. There's a problem. I don't think this is a good time for you and your aunt to be here."

But Drew was right behind her. "Nonsense, Maggie. We can't just stand around feeling depressed. Life has to go on." As Will looked questioningly at Maggie, Drew reached out his hand. "Drew Douglas. You must be Maggie's friend Will. We're glad you could come."

Amy then took charge. "I'm glad to meet you. This is a little awkward, and we haven't had a chance to get dinner started. But we all need to eat, and having company would make this evening easier for us."

Will still hesitated, looking to Maggie, and at the two police vehicles and the car from the medical examiner's office.

"If Drew and Amy say it's fine, then it will be. And your aunt?"

Everyone turned to see the tiny woman sitting in the front seat of the car. Will hurried over to open the door for her, a gesture she had clearly been waiting for. "Aunt Nettie, we seem to have caught these people at a difficult time. But they are insisting we stay. Would that be all right with you?"

"It will be just fine, if you introduce me," declared Aunt Nettie in a clear voice. "At my age where and what I eat isn't a quarter as important as who the company is I'm eating it with."

"This is Drew Douglas," Will said, as Drew bent down and shook Nettie's hand, "and this is Nettie Brewer, my aunt."

"Might as well call me Aunt Nettie. Half the town does already. And which one of these people is Maggie?"

Maggie actually blushed as she stepped forward. "I'm Maggie. And I'm pleased to meet you. This is my friend Amy Douglas."

"Well, now that everyone knows everyone else, let's get down to brass tacks. What's this problem everyone's looking so glum about? What are all these police cars doing in your driveway?"

"Maybe it's something they don't want to talk about." Will looked from Drew to Amy and back again and tried for levity. "When I talked with Maggie yesterday, she said you might have ghosts in the house. You all look as though you've just seen one."

There was silence.

Maggie hesitated, but Amy nodded slightly. It wouldn't be a secret for long. Having decided to have dinner together, they couldn't not mention what had happened. She hoped Aunt Nettie wouldn't be too upset. You never knew how older people would react at the thought of death. Especially the death of someone so young. And a relative of some sort too, Maggie remembered.

"Aunt Nettie, this afternoon the body of one of Amy and Drew's neighbors was found in the field behind the barn. The one between this house and the one where Shirley Steele and Tom Colby live."

"The matter's with the police now. We really shouldn't be talking about it," Drew added quickly.

Will ignored Drew and looked at Maggie. "Maggie seems to get herself involved with the strangest situations. Who died?"

"Crystal Porter."

Aunt Nettie gasped. "Rachel's little girl? Dead? How?"

"We don't know. She'd been helping out at our house, and she left yesterday afternoon to walk home. She never got there," said Amy.

"But her house isn't in the direction of Tom and Shirley's," Aunt Nettie said immediately. "What was she doing over behind your barn?"

"We don't know. We don't really know anything," said Maggie. "I tried to call and suggest we cancel tonight, but no one answered."

"Will was doing some errands for me, and I don't answer the phone unless I'm expecting a call," said Aunt Nettie. She smoothed out the skirt of her cotton Black Watch plaid dress. "And I'm sorry about little Crystal, but she was conceived in error, and perhaps it was God's way." She looked around at the startled faces of those listening to her. "What are we going to have for dinner?"

Will and Aunt Nettie had brought two bottles of burgundy and a blueberry pie for dessert. They all sipped wine while Drew and Will started the grill and Aunt Nettie and Maggie helped Amy in the kitchen. Maggie cut the steak in cubes and marinated it in dressing. Finding enough green peppers, onions, and tomatoes to make shish kebab was not hard to manage, and Amy added some garlic to a package of white rice. "Voilà! Dinner."

The early-evening wind blowing across the river was cool. After Aunt Nettie asked to borrow a sweater Amy decided to serve dinner on the slightly rickety kitchen table.

"We have so many things to do in this house," she chattered, clearly eager to keep the conversation away from more weighty subjects. "The kitchen has wonderful cabinets, but so little counter space. We want to find an old pine table, and some chairs to match. Our apartment in New York was full, but the furniture we had there hardly fills two rooms in this house! And we love the old fireplaces. Before next winter I want to get the chimneys lined so we can have fires in at least the living room and the master bedroom."

"I wonder what condition the old kitchen is in," said Aunt Nettie.

"Well, you can see," said Amy, looking around.

"I don't mean this room. I mean the *old* kitchen." Aunt Nettie spoke definitively.

"Isn't this the old kitchen?"

"One of them, of course," acknowledged Aunt Nettie, speaking as if she were educating a slow child. "Where we're sitting is actually part of the oldest kitchen. But when Captain Brewer moved the house over from the island in 1833, they closed it off. It was too old-fashioned. Just a fireplace; no stove. The new 1833 kitchen was in the ell."

"Where?" asked Drew. "There's a chimney there, and a brick wall. I didn't think of it as a kitchen though."

"It was the kitchen," Aunt Nettie said. "It was the kitchen until Charlotte inherited the house in, I think it was 1931. She's the one who decided to use this room as the kitchen again, and modernized it. She said she'd fix it up good enough to last until she died. And she did."

They all looked around. Certainly the 1931 appliances were still there. And operating in some sort of fashion. "They made good stoves in those days," agreed Amy. "And refrigerators."

"Just as good as the old iceboxes," agreed Aunt Nettie. "I just never understood why Charlotte used this end of the kitchen for her appliances when she could have used the old part."

"The old part?" Drew looked around. They were sitting at one end of the kitchen. The end where the cabinets were, and the sink. At the other end of the long room was the door to Amy's study, and the door to the outside. And two blank walls.

"Over there." Aunt Nettie pointed at the empty wall beyond the cabinets. "That's where the old fireplace was, before 1833. I remember my grandmother telling me they boarded it up before they moved the house. They put the new stove in the ell."

"In 1833," said Maggie. "So the original 1774 fireplace is still there? Behind the wall?"

"So my grandmother always maintained," said Aunt Nettie. "I told Charlotte, when she was fixing up the place, but she didn't want anything old. She liked new things. She's the one put the linoleum over the brick hearth."

"There's a brick hearth?" Amy started to get excited.

Will had already risen and gone over to the wall and begun tapping on it.

Maggie smiled at him. "An old fireplace! What a temptation. Will specializes in old fireplace and kitchen equipment, you know."

"Do you know anything about the construction of these old houses?" Drew had joined Will at the wall.

"I have a degree in construction. I taught woodworking for eighteen years before deciding to go into antiques full-time."

"Do you think we could do it? Take the wall down?"

Will tapped again, high and low. "I'd be willing to bet there are beams here, supporting part of the original structure, but we could work around them." He reached down to the flowered brown linoleum. As he touched the edge, a small piece of it broke off in his hands. He looked at Drew questioningly.

"Go right ahead," said Drew. "Here, I'll help you. That linoleum had to go sometime anyway." They both got down on their knees and started breaking off pieces of the flooring. Clouds of dust rose immediately.

"Look!" Drew pointed. "There are bricks under here!"

"Just as I said. They wouldn't have disappeared in only seventy or eighty years." Aunt Nettie sneezed. "But taking up any more of that linoleum's going to be a messy job."

"Tomorrow?" Drew asked, grinning.

"Tomorrow!" agreed Will.

Crystal's death had not been mentioned in several hours. Not that anyone had forgotten.

Chapter 12

———✺———

Malay Cock. Harrison Weir (1824–1906). Lithograph of rooster, published by Leighton Brothers, c. 1855. Weir was a noted British animal and poultry painter and illustrator whose work was extremely accurate to nature. He was also a friend of Charles Darwin's. 7 x 10.5 inches. Price: $60.

Maggie woke to the sound of the telephone. She glanced at her bedside clock: 1:30. The ringing stopped. It wasn't her house; the telephone wasn't in her room. But houses built in 1774 weren't insulated. Sound travels well in them. The telephone rang again at 2:00. At 2:45. And at 4:00. By the time it rang at 5:15, Maggie gave up on sleep.

Assuming that there had not been five emergencies, the mysterious caller must be back. And if she couldn't sleep down the hall from the telephone, Amy and Drew, with a phone in their bedroom, must have gotten very little rest.

She decided five-thirty was morning and pulled a bathrobe over the faded orange college T-shirt she used as a nightshirt. Maybe it wasn't time for bacon and eggs, but the craving for a diet cola was too much to resist. To her surprise, she wasn't the first one up. Drew was sitting at the kitchen table, sipping a large cup of coffee.

"Sorry about the phone calls. They woke you too?"

Maggie nodded. "Were they the hang-up calls Amy told me about?"

"Yup. Every one. I grabbed them as fast as I could, but no one was there. I finally turned the ringer off on the bedroom phone and came down here to turn this ringer off too, and the thought of coffee was too overpowering to ignore. Some for you?"

"Actually, I'm more the diet cola type. But I happen to know there are a couple of bottles in the refrigerator." She poured herself a glass and drank deeply. "There. That was almost worth missing sleep."

"There sure hasn't been a lot of sleeping done in this house recently."

"Not even mentioning your mysterious caller, and now Crystal's death. You and Amy have a lot going on in your lives."

"I don't know how much she's told you, but moving here hasn't been the stress-free experience we had both imagined. But we love this house, and we love Maine. I'm sure we'll get the house in order, banish whatever ghosts are around, and be able to re-create ourselves as normal people." Drew took a deep sip of his coffee. "It was Amy's idea to move, you know. I had my doubts. But I still think we can make it work, if only she would relax a little."

Relax? When her house was filled with ghosts, her drunken husband was sleeping with a teenaged neighbor, when she couldn't meet his need for a baby, and they had found a body in the backyard? No reason she could think of why Amy wouldn't be able to relax.

"Amy's always been so focused," continued Drew. "She's always known exactly what she wanted to do, who she wanted to be with, and where she wanted to go. I've never been that way. Oh, I worked hard enough to get through college and get a good job. I made money in the nineties, but who didn't? I never really felt it was part of a long-term plan. It was just what needed to be done right then. Amy has never eaten a sautéed shrimp without knowing exactly how it fit into her long-term plan for life."

"Amy told me you want children."

"That's one of the things we agreed about when we first met, long before we decided to get married. We each have our own reasons. I was adopted. I have a wonderful family. Sometimes I wonder what my life might have been like if I hadn't been adopted by them. I can't see anyone giving me a better life than the parents I had. I want to be able to give that sort of life, or maybe even a better one, to my children. And Amy had a rough childhood, so she felt the same, but for other reasons."

"Amy had a rough childhood? In Short Hills, New Jersey?"

"Well, I'm sure she's told you that her father died when she was little, and her mother remarried." Drew looked at Maggie as though she should know something else. "She and her stepfather had some issues."

Funny. Amy had never talked about her stepfather.

"Anyway, we both want children. But so far we haven't had any luck. Amy always wants to do things the right way. You know her. She's the sort who would never substitute margarine for butter in a recipe."

"Like your beautiful nursery upstairs. Perfect."

"Exactly. No baby, but a perfect nursery. That was one of Amy's long-term plans. My mother always said that we should wait, that it was bad luck to buy infant things before you had a baby. She didn't buy anything for me even though she knew she was going to adopt. She and Dad have a great story about stopping on the way home from the hospital where they picked me up and buying a crib." Drew smiled. "Babies don't care what kind of crib they sleep in. They care that someone holds them when they cry, and feeds them when they're hungry, and changes their diapers when they need it. But Amy didn't see it that way. She wanted everything to be just the way she'd always dreamed it." Drew sighed. "So here we are, in the perfect state, in the perfect house, with the perfect nursery."

For the perfect baby, thought Maggie.

"And now Amy even says she hears a baby crying in the house. She talks so much about it I even thought I heard it one night."

"Drew, I heard it too. The night before last."

Drew got up abruptly. "Then she's got us all going crazy." He looked at the wall clock. "It's six. We might as well get on with the day. I'm going to take a shower and then drive to the hardware store. Will said we could use some crowbars, and I don't have any. Why would I have needed a crowbar in New York City?" Drew shook his head. "The Waymouth hardware store opens at seven, so I'll get there and home before Will arrives at eight or eight-thirty. I'd better get some more vacuum cleaner bags too. If we're going to take up the linoleum and pull down part of a wall, there's going to be a lot of dust and dirt."

"For sure. I'll finish my cola, and claim the shower after you."

"Amy usually sleeps until eight or so. Why don't I bring

back some doughnuts and sausage and we'll have breakfast then. If Will arrives, there'll be plenty for him too."

"Sounds good." Maggie sat and sipped her cola as she listened to Drew's footsteps going upstairs. There were always two sides to a story, two sides to a marriage. What was really happening in this one? Maggie shook her head, as though to get her thoughts in order. It was none of her business what was happening inside this marriage. Unless it affected someone else.

Why did she keep thinking of Crystal, that beautiful young girl whose body had been lying in a field not far from this house? This house that everyone agreed was perfect. Except for a few little problems. The paint. The roof. The phone calls. The fire. And now—the death. How had Crystal died? Would they learn that today?

Maggie shivered. Thank goodness it was going to be a beautiful day. The sun's warmth would be welcome. She finished her diet cola and decided to try for a short nap before her shower.

The next sound she heard was Amy's voice. "Maggie! Maggie! Come quickly!"

Maggie shook her head. Seven-fifteen. She had drifted into a deeper sleep than she had planned.

"Maggie, please! Wake up!" Her door swung open. Amy's sleep-tangled hair was around her face, and she was still wearing her nightgown. "Didn't you hear the crash? There's been an accident down at the curve below the house. I can't see the car, but I can see the end of one tree that's down. I called 911, and they're coming. But someone should at least stand and make sure no other cars zoom around that corner right now!"

Maggie was already throwing on a light sweater and climbing into jeans. "Drew went to the hardware store."

"How do you know that?"

"Five-thirty coffee and cola break in the kitchen."

Amy's expression was one of open doubt.

"I didn't seduce the man, Amy. He drank coffee; I drank cola. We didn't even share a beverage. I couldn't sleep after all the phone calls."

"Sorry. The phone calls were awful."

"Why aren't you dressed?"

Amy looked down at herself in recognition. "Right. I need to get dressed."

Maggie shook her head. "I'll go ahead and make sure no power lines are down. Stop cars." She ran downstairs.

Outside on the lawn her leather sandals slipped on the damp morning grass. The Douglas home was on top of a steep hill; the grading to the road was almost ninety degrees at the corner. She wouldn't attempt it. She ran to the end of the driveway and turned down the hill toward the curve in the road. She saw the car almost immediately. Clearly it had headed down the hill and not made the turn; it had hit a tree instead.

Clearly it was Drew's Jeep.

Chapter 13

A Fair Chauffeur, *1900 lithograph by Howard Chandler Christy (1872–1952). Published by Charles Scribner's Sons, New York, 1906. Woman behind the wheel of early open automobile, with man seated beside her. Christy created "The Christy Girl" for leading publications of his day and during the 1920s painted portraits of world celebrities. From his folio* The American Girl. *7 x 9.5 inches. Price: $65.*

The ambulance and the police car got there almost simultaneously with Maggie. By the time Amy arrived the road had been blocked off, a tow truck called, and the ambulance team was maneuvering Drew onto a backboard. The Jeep had hit the tree and its body was folded back toward the driver's seat.

Amy hovered, wringing her hands, as she tried to stay out of the crew's way. "I'm fine, honey," Drew called softly, and clearly with some effort. "Don't worry."

"You're not fine. Just stay quiet and let us do the work," said the big woman pushing a board under Drew's buttocks.

"We meet again." It was Deputy Colby, the same officer who had been at the Porters' home two nights before and had given Maggie and Amy a ride home. "Any idea about what happened?"

"Drew was going to the hardware store." Maggie looked at the situation. "And, clearly, for some reason he didn't make the corner." She paused. "He couldn't have been going very fast. He had just driven out of the driveway." She pointed up the hill perhaps twenty-five feet.

"He doesn't seem to have used his brakes at all." Deputy Colby looked at the pavement.

There were no skid marks.

"He was lucky to hit that tree, actually. If he hadn't, he might have ended up in the river."

Maggie shuddered. Good thing Amy hadn't heard that. The medical team had Drew almost all the way out of the Jeep now. He was pale, and one leg was at a funny angle, but he was conscious.

"Are you in pain?" Amy asked, following alongside the stretcher.

"Sure am," answered Drew. "Strangest thing. I put my foot on the brakes and the pedal went all the way to the floor. Nothing happened. Nothing. The Jeep was fine yesterday."

"I'll have a body shop check out the brakes," Deputy Colby assured him. "Do you want to go with your husband in the ambulance, ma'am?"

"Yes, please." Amy was already climbing in.

"Where are you going?" Maggie asked as they started closing the doors. "I'll meet you there."

"Rocky Shore," answered the woman as the door slammed in Maggie's face. A tow truck was making its way down the hill.

"I'll leave a message later about the car. Their insurance company will need to know where it is." Deputy Colby made another note. "Do you know how to get to the hospital?"

"I have a friend coming." Maggie checked her watch. "Anytime now. He'll know."

"Good."

"Have they found out how Crystal Porter died? The girl they found yesterday afternoon?"

"I know who she is. Not too many people get murdered around here."

"Murdered!" Maggie stepped back. She had assumed something freakish had killed Crystal. A weak heart. An unintentional drug overdose. A snake bite.

Not murder.

"Kind of hard to hit yourself on the head," said Deputy Colby. "Can't give you any more details, of course, but sure didn't look like an accident or suicide. Medical examiner's office has the body. They may know more later today." He looked at her. "You folks are all from New York, right?"

"Amy and Drew are from New York. I'm from New Jersey."

"Wherever. You don't plan on going back there in the immediate future, right?"

"What?" Maggie stopped for a minute. Of course. A girl had been murdered on Amy and Drew's land. They were all suspects.

"No one's going anywhere, Officer. Except to the hospital."

"Good. Because Detective Strait from the state police will probably be looking to talk with you all later today, once we get a couple of other issues ironed out." Maggie could hear a car horn honking on the other side of the curve. The deputy had closed the road, and someone wanted to travel it.

"We'll be here," Maggie assured him. "Or at the hospital. No flights to Brazil on the agenda."

He looked at her sideways. "Was that a joke, lady?"

She nodded.

"Just checking. 'Cause it wasn't funny. This isn't New York City. People don't get murdered every day in the state of Maine. Here we take murder seriously."

Chapter 14

—⁓—

Osprey (or Fishing Hawk) Egg, *lithograph from* Nests and Eggs of British Birds *by the Reverend F. O. Morris, London, 1879. One large white egg, speckled with irregular brown marks. 6.75 x 10 inches. Price: $55.*

Maggie sat on the porch steps waiting for Will, another glass of diet cola in her hand. She probably drank too much of this stuff. A minor vice.

The morning mists were beginning to rise. The scene looked like a slighter softer and grayer version of a Monet painting. Herring gulls were circling; perhaps one of the lobstermen had just finished checking his traps. There was the loud hum of a boat on the river, and an occasional car drove by on the road below, but the sound of chickadees in the apple tree was louder than any other noise right now. Queen Anne's lace in the high grasses bordered the lawn. Goldenrod was beginning to bloom.

A perfect August morning in Maine.

The ambulance had left. The tow truck had removed Drew's car. The deputy had made a very obvious point of writing down the license numbers of both Amy's and Maggie's cars before he had left.

Today Drew and Will had planned to take up the cracked kitchen linoleum and try to remove the wall Aunt Nettie swore was in front of the original kitchen fireplace. Maggie had privately thought of taking off for an hour or two to check out an antiquarian-book store she'd seen in Waymouth. Her trip to Maine was to have been one for relaxing, and adding to the inventory. Not for murders and accidents. Not to speak of ghosts and phone calls in the night.

Will should be here anytime now. She ran a hand through her hair. Had she even taken the time to brush it this morning? Probably not. Her hands automatically smoothed the long, wavy strands and began braiding them. She needed to get to the hospital to see if there was anything she could do for Drew or Amy. Why wasn't Will here?

A sudden flush of anger hit her. Why wasn't he here when she needed him? He hadn't been there when Michael had been in an accident. There had been no one to help when she had gotten that call, when she had taken Michael's things to the hospital. She alone had heard that Michael's leg was healing. His leg was healing, but a stroke had killed him.

This was crazy. She hadn't even known Will when Michael had had his accident eight months ago. It had nothing to do with today. Or with Drew. Michael had crashed his car because he'd had a stroke. Drew couldn't have had a stroke. She was stressing out, between the past two days and little sleep. Was it only four days ago she'd been doing an antiques show in Provincetown and sharing a glass of sherry with Gussie? She hadn't even sorted through her cash box since then, or sent customers' checks to her bank. She needed to do that. Today, if possible.

Why did Drew's brakes fail?

Will's RV came around the curve and turned into the driveway. Last night he must have been driving his aunt's car. Will always carried his inventory in his portable motel, just in case. Just as Maggie's van was filled with cartons and portfolios. Antiques dealers! Insurance companies hated them: inventory values changed with the seasons, and even those with shops were constantly transporting valuable stock to and from antiques shows. Antiques dealers were not reckless drivers. One accident could not only total their vehicle, it could eliminate their business inventory.

She walked toward the RV. "Good morning! Do you know where Rocky Shore Hospital is?"

"Are you sick?"

"Drew was in a car accident about half an hour ago. The ambulance took him and Amy to Rocky Shore. I said we'd meet them there."

"How bad?"

"He was talking. His leg didn't look good."

"So you saw him. Where was the accident?"

"At the corner." Maggie pointed. "The one you just came around."

"He must have been going too fast and missed the curve. That's a bad corner. Where had he been so early in the morning?"

"He wasn't coming home. He was on his way to the hardware store to get a crowbar."

Will frowned. "How could he crash if he was on his way out? He would have just put on the gas to get the car started!"

"He said his brakes wouldn't work."

"Get in. We're taking a drive." Will drove carefully along the twists and turns that took the road along the river. "Maggie Summer, you're an amazing woman. Whenever I'm with you, things seem to happen. Those murders at the fair last spring. And now a dead girl and an accident."

"Not just a dead girl."

"Not *just* a dead girl?"

"The deputy who came to check out the accident said Crystal was murdered."

"Shit." Will swerved the motor home slightly as his mind momentarily left the road. "What else did he say to cheer our day?"

"Not much. Except that Amy and Drew and I are all suspects, since she was found on their property."

Will shook his head. "A few years back I imagine some folks in town wished her mother, Rachel, had disappeared. But not Crystal."

"There are crazy people in the world, and sometimes they hurt people." Maggie hesitated. "What did everyone have against Rachel?" Rachel seemed so quiet, so matronly; how could someone like that have provoked anger?

Will read her mind. "Remember? I told you. Rachel didn't always look or act the way she does now. She was, shall we say, very popular with a lot of young men when she wasn't too much older than Crystal."

Maggie nodded. "So she was popular. The young fellows in town were competing for her?"

"Not exactly. Her favors were pretty liberally distributed." Will grimaced. "She was an embarrassment to the family."

"Well, I guess Rachel calmed down."

"After she got pregnant with Crystal. She lived at home with her folks at first. They weren't really happy about that, but they didn't kick her out. Then her grandmother died and must have left her enough money to buy the house that she and Crystal live in. She works over at the library, you know. Never got a degree or anything, but she knows the books better than anyone."

"And her social life toned down?"

"Way down. She didn't go out with anyone for years, that I heard of. Until Johnny Brent. When you saw her yesterday at the auction, didn't she say something about Johnny?"

"That he'd asked her to help out."

"That I don't know about. Walter English owns the auction gallery so far as I know. Has for years. Inherited it from his dad, who was also an auctioneer."

"Is there anyone in Waymouth or Madoc whose family hasn't been here for generations?"

Will grinned. "Not many. Keeps things cozy."

Maggie was quiet as they drove through Waymouth, and down Route 1. "Poor Rachel. Then she didn't have anyone but Crystal. She was so upset when Amy and I were there the other night."

"You and Amy visited them?"

"Crystal hadn't come home on time, so Amy thought it would be a good idea for the two of us to follow the path from Amy's house to Crystal's, to see if she'd sprained her ankle or something. We didn't see her." Had Crystal been lying in that field, so close by, when they had taken that walk up to her house on Egret Point? Maggie shuddered slightly. If only they had looked in the other field.

"I wonder when she died."

"Deputy Colby didn't share that with me."

"We're here." Will pulled into a long driveway that ended in a circular drive in front of a low sandstone building. "You get out and check the emergency room. I'll park this monster in the lot and meet you there."

Maggie nodded. Signs to the emergency room pointed to the left.

Amy was sitting on an orange plastic chair, holding a white Styrofoam cup. "Maggie! I'm so glad you're here."

"Will drove me. He's parking his RV. How's Drew?"

"They're doing full-body X rays. The doctors think his head hit the side window and got a few bruises. He might have a slight concussion, but the major damage is to his right leg and foot. Exactly what is broken and how badly they don't know yet." Amy brought the cup to her lips and then, realizing it was empty, crumpled it and tossed it neatly into a nearby wastebasket.

"How are you doing?"

"I'm okay. For someone who had a body found in their back field last night and their husband injured in an automobile accident this morning, I'd say I'm doing pretty well."

Maggie smiled. "I'd agree." She hesitated. Should she tell Amy that Crystal had been murdered? There was no reason to disturb her further just now. She'd have to know later, but by then at least she'd have some idea about Drew's condition.

Will joined them a few minutes later, and Amy repeated what she knew about Drew. "It looks as though I'm going to be here for most of the day," she added. "And I'm doing all right. They have a coffee shop nearby, and I have my cell phone with me. Why don't you two go antiquing? I'd just as soon stay here quietly. You can give me your cell phone number, Will. If anything happens, or when I need a ride home, I'll call you."

Maggie and Will looked at each other. "Maybe we could

just do a few shops in Waymouth," Maggie said. "What do you think, Will?"

"For sure I don't think this is the day to take your kitchen apart, Amy." He looked at Maggie. "I suspect you'd like to see the antiquarian-book store."

Maggie nodded. "I'd hoped to."

"Then the two of you go. I'm fine, and they seem to be taking good care of Drew. After the last twenty-four hours, what else bad can happen?"

Chapter 15

—◠◡◠—

Behind the Scenes—How Stage Effects Are Produced.
*Unusual 1875 wood engraving showing "behind the
scenes" theatrical work, including men producing
"Shooting Thunder Bolts," "Stormy Winds," and "A
Shower of Rain." 8.75 x 11.75 inches. Price: $55.*

Maggie and Will spent the rest of the morning avoiding talk of the Brewer family, or Crystal, or even Drew's accident.

"That's five shops, and no buys for either of us," said Will as they left a small, red barn painted with a big ANTIQUES! CHEAP! sign. "But we haven't exactly been in shops featuring superlative pieces."

"Most of the stuff we've seen falls more into the 'collectible' or 'vintage' category," agreed Maggie.

"I'd say most of it falls more into the 'used junk' category," said Will.

"Only when junk is spelled *j-u-n-q-u-e,* of course."

"Of course."

"But you never know where we might find something. And we're looking for such different things." Maggie climbed up into passenger seat of the RV. "Although that last place was a total waste of time. Who told that guy that two-year-old *Time* magazines and bottles of sea glass were antiques?"

"Probably the same person who crocheted those pot holders in the shape of lighthouses. I'm surprised you didn't snap up a whole pile to give to fellow professors for Christmas gifts."

"I was tempted. But I managed to squelch the impulse," Maggie answered. "What about that Victorian house I remember seeing not far from Cut 'n' Curl? Didn't it have an ANTIQUES MALL sign on it?"

"That's one of Walter English's side operations."

"The auctioneer?"

"Right. Lots of dealers are his customers, of course, so several years ago he got the idea of making money on both sides of the balance sheet."

"So he auctions goods to dealers, they put the items in his mall, and he takes a percentage of the sales?"

"That's it. And, of course, he has someone there to answer questions about disposing of a collection or a special item. He even runs his 'free appraisal days' out of the mall."

Maggie shook her head. "In New Jersey there are antiques malls. But most of them are co-ops. Each dealer has his or her own area, almost like a small shop. In addition to paying rent for their space they volunteer to work in the mall one day every week or two. That way customers always have a few dealers on hand who can talk about the merchandise. And it saves the cost of sales staff."

"Have you ever taken space in a mall?"

"No. I've thought about it. But the co-op places would be hard for me because I have a regular job during the week and am off doing shows a lot of weekends. And prints are hard to display in cases. You?"

"I just started last winter. I use two malls. One in Buffalo, near home, and one in Westchester, where I share a booth with another dealer. I travel back and forth in New York State often enough that I can replenish the inventories in both places, or switch them around. I pay extra not to volunteer in the malls since I need to be free to travel to shows. Malls are a lot more convenient than having to be at a shop all the time, and less stressful than doing shows every weekend. I do almost thirty shows a year as it is. But now that I'm trying to make a living at antiques I needed to check out all possibilities for sales. The only major sales outlet I haven't tried yet is eBay."

"I haven't gone that route yet myself. But I know two dealers who've stopped doing shows and closed their shops and just sell on the Internet now. Let me know if the malls turn out to be good sales outlets for you."

"I'm monitoring them pretty closely. There are times this business is exhausting. But I got tired of teaching and never having enough time for the antiques. Somewhere there must be a middle line."

"I enjoy teaching, so I don't mind limiting the antiques to the dozen or so shows I do each year. And I do a little mail order to old customers, and the usual 'by appointment' sales. I have several New Jersey and New York decorators who've discovered my prints and become a good source of income. If I can keep what they're looking for in stock!"

"What's the big trend in decorator prints this year?"

"Botanicals and fruit are always popular. Birds are a favorite. And I can always sell prints of eggs. They fit in both traditional and modern decors. And at the moment cows are out; butterflies are in."

"And, I suppose, hunting prints for the gentleman's study."

"The gun lobby has changed that a bit. Hunting and fishing prints used to be popular. Then hunting became less popular; fly-fishing was the popular sport. Recently I've noticed that although fish still do sell, prints of golf and baseball are more popular than those of fishing. But it varies by the year. And, I suspect, by the area of the country. Golfing prints, especially those done by Arthur Burdett Frost, are in demand. Lots of people golf, and Frost lived in Convent Station, New Jersey, from 1880 until 1907, so some people in Jersey collect his work because it has a local connection. When I do New York shows, though, people could care less about golf. They're looking for prints of dogs or cats. Or tigers, if they went to Princeton! Everyone has their angles. I have one customer who is collecting A. B. Frost prints just because the artist was a distant cousin of the poet Robert Frost."

"It's the same regional differences as with my kitchen and fireplace equipment. In the city I sell Victorian fireplace sets, or large brass pans or kettles that people use for display, or as a base for flower arrangements. In the country people are looking for trammels or iron pots or trivets to hang in or near their fireplaces. Sometimes their hearths are authentic; someone is restoring an old house, like Amy and Drew. Or sometimes the home includes the twentieth-century equivalent of 'an authentic colonial' fireplace. But my best sales are to collectors. I know one man who has three walls in his house covered with match safes, those fireproof boxes that used to hang near fireplaces or stoves to hold matches."

"That sounds decorative. They were usually made of iron or tin, right? Or brass?"

"At first. But by the end of the nineteenth century some were made of redware or another sort of pottery, or even china."

"When did people start using matches?"

"Around 1830. They were called lucifers, then. They looked pretty much like modern matches; the heads were made of phosphorous, brimstone, powdered chalk, and glue, and they burst into flame when they were pulled across sandpaper. In fact, they lit so easily that the first match holders, or match safes, all had fireproof covers. Then, in 1856, safety matches were invented. They would only light when rubbed against special chemically treated paper."

"So match safes that have covers were made before, say, 1860?"

"Some were made after that. But if a match holder doesn't have a cover, then you know it's from the second half of the nineteenth century or later."

"I have a match safe. It's iron, has a lid, and has strawberries on it."

"And what have you done with your match safe, Dr. Summer?"

"I keep matches in it, of course! It's hanging in my kitchen, near my drawer of candles."

Will grinned. "So the print lady has a match safe she uses for matches!"

"Well, I've never seen your home, but I'd bet it has a few prints in it!"

Will hesitated. "My wife decorated the house. And, yes, there are prints hanging in it."

Maggie gave herself an invisible slap. Why ask a question that would remind Will of his wife? Once earlier that summer he had said his wife's death had been difficult for him, and after that he had not mentioned her. After a moment she said, "Shall we try the mall?"

"Fine with me. I'm surprised we haven't heard from Amy yet. I hope Drew's leg isn't worse than they thought."

"Hospitals are sometimes slow. And, of course, he could even end up needing surgery." Maggie hesitated. "Let's do the antiques mall, and then head back to the hospital and check in with her."

The large Victorian home was complete with wraparound porch, double doors, and at least three stories, not including the cupola. Maggie had a moment of house envy before she reminded herself of basic Victorian housing realities. Heating bills. No insulation. No air-conditioning. Roofing bills. Decorating costs. No wonder this beautiful house was being used commercially; at least this way it would support itself. Will held one of the stained-glass-paneled doors open for her. The front hall was high-ceilinged and held two Victorian oak coat stands, complete with mirrors. The rest of the hallway was covered with paintings and prints from floor to ceiling. Maggie did a fast assessment. Nothing too spectacular, and not a good place to display any of them; the walls were too high for customers to be able to see some of the paintings, and the hallway was too dark to show off anything well. Authentic Victorian decorating; not good marketing.

"May I help you?" A small, balding man rose from a 1930s oak desk in what had once been the front parlor. "Looking for anything in particular?"

"Thank you, no," answered Will. "We'd just like to browse." It was always a debate whether to ask for what you were really looking for, and risk doubling the price on it, or to wander, and possibly miss something that had been held back until a customer specifically asked for it. Maggie smiled to herself. She usually did what Will was doing. Especially in an antiquarian-book shop, where the owner might be less than anxious to sell to someone he knew was a print dealer. Print dealers might purchase a book and then take it apart. Destruction of a book was a sin in the eyes of most book dealers.

Will stopped to look at some early cookware hanging on a wall in the kitchen, while Maggie indicated she was going to check the upstairs. Seven large bedrooms were on the second floor. A large affluent family had owned this house. No doubt the third floor would consist of much smaller rooms for the help, and, possibly, a nursery. As on the first floor, prints and paintings were on the walls, but most of the prints were twentieth-century reproductions. Some were in authentic Victorian frames. She wondered if it was ever pointed out to customers that the frame was older than the print. She suspected not. Caveat emptor. The oil paintings and watercolors were generally unsigned and undistinguished. It was August, after all. Tourists and dealers had been checking this mall daily since early spring.

The white-painted stairs squeaked as she climbed the curving flight to the third floor. The oak stair rail went all the way up, which was a nice touch, but the house had no air-conditioning, and she suspected no windows were open. The temperature rose a degree or two with every step.

She turned to her left and entered the first open room. It displayed linens and quilts and Victorian clothing. Not her thing, although a nice variation to the other merchandise. Mostly furniture was displayed, covered with the clutter of china figurines, pieces of silver, pottery, frames, and the miscellaneous tabletop items that dealers called smalls. The second room was similar, with one wall covered with pencil drawings by someone whose work she immediately labeled "amateurish; not interesting enough to be called folk art." She just glanced in the other rooms. Their contents were similar.

Maggie headed downstairs toward Will. As she left the

second floor, she heard voices. Maybe Will had found something of interest? No; that wasn't his voice.

"How much more stuff is there like this?"

"Enough. I can't say."

"And you're sure you don't want to put it up at auction?" She recognized Walter English's voice from yesterday's auction.

Maggie smiled. Someone had no doubt brought in some items to be appraised, and the auctioneer was trying to convince him to auction them off. It wasn't a coincidence that usually it was auctioneers who offered "free appraisal" days. After everyone and their cousin Suzie had started watching *Antiques Roadshow* on television, half the population was convinced they had a secret treasure hidden somewhere in their attic or garage, if not in their living room. Unfortunately most family heirlooms were just that: heirlooms to family members, with little value to others.

"I'm sure. But is it valuable?"

"As I said. Very unusual. I would have to check my reference books, but I think there are such a limited number that they are cataloged and numbered. Finding one that is not cataloged would be unusual. Are you sure you have more?"

"I can get more." The other man's voice also sounded familiar.

"Then I'd strongly suggest you put them in a secure location. And if you should decide to auction them off, I would be more than happy to assist you."

Her curiosity got the better of her. She walked down the hall past the pantry, trying to follow the voices. Walter English was in the former dining room, as she suspected, but she was too late to see whoever had been speaking with him, and whatever he had brought. As she entered the dining room, she heard the front door shut.

"May I help you?" said English.

"I was just looking for my friend," Maggie said, and turned back toward the kitchen. The auctioneer obviously did not recognize her from yesterday's auction, which was not surprising. In addition to the regular attendees, at this time of year probably one or two hundred summer visitors were at each auction.

"If your friend is Will Brewer, he went out to the barn to look at the tools there."

"Thank you." And, of course, everyone in town seemed to know Will. Small-town living had its advantages and disadvantages. She walked through the kitchen and out the back door, heading for the barn.

"You found me!" Will straightened up from several boxes of tools he was examining on a carpenter's bench.

"If you wanted to hide, you didn't try hard enough. Walter English tipped me off that you'd be out here."

"Caught again. He came in while I was still in the kitchen and said they'd gotten some new things in back here that I might be interested in. He was right. I'm going to ask how much he'll take for this carton."

Maggie nodded. Old tools were not something that fascinated her, although she had seen some beautiful handmade teak levels and brass-handled planes. She peeked into the box. It was half-full of various sizes of clamps.

"Did you happen to see someone just leaving the house? I overheard an interesting conversation."

"I've been here for the last ten minutes or so. I can't even see the front of the house. What did you hear?"

"It sounded as though someone had brought in a valuable item to be appraised and implied there were more where it had come from. Walter English was trying to get him to agree to auction them off. I was just curious as to what the man had brought in."

"I have no idea. It could have been anything." Will hoisted the carton onto his shoulder. "I'm going to go talk with Walter."

"It was stuffy in the house. If it's all right with you, I'll stay outside and imagine what the gardens must have looked like a hundred years ago."

"Fine. I'll meet you at my carriage in a few minutes."

They exchanged grins and Will headed for the house as Maggie walked slowly up the driveway and admired the sunflowers bordering the fence. She couldn't get her mind off the conversation she'd heard. Who was the man talking to Walter English? Why was the voice so familiar?

The sunflowers were looking straight up. She checked her watch. Sure enough; it was close to noon.

Chapter 16

———⌇———

The Human Skeleton, *steel engraving, by Henry Winkles, 1857, from* Iconographic Encyclopedia. *Shows three complete posed skeletons—front, back, and walking—and details of some joints. 9.5 x 11.5 inches. Price: $75.*

Amy was still sitting outside the emergency room when Will and Maggie arrived, but she was smiling. "Drew's going to be fine. Two small bones in his foot were broken, and one in his leg. The doctor put a pin in the leg, and he'll be wearing a leg and foot cast for at least a month, but after the pharmacy here at the hospital fills a couple of prescriptions, we can take him home. Your timing is great; he'll be released within the next half hour."

"Doesn't sound as though he'll be having an easy time, though," said Will.

"No driving, because it's his right leg, and he'll have to use crutches for a while. The doctor suggested he avoid steps for at least a few days. Maybe you two could help me move a bed downstairs for him? We have a single bed in the corner of his study."

"Sure thing. With three of us it shouldn't be a problem."

"How are you doing, Amy? You got so little sleep last night, and now this." Amy was pale, and with no makeup and her hair limp, she looked waiflike.

"I'm tired, no doubt. I'm just glad the accident wasn't worse. I'll be relieved to get Drew home and then collapse. But you're both on vacation! Drew's accident should not be your problem. Did you find any great antiques this morning?"

"We stopped at several shops, but this time of the season they've been pretty well picked over. We didn't get as far as the antiquarian-book shop. We did visit that Victorian house Walter English has turned into an antiques mall. Great house, but no great bargains except for a box of tools Will bought."

"Did you look for my corner cabinet?"

"I did, and not a one. But there are a lot of antiques shops left."

Amy and Maggie were both glad of Will's help when they wheeled Drew out. Drew was not an enormous man, but with the crutches and the cast he was awkward. Amy and Maggie followed along as Will helped Drew, who was also feeling the effects of the pain medication, into the back of the RV so his leg could stretch out. Despite the pills, Drew winced at every bump they hit on the way home. They were all relieved when Will slowly drove around the corner where the accident had occurred that morning, and into the driveway. Amy went ahead to open the door and Maggie went up the steps directly to the porch. One of the chaises there would be perfect for Drew to sit in so he could keep his leg and foot up.

The porch curved from the side of the house around to the front. As Maggie walked quickly toward the side facing the river, where the chaises were, she almost ran into a man bending down at a window that opened from the porch into the living room. "Who—?" She started to say, as the man turned around. It was Tom Colby, the neighbor and Civil War reenactor. "I'm sorry; you startled me! And I didn't recognize you out of uniform." Maggie smiled. "May I help you?" What was Tom Colby doing here?

Drew, struggling with his crutches, and Will were right behind her. Drew sat down heavily on one of the chaises, and Will helped him move his foot up. Amy came out the side door and covered Drew's leg with a shawl. "I don't think I'm going to need this in the middle of the day in August. I'm not an old lady," said Drew. "Tom! What are you doing here?"

Tom had backed up a couple of steps. "I heard about your accident this morning. Rough luck. I just came to check and see if I could do anything to help."

Maggie looked at Tom. What had he really been doing on the porch? After he left, she was going to check the locks on the windows. But Amy and Drew didn't seem to find his presence surprising. Maybe he stopped in a lot. He did live just next door.

"I'm fine. Lucky, I guess. Just broke a couple of bones."

"Looks like you'll be laid up for a while."

Drew winced. "Yeah. It does."

"Maybe I could bring over those Civil War books I was

going to loan you. This would be a good time for you to get caught up with your reading."

"Thanks, Tom," said Amy. "But I think today Drew should just rest. He'd appreciate a visit more tomorrow." She walked with Tom to the end of the porch where steps led down into the yard. "Those books are a good idea. Drew has been wanting to read them."

"I'll stop in around noon tomorrow, then," said Tom. "Drew, sounds as though your wife is taking good care of you."

"The best," answered Drew, who had not stopped Amy's dismissal of Tom.

Tom waved and walked off toward the path in back of the ell that led to his house. The path near where Crystal's body had been found.

"I'll find us something for lunch," Maggie said. "We should eat." Amy nodded and looked relieved that Maggie was taking over for a few minutes. She sat down next to Drew.

Maggie scrounged quickly through the kitchen and came up with bread and canned salmon for sandwiches. Will joined her and they added potato chips and raw carrot and zucchini slices to the plates. Someone pounded on the back door.

"Mrs. Douglas?" asked the state trooper who stood in the doorway as Maggie went to the door.

"No; I'm her friend. I'll get her."

"May I come in? I'd like to speak with Mr. Douglas too, if he is home."

"They're both on the porch." Maggie led the trooper through the hall and living room. "Amy, Drew? There's someone here to see you."

Will followed in a minute with the sandwiches and cans of cola and iced tea.

"You folks've been having some problems, I understand," the trooper said.

No one said anything. Problems? He could have meant anything. Phone calls? Fires? Murders? Accidents? Maggie felt she'd lived a lifetime in the past four days.

"I'm Drew Douglas. I'd get up, but you can see I have a bit of a problem." Drew grinned ruefully. "I had an accident this morning."

"So I heard," noted Detective Strait.

"This is my wife, Amy. We've lived here for almost five months now."

"I'm Amy's friend Maggie Summer. I'm visiting from New Jersey. And this is—" Maggie turned toward Will.

"Will Brewer. I know." Detective Strait shook Will's hand. "How're you doing, Will? Haven't seen you this summer."

"Fine, Nick; I'm fine. Only been here a couple of weeks."

"Staying with Nettie, as usual?"

"Same as usual."

Detective Strait nodded. "And these folks are friends of yours?"

Maggie wasn't sure whether the tone of the phrasing meant he was expressing amazement at Will's choice of company or looking for an endorsement.

"I've known Maggie for a while," Will replied evenly. "Amy and Drew are friends of hers, and they seem like fine people."

"Glad to hear it." Detective Strait checked an earlier page in his notebook and then looked back at them all. "Frankly, folks, I'm a little concerned about your area of the world. You're new to these parts. Madoc is a pretty quiet place, as

I'm sure you've noticed. We haven't got a lot of people moving in and out. But we've got nothing against folks from away. Just want you both to understand that."

Amy and Drew exchanged glances. Maggie waited for the *but* in Detective Strait's little speech. It wasn't long in coming.

"But since you've been here, this property seems to have attracted a lot of attention." He looked down at his notes again and counted out the issues. "First, there were some telephone calls at strange hours that seemed to be a problem. Second, there was a fire of unexplained origin. Third, and certainly most seriously, a young girl's body was found on your property yesterday." He looked up from his list again. "You folks might not have heard yet, but Miss Porter's death has been ruled a homicide."

Amy gasped softly, and Drew sat up as far as he could. Maggie was glad she hadn't mentioned that earlier.

"And then this morning, you, Mr. Douglas, were involved in an accident."

"But that isn't the same thing. People are sometimes in car accidents. That's nothing like a murder." Drew looked as though he'd been accused himself.

"The deputy who responded to the 911 call this morning said your brakes hadn't worked well when you went around the corner."

"That's right. I know I put on the brakes, but the car kept going."

"Deputy Colby had your car towed, as you know, and he asked the mechanic to check out your brakes, Mr. Douglas." Detective Strait looked directly at Drew. "The rubber hose leading to the back brakes on your Jeep had been cut very neatly."

"No!" Amy jumped up. "I can't take this place anymore!

We wanted to move to a quiet, beautiful place, to start a new life, and to have a family. This whole move has turned into a nightmare! We should never have left New York!"

"Nice, safe, quiet place, that New York City," agreed Detective Strait. "And if you ever want to move back there, why, that would be your choice. But as long as you folks are here, then I think we'd better think real seriously about what's been happening."

"We have no enemies," said Drew slowly. His face, already pale from exhaustion and pain, was now even whiter. "We don't even know very many people here. We've met Tom and Shirley, next door, and Amy met Rachel Porter at the library and arranged for Crystal to come and help us out this summer. Rachel also helped us to find Brent Construction, and Giles and Brian Leary have been doing some work on the house. But we've hardly had time to meet anyone else. Maggie, who's known Amy since they went to college together, is the first guest we've had since we moved in, and we were pleased to meet her friend Will. And last night he brought his aunt for dinner."

"You brought Nettie over here?" Detective Strait grinned at Will, as though they were sharing a private joke. "Must have been an interesting evening."

"It went just fine," answered Will, almost as though the two of them were talking about a totally different subject from everyone else. "She told Amy and Drew a little about the history of the house. She's glad some young people are going to fix it up and raise their family here. Like folks did in earlier days."

As in the eighteenth and nineteenth centuries? Maggie thought. She wondered suddenly whether Detective Strait was part of the Brewer family somehow too. Everyone else seemed to be.

The detective turned back to Amy and Drew. "So, first of

all, you're sure you don't know anyone in town except for the few people you just mentioned, and you don't have any enemies."

"No!" said Amy vehemently. "We just bought a house and are minding our own business."

"And what would that business be?" inquired the officer. "Just for the record, you understand."

"In New York I worked in advertising and Drew was a stockbroker. We haven't decided yet what we're going to do here."

"So you're both unemployed." Detective Strait made another note and turned the page in his notebook. "And you bought this big house, and you're having work done on it."

"That's right." Drew's fist tightened. "Do you want to see our tax return, or our bank balances?"

"Not just now, anyway. But thank you for offering. I'll just assume you folks have a little income from your investments." The detective looked up at them innocently. "Would that be right?"

"Yes," said Amy.

Will's face twitched a little, and Maggie too realized that Amy and Drew had just confirmed what everyone in Madoc had probably already deduced: they were rich out-of-staters who didn't need to work for a living. She could visualize the Douglases' roof repair bill rising as word got out.

"So, you folks have no enemies in Maine. Do you have any enemies in New York? Anyone who might have followed you here? I've heard some folks in New York take things pretty serious."

"No one followed us from New York! We're just normal, quiet people!" said Amy. "And our life in New York was normal—quiet—no problems! Crazy things only seem to happen to us in this town! It isn't our fault! We haven't done anything."

"And what do you suppose Crystal Porter did, to get herself killed like that?" Detective Strait said quietly.

"I don't know. She was just a young girl. I liked her. We talked about New York." Amy burst into tears. "Why is all this happening?"

"Nick, can you tell us what happened to Crystal?" said Will quietly.

"I wish I knew, Will. Someone hit her pretty hard on the head and the medical examiner figures she fell and then lay out in that field for a while and bled to death." He paused. "Rachel was pretty upset when we told her. She was especially upset when we told her Crystal was pregnant."

Chapter 17

The Young Mother, hand-colored lithograph by N. Currier, c. 1850. (In 1857 Nathaniel Currier partnered with his brother-in-law, James Merritt Ives, and the firm of Currier & Ives was created and then prospered.) Woman standing and holding baby, while toddler holding spaniel sits in chair beside her. Draped background. 8.5 x 12.5 inches. Price: $125.

Will left shortly after Detective Strait, promising to take Maggie out to dinner later that day. Amy and Drew looked relieved, Maggie couldn't help but notice. They were exhausted and needed some time to themselves. Right now it was best for everyone if she was a houseguest who stayed out of the way.

Maggie yawned. Those telephone calls last night had kept her awake too. She headed for her bedroom to take a short nap.

But although her body clearly wanted to rest, Maggie's

mind was too active. And confused. As she lay, floating between the sleep her body craved and the awareness of her brain, her thoughts wandered from murders to babies; from fires to accidents; from broken legs to broken windows. She must remember to check the locks on the porch windows that opened into the living room. She must remember . . .

Amy woke her at six-thirty to say Will had called; he'd made a seven-thirty reservation at a restaurant in Edgecomb, just down the coast. Maggie nodded and headed for a hot bath. Lavender soap and one of those plastic sponges woke her up. She chose a long Indian cotton skirt and a long-sleeved blouse and pinned a favorite rhinestone *M* to her collar. A student she had advised had given it to her at graduation several years ago. She brushed her hair hard. That nap had helped.

Will had changed to slacks and sports jacket and a shirt that particular shade of blue that brought out the color of his eyes. Maggie wondered if he had selected it or whether his wife had done that. She had died eight years ago. It was crazy to be jealous of someone who was dead.

Like Crystal.

Maggie concentrated on smiling, and relaxing, and was secretly glad that Will had borrowed Aunt Nettie's compact car again. It was a little less conspicuous than driving the RV everywhere, and it was definitely easier to park.

Their table at the Sheepscot River Inn overlooked the water, and they arrived in plenty of time to enjoy a spectacular orange and pink sunset reflected in the river. The Soave was dry, just as Maggie liked it, and there was even a pianist playing softly in the background and a small candle on the table.

She raised her glass to him. "This is lovely. Just what I needed tonight."

"I thought of including Aunt Nettie, but she shooed me out the door."

"She's a special lady. I can see why you come back every summer. There really is no other place like the coast of Maine."

"It isn't hurried, like the Cape, and the commercialized parts are almost caricatures of Maine, as though the state is quietly making fun of itself."

"And, even more, making fun of all us out-of-staters."

"I've thought sometimes of moving here. Having New York State plates on the car has always been a matter of some embarrassment. Maybe I'll do it after I prove to myself that I can make a reasonable living off antiques. For now I'll keep my house near Buffalo, and my teaching contacts. Just in case."

"It's always good to have a fallback position," agreed Maggie. "I've always lived in New Jersey. Grew up there, went to school there, and now I teach there. I love that it's close to both New York and Philadelphia. But since Michael died, I've begun to think of other possibilities. In lots of areas." Maggie took a mental deep breath. Was she ready to share this with Will? How well did she really know him? "Amy and I were talking the other night, before everything seemed to get even crazier than it already was. She and Drew want to have a family. That's one reason they moved here. They thought Maine would be a good place for children to grow up."

"No doubt. Some schools are better than others, but that's true in every state. And the closeness to the land—the seacoast, or the mountains, for those who prefer winter sports—is more a part of everyday life than it is in most parts of suburban New York or New Jersey." Will sipped his wine.

"Talking with Amy made me think about children too," Maggie said. "I think; no, I know. I'd like to be a mother."

Will looked at her curiously. "Is that a proposition?"

Maggie backed off. "No! I didn't mean it that way! It's just that Michael and I always assumed we'd have children, but we were both so busy, and we just never sat down and decided that 'this is the right time.' And now I'm thirty-eight years old and . . ."

"Your biological clock is ticking."

"I guess that's it. But that makes it sound so simplistic. What I really feel is emotional. I want to have a child to read books to, and take to museums, and teach to ride a bicycle and . . ."

Will had moved his chair away from the table and was leaning back slightly. "I'm not sure why you're telling me all this, Maggie. I like kids. Hell, I was a teacher for eighteen years. A pretty good teacher, I think. But now I want other things in my life."

Maggie's mood fell. Will certainly had a right to his feelings. And their relationship was new. He lived in Buffalo and traveled a lot. She lived in New Jersey. They were two separate people. Why should his not wanting children have any effect on her?

"It's great that you want to be a mother. I'm happy for you." It was Will's turn to look out over the river. "My wife wanted children too. I wasn't sure. I wasn't as supportive as I should have been when she got pregnant."

"I didn't know you had a child, Will."

"I don't. She had an ectopic pregnancy. She didn't want to bother anyone when she started having pains. She thought everything would be all right." Will said the words mechanically, as though he'd pressed a button and the words just spit out. "She bled to death, Maggie. The baby died and she bled to death. I wasn't even there. I was away, doing an antiques show in Ohio. She had to call a neighbor to take her to the hospital."

"Oh, Will. I'm so sorry." She had hoped to share a special thought, a personal hope, with Will. Instead, she had opened a painful part of his past. "I didn't know. I didn't mean to remind you of such a sad time."

They sat silently, facing their own thoughts.

"Maggie, I wish you the best of luck in whatever you decide to do. But children are something for other people. Not for me." Will picked up the menu. "Now, shall we relax a little and discuss something important, like what we're going to order for dinner?"

Sharing a large platter of mussels steamed in white wine with garlic and herbs helped them both relax a bit. By the time Will's stuffed haddock and Maggie's shrimp scampi had arrived, they had finished more than half the bottle of wine, and the earlier conversation had been pushed to the side.

"Will, I've only been in Maine a few days, but an awful lot has been happening. You know this area; you know these people. Maybe I'm being ultrasensitive, but it almost seemed to me that your friend Detective Strait was warning Amy and Drew today."

"He was. Mainers don't take too kindly to people from away who arrive and want to change things."

"All Amy and Drew wanted to do was buy a house, fix it up, and live here in peace."

"Probably so. But even before they arrived their coming was upsetting to people who felt that house should have stayed in the Brewer family." Will raised his hand as he saw Maggie open her mouth to protest. "I know. Charlotte hadn't the money or didn't see the need to keep the house in as good condition as she might have. And it certainly wasn't Amy's or Drew's fault that Charlotte left the house to Lizzie instead of to Shirley, or that Lizzie sold it. But, nevertheless, they arrived at a time when nerves were on edge."

"And Crystal . . ."

"And Crystal. That's a whole horrible situation that probably has nothing to do with Amy or Drew or the house, but, of course, since her body was found there, it makes the situation even more awkward."

"Could someone be trying to get Amy and Drew to leave?"

"It's possible. The telephone calls, the fire. When Drew and I see if we can expose the old fireplace, I want to take a look at where that fire started. And then there are the brakes on Drew's car. Even Crystal's body being found on their property. It could all have been staged to scare them off."

"But Crystal was killed! And Drew could have been! I can understand someone in the family being upset by their living in the family home. But murder? Attempted murder? And Crystal was part of the Brewer family! You said she was a distant cousin of yours."

"A branch the family wasn't too fond of, but, yes, family. I agree. The phone calls, maybe. The fire? I want to check that out. But Crystal's murder and the accident were beyond the possibility of chance or annoyance." Will hesitated. "I know they're your friends, Maggie. But have Amy and Drew had any problems recently?"

"Problems like being murderers? Like cutting the brake lines on Drew's car? Will, no. That's impossible." Maggie took a sip of her wine and thought for a moment. "This move has been difficult for both of them. More difficult than I think either of them wants to admit."

"For example?"

"Amy's been really scared by the phone calls and the accidents in the house. And she told me Drew is drinking more than he used to. When you were there last night, he seemed all right, but the day before he definitely was drinking too much."

"Is that new behavior?"

"I don't know. I've known Amy for years, but I haven't seen her much recently. I'd only met Drew twice before I arrived this week." She paused, not sure this was the right time to bring up the subject of children again. "They both told me they want to have children. But Amy hasn't been able to get pregnant, and that's putting pressure on both of them. Will, they have a room on the second floor of the house decorated like a perfect nursery. It even has a canopied crib and shelves of stuffed animals."

"Maybe she was pregnant and something happened, and they were left with all the baby things."

Maggie shook her head. "Not based on what she told me. She said Drew gave her the crib as a wedding present."

Will leaned back and whistled a little. "Weird. And some pressure. Most couples don't even begin to buy baby things until the second trimester. Just in case."

Maggie nodded. "I agree. It's very strange. I thought maybe they were planning to adopt, but Amy told me Drew wouldn't consider any child other than one biologically his own. He was adopted as a baby and feels really strongly about genetic ties. But Amy has shelves of books on adoption in her study." Maggie didn't mention that some of them were now sitting on the floor next to her bed, and that she planned to look at them later that night.

"That's sad, but it certainly doesn't explain anything that's been happening. You know, there have always been stories about that house. When I was a little boy, my father told me there was hidden treasure in the house, and hidden secrets."

"Your aunt Nettie told me at Cut 'n' Curl that a woman with a baby walked the halls there."

"Oh, yes. The ghosts. I've heard that too, but I've never met anyone who's seen them."

"You have now."

"You?"

"I'm not crazy, Will. And I haven't seen the woman in white. But I did hear the baby cry. It woke me up two nights ago. Amy came running in. She heard it too."

"You know that's impossible."

"Maybe. But it happened." No matter how she tried to change the conversation, they kept getting back to babies. And neither of them had mentioned that other baby. Maggie plunged ahead. "Detective Strait said Crystal was pregnant."

"Yes. That news will get around town faster than the news of her death. Everyone will revisit Rachel's teenage years. And wonder."

"The father of the baby could be her killer. Maybe they argued; maybe he wanted her to have an abortion, and she refused. Or she wanted him to marry her." Maggie couldn't help thinking of Drew. Was it possible? Maggie wanted very much to know that there were other potential fathers for Crystal's baby.

"I assume the police will talk with a lot of people, but I'll check around. Being a member of the family means I might hear something that isn't common knowledge."

"Would you, Will? I think your detective friend is looking at Amy and Drew as possible suspects. And the sooner other suspects are identified, the better for them."

"I'll see what I can do. In fact, I think maybe I'll stop in to see the Learys tonight, after I drop you back in Madoc."

"The Learys who are working on the roof?"

"The same. Giles and Mary are my cousins. Of course, Maggie." He grinned at her incredulous expression. "I told you Aunt Nettie had a sister who married Silas Leary. In any case, they may have some ideas. And Brian was the one who found Crystal, wasn't he?"

"Yes. And they were good friends. They had a date planned for the night she was killed." Maggie looked up. "He could be the father of her baby, Will. He knew her well, and he was clearly upset about her death. Maybe he's the one responsible."

"For her pregnancy? Or her murder?" Will finished his wine. "I'll drop in and see how my cousins are doing, Maggie. But I can't believe a kid like Brian would kill his cousin." He paused a moment. "Maybe sleep with her. But not kill her. Brewers don't do that sort of thing."

"Well, someone did." Brian seemed like a sweet kid. But someone killed Crystal, and she hoped against hope, for Amy's sake, that the person responsible wasn't Drew.

Chapter 18

Pierrette. *French pantine, or paper marionette. Pierette is the female partner of French pantomime character Pierrot, both stylized figures introduced at the Théâtre des Funambules by Jean Gaspard Deburau in the early nineteenth century. Original uncut sheet. 11.5 x 15 inches. Price: $75.*

Maggie had gotten back to Madoc before ten, but Amy and Drew had left the door open and were already asleep. It had been a rough day. Maggie walked softly through the dining room to avoid the living room, where they had put a bed for Drew. The door to Amy's room was closed, but there were lights on in the hall and on the table next to Maggie's bed.

In New Jersey she would have been turning the air-conditioning to high. Here, the soft river breeze coming through the partially open window smelled slightly of pine and salt. A perfect night for sleeping.

But after the nap she'd taken this afternoon Maggie wasn't tired. The dinner with Will had been unsettling. He was the first man she'd allowed herself to be interested in since Michael's death, and a part of her had hoped that somehow he would be perfect. A perfect man would have embraced the possibility of children. But Will's past headed him in another direction.

It was unrealistic, she told herself, for one person to echo her every interest. She and Michael had been married for fourteen years, and they certainly hadn't agreed on everything. Why should she even fantasize that there was someone who would want exactly what she wanted, at the same point in their lives?

She picked up the pile of pictures of waiting children she had left by her bed the day before. They were still waiting. Babies, yes. But it was the older children whose faces she found most compelling. Faces that looked out from different worlds, asking for love. For a chance. A possibility. Dark faces; light faces. Faces born in Asia, Latin America, Africa, eastern Europe, and here in the United States. Sibling groups who didn't want to be separated. Children unlucky enough to be born imperfect.

Was she really ready to make that kind of commitment? A lifetime commitment to someone she had never met? But wasn't that what every mother did, before her child was born?

Maggie put down the sheaf of papers and picked up the books on adoption she had selected in Amy's study. She glanced through some chapter headings: "Finding Your Child"; "The Honeymoon Period"; "Early Childhood Trauma Disorder"; "Raising an Interracial Family"; "The School and the Adopted Child"; "The Adopted Adolescent"; "When Your Child Wants to Search."

Even the topics were intimidating. She put that book down and picked up the book on open adoption. What was that? As she started reading, she realized there were whole worlds of relationships she'd been unaware of. She had thought adoption was a contract in which one or both biological parents relinquished their parental rights and their child was adopted by another couple. Or by a single parent. The adoptive parents and child knew nothing, or little, about the biological parents, and the biological parents had no way of knowing what had happened to their child. Open adoption was totally different. In these adoptions, the biological parents, or mother, often actually chose the adoptive parents. And the biological and adoptive parents not only met, but agreed to stay in touch, so the child would grow up knowing both sets of parents.

Whew! Maggie lay back on the pillows she'd piled up. How would that work in reality? Were both sets of parents so unselfish and loving that they could accept each other? Could they avoid jealousy? What if the child played one set of parents against the other? What would the child even call each of his or her two mothers?

Maybe it would be the best of all possible worlds. But if it didn't work . . . Her professorial side wanted to see studies on how the two types of adoption turned out, twenty or twenty-five years later. At least in open adoption there would be no fantasies about biological parents; no people like Drew who grew up longing to meet a genetic relative.

Maggie picked up the third book. It was a how-to on the actual adoption process. She read about ten pages before realizing that she had read one paragraph three times.

She hoped there would be no telephone calls during this night.

She hoped there would be no more bad news.

Chapter 19

━━◦◦◦━━

Group of Snapdragons—Antirrhinum vars. *1893 British lithograph by Cassell and Company; included in* Cassell's Popular Gardening. *Print is in two perfectly matched pieces; divided where it was originally bound in book. 8.75 x 11.75 inches. Price: $85.*

Drew was still sleeping, drugged by his pain medication, as Maggie and Amy sat at the kitchen table planning the day.

"I should stop in to see Rachel," Amy said slowly. "It will be a difficult visit, but it's the right thing to do."

Maggie nodded. "Maybe you could get her some flowers, or a platter of cookies."

"Flowers! Yes. And would you go with me? I feel awkward about going, but even more awkward about not going. It would help to have someone with me."

"Of course I'll go with you." Maggie wondered what their reception would be. Crystal's body had been found on

Amy's property; she had disappeared while walking home from here. At least part of Rachel's mind could hold Amy and Drew accountable. "It might even be better if I were with you. In case Rachel . . ."

"In case she holds me responsible. I know, Maggie. I could hardly sleep last night thinking about it. Wondering who would have wanted Crystal dead. She was so young and innocent, in so many ways. She had so many dreams."

"Let's make that visit this morning. Maybe there is something else Rachel could think of that we could help with."

"Since Drew has to stay quiet for a while, maybe later today would be a good time for you to show us some of your prints."

"You said you especially wanted to see the Winslow Homers and the N. C. Wyeths, right?"

"Yes. And maybe some of the Thomas Nast prints you mentioned. I was thinking about something for the nursery. He did some Santa Claus engravings, didn't he?"

"He was the first person to picture Santa as we think of him today, round and jolly with a full beard. Some historians feel his Santa Clauses were self-portraits, except that Santa had a white beard, and Nast a dark one."

"I thought Clement Moore's poem ''Twas the Night Before Christmas' was the first description of Santa as round and jolly."

"It described St. Nicholas in words, but, of course, didn't actually picture him. Nast took Moore's ideas, added some details of his own, and created the American Santa Claus. His engravings were printed in the year-end issues of *Harper's Weekly*. In most of them Nast's home in Morristown, New Jersey, was the setting, and his children were his models. If you had a full collection of Nast Christmas prints, you could see his children growing up, year by year."

"Are there any prints with babies?"

Amy certainly hadn't lost her focus on infants despite everything that had been happening. "One shows Santa bending over a baby's crib. I'll pull them all out later so you can take a look."

"That should be fun! And very different from the last couple of days. Drew will like seeing them too, especially the Civil War prints."

Civil War. Maggie suddenly thought of Tom, the Civil War reenactor she was sure had been trying to open the window on the porch yesterday.

"With all of the problems you and Drew have had here, Amy, do you have any kind of security system? Locks on the windows? Anything?"

"In Madoc, Maine? You have to be kidding!" Amy looked at her. "And you're not. No, we have no security system. Most of the windows have the original 'locks': nails in the sides of the window frames on the inside. You have to press the nail head in to raise the window or it won't move. It's actually a pretty safe system." She looked down at the bandage she still wore on her arm. "But the nails have disappeared from some of the window frames—after all, it's been over two hundred years!—and some of the nails have been painted over, so the windows won't go up at all. That's what I was coping with when that window collapsed on me the other day and broke."

"Have you thought about getting a better system?"

"To keep the ghosts in? We haven't had any problems with break-ins, and securing the windows wouldn't help with the telephone calls. I haven't heard about anyone near here even talking about such a thing. What would anyone break in for? We haven't got anything terribly valuable. This isn't New York."

"At least there were no phone calls last night. Or I didn't hear any."

"Oh!" Amy jumped up. "I forgot to turn the ringer back on! Drew and I decided to turn it off last night." She switched the ringer on the kitchen phone to "on." "I'd better go see if there are any messages."

Maggie stretched and walked around the kitchen. Outside, she could see the grayness of lingering fog softening and blurring the trees and lawn. This would be the time for ghosts, she thought. Fog put the world halfway between light and darkness. And there was a lot of fog on the coast of Maine.

Amy came back, carrying her pocketbook this time. "I listened to the messages. Two hang-ups, but they might have been telemarketers."

Sure.

"Drew had a call from someone at his old office, so I left a note next to his bed. And Will called you, bright and early this morning. He said he had to go out, but he'd call back later. Something about a visit last night."

Maggie nodded. "After he dropped me off he was going to stop in to see the Learys. Just to see how Brian was doing."

"A good idea. He's a thoughtful man, Maggie. I like him."

Maggie wondered briefly if she could share Will's feelings about children with Amy. But this wasn't the time for girl talk. Besides, she wasn't comfortable talking about parenthood yet. Especially with Amy. "I haven't seen Brian or his father working on the roof recently."

"Drew told them to take the week off. I'm sure their boss has found something for them to do, but we just didn't think it would be good for Brian to come back here so quickly. Crystal was his friend."

"It's hard to believe she was pregnant."

"It must have been early. She certainly didn't show."

"She must have been so scared. Only eighteen."

"Maybe she had a plan. Some eighteen-year-olds think they have the world all figured out." Amy paused. "Or maybe the father of the baby had a plan."

"Which she might or might not have agreed with." Does Amy have any idea about Drew and Crystal? Maggie wondered. Could I possibly have been mistaken in what I saw? No; she was quite sure about what had been happening in that bedroom. Should she tell the police? None of the answers were ones she wanted to act on.

They were both silent for a few moments.

"Let's go and get those flowers. There's a florist's shop in Waymouth. Then we'll go and see Rachel. I don't know what we can say that will mean anything. But I'll feel better after we've done it."

They choose a large bouquet of white marigolds and delphiniums and baby's breath with a few daisies. The grouping looked young and innocent. Crystal had at least been young.

Other neighbors must have had the same thought; several cars were in the Porters' driveway.

"I'm nervous. Here I am, the neighbor from away who owns the home where Crystal was killed, and all of these cars probably belong to family and longtime friends." Amy sat for a moment.

"We don't have to stay long. Just pay our respects," Maggie said quietly. "If you don't go, then someone will question that too. And you did get to know Crystal well this summer." Or at least you thought you knew Crystal well, she added to herself.

They didn't need to knock on the door; Shirley Steele opened it. She looked Amy and Maggie up and down and then said loudly, in the direction of the rest of the house. "It's so nice of you to come. And you've brought flowers."

Rachel came out from the kitchen. She wore no makeup, and her hair was combed, but the part wasn't straight. Her face was pale and swollen, and her faded-gray flowered dress was crushed and hung loosely. She'd aged years in the few days since they had seen her.

Amy handed her the bouquet. "Drew and I are so sorry, Rachel. We wanted you to know that. And if there is anything we can do . . ."

Rachel nodded. "Nothing that can be done now. Except find whoever killed my little girl and make him pay."

They followed Rachel to the kitchen, where another woman took the flowers and filled a glass vase with water.

"Would you like something to eat?" Rachel gestured to the room. Besides Shirley there were two little girls, her twin daughters, Sorrel and Sage, Maggie immediately thought, and another woman. The table and the counters were covered with food. Two baked-bean casseroles, a plate of chocolate chip cookies, and another of brownies; a bowl of potato salad; a ham; a large plate of cranberry muffins; a blueberry pie and a lemon meringue pie. Theirs were the only flowers. Clearly sympathy in Madoc was said through the stomach. "Everyone has been so kind to bring food."

Except for the out-of-staters who hadn't expressed their feelings with the currency of the realm. But the flowers did look lovely. Shirley set the vase in the center of the loaded table, where her two girls were taking full advantage of the chocolate chip cookies.

"You took the biggest cookie." One of the twins pushed the other one slightly.

"You took two before that." The second push was a little stronger, and the girl moved to the other side of the table and stuck out a tongue covered with chocolate chip cookie crumbs.

"No, thank you," said Amy. "We just wanted to tell you how sorry we were."

"Sorry is as sorry does." Rachel sat down in a rocking chair, which had been set so its occupant could watch a small TV in the corner of the room. A large box of tissues was on the floor next to her chair. "Since you're here, and I know you mean well, you might as well look in Crystal's room and take the books you loaned her. I don't want anything about New York in my house any longer. All those dreams in her head helped to get her killed. I'm certain about that. Just thinking about New York did it. She didn't even have to go there."

Amy looked a little surprised. "Of course; I'll be happy to take them."

"Her room's just down the hall." Rachel hesitated. "The police were there already. It's messed up. But I'm not ready to cope with it yet." She started to cry. Shirley put a hand on her shoulder and gave her another tissue.

Maggie and Amy moved down the hallway lined with framed photographs of a pretty blonde baby, a beautiful toddler, a cute little girl, and a smiling teenager. Crystal's life. And Rachel's.

It was obvious which room was Crystal's. It had probably not been immaculate before the police searched it. But their presence had not helped.

The contents of bookshelves had been dumped on the unmade bed. Piles of boxes holding embroidery floss, children's games, Barbie dolls, and school papers were spread across the floor. They had most likely been in the closet, which was now open. Crystal's wardrobe seemed to have consisted mainly of jeans and T-shirts and wool sweaters; two pairs of three-inch heels had been kicked into the corner.

Open bureau drawers exposed an assortment of flannel nightgowns and cotton underwear.

"What were the police looking for?" whispered Amy.

"Drugs? A diary?"

"A diary!"

"Lots of teenaged girls keep one. It might have told them who the father of her baby was. Or who might have been angry with her."

No wonder Rachel had been upset about "New York." Travel posters of the Empire State Building, the Statue of Liberty, and Central Park were taped to the walls, along with magazine pages of young models. Supermarket makeup covered the top of the bureau.

Amy looked through the books on the bed. "I loaned her a couple of photograph books of New York. That's all. And I said she could take any magazines Drew and I had finished with." A stack of *New York* magazines was on the floor near the window.

Maggie glanced at them. This year's, and addressed to Mr. and Mrs. Drew Douglas. "Maybe you should take these. Rachel obviously doesn't want them here."

Amy hesitated. "All right. I've found my two books."

Maggie picked up the stack of magazines. Most of them were *New York*s, but she also saw two copies of *Adoption Today,* and on the bottom, several issues of *Baby Care.* She checked quickly. *Baby Care* had not been addressed to Amy and Drew. So Crystal had been researching possibilities in several directions. Rachel didn't need to see those other magazines. Her grief was strong enough. She didn't need to know what Crystal had been thinking. And, Maggie justified to herself, the adoption magazines had been Amy's.

Back in the kitchen the women sat quietly. Tears still ran

down Rachel's face. The woman Maggie hadn't met came over to them. "I'm Mary Leary, Giles's wife. He's been working on your house this summer. It was very nice of you to stop in, but I think Rachel needs to be quiet now."

Amy nodded. "I only found two books and a few magazines that had been Drew's and mine. She wanted me to take them."

"Then you do that. The police have been through everything, and she's still in shock, of course." Mary glanced at the books and magazines Amy and Maggie were holding. "She had so many dreams, didn't she?" A tear started down her cheek.

"We'll be going now," said Maggie, moving Amy toward the door. "If anyone thinks of something we can do to help, please do call."

"We will." Mary paused. "I was sorry to hear about your husband too, Mrs. Douglas. There have been a lot of accidents at that corner."

Amy nodded. "Thank you. He'll be all right."

They all thought of Crystal. She wouldn't be all right. Ever. Maggie wondered how Rachel would be too. No husband, no other children. Despite having neighbors and friends, she must feel very alone. Being a single mother mustn't be easy even in the best of circumstances. And these were the worst.

They headed home in silence. Amy said finally, "Rachel might not really have wanted me there, but I'm glad I went."

Maggie nodded. "It was the right thing to do. But I'm sure she connects you and Drew with Crystal's death. She couldn't help but do that."

"Crystal was so fascinated with New York. She asked me questions about everything from the subways to the Statue of Liberty. There were days she drove me crazy! 'Does everyone eat bagels for breakfast in New York?' 'Do people really get shot in the subways?' 'Is Macy's really the biggest store in the world?' 'Are there famous people everywhere?' 'Have you ever been to Tiffany's?' Some days it felt obsessive!"

"She was a teenager. She was dreaming. Doing her own kind of research."

"She thought Drew and I had led glamorous lives in the city. I once found her looking in my closet, and then she asked me how many evening dresses I had."

Maggie smiled. "You had a few, I'd guess."

"Three, I think. I had her put them in an old wardrobe in the attic space. There isn't much call for them in Madoc."

"Nor in the New Jersey community where I live, except when there are special events at the college. And even in New York you can go to the opera dressed like Lauren Bacall or dressed in jeans."

"With most people wearing whatever they've worn all day to the office, in any case. I think Crystal had watched a lot of movies made in the 1940s and 1950s."

"No doubt. And there are certainly a lot of sides to New York."

"She just wanted to be grown-up, to move away from Madoc. To live a life more glamorous than making blueberry pies or helping me unpack boxes." Amy dabbed at her eyes. "Getting pregnant must have blown all of those dreams into fantasies. Do you think she would have stayed here and had the baby? Or had an abortion?"

Maggie decided not to bring up that Crystal had obviously borrowed some magazines on adoption too. One more alternative. Whatever decision she would have made was going to influence the rest of her life in some way. "And who knows what the father of the baby had in mind. If anything."

"A teenage boy confronted with that kind of reality usually runs like crazy. Or denies. Or blames."

Amy too had been pregnant as a teenager. Maggie touched her own abdomen. How would it feel to know you were carrying a child? To know you were responsible for another life? Whatever your decision was, it had to change the way you looked at the world.

And the way the world looked at you.

The back door was open when they arrived at the house. Drew must be awake. They heard another man's voice as they walked in.

"Tom! How nice of you to come over." Amy looked around the kitchen and started piling dirty coffee cups in the sink. "You and Drew must have had coffee and"—looking at the crumbs still on the table—"doughnuts."

"Yup. I just stopped in to see how he was doing."

"I'm all right, I guess," said Drew, standing awkwardly in the doorway with his crutches. "The throbbing isn't as bad now, but I'm not exactly ready to run a marathon."

"Nor should you even be standing." Amy went over and herded him back to the living room, where clothing and bedding were strewn in various directions. "Why don't you sit on the couch and put your leg up, as the doctor said? I'll straighten the room. You don't want to trip on anything."

"Tom got here just when I was waking up," Drew continued, sitting heavily on the couch. "He went upstairs and got me a clean shirt too. And a pair of shorts."

Of course Drew wouldn't be able to wear his jeans or even sweatpants; they wouldn't fit over his cast. Luckily, this was August. The shirt Tom had found him was dark green, embroidered in orange with a corporate logo of some sort suitable for a golf course in Short Hills. The shorts were a purple and yellow plaid. Maggie wasn't sure precisely where they would be suitable. But at least Drew was dressed and seemed comfortable enough.

"You're going to sleep downstairs for a while, then?" Tom said.

"I'm not supposed to try steps for at least a few days. Pretty boring, but I'm supposed to stay off my foot and leg. I'm already getting restless. Amy, maybe you could go to the library and pick up some books for me."

"Sounds like a possibility," said Amy. "Maggie agreed to show us her Homer and Wyeth prints later today too. We have the whole day in front of us." The telephone interrupted her. It was Will.

Maggie could hear the smile behind his voice. She imagined him sipping coffee in Aunt Nettie's kitchen, with a row of white and purple African violets in bloom on the windowsill behind him. "Good morning! Sorry I missed your call earlier. Drew turned off the ringer so everyone could get a good night's sleep."

"I had an interesting visit last night with Giles and Mary Leary. And Brian. I'd like to tell you about it."

"Here I am. Listening."

"I know. But telling you isn't so easy just now."

Maggie suddenly realized that her vision of African violets might be a fantasy, but Aunt Nettie's presence probably wasn't.

"Would you like to stop in here? Or maybe I could meet you somewhere. Amy may go to the library." Maggie hesitated. "Rachel isn't the only person who works at the Waymouth Library, is she?"

"I don't think so."

"Because she's at home this morning. Amy and I made a condolence call. In fact, Mary Leary was there too. And Shirley and her twins."

"The whole gang, eh? Any lynchings?"

"No. But I think we broke local tradition by bringing flowers instead of food."

"An unforgivable sin. Why don't I come over there this afternoon? We can take a short walk. And I'd like to check out that area in the ell where Drew said the fire started."

"That would be fine with me. Hold on one moment." Maggie held her hand lightly over the receiver. "Amy, could Will stop in this afternoon?"

"Tell him he has to bring his own crowbar if he wants to do anything with that wall! I never did get to the hardware store," Drew called back. "Does he like Homer prints too?"

"I heard that," Will said. "Tell Drew I have a couple of crowbars, but at this point I think we should wait a few days before disrupting his home. What was that about Homer?"

"Amy and Drew wanted me to show them my Winslow Homer wood engravings this afternoon."

"Sounds good to me. Have you ever gotten to that antiquarian-book store?"

"Not yet."

"Then why don't we meet there about one; I promised a friend in Buffalo I'd keep my eyes open for some New York State history books, and you can look over the dealer's stock while I'm bothering him with obscure requests. It would also give us a few minutes to talk before we go back to Amy and Drew's."

A few minutes to talk. What had Will learned that he wouldn't say in front of Amy and Drew? Or Aunt Nettie? Maggie wasn't sure she wanted to know.

Chapter 20

—⁓—

Vaccinium macrocarpon: American Cranberry, chro-molithograph published by Prang, Boston, 1878. Shows plant, including root and cutaway of fruit. Information from book (The Native Flowers and Ferns of the United States in their Botanical, Horticultural, and Popular Aspects, *by Thomas Meehan) in which this plate was found includes natural habitat of cranberries, poetry written about them, and details about the cranes that are attracted to them. Information attached. Few nineteenth-century renderings of the American cranberry exist. 7 x 10 inches. Price: $70.*

Maggie had already perused the Medical and Children's shelves at Books Older Than U when Will came up behind her. He reached around and hugged her, including the two books she was holding. She leaned back against him and, for a moment, felt safe, and far from Crystal and babies and car crashes and the challenges of relationships. A hug from a large man was reassuring in a primal way.

"Found anything good?" The voice in her ear was just lascivious enough to imply something more than a book worth purchasing.

Maggie stood up straight and turned around. "You, sir, have a slightly dirty mind."

"Only slightly? What have I done wrong this morning?"

Maggie held up one of the books. "An Arthur Rackham. *Peter Pan in Kensington Garden.* One of my favorites, and I'm almost out of stock of these illustrations."

Will peeked over her shoulder at a picture of a baby sitting up in a tree discussing life with a crow of approximately the same size. At the base of the tree, two lifelike mice (except that they were wearing blue-polka-dotted ties and blue-and-white-striped socks with their shoes) were listening in. "Nice. And what a sense of humor." He pointed at one mouse that was using a miniature shoehorn. "But the colors are so muted and the details so tiny! Do people buy prints like those to frame and hang?"

"They do. Often. Rackham is one of the few early-twentieth-century illustrators I carry. His work is unmistakable. No one else drew fairies and ghosts and small woodland creatures and elves the way Arthur Rackham could. My personal favorites are his series of mermaid illustrations for *Undine.* They're very art nouveau and very hard to find. Rackham has become much more popular during the past fifteen years. You used to be able to pick up a book like this for around twenty dollars. This one is a third edition and reasonably priced at one hundred and twenty-five dollars. I've seen first editions for three hundred dollars or more in New York or New Jersey. *Undine* had a small printing and would go for several times that. And a friend in England tells me Rackham prices in America are considered bargains. In the U.K., prices for the books he illustrated have gone through the roof. The only thing you have to be careful about is that Rackham's work has been reprinted within the last twenty years. Some print dealers might be tempted to sell those reproductions as originals."

"Not you."

"Not me. I guarantee the dates on my prints. But some of the later-twentieth-century reproductions were done well. I wouldn't buy any loose Rackham prints myself. I prefer finding the original book. Then I know for sure what the date is."

"So you've found something already. Need more time?"

"I haven't even checked the shelves of natural history!" Maggie turned back and then added, "I saw some shelves of modern secondhand paperbacks in the front. Would you see if there are any suspense or mystery novels there that Drew might like? He's already getting bored."

Maggie headed for the Natural History section, where she most often found books with color plates. She overheard Will asking the owner for several history books.

Most of the shelves she scanned quickly. The bindings were obviously twentieth century, which meant the illustrations were too recent for her—and, most likely, were photographs. She didn't carry photographs, not even early ones. That required knowledge that she had found neither the time nor the interest to acquire. But prices of daguerreotypes and early photographs were skyrocketing. She'd already missed out on any dealer's window of opportunity. All she knew were the basics: the earlier the better; the more identifiable the subjects, the better; men in uniforms, especially Civil War uniforms, were good; Native Americans and

African-Americans from the mid–nineteenth century were good; animals and children were good. The chance of getting any real bargains on early photographs was rare today.

Her hand stopped on a set of four leather-bound books titled *Flowers and Ferns* by Meehan. She opened one of the volumes carefully. It was beautifully bound, but a number of the illustrations had come loose. Not good for a book dealer; not bad for a print dealer. Although she would hate to hurt these bindings.

The cover page listed the actual title as *The Native Flowers and Ferns of the United States in Their Botanical, Horticultural, and Popular Aspects.* So far so good. She hadn't heard of this book. Most of the ferns she had were from the British Cassell's series and were beautifully lithographed, but they were European. American customers wanted American subjects. Prang was the publisher of these volumes. Maggie's smile widened. Prang, located in Boston, was an outstanding American printer of chromolithographs. Chromolithography had been perfected in Germany and Switzerland, but Prang had come close to reaching that perfection. The technique was time-consuming and expensive and was used for a window of perhaps thirty years. She checked the date: 1878. For an American chromolithograph, that was early. She looked carefully through the pages, which had some foxing, the yellowish brown discoloration that meant the book had at some time been exposed to dampness. For the book's age the foxing wasn't bad. Some customers saw foxing as a distinguished sign of age, much as an elderly gentleman would not be embarrassed by fine lines on his face. But a dealer also had to keep in mind that some customers would reject a print with any foxing. Some of these chromos were beautiful; others would not be salable.

Maggie started paging through the four volumes to get an

estimate of how many of these prints would sell well. She would then divide that number into the dealers' price for the set of books and make her decision as to whether it would be a good purchase for her.

Remember, Maggie, she said to herself, you still have to remove these and mat them. And they'll have to be matted individually because the chromos fill the pages to different degrees. No measuring one print and then cutting three dozen mats to match. These books would consume hours of time before she could get them close to a customer.

There were 45 to 50 chromos in each book; perhaps 190 total. But some were badly foxed; some of those that were loose had torn edges. And some of the subjects would sell much faster than others. Customers wanted big, bright flowers for their walls, not tiny, delicate ones. She hesitated again. This collection showed the plants' roots. That would turn off some buyers, although someone truly interested in botany would consider it a plus.

Unfortunately, not that many botanists were looking for nineteenth-century prints.

The dealer was asking $1,000 for the four-volume set. She did the math in her head: 180 prints, but perhaps only half of those would sell well. So—90. A little over $10 a plate. She looked through the second and third books again. She could probably get $60 a plate for the better plates. But not for all. A good profit, but not a guaranteed one. And first she'd have to do all that matting.

Let's say that after matting she could make an average of $40 a print. Optimistic. She'd then have to sell twenty-five flowers or ferns to get her initial investment back.

Maggie put the books back on the shelves. It was a nice printing. She hadn't seen it before; no doubt it was a limited edition.

But she already had the Cassell's ferns, which were slightly larger, and brighter, and therefore more salable even though they were European.

And she didn't relish the idea of hours of matting these particular prints. The leather bindings were beautiful. Maybe this dealer would find someone who would value the whole package. She hoped so, because it was a special set. But, no, not quite right for her.

Maybe she just wasn't in the right mood to spend that much money. She had just bought the Wilson birds at the auction.

Will was at the front of the store sorting through a stack of used paperbacks. "This is a great collection of bestsellers for vacation reading. Only one dollar each. Bargains!"

Maggie agreed, and they chose ten books for Drew, and several each for themselves. Will had found one of the books on his friend's list: an early Washington Irving in acceptable condition for someone interested in the content, not the binding.

"Not a bad shop," said Maggie, as they left. "Maybe I should have bought those flowers and ferns."

"Stick to your initial instincts. My experience so far with you, Maggie, is that your instincts are usually right."

"I wish I had better instincts about what is happening with Amy and Drew."

"Let's put the books in our cars and go and sit over by the water." Will pointed at some large rocks comfortably situated so they had a full view of Waymouth Harbor. "I want to tell you about my visit with the Learys."

"Giles Leary is your second cousin? Third cousin?"

"Close enough. I've never been into genealogy that much. He and I are about the same age and spent a lot of summertimes together when we were growing up. 'Hanging out' the kids would call it now. We called it fishing and rowing and clam digging and perfecting our curveballs."

"A childhood from the dim, dark ages," Maggie said, smiling. "Before video games. So you and Giles go back a bit."

"That's why I felt comfortable stopping in. He's done all right over the years; hasn't made a fortune working for Johnny Brent, but he and Mary have a nice little house not far from Aunt Nettie's, and they have Brian."

"Brian was a close friend of Crystal Porter's from what I gathered."

"More than a close friend. Turns out I got there just in time last night to hear part of a major argument he and his dad were having."

"About Crystal?"

"And about who was the father of her child." Will hesitated a moment. "Brian said that he must be, but she hadn't told him she was pregnant. He was really furious at her. Kept saying he would have married her. He loved her. He would have taken care of her."

"Well, that explains the pregnancy." Maggie hoped it did. Crystal had been sleeping with Drew. And now Brian. Could there have been any other man involved? And was Brian really the father of her child? Crystal hadn't told him. Or maybe she didn't really know. "And his parents' reactions?"

"Mary was pretty quiet. She tried to calm both Brian and Giles. She said Crystal was gone; they should mourn her and do what they could to find her killer. Her pregnancy was water under the bridge, and Brian should just keep quiet about his role in her situation."

"They said all that with you there?"

"Well, part of it they said while I was still on the porch, ready to knock. Voices go right through screen doors. But I did knock, and Mary let me in. Everyone was pretty quiet for a few minutes, and then Brian went stomping off."

"Sounds like a teenager's reaction."

"Mary knows Giles and I are old friends. She got us some coffee and then excused herself. She looked pretty tired."

"And torn between her husband and son. Did you and Giles talk?"

"We said polite things for a while, and then we added some cognac to our coffee and talked about when we'd been young."

Maggie looked out to the harbor. A teenaged boy had just rounded the point downriver in a small, bright green speedboat and almost swamped two kayakers. Kids. Taking risks that could so easily get out of control.

"I found out what Giles's real problem was."

"Other than having a son who didn't practice safe sex and whose girlfriend was just murdered? That sounds real enough to me."

Will ignored her sarcasm. "Giles had told Brian time and time again to stay away from Crystal."

"Because she was trouble?"

"Because she might be Brian's sister."

Chapter 21

The American Tar: Don't Give Up the Ship. Hand-colored lithograph of young, bearded American sailor dressed in traditional white pants, blue sea jacket, and middy, posed on a blue sea chest with the American flag in the background. (Tar, from tarpaulin, *was a slang expression for a sailor.) N. Currier, 1845. (Pre–Currier & Ives partnership.) 11.14 x 8.8 inches; small folio. Price: $600.*

"Crystal was Brian's sister?" Maggie thought back quickly. "You said Rachel hadn't told anyone who the father of her baby was. So it was Giles?"

"He thought it might be. He hadn't told Brian that, of course. He just told Brian that Crystal was his cousin, which she was in any case, and he should lighten up the relationship."

"And he didn't."

"I asked Giles if he was sure Crystal was his daughter. He wasn't positive. But he thought there was a good possibility."

"I remember you said several young men around town were glad when Rachel didn't name anyone as Crystal's father. So it could have been someone else too."

"It could." Will looked at Maggie. "For example, it could have been me."

Maggie just sat.

Everyone had a past.

But sometimes it was easier not knowing about it. "You? You walked out on a pregnant girl knowing she might be having your baby?"

"I'm not proud of it, Maggie. I had just graduated from college, and my mind was on my future. I figured Rachel was the only one who knew for sure, and if she'd wanted my help after the baby was born, she would have said so. She never said anything."

"Did she say anything to Giles?"

"Nope. I asked him, and he said the same thing. That after Crystal was born he was waiting to be called on the whole situation. Rachel didn't open her mouth."

Maggie sat for a moment, trying to absorb this new information. Her own feelings about Will's actions were getting in the way of her logic. She must remain calm. She must think. "Rachel is the only one who really knows who Crystal's father is."

"If she did know for sure. There were several of us around that year. It might not have been Giles or me."

"Who else could it have been? For example?"

"Tom Colby."

"Who was also Rachel's cousin. Right?"

"Right."

"Do you think Rachel ever told Crystal who her father was?"

"I doubt it. If she had, I suspect Crystal would have told someone else or contacted her dad to say hi. I don't think she knew."

"Do you know if Rachel tried to break up Crystal and Brian?"

"Giles said she did. But it might just have been any mother trying to keep her daughter away from boys."

"The detective who came the other day, the one you knew?"

"Nick Strait."

Maggie looked at Will. "He's about your age, and Giles's. I suppose he's also a possible candidate for fatherhood?"

Will grimaced. "No, Maggie. Not everyone in the state of Maine. Just a few of us, that one summer."

"He said Rachel didn't know Crystal had been pregnant. But when Amy and I were in her room—Rachel asked Amy to take back some books Crystal had borrowed about New York—I saw magazines about baby care. And adoption. If her mother had seen those in her room, she would have at least suspected the pregnancy."

"What did you do with the magazines?"

"I took them with me. The adoption magazines were Amy's and I didn't want Rachel seeing the other magazines if she hadn't noticed them before."

"Rachel would have been plenty mad if she'd known Crystal was following in her footsteps."

"And if she thought there was even a possibility that Brian and Crystal were brother and sister . . ."

"How angry can a mother get? How worried?"

"I don't know, Will. Upset enough to kill her own daughter?"

They both sat on the rocks in silence for a time. A lobsterman checked his traps nearby. A young couple jogged down the road. Two crows squawked a warning to a nearby chipmunk.

"Will, you told me a secret. I'm not happy to know it, but I am glad you trusted me enough to tell me." Maggie stared out at the river. The waves made by the small motorboat's wake were now lapping the shore. "I know something too that I haven't told anyone." She turned and looked at Will. "Crystal also slept with Drew Douglas. I don't know how often, but at least once."

"How did you find that out?"

"I saw them." Maggie avoided looking at Will.

"Did you tell Amy?"

"I couldn't. I just couldn't. And now Crystal's dead, and I'm not sure what I should do. But if the afternoon I saw them wasn't the only time, Brian might not be the father of Crystal's child."

Will reached over and took Maggie's hand. After a few minutes she took it back. "Will, we have to think. Who would have had a reason to kill Crystal? Her mother could have known she was pregnant and been so furious she did something unthinkable. Brian talks a good story now, but he wouldn't have been the first teenaged boy to turn on a pregnant girlfriend. Could Giles have known? Or maybe he was trying to break them up and got into an argument with Crystal. He was there working on Amy and Drew's home too." Maggie felt totally confused.

"And what if Crystal had threatened to tell Amy about her relationship with Drew?"

"Oh, Will. If Crystal was carrying Drew's child, how would Amy feel? She's been trying so hard to get pregnant. I can't tell her."

"Someone is pretty mad at Drew if they cut the brake lines on his car. Are you sure Amy didn't know about him and Crystal?"

"And what about the fire earlier, and the telephone calls?

Maybe Brian suspected something and was getting back at Drew."

"If you start assigning blame for actions like those, you could even put Crystal on the list. Maybe she was jealous of Amy."

"You said Shirley Steele was pretty put out when Amy and Drew moved into the house. Maybe she's strongly suggesting they move on."

"Or Tom Colby thinks the Douglas house would be a great place for sister Shirley and her kids to go."

"Even if Drew and Amy left, that doesn't mean Shirley, or anyone in the family, would get the house."

"No."

They both sat in silence, knowing they were expected back at Amy and Drew's house soon. And that right now that was the last place either of them wanted to be.

Chapter 22

———∿———

Great Fire in Portland, Maine: Tents Among the Ruins, *and* Great Fire in Portland, Maine: Distributing Food to the Citizens at the Old City Hall. *Two wood engravings by Stanley Fox on the cover of* Harper's Weekly, *July 28, 1866, including the* HW *title art: "A Journal of Civilization," with an artist's palette, a telescope, a book, a globe, a pen, and a lyre. (The Portland fire was the result of mismanaged fireworks on the Fourth of July and destroyed about one-third of the city.) Full page, 11 x 16 inches. Price: $75.*

"You're finally here! I was beginning to worry." Amy met them out on the lawn. "I've been back from the library for over an hour now, and I thought our schedules were pretty well coordinated."

Amy and her schedules!

"I'll bet you found all sorts of bargains at that bookshop or just took off for some . . . personal time." Amy looked from Maggie to Will and then back again. "That's it! I'm sure! You just wanted some time on your own. Well, why not?"

"We found some books to add to Drew's reading list," said Maggie, handing Amy the bag of books. "And we each found a couple of the volumes we were looking for too, so it was a successful bookstore visit."

"Drew will have a vast selection, now," Amy agreed, looking into the bag. "Between what I found at the library and these, he may not even mind having to keep quiet for a while."

"How is he feeling?" asked Will.

"He's still a little dopey from the medication and the pain. And frustrated by the whole situation."

"Frustration sounds like a good sign. It's better than boredom," Will said. "Why don't I go in and say hello, he's probably feeling very left out with us talking here on the lawn."

"What's next on the list, Amy?" Maggie asked.

"We were going to look at your Homers. But Drew said Will was going to check out the old kitchen. They talked about it the other day. Drew's still concerned about the fire we had earlier this summer."

"I can understand that. Especially now. He wouldn't exactly be able to leap out of the house were there a problem."

"No."

"And how is your arm, by the way? We've been so focused on Drew's leg I forgot to ask."

Amy held her elbow out to display. "It's doing all right. Just takes time. And it's been less than a week."

"And a week ago I was still doing an antiques show in

Provincetown. Which reminds me that later tonight I'd like to call Gussie. I promised I would."

"Whenever you'd like."

Drew and Will were deep in conversation in the living room. "Do you know when they stopped using it as the kitchen?"

"No. From what your aunt said, maybe as late as the early 1930s."

"And have you had the chimneys cleaned and inspected since you've been here?" Will was clearly quizzing Drew.

"There are two chimneys. The one over the ell, which would have gone to the old kitchen, we haven't had checked at all, other than Giles and Brian tarring around it when they were working on the new ell roof. The main house has five flues—one for each of the old fireplaces—all in one central chimney."

Maggie, listening, thought quickly. The old kitchen, living room, dining room, and the two master bedrooms. A classic colonial mansion.

"And have you had that chimney checked?" Will was pressing a point Maggie wasn't sure of.

"The flue that originally led to the dining room fireplace had been closed off whenever Charlotte put in central heating. We had the company that supplies our oil come and clean and check that one. It was dirty, but structurally okay. The guy who came took a fast look at the other flues. He said they'd need to be lined before we could safely use the fireplaces."

"And so you haven't."

"No. Of course not. We may be from the city, but we know an old frame building could go up quickly. That's why we were so concerned over the fire in the ell. Would you mind taking a look?"

"There are a couple of possibilities. You said the fire department couldn't locate the source of the fire."

"They said it wasn't electrical. The only electricity in that room is one lightbulb hanging from the ceiling. But some material burned. Luckily, it gave off a lot of smoke, and one of the first things we did when we moved in was install smoke detectors."

"Let me get the flashlight I have in my car. The room is in the center of the ell?"

"I'll meet you there," said Drew, pulling himself to his feet and standing on his crutches, despite Amy's glares. She and Maggie followed him out through the kitchen to the series of small rooms that in many New England homes connected the barn with the main part of the house. Ells were originally designed to make it easier to care for animals and get supplies into a house in bad weather.

Maggie smelled the lingering odor of smoke as soon as they stepped across a low threshold into the room, empty except for smoke marks on the walls and ceiling, and a spot about three by four feet where the pine floor had charred, and the center had burned through. That spot was close to the brick wall Aunt Nettie had mentioned. Maggie crouched down near the hole; there was earth just below it. "There's no basement under the ell?"

"No."

Maggie reached down and touched the ashes and dirt below the flooring. "It's damp!" she said, surprised. There had been no rain since she had been in Maine.

"The fire department guy said that was one of the things that saved the house. Along with our hearing the smoke detector, and Amy's calling 911 immediately while I used our kitchen fire extinguishers. There might be a spring under the ell. That would also explain why no one dug a basement here."

Will came in at the end of Drew's explanation. "That makes sense too when you look at this wall. Aunt Nettie said this was used as a kitchen in the 1830s. A kitchen then would need the same things a kitchen would need today: water, and a way to cook. She said there had been a stove in this room. A wood-burning iron stove would have been the height of modern kitchen appliances in the 1830s." Will got down on his hands and knees and crawled along the floor, looking at it closely. "I'd say this floor has been replaced at least once, maybe more often, since 1830. With the dampness underneath, probably it rotted out periodically. It wouldn't have been hard to replace. But because this isn't the original flooring, we can't see exactly where the stove was."

He stood up again. "But we know it had to be vented through a stovepipe to the chimney over this section of the ell, and the brick wall was a part of that." He opened each of several iron doors in the brick wall. "The compartment behind this door"—he pointed to the lowest one, which was almost on the floor—"probably was to store foodstuffs so they wouldn't freeze. Anything needing what we would think of as refrigeration would have been put in the cellar of the main house. I'll bet there are remnants of bins or storage containers there, right?"

Amy nodded.

"This door," Will continued, moving up the wall, "was probably for the stovepipe." He got out his flashlight and beamed it up into the space. "I can't tell for sure, but I'll bet this is a straight track to the chimney you haven't had checked, on the ell roof."

"What is this big depression in the bricks, lined with metal?" Amy asked. "It's big enough to bathe a baby in!"

"And might have been used for that. But, more likely, considering that personal cleanliness was not considered as vital in the 1830s as it is today, it was used to wash dishes or clothing. Today there are no entrances or exits for water, but I'd be willing to bet that at some point in the past there was a pump near here, to bring the water from that underground spring you mentioned into this room. The water would then be put in this container to warm it; the container would have been near the stove, remember, and on the same wall as the stovepipe. And there might have been an outside drain at some point. That could have been covered or torn out when the floor was replaced."

"That's interesting," said Drew. "You obviously know your old kitchens. But how could a fire have started?"

"The fire was here, right?" Will pointed at the hole in the floor.

"Yes."

"So the fire was pretty much where the old stove must have been."

"All right."

Will hesitated. "Now, I'm guessing. I haven't been up on your roof, and I haven't examined your chimney. But you said the fire was in material of some sort."

"At first I thought we might have left some cleaning cloths out here, while we were emptying these rooms." Drew hesitated. "There was some junk in the ell that we took to the dump. Wooden crates and cardboard boxes and hundreds of old bleach bottles and peanut butter jars."

"We assumed Charlotte was saving them to use for canning," added Amy.

"Most likely. Most women up here can vegetables in summer, and although Charlotte didn't do any preserving in her last years, she probably would have kept the supplies out of habit. But you decided no cloths had been left."

"We didn't think so. We told ourselves that somehow we

must have left something here, though, or nothing would have ignited."

Will shook his head. "I can tell you're pretty careful people. I don't think you left any cleaning cloths here. I think someone put some cleaning solvent on some rags, perhaps wrapped the rags around a small child's bouncing ball that would keep everything moving, and dropped them down the chimney from the roof."

Amy went over to the brick wall. "But the iron door was closed. The material wouldn't have gone anywhere."

"Wait a minute, Amy." Drew hobbled over to the site of the fire. "I think Will is right. The door was open that night. I remember one of the firemen closing it to stop any drafts from accelerating the fire."

"We always closed it," Amy pointed out. "I thought there'd be dust up there, and I didn't want it coming down into a room we'd just cleaned."

Will spoke slowly. "I think someone came into the house, opened that door, and then left. Then either the same person, or an accomplice, dropped the fiery cloth down the chimney, hoping it would start a blaze. You've been having roof work done, right?"

"All summer," said Amy. "Different parts of the roof, of course."

"So there have been ladders around."

Drew inhaled deeply. "Someone tried to burn the house down. And we were in it."

Will nodded. "I'm not an expert, but the possibility fits the circumstances."

"And that someone was able to get into the house without our knowing it."

Or with their knowledge, Maggie thought. The construction crew, Giles and Brian, had been in and out all summer.

Tom Colby, from next door, seemed familiar with the house. Crystal had been there.

Of course, half of Madoc was familiar with the house. It was the Brewer house.

"Let's go back to the living room," Amy said. "Drew should have his leg up. And I think we should all have a drink."

"Or two," added Drew.

Will and Maggie waited a minute before following them.

"You've really scared them. And me," said Maggie.

"But they need to know. And"—Will gently touched Maggie's cheek—"I'm not too thrilled you're staying here just now."

The touch wilted Maggie for a moment. She wished he would hold her and make all the problems connected with this house disappear, if only for a moment. But she was a realist. "I'm not going to be scared off, and neither are Drew nor Amy."

"Now the question is . . . did whoever set the fire have any connection to Crystal's death?"

Despite the August heat Maggie shivered slightly as they walked back through the ell to the kitchen, where she could already hear the tinkling of wineglasses. For once she wasn't interested in diet cola.

Chapter 23

The United States Arsenal at Augusta, Maine. *Wood engraving by Kilburn, published in* Gleason's Pictorial, *1857. Shows arsenal, American flag, and the Kennebec River entry to the arsenal, including two small boats. 6 x 6 inches. Price: $45.*

Despite his words, Drew knew he shouldn't drink while he was taking medication. "Someone may be trying to get us, but I'm not going to make it that easy for them," he joked.

The other three sipped a fragrant burgundy on the porch, watched a lobsterman pull three of his traps and check them as herring gulls followed in expectation, and tried not to think too hard about the possibility of someone's getting access to the house. Access to Drew's car would not have been a problem. It had just been parked in the driveway. This was Madoc. It hadn't even been locked.

Maggie turned from the river scene to the ell. "What is above the old kitchen room and the other rooms in the ell? I just realized there is space there."

Amy answered, "Lots of space. That's the attic. Someday we might want to finish it off, but for now we've just started cleaning it out, especially where there were leaks. Some trunks and boxes are there, and we've put our winter clothes and Christmas ornaments in the corners we've cleaned. After living in New York City, having that much space for storage is a real luxury."

Will and Maggie looked at each other.

"What sorts of things are in the trunks and boxes?" Will asked.

"Papers, mostly. Some look like old captain's logs." Amy put up her hand to stop Will's words. "I know; they probably belong in your family. They shouldn't have been left here. But they were, and I had planned to check through them, just to see what we could learn about the people who lived in this house, and then donate them to the Waymouth Library. Their archives could use the local history information, and that would make the papers available to anyone who wanted to study them."

"An excellent plan, Amy," said Will. "I wasn't trying to interfere. In fact, that's what the family should have done years ago, since my guess is the heat and cold in that attic space haven't been kind to those papers."

"You're right. And there were several cartons of papers I just threw out, because mice or red squirrels had chewed them up, probably for nesting materials."

"But what fun to look through the things!" Maggie felt more relaxed now. Going through old boxes of what someone had once considered a treasure was a familiar and potentially exciting task. "Amy, would you mind awfully if Will and I took a look at the attic? Just in case there's something there you might not have noticed."

Amy hesitated.

"I promise! We won't touch anything without your permission."

"I was just thinking. Crystal helped me put some clothes and boxes up there to store, and we had to move some of the really horrendous stuff. There was a chair whose seat had totally mildewed from the rain dripping down, and whose wooden frame is water-stained and warped. And there was a box of old toys Crystal looked through one afternoon. I gave her a small carved boat that she particularly liked." Amy looked over at Drew, who was dozing a bit after his most recent dose of pain medication. "Why not? Come on. It will take our minds off other things."

"Wasn't one of the rumors about this house that there was treasure hidden in it?" said Maggie. "Seems to me I heard someone say so. Maybe Shirley."

"Unless Shirley thinks pickle jars filled with dust and dead flies are a treasure, or she really values stacks of green plastic blueberry baskets, I don't know what in the attic would meet the criterion of 'treasure.' But why not look? If you both don't mind getting a little dusty."

The attic space was as Amy had described it. Larger than Maggie had imagined, and, although she could see some parts had been cleaned out and the floor swept and new cartons stacked, most of it was still untouched.

"When we bought the house it was supposed to be empty. But at the last minute the Realtor said the owner hadn't had time to clean out this area." Amy shrugged her shoulders a bit. "We thought the same thing you did—maybe treasure! But that was before we started going through it. We haven't checked everything. And the papers should go to the library. But what is really needed up here, I'm afraid, is a direct slide to a Dumpster. We took several carloads of stuff to the dump, and Giles took a truckload for us one weekend. But we just haven't had time to get into a lot of this stuff. We had to clean out the rooms below here too, you know."

The attic was hot and stuffy. Will tried to open one of the low windows that lined the room but gave up. "They've been painted closed. Many times. They could be opened, but it would take a while."

"We just thought we'd leave them that way for now," Amy said. "At least in the winter we won't worry about too many breezes blowing through here. There is so much that has to be done in this house that the windows in the attic just didn't seem a priority."

"At some point you should do them, though," said Will. "There's very little ventilation in here. Not good for whatever you're storing, and . . ."

"Possibly a fire hazard," finished Amy. "You're right. But not this afternoon." She gave them a brief overview. "Crystal and I did try to organize this corner. There"—she pointed at a carton in a corner—"is the carton of toys. And there are the three trunks of papers I told you about."

Maggie walked toward them, totally entranced by the idea of trunks full of nineteenth-century papers, but Amy continued her tour. "We didn't get all the way back into that corner, but there are several boxes of old picture frames. And a lot of broken glass."

"Are any of the frames Victorian?" Maggie asked. "Gilt? Or Currier and Ives frames?"

"You can check that out for me. Just be careful not to cut your hands on all the broken glass." Amy glanced down at the bandage on her arm. "Crystal and I piled all the parts of chairs over there. It looks as though every time a straight chair was broken they stuck it up here. It's like a giant Lincoln Logs set. Maybe some of the pieces could be put together to form a full chair. But I don't know if any of the chairs would be worth the time. That pile over beyond the chairs is just old cardboard and boxes. Crystal and I thought we'd take them to the dump some afternoon." Amy paused a moment. "There's an old bureau in the corner, but it was under a leak, and it's so warped we couldn't open the drawers, so maybe your treasure is in there. The rest of the stuff"—she gestured at piles of broken electric fans and heaters, a large carton of moth-or-mouse-eaten yarn, a small collection of used marker buoys, some clam baskets, and an assortment of unidentifiable wooden and metal objects— "well, you're welcome to look through it." She grinned. "And don't forget to check all the boxes of birds' nests and eggs and dried seaweed and sea glass and shells. This place is full of treasures." She started sneezing. "And my allergies are another reason we didn't spend more time up here. I must be sensitive to dust. Would you mind checking this stuff on your own for a while?"

"No problem," said Maggie. "While we're up here, would you like us to fill some garbage bags or boxes with stuff like the old birds' nests? They're not going to help your allergies and should be disposed of."

"I'd love it!" She reached up on top of a wardrobe near the door and handed them a box of supermarket plastic garbage bags. "You see, I just happen to have some handy. Have fun, both of you. If you find any diamonds or emeralds, let me know. And—I'd prefer the emeralds. They're my birthstone!" Amy sneezed her way out of the attic and down the stairs.

"Wow." Will looked around. "And this is part of my

family's heritage too. Maybe my great-grandfather sat on one of those chairs and broke it."

"If you're going to get sentimental, Will, that's fine. I suspect Amy might even let you take that broken chair as a souvenir. She was right; this place is really dusty and hot. I don't think we'll want to spend a lot of time here."

"But we certainly should check some things." Will lifted the wooden lid on one of the trunks. "It would be easier to go through the papers downstairs. The light would be better, the dust would be minimal, and they are going to the library anyway."

Maggie sadly agreed. "So we'll put those off for now."

"Why don't you check out the frames, and I'll look under some of these junk piles and make sure there's nothing of value that Amy and Crystal missed."

Maggie picked up one of the empty cartons and shook it to get at least some of the dust and dead insects out. "A garbage bag would be no good for glass, and I've been warned. I'll at least isolate the large pieces so they can safely go to the dump without harming anyone. There have been enough accidents around here already."

Will took a garbage bag. "My good deed will be disposing of some of these birds' nests and small pieces of driftwood." The attic beams were covered with rows of them. "Even if my great-grandfather collected them, I think their time is over." He reached up and took the nearest one down and dropped it in the plastic bag.

"Make sure to check for Amy's emeralds before you throw anything out, now!"

"This was my family's home, remember? I don't seem to remember any family jewels, missing or not missing. If there is treasure here, I don't think it's a bird's nest full of diamonds." Will reached up to take another one down and started coughing. "Although that would have been a good hiding place. I don't think these things have been touched in a hundred years."

"I was surprised at the box of toys. Everyone has said there were only single women who've lived here for the last hundred years."

"Which means, of course, that those toys are definitely going to be checked out," Will agreed. "Although some of those ladies could have kept some toys around for nieces and nephews and cousins to play with when they visited. Being unmarried doesn't mean being a hermit."

"I certainly hope not," Maggie said quietly to herself. That was a nice thought. The unmarried ladies of the house keeping a box of toys for visiting children. She worked her way through to several cartons filled with frames. "This is going to take more than a couple of minutes."

"Not to worry. There are plenty of birds' nests here to keep me occupied." Will was happily working his way down the beams and already had half a garbage bag filled.

It was peaceful in the attic, and despite the heat, Maggie and Will worked comfortably together.

Within an hour they had two cartons of glass and five garbage bags of junk ready for the dump, and Maggie had chosen about a dozen frames that were worth saving. The box of toys had yielded some iron wagons and cars that had some value; several of them more than "some value" Maggie suspected, although she wasn't a dealer in toys. But she had been going to call Gussie sometime today anyway. She'd ask an expert.

Will found one small nineteenth-century iron fireplace set—"Probably originally used in one of the bedrooms!"—and had filled several Mason jars with sea glass. "In case

Amy and Drew are the sort who like to display it in their windows. If not, it's all set for the dump."

They took one more look around and decided it was time to share their treasures with Amy and Drew.

No emeralds, but some progress had been made, and they'd found a few things that could be recycled into the house if Amy and Drew chose to do so.

"These picture frames are good ones?" Amy looked interested, if a bit doubtful.

"Definitely. You wanted some nineteenth-century prints. When we get to those, maybe we could match up some frames and pictures."

"It would be nice to hang some of the same picture frames that were originally in the house," Amy agreed. "But the gold on these frames is flaking off. They really don't look that good, Maggie."

"Gold leaf will solve that problem. An art store should have some, and I'm sure someone there can give you lots of advice on how to restore these. I've seen elaborate gilt frames rebuilt and restored, and none of these have major problems."

"And the wooden frames? They're so dingy."

"These three are oak, and this other one I think may be cherry. Liquid Gold is the solution."

"Gold?"

Maggie laughed. "You can get it at the supermarket. It's a very rich oil that you could put on these frames. Probably several times. It will almost erase the use and will put the moisture and richness back in the wood. Just make sure you put the frames on top of some heavy plastic before you put the Liquid Gold on them, because it seeps through anything porous and can make a major mess."

"And the toys?"

"If you don't mind, I'll ask Gussie about them tonight when I call her. She would know how valuable they are. It's up to you whether you keep them or sell them, but you should know what you have."

"I'd like to bring those trunks downstairs to one of the empty rooms in the ell. The light is better there, and Maggie knows paper more than I do. I'm curious because it's my family. But maybe we could all look through them. And at least two of those trunks could also do with some Liquid Gold and would make great coffee tables or blanket chests." Will looked ready to go back for the trunks that moment.

"Do you think the three of us could lift them?" Amy glanced at where Drew was sitting with his foot up.

"I think so," said Will. "If they turn out to be too heavy, we could move some of the papers to cartons and just bring those down."

Agreed, the three of them headed for the attic. The first trunk was embossed metal over wood, and lighter than they anticipated. But taking it downstairs was still a challenge. "There is no way this is simple," Maggie said, laughing. "If Will takes the bottom weight, then he has to walk backward, and we have less weight, but we have to practically bend double to get the stuff down."

"Maybe we could just bump the trunk down from step to step?" Amy asked hopefully.

"No way! That might damage the trunk, and we haven't had a chance to really check it out yet," said Will.

The second trunk was heavier because it was solid wood.

Before they moved the third trunk they all stood in the attic for a moment. "You guys did a great job in only an hour." Amy looked around and only sneezed once. "The birds' nests are down, and I hadn't been able to reach them.

And so much of this other stuff is organized better. And I love the iron fireplace set you found, Will! It must have been hidden under that other metal stuff."

"Most of which really is junk," agreed Will. "But it will be fun to have the set back in one of the fireplaces when you have the chimneys cleaned out." He looked down at the trunk they were to move. "Did you say you and Crystal had moved these trunks before?"

"They were over by that outside wall, but there was some dampness there, so we pushed them to the center of the room."

"Have you moved them since then?"

"No; they've just sat here."

Will squatted down and smoothed his fingers over one of the boards in the floor.

"This board looks as though it's been moved recently. There's not as much dirt along the edges as there is near the other boards." They all got down on their hands and knees and looked. Will was right.

"Have you had any of the boards in this floor replaced?"

"No. A couple will need to be, but that's another thing far down our 'to do' list. We figured getting the roof fixed first was most important, since the boards in the floor were getting worse with the dampness. Once the roof was fixed, things would stabilize until we had time to fix them. Were we wrong?"

"You were right. But I think this board has been taken up. Recently."

Will got up and went over to the pile of rusted metal bookcases and pieces of metal and selected one aluminum strip that was thin but sturdy. "Might have been part of a clothes rack at some time," he commented. "Would you mind if I tried this on the loose board? If it's nailed down well, I won't force it. But it's a wide old pine board, and it looks pretty sturdy."

"Go ahead," said Amy. "But I don't know what you're going to find."

"I don't either," said Will. "But I'm curious. There is something different about this board. I want to find out what it is."

He took the piece of metal and slipped it into the crack between the board he was looking at and the next one. He had been right. It was an easy fit, and there was little dirt. Thick dust had settled between the other boards. Maggie and Amy were down on the floor watching as Will pried the board up with remarkably little effort.

"No nails," he said, examining the board. "Or they were removed long ago. No new marks." He put the four-foot board next to what was now a hole in the floor.

The hole was a space perhaps eight inches deep and four and a half feet long, and it had been lined with a quilt. Many years ago, Maggie noted, as she reached out and touched the edge of the quilt. It was linsey-woolsey, and the soft fibers fell apart in her fingers. But what they were all looking at was what was on top of the quilt.

Five rifles.

"There is your treasure, Amy," Will said softly. "If those guns are what I think they are, they may not be emeralds, but they are definitely treasures."

Chapter 24

———⁓———

Eldorado Blackberry, *1892 lithograph, drawn by D. G. Passmore and included in the* Report of the Pomologist, U.S. Department of Agriculture. *One branch of blackberry bush, with fruit and leaves. 5.5 x 9 inches. Price: $48.*

They removed the guns carefully, so the metal would not be scratched. The stocks were walnut; Amy immediately thought a little oil would help. "You said there was an oil that would make the frames look better. Maybe it would help the wood on these rifles."

"Don't even think about it!" said Maggie. "I'm definitely not an expert on firearms. But I know enough to be able to give an educated guess as to what these are, and to know that the less we handle them the better. They are in extraordinary condition. They may never have been used."

They put them carefully next to each other on the living room coffee table so Drew could see them too.

He reached out and touched one, then withdrew his hand. "Watch out! These have angular bayonets. But most nineteenth-century rifles had some sort of bayonet attached. Why would these be so special?"

"Any rifle—any gun, for that matter—made in the nineteenth century was made for heavy and regular use. Like Will's cast-iron pots or brass trammels, they were tools, and they were made to last. They weren't for display. Their construction could mean life or death for someone. So it would be very unusual for a finely made rifle never to have been used. And, of course, that would make certain types of collectors value it very highly." Maggie looked carefully at the rifles. Could they be . . . She knew very little about firearms. But she did know about the Civil War. She looked at Will. "Is it time for me to get out those Winslow Homer prints?"

"I think it is." They smiled at each other, connecting with something to which Amy and Drew did not have a clue.

"Before we start going through prints, I think we should be thinking of dinner," said Drew. "Just because you all had wine early doesn't mean we need to eat at a sophisticated ten o'clock. This is Maine, where the evening news starts at five. And I'm getting hungry!"

Maggie glanced at her watch. It was almost six-thirty. She was hungry too, now that she thought about it.

"Do you folks like fried food?" asked Will. "Because there's a place in Waymouth where they specialize in it. And they do takeout."

Maggie smiled. "Totally evil, and totally delicious, if I'm thinking of the right place."

Will nodded.

"Will took me there the day of the auction preview." The

day he told her about this being his family's home. And she'd asked him about ghosts. At least the ghosts hadn't made a visit in the past couple of days. Although she had heard that baby cry. Maggie realized she hadn't even thought about that today. There had been too many more immediate issues to concentrate on.

"Take-out fried food sounds like a wonderful idea. And we should really learn more about the local places to eat. Can we call and order ahead?" said Amy.

"Absolutely. And I'll even play delivery boy and pick up the dinner." Will headed toward the telephone. "That will give you time to get out the Homer prints, Maggie, before I get back."

"The man has a one-track mind," grumbled Maggie.

They decided to make it a buffet. Fried scallops, fried clams, fried haddock, fried shrimp, and onion rings, plus two salads, which they planned to combine. "We'll have more than enough," Will cautioned. "Their portions are generous. But they do make a great blueberry pie too."

As Will took off for Waymouth, Maggie headed for the Shadows inventory in her van to find the Homers. She might as well bring in the Wyeths too, since Amy and Drew had asked about them earlier in the week. It took a few minutes; her portfolios were lined up and tightly packed. Although she had only three portfolios of Homers, and one of Wyeths, she had to move two dozen other portfolios to get to the ones she wanted. Had it only been five days since she'd packed up the van after the Provincetown show? It seemed years. She hardly remembered what she'd sold at the show. As she moved portfolios out of the way, she saw the one labeled "Nast—Christmas." Amy had asked about one of those prints, possibly for the nursery. She pulled it out too and leaned it against the car next to the "Homer—Civil

War" and "Homer—Other" portfolios. She still had to find the Wyeth and the "Small Homers" portfolios.

Amy was pleased: the timing was perfect. By the time Will had returned bearing tubs of fried seafood, Amy had set the table and Maggie had found the requested portfolios and put them in the living room.

The kitchen smelled irresistible. Only one thing would have made it even better. "Do you have any beer to go with all this fried food?"

"Maggie! No diet cola?" teased Amy.

Before Maggie could answer, Will pulled out two six-packs of Sam Adams. "Great minds, and so forth. I thought someone might be interested in beer."

"Perfect!"

They sat and ate the fried food with their fingers, saving the formality of knives and forks for their portions of the enormous salad that two orders had turned out to be. Dishes of fresh tartar sauce Amy had mixed up were soon almost finished. For the moment, words weren't important.

After dinner Drew settled himself back on the living room couch. "Now what's the connection you and Will obviously found between Winslow Homer and some guns in our attic?"

Maggie went over to the "Homer—Civil War" portfolio and leafed through the prints. She pulled out a matted wood engraving and handed it to Drew.

The print showed a young Union soldier sitting high in a tree, his rifle balanced on a branch, poised to shoot. "'The Army of the Potomac—A Sharp-shooter on Picket Duty' I've seen this somewhere before."

"No doubt. Probably in your college survey-of-art course. But you're remembering the oil painting Homer did of this same scene. That oil painting was his first to be exhibited.

After that, he did a wood engraving of the same scene. The painting is a classic depiction of innocence—the young man—and death—the rifle—and became so popular that the wood engraving is also one of Homer's best known."

"Which no doubt accounts for the seven-hundred-and-fifty-dollar price tag I see on it."

"True."

"I know enough about the Civil War to know a sharpshooter was a Union soldier whose job was to go ahead of the other troops and pick off the Confederate officers or any other specific men they felt would make a difference to the battle."

Maggie nodded. "Right. There were two sharpshooter regiments. And they used special rifles. Extremely accurate percussion, straight-breech models with double-set triggers. Although several major companies supplied rifles for the Union Army—the Army of the Potomac, as it was known at first—the most accurate were considered to be a special group of the 1859 model of the rifle manufactured by Christian Sharp."

Drew's interest was obvious piqued. "I always thought a sharpshooter was someone who could shoot sharply. As in 'look sharp!'"

"That's what most people think. But actually the Yankee sharpshooter regiments got their name from their Sharps rifles."

"Incredible." Drew looked from the wood engraving to the rifles on the table and back again. "And you think these rifles are the same as the one in the engraving?"

"I don't know for sure. But I've a friend in New Jersey who collects guns, and I've learned a little from him. No matter what these rifles are, they're mid–nineteenth century in mint condition, and that gives them value. But we know they're made by the Sharps Rifle Manufacturing Company in Hartford. It says so on the barrel. What really got me excited was that on the top of the barrel, near the breech, it says 'new model 1859.' I think that's the group of two thousand rifles that were issued in 1862 to Colonel Berdan's First and Second Regiments of sharpshooters." Maggie hesitated. "One thing I don't know: why the letters *J* and *T* are on the buttstocks of all five rifles."

"Would your friend know about the serial numbers?"

"I think he could look them up. There are books tracing the rifles. I once saw a list researched to the point of knowing which serial number had been issued to which Union soldier, and what happened to the soldier. But these guns are different. Because they look so new, they may never have been issued. Or"—Maggie hesitated—"I hate to accuse any of your ancestors, Will, but someone might have lightened the munitions supply a little."

"I know there were a couple of people in the family who fought in the Civil War. Tom would know their regiments. I'd never heard any of them were sharpshooters, but they might have been. There were members of Berdan's regiments from Maine."

"If these rifles are what you think they are; if their serial numbers agree they were some of the guns issued to Berdan's sharpshooters, then how much would they be worth?" Amy sat on the floor next to Drew's couch and held the wood engraving he'd handed to her.

"I don't know. Especially if these rifles were—liberated— during the Civil War and then hidden for some reason. They may be the only ones in this condition. There would be no comparables. We'd probably be talking in the thousands." Maggie hesitated. "But that isn't an estimate, and we haven't checked the serial numbers. You'd need a firearms expert to confirm my suspicions; someone who was an expert would also have a knowledge of current values."

"We understand," said Drew. "But obviously until we know for sure what these rifles are, and have decided what we're going to do with them, we need to get them out of sight and into some safe place."

"You're right. And that's one of the things that's bothering me," put in Maggie. "Will found these because we moved the trunks and he noticed that one of the boards in the attic floor was different. It had been moved before. Not long ago. If these rifles were hidden there after the Civil War and not disturbed until now, there would have been plenty of dust around that board, just as there was around the other boards upstairs. I think Will is right, and someone else found these before we did."

"Chances are it was pretty recently, then," said Amy. "Because that attic was totally crammed with boxes and cartons and broken furniture when we moved in. Those piles had been there for years."

"When did you and Crystal clear out the space in the middle of the attic and move the trunks?"

"About three weeks ago. It was just after we'd moved some of Drew's and my winter clothes, and those formal dresses I told you about, Maggie, into the old wardrobe in the attic. I noticed the dampness near the trunks and wanted to prevent any further damage to the papers, so Crystal and I spent the rest of that day, and the next one, cleaning out."

"That was about the middle of July," Drew said. "I remember taking several loads of the junk you found to the dump."

"So there were only one or two days when that space was empty: after you took the junk away, and before you moved the trunks."

"That sounds right."

Maggie hesitated. "Do you remember whether you moved the trunks before or after the fire?"

"It happened right about that time," Amy said slowly. "I remember thinking that, thank goodness, we had gotten a lot of stuff out of the attic before the fire, so at least that wouldn't have added to the flames."

"So whoever set the fire could have found the rifles," Drew said.

"It's possible. But if they did—and knew their value—then why wouldn't they have taken them?" Amy looked unconvinced.

"Maybe they didn't know the value. Maybe they didn't have time."

"Or maybe they did take one, to find out how valuable they were. And, if they were valuable, whoever found them planned to come back for the others."

"That sounds silly. Why not just take them all at once? Especially if the person set the fire. If the building had gone up, so would the rifles." Amy shook her head.

"Maybe because you and Drew found the fire much faster than anyone thought you would. Maybe there wasn't time," Maggie said.

"Wait a minute. I don't see how the fire and the rifles could really be connected. Will said maybe the fire could have been dropped down the chimney from the roof. That would mean someone climbed up a ladder to the roof, and then got down fast, so no one would see him. Before he might get caught in the fire." Amy was making a mental itinerary. "But someone had to have been in the house before that to open the iron door to the flue."

"But those are separate levels. The iron door is on the first floor. The rifles were in the floor of the attic, which we saw this afternoon wasn't accessible through a window. Someone would have to have gone up the stairs, through a couple of empty rooms, and into the attic." Drew shrugged. "I think we're trying to connect events that just aren't related to each other."

Maggie thought a moment. "Maybe. But the timing is certainly close. Were Giles and Brian working on that part of the roof then?"

"They might have been," Drew said. "I don't remember. They were on the roof of the main house in the early part of July; there was a lot of rotten wood there to replace. But not as much as on the ell. They've been up on the ell roof since, well, it could be mid-July. They've just about finished."

"During the roofing there might have been a time when there would have been an opening from the roof to the attic."

"Giles and Brian wouldn't have left a hole in the roof even for one night," said Amy. "They've been so careful about everything."

"But they might have left part of the roof tarped for one night, especially if no bad weather was predicted. I've done that when I've been roofing," said Will. "Lots of people do."

"I can't believe Giles and Brian would have set a fire, or looked for rifles, though! It doesn't make sense," said Amy.

"There are a lot of things that don't make sense," Maggie said. "But for right now I think we'd better hide these rifles somewhere in the main house."

"If someone were checking to see their value and found out they were worth money, they would come back for the rest." Drew looked around the room. "Well, one thing we haven't had so far in this house is a burglar."

Maggie remembered Tom Colby, the Civil War reenactor, looking through the window. And something else clicked into place. But accusing anyone now would be pointless. Tom was Will's cousin, and Drew's friend. It might be nothing.

"Let's just put the rifles under our bed, upstairs," said Amy. "No one would look there, and they'll be safe until we have them checked out."

While Amy and Will put the rifles away, Maggie returned her print to the portfolio. "I'm weary," she said. "I'll admit it. This has definitely been a full day. And I do want to call Gussie tonight. Shall we call it an evening?"

"Make sure you ask her about the toys," said Amy.

"I will. And, if you'd like, I could try to reach my friend about the rifles."

"Would you try?" said Drew. "I'm curious."

"I wrote down the serial numbers and the identifying information," Maggie said. "I'll see if he's home. He may have an interesting story to tell us."

Chapter 25

—◦—

Four Snakes, *German chromolithograph, c. 1870.*
Brown and yellow-marked snakes (python, cobra, black
snake, green snake) coiling dramatically around fallen
tree on the ground. One snake holds a struggling frog in
its mouth. 10.5 x 14.5 inches. Price: $90.

Maggie closed the door of Amy's study. She sat in the brown leather executive desk chair and spun around. She wanted a few minutes to think.

She and Gussie, the owner of Aunt Augusta's Attic, an antiques business specializing in toys, had met at an antiques show and had been friends for ten years. Gussie was coping well with the effects of postpolio syndrome that were now keeping her closer to her home, and to her motorized wheelchair. Just last weekend they had both done the Provincetown Antique Show, Gussie assisted by her nephew Ben, and by the current man in her life, lawyer Jim Dryden. Talking with Gussie always helped Maggie put life in perspective. She could really use some perspective now.

Maggie shook her head slightly and began drawing circles on a pad of paper. She labeled the circles, remembering an old creativity exercise she'd learned years ago. Isolate the elements; then see where they interrelate. She labeled the circles with the strange happenings at or near the Douglas home.

Circle One: Amy had seen a ghost. Maggie forced herself to go on to the next circle.

Circle Two: Annoying telephone calls. Usually at night. That was verifiable; Maggie had heard them.

Circle Three: A fire without specific origin. Maggie thought about that one for a while. If Will's theory was right, then someone, or some people, were not only willing to risk hurting Amy and Drew, they were willing to risk hurting this house. Since this home meant so much to the Brewer family, that would seem to rule out a family member.

Circle Four: Crystal's murder. And Crystal's pregnancy. Were the two related? Maggie reached for an eraser and separated the two.

Circle Five: Crystal's pregnancy.

Circle Six: Brakes cut on Drew's car. That must have been done by someone specifically looking to injure, or even kill, Drew. And Amy, or even Maggie, might have been a passenger in that car.

Circle Seven: Possibly valuable rifles found in attic. Rifles, Maggie added, that might have been found by someone else before today. Were the rifles possibly the "treasure" that was rumored to be in this house?

That was it. Drew drank a little too much sometimes, and he and Amy wanted to have a child. Issues, perhaps, but not life-and-death issues.

No. One more thing.

Circle Eight: Members of Brewer family upset that home sold out of the family.

That would be Shirley Steele and Tom Colby, who lived next door. Other members of the family might have felt the sale wasn't appropriate, but they weren't advertising their feelings.

Maggie carefully made the circles darker, thinking about each one.

There were overlaps. Crystal was a member of the Brewer family. The telephone calls were harassment and might be connected to someone unhappy about the Douglases buying this house, but they weren't violent.

Cutting the brakes on the car and setting a fire were violent acts, but acts of someone who was still at a distance, relatively impersonal.

Crystal's murder was violent and very personal. Her pregnancy was very personal.

And the Brewer family relationships could include issues mixed with her pregnancy. But who had known she was pregnant? Maggie had heard of no one who said, "I knew Crystal was pregnant. She told me." Her mother might have guessed; Brian was sorry he hadn't known. At least that's what he said. Crystal, of course, must have known, although Maggie had read all too often about girls who didn't figure out that they were pregnant until it was too late.

Too late for what? Good prenatal care? An abortion? An early wedding? Any of the above. It was definitely too late for Crystal. And the magazines in Crystal's room pointed to her knowing she was pregnant. Or at least thinking about pregnancy.

Maggie picked up the telephone. It was after eleven, but Gussie usually read late. She needed to talk to someone far away from Madoc, Maine. Someone who could help her make sense of all this.

Gussie answered on the first ring.

Maggie could feel herself relaxing, just hearing Gussie's voice. "I'm fine, Gussie. And guess who else is here? Will Brewer!" Gussie had met Will when they'd all done the Rensselaer Antiques Fair over Memorial Day weekend.

"Turns out his relatives used to own the house Amy and Drew bought. Gussie, there is a lot going on here. But, first, before I forget, this afternoon Will and I went through some of the things in the attic of this house. Generally, a lot of junk. But there was one box of toys."

"Yes?" Gussie's voice had brightened from friendly to alert.

"I'm no expert, but some of them look good. Most of them are iron: a miniature woodstove with iron pots, an elephant-shaped bank, several cars. No dolls. One pretty ragged early teddy bear. A board game; I didn't check to see whether all the pieces were there. A pack of cards, ditto. And a couple of what look like lead British soldiers. In any case, I don't know what Amy will decide to do with the stuff, but I wondered if you could give me a fast telephone appraisal."

"Based on what you've said, not really. Sounds like most of those things would be from about 1890 to 1915. Iron toys, especially iron vehicles, are good. Banks are good. But condition is critical. If they have any of the original paint, that gives them more value. The more paint, the more value."

"What if someone stuffed the miniature woodstove with toothpicks instead of kindling?"

Gussie laughed. "Well, the toys were played with! That says good things about the family in the house, but not for the value of the toys. The teddy bear could be the highest-valued antique you mentioned. If it really is a period teddy bear, say 1910 to 1920, then it could be worth several hundred dollars even in pretty crummy condition. Mint teddy bears are getting thousands at auction now."

"So what should I tell Amy?"

"Tell her to keep anything she really likes. It would be nice to have the toys stay where they were played with and loved. But if she doesn't want something, either take it to a local auctioneer for an appraisal and auction it off, or send me pictures and I'll make her an offer. Although I'm not sure any of those things are really for me. Condition is the key."

"I know." That was true of all antiques. And Gussie was particular about only buying toys in near-mint condition for her business.

"So. That wasn't hard. Now what else is happening? Amy was so upset when she called you!"

"It's complicated, Gussie. There's a lot going on." Maggie looked down at the circles she'd drawn on the pad in front of her. "I'm having trouble sorting it all out. Knowing which details are the important ones."

It took at least fifteen minutes just to explain the basics of what had happened.

"Maggie, now, tell me the truth. Are you in any danger?"

"I don't think so. Unless, of course, someone sets another fire. But I'm not so sure about Amy and Drew. I have to believe that someone wants them to leave. That may have to do with keeping the Brewer house in the family, or it may have to do with just getting rid of people from away. I don't know. Crystal was the one murdered, and she didn't own this house. In fact, she was part of the family that has owned it. That's why I'm so confused. I can't decide which details are important and which are not. And I'm worried about Amy and Drew." Maggie paused. "And one more thing, Gussie, and it may be important."

"Yes?"

Maggie lowered her voice, just in case Amy or Drew was still awake. "Drew and Crystal were sleeping together."

A pause. "Are you absolutely sure about that?"

"I saw them."

"Maggie, you have to tell someone. If you don't, it might be withholding evidence."

"I really don't think Drew killed Crystal, though. And it would be so awful to tell Amy. She's already feeling her marriage is unstable because she can't get pregnant."

"Maybe she's right to feel that not all is well. Wouldn't you have wanted to know, if Amy had found out something like that about Michael?"

Maggie thought. "I don't know, Gussie. I just don't know."

"Think about it, Maggie. If you don't tell Amy, then at least talk to Drew. See what he says."

"That sounds like blackmail."

"Give him a chance to tell Amy himself. If she has to find out, and I think she does, then it would be best if he did the telling."

Chapter 26

———⟿———

The Fog Warning, 1893 lithograph of Winslow Homer oil on canvas completed in 1885; one of three Homer oils depicting North Atlantic fishermen displayed at the World's Columbian Exposition in Chicago in 1893. Lithograph published as result of that exhibition. Man in fishing gear rowing a dory filled with halibut in a rough sea as fog rolls in, obscuring his view of the vessel he must return to. 7.5 x 10.25 inches. Price: $210.

Sleeping was difficult. Maggie tried to think of what she would say about Drew's relationship to Crystal. And to whom she would say it. By morning she was still weary and had come to no satisfactory conclusions.

As Amy scrambled eggs, Maggie made toast from anadama bread and shared Gussie's comments about the toys. Drew paid more attention to the morning's *Portland Press Herald* then to Maggie. "The only mention of Crystal's murder is a small article on page twelve saying the investigation is ongoing."

"I had hoped they would solve it quickly. How horrible for Rachel to have to live through days of waiting to find out who killed her daughter." Amy put some butter and raspberry jam on the table next to the plate of toast.

"Not to speak of no one's being able to settle in to getting any work done. When will Giles and Brian be finishing the roof, did they say?" Drew folded the newspaper and put it down on the table.

"They should be back next Monday. Remember, you gave them the week off." Amy divided the eggs three ways and Maggie poured herself a diet cola to start the day as Amy and Drew sipped coffee.

"I'd like to take those toys over to Walter English to appraise, as Gussie suggested," said Amy. "I really don't want to keep any of them, except maybe the little woodstove. That's cute, and decorative. But I want our baby to have all new toys, bright and shiny. Who knows what germs old toys might carry?"

"That's fine with me. One more carton out of the attic, and a little extra money would be a help now. Fixing this house is costing a lot more than we'd thought, and we've only started." Drew put his cup down next to the newspaper. "It would be nice if the house would contribute a little to its own upkeep."

They all thought of the rifles under the bed upstairs.

"We knew when we moved here that it wouldn't be easy," said Amy.

"But we had no clue it would be this involved and expensive," said Drew. "Between your infertility treatments and the stock market decline, funding this move has not been simple."

A knock on the door interrupted that thought. Maybe it's Will, Maggie hoped.

It wasn't Will. It was Detective Strait, and his visit was not a social call. Will had helped smooth things the last time Strait had been here. There was no help now.

"Mr. and Mrs. Douglas, Ms. Summer. Sorry to disturb your breakfast, but I need to ask you all a few more questions."

"We'll help in whatever way we can," said Drew.

"It appears that Crystal was assaulted between three and four in the afternoon. None of you remembered when she left this house, but, considering where her body was found, she probably encountered her killer shortly after leaving here. I need you all to think back about what you were doing that afternoon."

"Brian and Giles Leary were here, too," said Amy.

"I've already talked with them. They say they left a little early that afternoon to pick up new supplies. Their story checks out. They were at the hardware store in Waymouth between three and three-thirty that afternoon."

"They could have stopped back here, to drop off whatever they'd bought."

"Could have, but didn't. They went over to help Mrs. Leary set up tables for a church supper."

A church supper, thought Maggie. Pretty good alibi. No wonder the detective was here. She, Drew, and Amy were apparently the only people on the premises when someone hit Amy on the head.

"What about a hitchhiker, or a biker, or someone just wandering through the area?" Drew asked.

"I've checked with everyone who lives in this neighborhood, and no outsider was seen. Although Crystal had been sexually active, there were no signs of sexual assault, so the sex was most likely consensual. And she carried no valuables. So we have no motive. Let's just go over the time frame again. Ms. Summer, you had just arrived in Madoc the day before."

"That's right."

"Had you any contact with or knowledge of the deceased young woman before you arrived?"

"I live in New Jersey and haven't even visited Maine for years. I hadn't heard of Crystal until I arrived here and Amy introduced her."

"And what did Mrs. Douglas say?"

"She just said, 'Crystal, this is Maggie, a college friend of mine. Maggie, Crystal's helping me with some things in the house this summer.'"

"So you assumed she was a maid of some sort?"

"Not a maid exactly. A teenager earning some extra dollars. She was working in the kitchen when I saw her. But she and Amy—Mrs. Douglas—seemed to have an informal, friendly relationship. I didn't think much about it."

"And when did you next see Ms. Porter?"

"Not until the next day."

"In the morning?"

"No. She wasn't here, or at least I didn't see her, at breakfast time. I left the house and went to an auction preview, and then had lunch with a friend."

"That friend being?"

"Will Brewer."

"And when you returned from your lunch?"

Ouch. Maggie couldn't see a way out of this. Even Gussie would not have anticipated a detective's cross-examination being the way she'd tell Drew and Amy what she knew. "I walked in the house. The kitchen door was unlocked."

"And where were Mr. and Mrs. Douglas and Crystal?"

"I assumed Amy wasn't home; her car wasn't in the driveway. There was no one in the kitchen."

"And?"

"I went upstairs to my room to lie down. I hadn't slept well the night before."

"Did you see Mr. Douglas or Ms. Porter anywhere?"

Amy was sipping her coffee. Drew was listening closely. Did he have any idea of what she'd seen? Had he heard her steps on the stairs? "Yes. I saw them."

"Where were they?"

"In the master bedroom."

"And what were they doing in the master bedroom?"

Maggie hesitated a moment and then knew she had to say it. "They were having sex."

Chapter 27

—⁓—

Fulmar Petrel, adult and young, 1826 hand-colored engraving by Prideaux John Selby (1788–1867), British painter and member of the Royal Society of Edinburgh, who painted natural history subjects. Birds on rocks by sea; icebergs in distance. 15.5 x 22 inches. Price: $975.

Will stood outside the door, a grin on his face and a crowbar in his hand. "Morning, Maggie. Hope I'm not too early. Drew and I thought we'd do some work on the kitchen this morning." Detective Strait appeared behind Maggie.

"Will, I need to question Mr. and Mrs. Douglas about some details connected with Crystal Porter's murder. I think, Ms. Summer, that I won't have any other questions for you just now. But don't go too far away."

Maggie walked out into the yard as Will put the crowbar down by the door.

"What was happening in there? You look as pale as one of those ghosts Amy says she's seen."

Maggie took Will's arm and headed him farther out into the yard, where they couldn't be overheard. "I may just have told your friend Nick Strait something that would give Amy or Drew a motive to kill Crystal."

"You told him Drew and Crystal were sleeping together."

"He was asking me moment by moment when I'd seen Crystal, and I couldn't lie. Will, it was horrible."

Will put his arms around Maggie. She leaned into him, wishing everything in life were as simple as this moment. She wished they could stand that way forever.

Will broke the embrace. "You had to tell the truth, Maggie. You did the right thing."

"But I should have let Drew or Amy or both of them know ahead of time. To blurt it out in front of a detective! How can I face them again? I just want to get in my van and drive to Timbuktu."

"Last time I checked there was an ocean between us and Timbuktu. Besides, I think I heard Nick asking you to stick around."

"He did."

"Do you really believe Amy or Drew killed Crystal?"

"I can't think that! But your friend Nick sounded as though he was out of suspects. He's looking for someone who had a motive."

"And you gave each of them one."

"Right! Amy could be jealous; Drew could be covering an affair."

They both looked back at the house.

"I suspect there are some very interesting conversations going on in there right now."

"Oh, Will. This is horrible."

"What Drew did was horrible." Will's voice was no longer gentle. "How could he possibly justify taking advantage of a young girl who was working in his own home? There is no way he didn't know that what he was doing was wrong. And now Crystal is dead. I don't know whether that's his fault, Maggie, but Drew ought to be punished in some way no matter what. He did an unforgivable thing." Will's anger was real.

Was he thinking that Drew could have been sleeping with his daughter? Maggie pushed some hair out of her face and wished she could as easily push this whole situation far, far away. They walked several steps farther away from the house, looking over the road toward the river. The water was a brilliant blue and wind was blowing the tops of the waves into small whitecaps. How could life be so complicated and still so beautiful? "What can we do?"

"We can think about something else. Were you able to get in touch with your friend who might know about those rifles?"

"Yes. The serial numbers match. Assuming that no one went to the trouble not only to reproduce rifles and serial numbers, but also to hide them in old material in the attic of an old house, those five rifles were among the two thousand purchased by the Army of the Potomac and issued to Colonel Hiram Berdan's First and Second Regiments of United States sharpshooters in 1862. But it turned out that serial numbers aren't always as easy to document as I'd thought. The key is that the rifles have *JT* stamped on their buttstocks. That meant John Taylor, the army inspector for that period, had checked them. Other initials would mean one of his civilian employees had checked them. John Taylor personally inspected those key two thousand rifles."

Will inhaled. "So they're as valuable as we suspected?"

"My friend wouldn't even guess at a figure. Auctions are unpredictable, and they'd have to be authenticated by an expert in antique American firearms first. But they definitely are valuable rifles. The mystery is how they got into this attic."

"Not a mystery, Maggie. I asked Aunt Nettie about it last night. She said three Brewer men fought in the Civil War. Two came back. One was a sharpshooter."

"But how could he bring back weapons in unused condition . . ."

"We'll probably never know. And I'm not sure I want to know, considering that it is an ancestor of mine who did the deed, and knowing the Union shortage of Sharps rifles."

"What did Aunt Nettie think?"

"She was embarrassed for the family, of course. Said she hoped Amy and Drew wouldn't publicize the find. Although whether they go to Walter English Auctions in Waymouth, or to Sotheby's in New York, this sort of find is going to be covered at least by the antiques press and the Civil War publications, and quite possibly by the mainstream media. Hidden rifles like those pictured in a famous Winslow Homer painting: it's too good a story to be ignored."

Maggie nodded. "You're right. And I assume Amy and Drew will want to sell the rifles, so I'm sorry for your family, Will."

"All families have parts of their history they'd like to forget. The Brewers will survive. The real mystery is who else knows about the rifles."

"You really think someone was there and found them before we did, don't you?"

"The more I thought about it last night, the more I was sure."

Maggie walked a few more steps. "I think I know how we could find out, Will. But with everything that's happening here now, I'd like to wait. We've hidden the rifles. There are so many other issues that seem more important." She looked back toward the house in time to see Detective Strait driving away.

"At least he didn't take either of your friends away in handcuffs, Maggie."

"How can you joke about something like that?"

Will looked down at her. "I know Nick Strait. I wasn't joking."

Chapter 28

———✍———

The American Tar: "Don't Give Up the Ship," 1845
hand-colored lithograph by N. Currier. Classic image of
American sailor in short navy wool jacket and middy
shirt with scarf, seated on sea chest; cannon, American
flag, and sailing vessel in background. Captain James
Lawrence's dying words to the crew of his ship, captured
by the British in 1813, became the rallying cry of the
U.S. Navy. 8.8 x 11.14 inches. Price: $400.

Will and Maggie walked slowly back toward the house. Neither of them was in a hurry to see Amy or Drew.

"Will! I'm glad you came," Amy greeted them, as they walked into the kitchen. "You're just in time to join us for a cup of coffee."

"Morning, Will," Drew added. "Another beautiful day."

Will and Maggie exchanged glances. Where was the hysteria and anger they had imagined they'd find here?

"A cup of coffee would be great," said Will cautiously. "Maggie was just telling me that she'd reached her friend who knows firearms."

"And?" asked Drew.

"He thinks yours sound legitimate. But without seeing them he couldn't be absolutely positive."

"Great!" said Drew. "Maybe we just paid for the roof and could have some plastering done inside."

"And new wallpaper for another bedroom," added Amy, as she handed Will his coffee. "You don't take sugar, right?"

"Just milk, thank you." He accepted the cup and poured some milk from the pitcher on the table. "But to handle the rifles the right way you'll need to have them authenticated. If I were you, I'd call Sotheby's in New York, tell them the story, and ask if they would handle them. They have experts on call in all areas, and the publicity they could generate would be good for the sale price."

"I'll have to go back to the city in a couple of weeks. Maybe I could take one down," said Drew.

"Check with your airline. I don't think anyone would be enthused about your flying with a rifle, even one from the nineteenth century, and you wouldn't want one damaged in checked luggage."

"I'll call Sotheby's and ask them what they'd suggest."

"Good idea."

Maggie sipped some cola she'd left at her place and reached for a piece of toast. Wasn't anyone going to say anything about what had happened? This was almost worse than being thrown out of the house. Amy was always in control, but Drew too? Maybe they didn't think Maggie would have shared what she knew with Will, and they were just waiting until he left to let her know what they felt. Maybe she should pack her suitcase now.

"I brought my crowbar over this morning. In case you decide we should go ahead and try to uncover your hearth and fireplace." Will hesitated. "I know this might not be the best time, but I would love to help. And I'll only be in Maine a few more days."

Maggie looked at him. She was sure he'd said he'd be in Maine another ten days to two weeks.

"I had planned to stay longer, but last night I got a call asking if I'd replace a dealer in a Rochester show next week. It's a show I've been wanting to get into, so I couldn't say no."

Amy beamed. "Then let's go for it! I'm dying to know what's under the linoleum and behind that wall, and you know more about what we'll be getting involved with than anyone. I'd like to have you here when we make the grand attempt."

"I'm afraid I won't be as much help to you as I'd hoped, though." Drew grimaced at his leg. "The pain isn't as bad today, but this cast is pretty limiting."

"Maggie and I can pull down plaster," said Amy. "Be a great way to get out anger and aggression!"

Maggie winced, but Amy didn't look at her.

"Besides the crowbar, we could use any long chisels you might have, or screwdrivers, and hammers," suggested Will. "We're going to make a mess. Do you have a small vacuum cleaner? Probably we should close off the rest of the house so the dirt stays in the kitchen. Some duct tape and several garbage bags would do that if we tape them over the door frame."

Maggie looked around. "Before we do anything, we need to clean up this kitchen and get any food far away from the dust."

"The refrigerator," agreed Amy. "Let's put anything open,

even the boxes of crackers or cereal in the cabinets, into the refrigerator."

"All our hammers, chisels, and screwdrivers are on the workbench in the barn," Drew said.

"I'll find them." Will headed out toward the barn.

By the time Will had returned the women had cleared away the food. Amy had moved a vase full of dried flowers to the dining room. "Can you imagine what these flowers would look like covered in plaster dust?"

They pulled Amy's office chair from her study for Drew, and he propped his leg on one of the kitchen chairs.

Will examined the floor and wall, tapping it, measuring, then checking both the wall and floor with a level. "The level was a ridiculous idea," he said. "Everything in a house this age is uneven."

Drew agreed. "Half our furniture has at least two of its legs propped up by little pieces of wood."

"Or paperback books, for now," said Amy. "And every time the wind blows hard across the river my lipsticks roll off the dresser."

"More little blocks of wood," said Will. "And don't do it by eye. Use a level. It's the only way you can really see just how different in height the boards in the floor are. This house has wonderful wide pine boards, but most weren't cut to precision thickness, and some have warped over the years. Not to speak of the general settling that happens in any structure. Or the buckling in the plaster." He ran his hand across the wall Aunt Nettie had said hid the fireplace. "This house was well made. And it has already lasted through two hundred Maine winters and summers and a move across the river. It will no doubt survive today's attempts to bring back the past."

Maggie watched as Will checked and measured one more

time. Finally he said, "We should take up the linoleum first, because it went down last. We'll see how easily we can remove it before we decide whether we should do the whole room or just this corner."

They all seemed totally engrossed, thought Maggie. Was it possible that a detective had been here an hour before, questioning them about a murder and adultery? Where were the shouting, screams, tears, and recriminations? Instead, Will was handing a chisel and hammer to Amy. They were going to take up linoleum.

The seventy-year-old linoleum was brittle; so brittle it broke off easily in irregular chunks. Below it, seventy years of dust had settled through the seams and edges of the flooring. Amy, Will, and Maggie were down on their hands and knees. Amy and Maggie both wore latex gloves that Amy kept in her kitchen, and Amy had tied a silk scarf around her face, but she was still sneezing. Drew supplied the required tissues.

Below the linoleum and the dust were pine boards, as Will had predicted. They used their screwdrivers and chisels as gently as possible, sliding them beneath the linoleum with the help of a hammer when necessary, then raising the linoleum until it chipped off. The work went so well that they decided to finish the entire kitchen floor. That meant a break to move out the kitchen table and chairs, and a related decision to leave the linoleum as it was below the old appliances. "We can take up those pieces when we get new appliances," said Amy. "We have enough work already clearing the floor."

About every twenty minutes Amy would decide she had to breathe fresh air and would stand by the door for a moment, or work vacuum cleaner duty, trying to pull out some of the dust deeply embedded in the pine floor's grain.

"Just get as much dirt as you can," Will said. "When we take down that wall we're going to cover everything with plaster dust and soot, unless they totally closed off the flue in 1833 and it has stayed closed." Will stood up and stretched. "That is highly unlikely."

It was noon before they finished.

"I'm not sure this would be termed 'finished' by a contractor," said Maggie, laughing, as they all stood back to admire their handiwork and sipped from cans of bottled water or cola that had been in the refrigerator, safely out of reach of the dust.

"If Johnny Brent's crew said this was 'finished,' I think we'd have a little discussion about payment terms," said Amy.

What had been the linoleum was now tied up in nine heavy-duty garbage bags. Except for the pieces left under the refrigerator and stove, the 1930s flooring was gone. What was left was an unevenly colored pine floor. The floor had been vacuumed half a dozen times but the air was still colored with dust, and it was settling on everything.

"Just as we predicted," said Drew. "Thank goodness you put the food away."

"And I don't want to take any out right now," said Amy. "We need a break, and we need some lunch." She grinned as she looked at everyone. "And look at us! I was going to suggest we go out somewhere, or at least go and get something and bring it back, but we're all covered with dust." As if to confirm her point, Amy sneezed.

"Hello? Anyone home?"

"We're in the kitchen," yelled Drew in the general direction of the porch. Whoever had arrived was coming in that way.

"All right if I join you? Just thought I'd meander over

with these Civil War books you wanted, and find out if you were resting." Tom Colby stood in the doorway and looked around the kitchen in surprise.

"Thanks. And you're welcome to join us. If you dare." Drew grinned. His black hair and eyebrows were now brown with dust.

Tom just stared. "Are you folks taking the house apart?"

"Just looks that way, Tom. We got rid of the old linoleum." Drew spun around on Amy's swivel chair. His leg dragged on the floor and created a small spray of dust in its wake.

"Yup. I figured that out," said Tom. "What're you goin' to do now? Take a group shower, or just hose everything down?"

"Sounds like two good ideas, Tom!" Amy tried to laugh, but started sneezing again.

"Actually, we were just trying to figure out how to get lunch without having to either take showers or get dust on the lunch."

"That's a problem," said Tom.

"We could just take bread and cold cuts out on the porch," suggested Amy, her voice emerging from the tissues she was holding near her face.

"Or one of us could shower and go back for some more of that fried food," said Maggie. "Although I'm not sure fried food twice in two days is optimal."

No one seemed too excited by either of those ideas.

"This is one of those moments I miss New York," said Drew. "Take-out places! Delivery!"

"We've got most everything New York has right here," said Tom with a quiet smile.

"How about pizza delivery? That's something I haven't heard of up here."

"Yup. We got it."

Amy looked at Tom. "From where? I don't remember seeing a pizzeria within ten miles!"

"No pizzeria. Just pizza. You call Annie Wilde. She'll do it up, and her boy, Clyde, he'll bring it to you."

"And where is this Annie Wilde's restaurant?"

"No restaurant. Just Annie's house. She's up on Heron Point. If someone were to call her, it'd probably take forty-five minutes for the pizza to arrive. She does 'em up to order, and that takes a bit of time."

They all exchanged glances. It was unanimous.

"Pizza!"

Chapter 29

———

Untitled. Print of anonymous nineteenth-century
woman. N. Currier hand-colored lithograph, 1846.
Woman in simple off-the-shoulder dress; ribbons in dress
and woman's eyes are blue; otherwise, print is black and
white. 9 x 12.5 inches. Price: $95.

Tom voted himself a member of the demolition team as they
sat on the porch breathing fresh salt breezes into their dusty
lungs and devouring the best pizza Maggie had eaten in
years.

"Annie makes her own tomato sauce of course, out of her
garden, and the cheese is from Amos Dodge's farm over to
Warren. Fresh vegetables from over to Skillins's garden
stand. Pretty good stuff." Tom was obviously enjoying the
appreciation of these folks from the big city who were
amazed to find pizza this good four hundred miles north of

New York. "You can find just about anything in the state of Maine, you know. You just got to know where to look."

Amy and Tom started talking about the very best place to get home-baked Italian bread, while Will leaned over toward Maggie. "Pretty cool friends of yours, considering the circumstances. I thought I might have to run a rescue mission and find you a bed at Aunt Nettie's." He leered with a wink. "Course, that wouldn't be a problem except for Aunt Nettie, you understand."

"I have no clue what is happening," Maggie whispered back, hiding behind the pizza slice covered with fresh tomato and mushroom slices and Italian olives. "But we are making progress on the kitchen, if not on crime detecting."

"This is more my style anyway," Will said. "Antiques. Construction. History. Pizza. All areas I feel some sense of control over. Why is it that when I see you people seem to get themselves murdered?"

"You're exaggerating. No one was murdered the day we went to the exhibit at the Metropolitan," Maggie pointed out.

"True. Good point." Will's blue eyes twinkled as he looked down at Maggie's dust-covered hair and body. "Hope they've got a good deep well. We haven't even started on the wall, and look at us. Long showers are going to be in order later today."

"At least you and Tom will be on separate wells," said Maggie. Truth be told, she had about used up her energy for old-house improvements today. She would have enjoyed taking that shower right now and then settling back on this porch with a book. But the group consensus was definitely in favor of finding the old fireplace.

"If Aunt Nettie said it was there," Tom said for about the third time, "it must be there. Aunt Nettie knows this house and its history and the Brewer family better than anyone else. Be something if it really is behind that wall, and been there all these years. It would have been the fireplace used when the house was first built over on the island."

"Right, 1774," said Drew. "I wonder what condition the bricks will be in after all these years? They could have crumbled into nothing."

"Or be in pristine shape. No way to tell until we take that wall down." Will rose and made a minor attempt to wipe dust and pizza crumbs off his beard with a couple of paper napkins. "Pizza's gone, and I'm ready. Anyone care to join me?"

Amy had brought out paper plates and lunch was cleaned up quickly with the help of another garbage bag. By the time everyone had made some attempt to wash up, Will was standing in front of the wall with a chisel and hammer.

Amy had covered her nose again. The first gentle taps of the hammer brought down powdery plaster. And then more plaster. And more. Chunks fell easily, as the old mixture of powdered clams and oyster shells, water, and sand crumbled. After a few minutes Amy had to leave the room. The heavy dust filled the air. Tom happily joined Will at the wall, while Maggie chased after both of them with a whisk broom and dustpan, trying to get at least the larger pieces of plaster into garbage bags before the dust invaded the whole house.

Within minutes it was clear Aunt Nettie had been right. The plaster coated thin strips of lath. Behind the lath was a brick wall.

Drew kept out of the way and joined Amy on the porch when he realized plaster dust was seeping into both the top and bottom of his cast. The doctor would probably not be thrilled.

Will handed Maggie a small saw and she started cutting away the lath. It was soon clear that one of the issues was how much plaster and lath to cut. They made a rough vertical line just beyond what might be the mantel: a smoke-stained, two-inch-deep board set into the middle of the wall. Above the mantel the fireplace flue tiered to the ceiling and beyond, but the brick wall continued in back of it. Below the mantel, plaster dust was only the beginning of the dirt problem. Over the roughly 170 years since the lath and plaster had closed up the fireplace, soot, dirt, and anything else that had come down the flue had piled up. Rain and snow had bonded the dirt and soot to some degree, but piles of that black mixture, chimney plaster, and the occasional bones of a dead bird or bat that had fallen down the chimney now poured out onto the kitchen floor.

"Stay away!" called Maggie, as Amy peeked her head around the corner. "You do have a fireplace here. The bricks are filthy, but in great condition, but there's a little problem with soot."

Amy ducked back out.

"You're going to have a terrific kitchen!" yelled Maggie after her. "Someday!"

Will and Maggie and Tom, now covered in layers of brown dirt, gray plaster dust, and black soot, took turns trying to scoop up the debris, which kept coming.

"How far up in the chimney was this stuff piled?" asked Tom, shaking his head. "This is the dirt of the ages."

"Exactly," agreed Will, whose hair and beard and face were now blacker than the crows who were complaining about the lack of seeds at the feeder outside. "One hundred and seventy years of dirt. Even at one inch a year . . ."

"One hundred and seventy inches of this?" Tom shook his head, shaking some of the soot from his body. "It's going to be impossible to get all this stuff up. And it's sinking into the floor. They'll never get that floor clean again."

"It will have to be power scrubbed and then sanded," agreed Will. "Gently, because it's pine. But the floor we uncovered is a different color from the boards in the rest of the house in any case, so Amy and Drew will have to decide whether they'll stain them all to match, or be authentic and paint them all a dark color."

"Oh, they shouldn't paint these boards!" said Maggie.

"In the nineteenth century people did. Brown, mostly. And then put braided or hooked rugs or Oriental carpets on top of them. Helped keep the dust down and the breezes out."

Twenty-three garbage bags were now filled and ready for the dump. The last few were heavy enough that it took two of them to lift the bags and get them out of the kitchen and into the yard.

Finally the flow from the chimney was beginning to slow. Maggie held up a hand. "Stop! I hereby declare a major break! I have got to have something to drink to wash this stuff in my throat down, and Amy and Drew have to come in to see what we've found!"

"Thank you, lady!" Tom hesitated not a moment before putting down the garbage bag he was filling and leaning against the wall. "Is there any beer?"

"There was some yesterday," Will said. His black fingers left distinctive marks on the refrigerator door as he handed Maggie a diet cola and took out beers for Tom and himself.

If Will were a suspect in anything, those fingerprints would be great evidence, thought Maggie. This didn't seem the moment to say that out loud.

"Amy! Drew! Come look!"

Amy and Drew had been sitting on the porch, frustrated

that they couldn't be more of the process. Amy had gotten a long sock and pulled it over Drew's cast to protect his foot from any more dirt. He limped in after her and Maggie pulled up a chair for him.

"Wow." Amy looked at the fireplace. It was intact, and real, and large enough to sit inside, should someone have wanted to crouch on top of the soot that was still sifting down like soft black snow flurries. "It's gorgeous!"

"It will be," agreed Will happily. "Once it's all cleaned up, and you furnish it with some great colonial kitchen copper and iron pots. And I think there is a real treasure back here. I wanted to wait until the owners of this estate were present to confirm, but I've kept my eye on a line in the back of the fireplace."

He reached in through the dirt and grime and pulled out a triangular-shaped piece of iron, thick with soot. "I was right! Whichever Brewer closed up this fireplace was either smart or lazy. And you're the beneficiaries."

Silence.

"See? It's the original crane!"

"Wow!" said Amy. "And it fit into the fireplace?"

"Absolutely. Blacksmiths made these beauties to order when someone was building a house. You never see them outside of their original locations because there would be no reason to take them. If this hadn't been left in the fireplace, you would have had to pay a blacksmith big bucks to make one that would fit, and, of course, it wouldn't have been authentic." Will looked at the dirty piece of triangular-shaped iron in his hand appraisingly. "A nice job too. Fine smithing." He smiled softly. "And one of my ancestors commissioned this piece, and my family ate food cooked in pots hung on this crane back in the 1780s and '90s."

Tom took it from Will, and they exchanged a glance. They were both Brewers. This was a Brewer fireplace. And they had uncovered it. It was a moment of shared pride.

"As soon as it's cleaned up, we must invite Aunt Nettie back to show her," said Amy.

"She'll be very pleased," Will said.

"Could anything else be in the fireplace besides the dirt?" asked Amy.

"A *lot* of dirt," said Maggie. "Incredible how much dirt."

"Well," Will said. "Sometimes there were hooks up in the chimney above the fireplace, where bacon or ham could be hung to cure. They would have been mortared in, so it's possible there might still be one."

Will got into the fireplace with a flashlight in his hand. His jeans would never be the same, Maggie thought. He bent over and then peered up the flue. "No hook. They either didn't have one, or took it out, or at some point it fell out." He turned the light slowly from one side of the chimney to the other. "But there is something up here." Carefully he reached, pushing his big body up the chimney opening.

I hope he doesn't get stuck, Maggie thought. Santa Claus he isn't. His beard was now black.

"There's a brick shelf." Will's voice echoed a bit. "Just a minute. Almost." He pulled himself out of the fireplace. In one hand was the flashlight; in the other, a wooden box a little bigger than a man's-shoe box. "Someone left this up there. Sometimes there were hiding places in these old kitchens. Or niches where they might put a ham to smoke. I've never heard of putting a wooden box in a chimney, though. It would have burned."

"Unless someone put it there just before they closed off the fireplace. They'd know there would be no fires then."

"True."

"Maybe the family put together a time capsule of items that were significant to them in, when was it? About 1833."

"Or maybe a woman in the family hid her jewelry here, or her silver."

"Or her love letters," put in Amy.

"And no one knew, and they sealed up the fireplace."

They all stood, looking at Will holding the box. It was filthy and, despite some of the soot falling off as Will moved it, certainly still an inch deep in dirt. He took his hand and wiped most of it away. "I suspect these aren't diamonds or, sorry, it was emeralds you desired, right, my lady Amy?"

She smiled at him and bowed in response.

"But whatever treasures this box contains are yours by right of ownership."

Nice touch, thought Maggie. Since Will and Tom were the two people in the room who had any claim other than possession to whatever might be in the box.

Will handed the box to Amy. She took it carefully and, kneeling in the dirt and plaster that still covered the floor, put it down. Her light brown eyes shone with excitement as she carefully located and then cleaned off a small tarnished brass latch. The box opened easily. Everyone leaned in to see what treasures it might contain.

Inside, wrapped in what might once have been a piece of blanket, was the skeleton of a baby.

Chapter 30

—~~—

The Praying Mantis, *E. J. Detmold illustration for*
Fabre's Book of Insects, *1921, New York (translation
of* Fabre's Souvenirs Entomologiques*). Delicate pastel
rendering of elegantly posed mantis. Frame border.
6 x 7 inches. Price: $65.*

"Oh, my God," Amy gasped. She pushed the box away from
her but still stared in horror. "My God."

"It's a little coffin," Tom said quietly.

"But who is it?" Drew asked. "Why would anyone put a
baby's body in a chimney flue?"

They were all silent. Maggie reached over and put the
cover back on the box. "Someone who was scared. Someone
who was hiding something. Someone who was angry. There
are so many reasons why. And there are no reasons. We'll
never know."

Amy started crying, a few tears slowly making their way through the dust on her face. She started sneezing again.

A heavy knock on the door brought them all out of their thoughts. Tom was closest to the door.

"Tom! Didn't expect to find you here. Just had a few more questions to . . ." Detective Strait walked in the room. "What happened here?"

Maggie rubbed at her wrist to brush the soot off her watch. It was eight hours since the detective had left them this morning.

"We found the old fireplace," said Drew quietly.

"So I can see." Detective Strait walked closer to check out the details, his large shoes leaving deep footprints in the soot. "Even the hearth is still intact. Very impressive." He looked at them all. "And you did this all just today?"

Tom nodded. "I don't suppose," he said quietly, looking at the others in the room, "I don't suppose the police would be interested in a body we found?"

Detective Strait turned around quickly. "What did you say?"

"Nick, it's nothing," said Will. "Nothing in your department, anyway." Will picked up the box and carefully removed the cover and showed the contents to Nick.

"You found . . . that?"

"On a shelf inside the fireplace flue. It must have been there since the fireplace was closed up in about 1833."

"You're right. Out of my jurisdiction." Detective Strait reached out a finger toward the tiny skull, then pulled his hand back. "Will, you and Tom are Brewers. I'm assuming this child must be too. You'll be taking care of it?"

"I guess."

"I don't think it's necessary to report this officially. For the family's sake."

"We'll need to bury it, sure," said Tom. "Have a nice ceremony. Put it in the family plot up at the old cemetery at Spruce Point."

"The body is a baby. Not an 'it.'" said Maggie. "The child deserves a proper burial." Her mind was a whirr of dirt and grime and faces of unwanted children. Someone had loved this child enough to try to keep him safe. She shuddered slightly, not even wanting to voice the possibility that the baby had been alive when the box had been put in the fireplace. That would have made even less sense. The infant had died and for some reason had not been buried. Instead, he or she had been entombed in this house. Soot must have gotten into Maggie's eye. She found herself blinking, then tearing up.

Will took charge. "Nick, it's late. And"—he gestured toward the box—"there's been a death in the family. Is it critical that your questions be asked now? Because if they can wait until tomorrow, I think it would give us time to get cleaned up, and to notify the rest of the family."

Nick nodded and took off his hat in respect. "That'll be all right, Will. Questions can wait. Sorry about . . . what you found." He started toward the door. "But I will have to talk with you all tomorrow morning." He looked over at Tom. "You too, Tom. Just verifying some times and places."

"Tomorrow morning will be fine, Detective," said Amy. "Thank you for understanding."

"Tomorrow morning at eight."

"We'll all be here."

"Not Will. I don't need him. But the rest of you."

Detective Strait put his hat on and walked out the door.

"What are we going to do now?" asked Drew.

"I am going to go home and talk with Aunt Nettie and tell her what happened," said Will calmly. Still in charge. "She's active in the church. She'll know whom to call."

"I'll go home and tell Shirley, and then I'll call the rest of the family," Tom said. "I need to get cleaned up too."

"Tom, do you know the person to call at the cemetery?" Will was already planning.

"Yup. I worked with the Spruce Point committee last fall, cleaning up some graves."

"Let's do it quickly. Not too many people involved. No press."

"Right. Just the family. That's what's right," Tom said.

"What . . . what should we do with . . . it . . . now?" Drew hesitated, looking at Amy, who was still crying quietly.

Maggie suddenly wanted to reach out, to claim the child. She would keep the box in her room, even for just the night. But it was Amy's house and Will's relative. It was not her place to say. There were people to claim this child now. A family to be called.

"I'll take the child," said Will. "I'll take him to Aunt Nettie." He held the box gently with both his hands. "See what you can arrange for tomorrow afternoon, Tom."

Chapter 31

—⟡—

Untitled. Wooden toy soldiers. From folio by Roberta Samsour titled Czechoslovakian Folk Toys, *printed in Prague, 1941. 8.5 x 10 inches. Price: $60.*

Will and Tom had taken the stacks of garbage bags out to the barn before they left. Amy and Maggie cleaned up the kitchen as well as they could and decided to drive to the local lobstermen's co-op for dinner.

Amy then announced that Maggie could not possibly stay in Maine one night longer unless she had eaten lobster. And the lobster at the co-op was the best: caught that day and steamed to order, with all the traditional accompaniments— steamed clams, potatoes, corn, blueberry pie, and salad.

"Sounds wonderful," said Maggie, although she would really have preferred going straight to bed. She dreaded being alone with Amy and Drew. Right now she was just too tired to deal with their anger about her telling Detective Strait she had seen Crystal and Drew together. And Amy must be feeling twice that anger . . . there would never be good circumstances under which to hear your husband had been unfaithful. Maggie knew that from personal experience. But surely these particular circumstances were among the worst.

"You'll love it!" Amy said. "A great view of the harbor at sunset, and all the boats. Just put on your old jeans and a T-shirt, since eating lobster is messy!"

"Messy" seemed an understatement to describe this entire week.

Maggie stood in her room, conscious that she'd leave a mark if she sat anywhere. She hoped Amy wouldn't take long in the shower. Her skin felt gritty with dirt; her fingernails were black; and her long hair was tangled and stiff. The joys of restoring an old house.

Despite the way the day had begun, what a lot they had accomplished. And how beautiful the old fireplace would look after the dirt had settled and the bricks were carefully scoured.

Although Maggie knew she would never look at the fireplace without thinking of the box that had been hidden within it. Why would someone put a baby's body in a fireplace? It was the sort of thing a young, unmarried mother might have done. A young woman like Crystal.

Detective Strait would be back in the morning. A killer was still out there.

And Will and Tom were planning a funeral for a child who had died perhaps 170 years ago. Maggie's thoughts blurred together. When would Crystal's funeral be? Had the medical examiner released her body yet?

"Maggie? Your turn in the bathroom!" Amy's tap on the

door brought Maggie back to the moment. Everything would look clearer after a hot shower.

They ordered their lobsters, collected three bottles of Shipyard ale, and sat on the rough, weathered, gray picnic tables overlooking the harbor, waiting for their number to be called. "Just one bottle for me, since I'm driving, and one for you, Drew, so you can take that pain medication to help you sleep tonight. But Maggie can have all she wants!" Amy was organizing everyone, as usual. Still no talk about what had happened that morning.

Maggie looked out over the harbor. Did Amy think giving her permission to drink meant Maggie would down half a dozen ales? Amy did like people to do as she directed.

The sun was low, its reflection orange on the now dark blue waters of the harbor. A large sailboat was just coming into dock on the far side of the protected water. Several large cruisers were anchored closer by, along with an assortment of smaller vessels, and perhaps a dozen lobster boats. A young couple in a purple canoe paddled by the dock where Amy, Drew, and Maggie sat among tourists and locals, waiting for their lobsters. A herring gull perched on a railing, watching to see if he could scrounge his dinner. A large hand-painted sign next to him read, "Beware of gulls! Protect your food!" A mother chased a toddler away from the railing.

Amy was the one to break the silence. "Maggie, I know what you're thinking. About what you told the detective this morning. But it's all right. Truly. Drew and I have some issues . . ." Amy shot a sidelong glance at Drew, who was looking out at the harbor and ignoring them both. "But we're going to be fine. Our marriage is too strong to be hurt by a little thing like adultery. Drew and I have the same goals, and working toward them together is what is keeping us together." She reached over and patted Drew's hand.

Maggie just looked at her. A little thing like adultery? It hadn't seemed like such a little thing when it had been her husband who was sleeping around. How could Amy say something like that?

"Just enjoy your lobster, and let's not talk about it again. We'll all just pretend it never happened."

No one else said anything. Perhaps there was too much to say to even begin. Amy stretched her shoulders and Maggie flexed her hands. She ached all over. Starting with her head.

"Thirteen!"

"Our number!" Amy and Maggie rose together to retrieve their dinners. Tonight thirteen was a lucky number; the lobsters were steamed to perfection, the clams were sweet, the corn and potatoes done just right. And all was served with plastic cups of melted butter, and piles of paper napkins. They happily dug in, and Maggie found she was hungrier than she had thought. She wished Will were with them.

But Will was planning a funeral.

By the time the beer and lobster and corn were gone and the blueberry pie had all but disappeared, they had all revived. "We still haven't looked at your prints, Maggie," Amy said. "Why don't we do that when we get home? I'm not ready for bed, and we seem to find other things to do during the day."

Wasn't that the truth.

Back at home Maggie pulled over the portfolios she had brought in from the car only yesterday. "I brought in the Winslow Homer wood engravings. This portfolio is full of his Civil War prints, done about the same time as his *Sharp-shooter*, which we looked at yesterday." Rifles, Maggie reminded herself. She needed to check something about rifles. There had been no time today. "The other portfolios are of subjects not related to the war. Most were published in

Harper's Weekly, but some in other newspapers. He also did some smaller prints, for newspapers and book illustrations. I have those in a separate portfolio." She pointed at each of her bulging brown portfolios in turn. The portfolios were well used; the handles on one had torn off. Paper was heavy.

"What about those other portfolios?" asked Amy, pointing at the two other portfolios Maggie had brought in.

"One contains N. C. Wyeth's illustrations for Kenneth Roberts's *Trending into Maine,* that we mentioned the other day. And the other one has the Thomas Nast Christmas engravings we talked about." Maggie wasn't sure this was the time to mention that Amy had wanted to see the Nast picture of Santa Claus and a baby. But that was the one she remembered.

Amy remembered too. "Oh, please, let's look at the Nasts first. Christmas is such a happy time of year, and we could use some happiness today."

No argument there. Maggie got out the large portfolio and put a pile of matted wood engravings on the coffee table.

"You'll remember that the European St. Nicholas was rather a skinny fellow, with a long beard. No artist had depicted him as a round-faced, smiling Santa with a wide white beard until Thomas Nast. Nast actually was born in Germany, but he immigrated to New York with his family when he was six. When he was fifteen, he got his first job as an illustrator, working for *Leslie's Illustrated,* a popular newspaper. By the time he was twenty-two he was hired away by *Harper's Weekly* to be a Civil War correspondent."

"So he did the same sort of work Winslow Homer did?"

"They had the same employer and are the best known of the Civil War artists. But after the war they went in very different professional directions. Homer turned to painting and by 1874 was working full-time as an artist specializing in oils. Nast stayed with *Harper's Weekly*. Although his Christmas scenes were loved and are the most well known of this work today, Nast was famous in the nineteenth century as a searing political cartoonist. I did my doctoral thesis on his influence on New York politics from the late 1860s through the 1870s, especially the pressure his cartoons put on the New York City government, which eventually took down Boss Tweed. Among his other lasting contributions to American culture were symbolizing the Democratic party as a donkey, and the Republican party as an elephant, and picturing Uncle Sam. He was a real political power with a pen."

"Whew! But these"—Amy was looking through the prints Maggie had brought—"are just his Christmas prints."

"They're his most popular. I have some of his Civil War work and cartoons at home; I use the cartoons in one of my classes. Most people today are just interested in his Santas."

"They look familiar."

"Because they've been reprinted on everything from stickers to Christmas cards to coloring books."

Amy looked carefully, then handed the prints to Drew. "You know what strikes me as strange? In almost all of these Christmas pictures Nast has included toys that are symbols of war: drums, flags, toy soldiers, toy guns, bugles, and maybe I'm imagining, but even the wooden horse in one of these prints looks like the Trojan horse."

"Good catch! Why he did that I don't know; certainly those were popular boys' toys of the Civil War period, which is when he started drawing the Santas. And Nast was a great one for symbols," Maggie said. Amy looked over Drew's shoulder as he carefully examined the pile.

"Here's one in color! I thought they'd all be in black and white, like the Homers."

"They all were originally in black and white. But over the years some people have hand-colored the engravings. Those Victorian ladies who liked to color prints were much more apt to color Santas than they were to color Homers. Although I do occasionally see one of Homer's engravings that someone has colored."

"Are they worth more if they're colored, or if they're as they were originally meant to be?"

"Value is in the eyes of the beholder. Purists would never accept a colored print, but some collectors like the colored ones. It really is personal choice. And," Maggie added, "the skill of whoever hand-colored the engraving. I've seen some coloring that is much too bright, or just not in appropriate colors for the period. I wouldn't buy prints poorly colored, and I don't think my customers would want them. Hand-coloring, no matter when it was done, needs to be done well."

"Are you implying that some people are hand-coloring old prints today?" Amy looked up in amazement.

"I'm afraid so. No one needs to worry about the coloring on Currier and Ives prints, or on early botanicals or other natural history prints. Those prints were hand-colored as part of the production process before they were sold or bound into folios or books. The ones that people color today are engravings, like Nast's, that were in mid-nineteenth-century newspapers. Or occasionally steel engravings from earlier books. I would certainly never endorse coloring an old engraving. But some customers do like the Nasts colored. Maybe because all the reprints you see today, all those post-cards and Christmas cards, are in color. People expect Nast's originals to be in color too."

"So none of his original engravings are colored?"

"Not the ones that appeared in *Harper's Weekly*. In the

1880s and 1890s some of his Santa Clauses were reproduced as lithographs and printed as children's books by
McLaughlin Brothers, in Boston. Those lithographs are well
done. And they are in color."

"I love the one of the little girl talking to Santa on the old
telephone," said Amy. "And the patriotic Santa, with the
flag in back of him and the children."

Maggie looked over her shoulder. "Those were Nast's
own five children."

"And this one." Amy smiled. "This is the one you told me
about. Oh, look, Drew. Wouldn't this look wonderful in the
nursery?"

Maggie watched as Amy and Drew looked at a large print
of a chubby baby sleeping peacefully in a crib. A sprig of
holly lay on his blanket, and Santa Claus was smiling at him
through the bars of the crib. It was titled *Another Stocking
to Fill*. After all that had happened today . . . how could they
still be focused on filling that perfect room upstairs?

Drew leaned over and kissed Amy on the forehead. "I
think you've made a sale, Maggie. Although I really like the
telephone one too."

"It would look wonderful if we could find an old wall
telephone set to hang near it, wouldn't it?" Amy said.

"Well, when we do, then we'll call Maggie," said Drew.
"For now, one Santa Claus in the house is enough. But I
would like to see those Civil War Winslow Homers."

Maggie packed up her Nasts, leaving out the print Amy
and Drew had liked. They were still buying pictures for the
nursery? But she certainly wouldn't turn down a sale. And
the $350 price had been right on the mat.

Maggie pulled out the Civil War Winslow Homers. "You've
already seen the most famous of his Civil War engravings, *The
Sharp-shooter*. Most of Homer's war engravings are based on

events behind the lines: men lining up at the sutler's tent to buy supplies, the surgeon with wounded men, soldiers opening boxes for Christmas, soldiers playing football." As she spoke, Maggie handed them the prints she was describing.

"Football! I wouldn't have thought of that as a Civil War print!"

"Actually, football was developed as a sport by soldiers during the war. It wasn't an intercollegiate sport until 1869," said Maggie. "As far as I know, Homer's engraving of football in 1865 is the first one anyone did of that sport. In addition to his 'behind the lines' engravings, Homer did two other sorts of Civil War prints. There are two battle scenes." Maggie took them out and placed them side by side: *The War for the Union, 1862—A Cavalry Charge* and *The War for the Union, 1862—A Bayonet Charge.*

"Wow," said Drew, looking at them closely. "These are wonderful! Is the bayonet charge the Twentieth Maine's famous charge at Gettysburg?"

"No; that didn't happen until a year later. Both of Homer's prints were done as public relations for the Union side, to show the folks at home how well their forces were doing. Neither of the scenes is based on a specific battle. But they are realistic."

Amy pointed at the rifles pictured in *A Bayonet Charge.* "Are those the rifles we have, Drew?"

He looked closely. "Some might be. It's hard to tell."

"The battle scenes are wonderful, but I don't think I'd want them in the living room," said Amy.

"That's good, dear, because they're going in my study," replied Drew. "Put those in the pile with the Nast Santa and the baby, Maggie."

"What about the non–Civil War wood engravings?" Amy looked over at the other large portfolio they hadn't opened.

"There are some that would be especially appropriate for Maine." Maggie bent down and flipped through them quickly. "Here's one of my favorites: *August in the Country— The Seashore*. It's an early one, so not technically as strong as some of the later ones, but it's delightful." The print showed fully dressed women and children on the beach. An elegantly attired gentleman was trying (unsuccessfully) to scare the ladies by waving a lobster at them, while a plump little boy was angrily trying to remove a crab from his finger.

"You're right. I love that one. See the woman sketching on the dune?" Amy put that one aside.

"There are other beach scenes." Maggie pulled out *High Tide* and *Low Tide*. "This makes a good pair. And here's one that's hard to find because it wasn't published in *Harper's Weekly*—it was published in *Every Saturday*, which didn't have as wide a circulation. But I love it. It's called *A Winter- Morning: Shoveling Out*."

The print showed a small New England house with snow almost up to its roofline. Two men were digging a path through the deep snow with heavy wooden shovels, while a woman threw crusts and crumbs to some birds.

"I like that one too," said Amy. "Are there any maritime engravings? I always think of Homer as an artist of the sea."

"He didn't move to Maine and do his studies of the sea until after he had finished with his wood-engraving period," said Maggie. "Only three of his works from this period are at sea. *At Sea—Signaling a Passenger Steamer* is dark. I know it's a storm, but I don't care for it as much as some of his others. There is also *The Approach of the British Pirate Ship* Alabama, which focuses on the people on the ship, not on the sea. And *Homeward Bound*, showing the deck of a sailing vessel. He did that one on his way home from Paris, where he'd been studying for a few months."

"Yes," Drew and Amy said together.

Drew added, "Definitely that one. You can feel the spray, it's so realistic! I love the slanted deck and the elegant passengers."

"Now, before you decide, you should know about Winslow Homer's Gloucester Series," said Maggie. "Those are—next to *Snap-the-Whip*—his most popular wood engravings. Unfortunately I don't have all of them in stock. As soon as I get them, they sell. I even have a waiting list for *Dad's Coming*. That one shows a boy sitting on a beached dory. His mother and little sister stand near him, and they're all looking out to sea. *Gloucester Harbor,* shows a scene like the one we saw at dinner tonight: several boys in two skiffs, rowing through a harbor with two sailboats in back of them."

"Which do you have?"

"I have *Sea-Side Sketches: A Clambake,* and *Ship-Building, Gloucester Harbor.*" Maggie put them next to each other on the table.

"I understand these are the most popular, and I do like them, but I really like the winter scene and the one on the ship better," said Drew. "What do you think?" He looked at Amy.

She nodded. "I agree. I do want some Homers for the house, and those seem just right. For different rooms, I think. And you still want *A Cavalry Charge* and *A Bayonet Charge* for your study?"

"Definitely. And if I ever do become a history teacher, they would be wonderful for a Maine classroom, even if Joshua Chamberlain's victory was a year later."

"So write us up a bill, Maggie. I don't even want to look at the rest. You've just sold a Nast and four Homers."

As Amy went into her study to find her checkbook, Maggie put the unwanted prints back in her portfolios. Wow! Those purchases just paid for her trip to Maine, and then some: $325 each for the two battle scenes; $375 for *Homeward Bound,* plus $300 for *Shoveling Out.* Plus the $350 Nast. A total of $1,675.

"I'll give you guys ten percent off, and even it off, since you're friends," Maggie said, as she added it up. "That would bring the total to an even fifteen hundred dollars. You have some wonderful selections here. They'll look perfect on your walls. They look well matted in black or off-white, and I like gold frames, but that's your choice. Just make sure whoever does your framing mats them in acid-free boards. Most framers know to do that, but it never hurts to remind them. That will prevent any deterioration. And antireflective glass would be a protection too, if you're going to hang them anywhere near direct sunlight."

"What a day!" Amy wrote out the check and handed it to Maggie. "I've just about had it. And that detective fellow said he'd be coming at eight in the morning, didn't he?"

"He did. And then I think we'll have a funeral to attend in the afternoon." Drew pulled himself up on his crutches.

By the time Maggie crawled under the two light blankets she needed on this August night she was exhausted. But after fifteen minutes of tossing and turning she realized her body was tired, but her mind was still working. She switched on the lamp next to her bed and looked at the pile of adoption books and pictures on her floor. She picked up one book, thinking she might read for a while, but then her mind started on a path she didn't like following.

She didn't like it at all.

Chapter 32

Scene in Dearborn Street When the Fire Reached the Tremont House, *hand-colored wood engraving of the Great Chicago Fire, 1871. From* History of the Great Fire. *8.5 x 10.5 inches. Price: $65.*

Morning did not dawn bright or early. Madoc was faded by heavy billows of fog blowing across the river. It was not a morning to rise early, and no one did. Maggie had hardly started sipping her diet cola, the coffeepot was still dripping, and Amy hadn't even started her "to do" list for the day when Detective Strait arrived.

"I'd like to talk with each of you separately," he said. "You do realize you are all suspects in the murder of Crystal Porter. And I am also trying to establish a motive for the brakes on Mr. Douglas's car being cut."

"You can't believe Maggie or I would do that to Drew!" Amy said. "What possible reason would either of us have to hurt him! And, besides, either or both of us could easily have been in that car."

"That's why I need to talk with both of you, ma'am. Separately."

"You can talk with me first. Amy and Drew haven't even had their coffee yet," said Maggie. "Is the porch private enough?"

"That would be fine."

"Ms. Summer, how long have you known the Douglases?"

"I've known Amy since college. We were roommates. That was about sixteen years ago."

"And you've kept closely in touch with her since then?"

"We talk on the phone every few months, and perhaps once or twice a year we get together. Amy lived in New York City, and I live in New Jersey."

"And Mr. Douglas?"

"I met him once when I saw Amy in New York, and then at their wedding three years ago. I hadn't seen him since then until this week."

"As far as you can tell, as a close friend of Mrs. Douglas, do she and Mr. Douglas have a happy marriage?"

Maggie hesitated.

"In your opinion."

"They decided to move to Maine, and to start a new life. To have a family. Change is stressful. It puts pressure on a relationship."

"You sense stress in their relationship."

Did adultery fall under the heading of "stress"?

"I think they care a great deal about each other and are planning their future together. But, yes, there have been a lot of stresses in their lives recently—the move, their wanting to have a family, the fire, the phone calls—and now, of course, Crystal's murder." Maggie looked out toward the river. The pine trees were silhouetted in the fog like the ferns Victorian ladies pressed into their memory books.

"Did you talk with Crystal Porter while you were here?"

"Just to say 'hello,' and 'nice to meet you.'"

"How did she seem to you? Was she angry? Relaxed? Anxious?"

Maggie thought. "I didn't pay much attention. She seemed comfortable with Amy. On the afternoon I arrived, Amy told her she could go home early, and she said no, that she'd wait because Brian Leary was going to give her a ride home."

Detective Strait made some notes. "That was the day before the murder."

"The day before she disappeared. Yes."

"And could you tell me more about the circumstances in which you saw her on the day of the murder?"

She knew he'd want to go over that again, but Maggie hated the whole situation. "I had been out. When I drove in, I noticed Amy's car was not here, but Drew's was. I knocked on the back door but no one answered. It was unlocked, so I just walked in. I didn't see anyone. I decided to go to my room and lie down for a half hour or so." Maggie hesitated and then forged ahead. "As I was walking up the front steps, I heard noises."

"Voices?"

"More like sounds. I could see from the stairs that the door to the master bedroom was open. I thought Amy and Drew were in there and walked softly, so they wouldn't be disturbed or embarrassed."

"You walked by the open door."

"Yes."

"And you looked in?"

Maggie blushed. "Yes."

"And what did you see?"

"I saw Crystal's clothes on the floor, and Drew and Crystal on the bed. They were—making love." *Making love* wasn't the phrase Maggie wanted to use, but it was the one she was most comfortable saying to a detective.

"What did you do?"

"I was surprised. Shocked. I didn't want them to see me. I walked as quietly as I could to my room and closed the door."

"And what did you hear after that?"

"I didn't hear anything until Amy knocked on my door."

"And when was that?"

"Perhaps half an hour later."

"And she came into your room?"

"Yes. She was very relaxed. She said she'd been shopping and now had some paperwork to do; she'd be in her study for the next thirty minutes or so, and then maybe we could go for a walk." Maggie didn't mention that Amy had appeared to want her to stay in her room. Not yet. And Amy hadn't said that specifically.

"Did she say anything about her husband? Or about Crystal Porter?"

"She didn't mention either of them." Amazingly enough, Maggie added to herself.

"And did you tell your old college friend what you had seen while she was grocery shopping?"

"No. I didn't want to upset her, and I really didn't know what to say. I didn't say anything."

"And the last time you saw Crystal was when she was in the master bedroom with Mr. Douglas."

"Yes."

"Did you stay in your room for the thirty minutes?"

"Closer to forty. I wanted Amy to have the quiet time she needed."

"And when you came downstairs, where was Mr. Douglas?"

"I didn't see him. I assumed he was in his study, or on the porch."

"But you don't know for sure where he was."

"No."

"And Mrs. Douglas?"

"She was in her study. She put away her paperwork and we went for a walk."

"And from that point on you were with Mrs. Douglas?"

Maggie thought carefully. "We went for a walk. When we got home, we joined Drew on the porch. We had some wine. After a while Amy went into the kitchen to start dinner, and the telephone rang. It was Mrs. Porter. Crystal hadn't come home. Amy was concerned. She suggested to Mrs. Porter that she'd walk up to their house to see if perhaps Crystal had fallen on the way."

"And you went with her?"

"Yes."

"Which way did you take?"

Maggie got up and walked to the end of the porch. She pointed past the driveway, toward the field she and Amy had crossed. "Across that field, and then through a woods."

"You didn't go into the field in back of the barn; the field between this house and Tom Colby's house, next door."

"No." That was the field where Crystal's body had been found.

"Why did you go the way you did?"

"Amy said that was the way Crystal usually walked home."

"Was it a clear path?"

"No. Not until we reached the wooded area."

"And you didn't walk back."

"Deputy Colby gave us a ride back home. He was at the Porters'. Rachel Porter was very worried about Crystal."

"Can you think of anything else that might be helpful for me to know, Ms. Summer?"

Maggie hesitated. "Tom Colby and Will Brewer are arranging a funeral for the child whose bones we found yesterday. I think it will be this afternoon. Will you be there?"

Detective Strait looked at her. "Should I be?"

"I think that might be a good idea," Maggie said softly, but intensely. "I think you should be there with the family."

"Are you sure you have nothing else to tell me? There is obviously something you're not saying."

"Because I'm not absolutely sure. And because it would be difficult to say."

"You're not withholding evidence."

"I don't have any evidence. But I might find something out between now and this afternoon."

Detective Strait looked at her. "Will Brewer told me you helped solve two murders down in New York State earlier this summer. You wouldn't be having any ideas of interfering with an official investigation, would you?"

"Certainly not, Detective." Maggie smiled her most beguiling smile. She hoped. "But if by chance I should find out something that would help you, then I'd like to know you'll be close this afternoon."

"At the funeral."

"Yes."

"Will also said you were a stubborn woman."

"Did he?" Then the detective and Will must have talked for a few minutes about her. That was flattering. She hoped.

"Can I trust you not to do anything stupid? And to tell me if you should—by chance—find out something?"

"Of course, Detective. You're in charge."

Of course . . .

Chapter 33

~~~

A Maine Sea Captain's Daughter, *lithograph by N. C.*
Wyeth for Kenneth Roberts's Trending into Maine,
1938. Portrait of a Victorian woman sipping tea
by a window overlooking a Maine seaport. The
woman is said to have been based on a portrait of
Kenneth Roberts's grandmother. 5.5 x 7.5 inches.
Price: $60.

Maggie and Detective Strait looked at each other, both of
them determined.

"Withholding evidence is a crime," he said.

"A woman's intuition isn't evidence, wouldn't you agree?"
Maggie stood up. "There are no facts I haven't told you."

"Ms. Summer, be careful. A girl was murdered, there's
been a suspicious accident, and there was a fire that might
have been arson. I don't need to deal with any more bodies."

"And I certainly wouldn't want you to. You'll be at the burial this afternoon?"

He nodded. "I will."

They returned to the kitchen just as Amy was putting down the telephone. "Will called, Maggie. The burial is to be at two, and Aunt Nettie has invited all of us to her home afterwards for tea or sherry."

"I'm glad Tom and Will were able to arrange it. Will everyone in the family be able to come?"

"I didn't ask specifically, but it sounded that way."

Maggie nodded slightly. "I need to do a couple of errands this morning. Detective, are you through questioning me for the moment?"

"Yes. But I need to talk with Mr. and Mrs. Douglas."

"Then I'll excuse myself. Amy, I'll be back later this morning, in plenty of time to change for the cemetery."

"All right. Where are you going?"

"I saw something at one of the antiques shops Will and I visited the other day that I'd like to look at again. That's all."

And that might indeed be all, Maggie thought to herself, as she walked through the fog-dampened grass. Her well-used blue van looked even more faded than usual in the gray of the morning. The fog was beginning to lift, but as she looked back at the house, it was still shrouded in wisps of gray.

She arrived at the Victorian house where Walter English sold antiques before it had opened.

As she paced restlessly up and down the narrow street, she wondered, Was she right even to ask questions? What if she was wrong? Would she get innocent people in trouble? Should she get involved? But then she thought of Amy, and of Drew, and of the child they might have someday. And of the child whose bones had been hidden in the fireplace. The child who would finally be put to rest this afternoon.

Generations of Brewers had lived in that proud white house on a hill in Madoc, Maine. Their descendants still watched the tides rise and fall on the Madoc River and buried their dead in the same cemetery.

This was a different world from the one she had grown up in, the world of suburbia where everyone came from somewhere else and was on their way somewhere farther still. The world in which her parents had lived and died. The world that most of her students had grown up in, and in which she and Michael had chosen to make their home. The high schools where she lived prepared 96 percent of their graduates to leave home, attend college, and find careers elsewhere. Their homes were, by and large, clean and painted and furnished comfortably. Their bookcases were filled. Their grass was cut. And the names of the homeowners changed from year to year. She and Michael had owned their home for twelve years, and they were the only people—she was the only person, Maggie corrected herself—who had lived on their block that long.

Here, someone who had lived here only twelve years was a newcomer. If you had not been born here to someone who had been born here you would always be "from away." The air was fresh; the street she paced this quiet morning seemed peaceful. But Amy and Drew had not found peace here.

Was it Maine? Or had they brought the unrest with them? She needed to find out.

For herself, and for Amy. Whatever was happening had to stop.

After Walter English arrived to unlock the door, Maggie gave him a few minutes. For better or worse, she thought ironically, as she entered the antiques mall. She needed some answers.

Chapter 34

———∽———

Kilmarnock Weeping Willow, *Roch Lithograph Company, Rochester, New York, 1895. One in a series of lithographs of American trees. During the nineteenth century weeping willows were often planted in or near graveyards, and their presence (in life or in art) was symbolic of death and grieving. 5.75 x 7.5 inches. Price: $48.*

The Douglas house was quiet when Maggie returned. She had gotten one answer. She just needed to put the rest of it together.

She took the portfolios she had left in the living room, checked a few details, and then returned them to her van.

Drew was on the porch. "Did you get your errands done?" he asked.

"Yes. I did." Maggie hesitated. But it wasn't quite time. "Where's Amy?"

"She went next door to ask Shirley what people would be

wearing this afternoon, and to make sure we'd be welcome. She suddenly had the feeling that since we weren't Brewers, perhaps we wouldn't be wanted."

"Will called here this morning, so I think he would have said something if we hadn't been. The child was found on your property, after all."

"Yes." Drew looked out over the river. "The fog's risen. Funny. When we lived in New York, I never paid attention to weather except to check whether to wear a raincoat or a topcoat. Here every day seems to define itself by the weather." He smiled at Maggie. "I like it."

"I'm going to go and get dressed," Maggie said. "And I have some papers of Amy's I want to gather and return to her." Upstairs, she once again looked through the piles of pictures of children waiting for homes.

Then she put on the only dark clothes she had brought: a navy blue linen skirt and a matching top she had packed as an extra outfit to wear at the antiques show, or perhaps to wear out to dinner in Maine. She had navy sandals too. She took her large canvas bag and tucked one of Amy's books into it. She would return that one later.

The other books and papers she carried downstairs and put on Amy's desk. Everything was as Amy had left it. Neat. In piles. Waiting for Amy to get to the next column on her "to do" list.

All there was to do now was wait.

By two that afternoon the fog had completely lifted. The sun reflected brightly off the polished surfaces of the newer granite or marble headstones in the cemetery. The older, rougher stones were of various sizes and shapes. As she and Amy joined the small group of people walking toward the back of the cemetery, Maggie noticed one white marble headstone topped by a carved lamb. A child's grave, Maggie knew immediately. Probably from about 1870. She would have liked to have spent more time here. There were stories everywhere. The man buried next to three consecutive wives, and his five children who had died as infants. The family of seven who had all died within one week. Epidemic? Fire? Maggie longed to know. She hoped someone knew. These were people who had lived in Maine and had died here. Had watched the sunsets and gauged the heaviness of the fog; had loved and hated and learned and forgotten. And, now, perhaps had been forgotten.

Having a family to remember them, even centuries later, was important. There was a deep truth and continuity to this place that she had not felt in more pristine suburban cemeteries.

She and Amy walked slowly, so Drew could keep up on his crutches. Looking ahead, she saw Will's strong shoulders bend slightly as Aunt Nettie held on to his arm with one hand and balanced herself on her cane with her other. Shirley had Sorrel and Sage with her, dressed in identical red dresses. Red wasn't usual for a funeral, but this wasn't a usual funeral, and children shouldn't have to wear black, Maggie agreed. Tom Colby was there, in his uniform, complete with rifle. She smiled. Why not? Although it was likely that this child had been born and died before the Civil War. Giles and Mary Leary were there too, with Brian, whose navy suit jacket was a little short for his arms. And, to her surprise, Rachel Porter was here. Here to mourn another child, before hers had been buried. There were one or two other people she didn't know; one of them must be the minister. And, there, to the side, was Detective Strait. He had come. He raised his hand slightly in greeting when he saw her. She nodded back.

There were no paved or even graveled paths in this cemetery. They all made their way slowly over the uneven grass, around the stones that were set in irregular patterns. Some were upright; some were on the ground. There were a few monuments of size, but most stones were modest, listing only a name and dates. The closer they got to the back of the cemetery, the oldest part, the more stones were carved with the name Brewer. This was the family burial ground and clearly had been so for over two hundred years. The dates told the stories. Would Will choose to be buried here, among his ancestors? Maggie wondered. Were his parents here, or had they been buried near Buffalo, where they had lived?

Those ahead had stopped. A small hole had been dug near a Brewer who had died in 1840. Good, thought Maggie. Perhaps whoever was buried here would have known this child.

A slim young man began saying a prayer. Maggie couldn't concentrate. She crossed the fingers held demurely in front of her. Did she have the right to do what she was planning? But, on the other hand, did she have the right not to?

The minister ended a short reading. Maggie started as Tom Colby fired a salute over the grave. Then Sorrel and Sage each went forward and dropped daisies on top of the tiny coffin. Did they understand that this was a child being buried? A child who had lived and died many, many years before they had even been born? They must understand something, Maggie thought. The box was so small. Then Rachel went forward and also dropped a flower: a white rose. Rachel was crying. So was Amy. Maggie's eyes were damp. She put her arm around Amy and hugged her briefly as they all turned and walked slowly back through the graveyard to their cars. It had been a short ceremony, but it had been appropriate. How many of these people were thinking that someday this would be their place too? Maggie had never thought about where she would be buried.

Michael had been buried in a plot in Ohio near his parents. She would not be buried there.

Will's hand on her shoulder brought her back to the moment.

"You got my message? You're all coming back to Aunt Nettie's?"

"Yes." Maggie looked up at him. Will was a man who knew his roots. She wondered what it felt like to have a place to come home to. A place you'd returned to every summer since you were born. A place you were known; a place you belonged.

"Is Amy all right?"

No one else Maggie could see was crying. "She'll be all right. It's been a difficult week. She's probably just reacting to it all."

Will nodded. "Follow the other cars; everyone is coming. We'd be disappointed if you didn't come."

"We'll be there. And I hope you don't mind, but I asked Detective Strait to join us."

Will stopped and looked at her. He knew her too well. "You found out something."

"I have some ideas."

"This is my family, Maggie. We've lost Crystal this week, and now this baby."

It was Maggie's turn to take Will's arm. "It will be all right, Will. I promise. It will be all right."

It was a good thing he couldn't see her crossed fingers.

Chapter 35

———⟆———

Court House, Augusta, Maine, *1869 wood engraving from* Gleason's Pictorial. *Courthouse on corner, with elegantly dressed man on horseback, and family walking in road in front of building. 4.5 x 5.5 inches. Price: $35.*

Aunt Nettie's house was smaller than Maggie had assumed, and the crowd arriving from the cemetery filled it. Aunt Nettie gave Maggie a special hug as she entered. "You take good care of my boy," she whispered with a pat on Maggie's arm.

Will grinned at Maggie from the other side of the room where he was presiding over the "iced tea, lemonade, sherry, or soft drink" table and winked. Maggie steeled herself. The players were here. All she had to do was get some answers. It shouldn't be that hard. Just in case, she glanced over at Detective Strait, who was sipping iced tea as he chatted with Will. No one seemed to pay any attention to the detective's being there; everyone must know him well. Better this week than before.

The advantage of approaching people in a crowd to discuss a difficult situation was that they wouldn't want too much attention to be drawn to themselves. And walking out would mean explaining themselves to everyone, or at least to the host. Of course, the disadvantage was that anyone could walk up and interrupt a delicate conversation.

Maggie felt like Amy, with a list. She took a deep breath and headed in the direction of Tom Colby, who had leaned his rifle up against the windows in back of the drinks table. He asked Will for beer and got a smiling shake of the head. This was Aunt Nettie's gathering, not Will's.

"Tom, could I talk with you for a moment?" Maggie herded him toward a corner not far from the table, but far enough so they wouldn't be overheard. "You did a wonderful job of organizing the burial, Tom. It was lovely."

"Fog burned off; that was nice. And we got a good group of mourners too, at pretty short notice." Tom looked around the room proudly. The buttons on his uniform shone.

There wasn't much time. No one would stay long sipping lemonade, or even eating the cookies on the coffee table. Sage and Sorrel were doing their best to ensure those plates would soon be empty. "Tom, several days ago Will and I went to Walter English's antiques mall. You were there."

"I go there once in a while. Walter sometimes finds Civil War pieces that I'd be interested in."

"You were showing him a rifle. A Sharps rifle."

Tom backed up a bit. "Maggie, now what do you know about rifles?"

"I know Homer's *A Sharp-shooter*. And I know there were

half a dozen Sharps rifles hidden in the Douglas home. Now there are five."

Tom paled. "Why are you asking me?"

"Because you know their house; you live next door; and you're the only one who's been in and out of the house this summer who would recognize a Sharps rifle and know its value."

Will had edged his way over to the corner of the table and was listening to them both.

"Tom? Is Maggie right?"

Tom shrugged his shoulders in a grand gesture. "Will, you know me. I wouldn't take nothing. Maggie's right, and she's wrong. I did know about the rifles. And I took one to Walter, to see if he could verify it. But I didn't take it from the house. Shit, Will. 'Scuse me, Maggie, but I don't even know where it came from in the house." He looked down. "At first I was all excited. It being probably one of *the* Sharps and all. You would know, being antiques dealers and knowing about history. But I knew it wasn't mine. I would have put it back, surely I would have, if I'd known where it came from. It's at my house right now, on the top shelf of the closet in my bedroom. Put away so the girls wouldn't find it. None of today's bullets would fit in it, but I don't want Sorrel and Sage thinking they can play with firearms. I'm always careful with my guns."

"How'd you get it, Tom?" Will asked.

Tom shifted his weight from one foot to the other. "I don't like to be in this situation, you understand? I did a favor. I told her it wasn't a good idea, but she said she'd tell everyone if'n I didn't."

"Who'd tell? What?" Maggie could guess one, but she was lost on the other.

Tom glanced up, to make sure no one else was near. "I don't like to say ill of the dead."

"Crystal." Maggie had been almost sure, but now she knew. But what had Crystal threatened to tell?

"She said she'd found it in the house when she was helping Amy clean out. She said there were more too. She wanted to find out what they were worth, and she asked me. She needed the money, she said. She had plans. To go to New York. She knew no one would ask too many questions if I had an old rifle. I already had a few."

"So you took the rifle to Walter?"

"He told me it was probably worth more than Crystal ever dreamed." Tom stopped a minute. "Made me think, I have to say. A person having six of those beauties to sell could do a lot." He looked like a boy embarrassed at being caught sticking his tongue out at the teacher. "A person could even help his sister buy her own house so he could be left in peace again."

Maggie glanced over at Sage and Sorrel. They were arguing over whose cookie was bigger, and Shirley was threatening to take them both home. This instant.

"But of course I couldn't do that. Because I didn't know where the other rifles were. Only Crystal knew that. And I knew if I sold the gun and didn't give her the money, well, then, she'd tell."

"Tell what?" Would whatever Crystal had to tell have disappeared after her death? Then all Tom would have had to do was find the guns.

"Will, you'd understand! You were there!" Tom looked at Will, as though for help.

"I was where?" Will had moved around the table and stood so Tom's back was against the wall, and he and Maggie were blocking the rest of the company.

"You were around that summer Rachel got herself in the family way." Tom took a chug of his iced tea as though it were Jim Beam. "Well, she'd told me. That I was the daddy of that little baby."

Will's face flushed. "Rachel told you that when?"

"When she was maybe three months gone. She asked me for money to, you know, take care of the situation. She told me she'd never tell no one, and so far as I know she never did. Only I knew Crystal was my little girl. I wanted to do what I could to help her."

"Tom, how much money did you give Rachel, back then?"

"She needed five thousand dollars. I remember, because it was a lot of money, and I was still in school. Had to take a loan, and work a lot of overtime to get that money. Didn't want my folks to know." Tom hesitated. "Rachel told me she was going to have an abortion. But when she didn't, I daren't say a word, since I didn't want anyone to know. But all these years I've been looking out for that young lady. And she was a beautiful thing, wasn't she?" Tom's eyes filled with tears.

Will ran his hand through his thick gray hair. "Tom, I need to tell you something. Something I've never told anyone." He looked at Maggie and then back at Tom. "Tom, Rachel told me the same thing."

"What?"

"She told me I was the father, and she needed five thousand dollars for an abortion. And I got her the money."

"Did she ever say anything else about it?"

"Never. I was real angry at the time when the baby was born, but she never said a word. I saw Crystal every summer, and Rachel seemed to be doing a good job of raising her. Never asked for any money or anything. I sent Crystal and Rachel nice Christmas gifts every year."

"You mean I wasn't that little girl's father?" Tom looked totally bewildered.

"I don't know if you were. I just know Rachel told me the same story."

Both Will and Tom looked across the room to where Rachel stood, sipping sherry, and receiving condolences.

"She was a good mother to Crystal."

"She was." Will hesitated. "But, Tom, I have a feeling Rachel told that story to someone else, too."

Maggie and Tom and Will all looked over at Giles Leary. Will said softly, "You see, Tom, Giles told me he thought he was Crystal's father. That's one reason he didn't want Brian spending time with her. Maybe he thought so for the same reason we did."

Maggie thought a moment. "That could explain where Rachel got the down payment for the house she bought. Remember you once wondered how she had managed to get that much money together when she was so young, and a single parent; that maybe her grandmother had left her some money?"

They were all quiet. Then Maggie shook her head. "Tom, I believe you didn't take the rifle. Crystal had the opportunity. But who would have killed her?"

"Not me!" Tom said. "I thought she was my own daughter. And she said she'd tell a secret if I didn't get her the money for the rifles. I figured Rachel had told her I was her father, and she was going to tell everyone. It's an old story, but I'm a teacher. I didn't want it getting around that I had done something like that when I was young. I'm supposed to be a role model. And Rachel was my second cousin."

"Mine too, Tom. Mine too." Will looked around the room. They were all silent.

Drew and Amy were talking with Aunt Nettie. "Will,

Tom, would you find an excuse to talk with Drew? I need to talk with Amy privately." Maggie looked at both of them. "It's important. Please."

Will picked up an extra glass of iced tea and the two men went over to where Drew was sitting. In a few minutes they were deeply involved in a discussion of something. But whatever topic they'd chosen, perhaps the Civil War, didn't interest Amy. She headed for the refreshments table and a glass of sherry.

"Not exactly a lively party, Maggie." Amy raised her glass in salute. "But we won't have to stay much longer. We're just putting in an appearance."

Maggie moved a little closer and took Amy's arm. Amy's breath was heavy with sherry. The glass she had just poured was not her first. "Amy, you're a dear friend, but I know what you did. I think I know why. And you are going to have to turn yourself in to Detective Strait. It will be much better for you if you do. He's over in that corner. You can do it quietly and no one will even know."

Amy pushed Maggie away abruptly, moving back so suddenly she hit the table in back of her. Two glasses of iced tea fell over, and a small pool of brown liquid spread across the white, embroidered linen tablecloth and toward the floor. No one paid attention.

"What do you think you're talking about?" said Amy, her voice low.

"You killed Crystal Porter."

Amy suddenly broke into a raucous laugh that drew attention from everyone throughout the room. "You're out of your mind! How can you even imagine something like that? Me? You're crazy, Maggie. Me?"

Maggie moved closer again and spoke softly. "Amy. Turn yourself in. It will go much better if you do that now."

Amy slid away from Maggie and pushed the table again. The crystal glasses on the table glistened in the light from the window. A rainbow was on one of the curtains.

Amy's eyes flickered like those of a trapped animal. The room was full of people. Right now most of them were looking at her. She looked to the right, then to the left, as though seeking a way to escape. Then she pulled the table forward and moved in back of it, grabbing the rifle Tom had left there. Maggie reached across the table, but before she could reach Amy, the rifle was pointed directly at her.

No one in the room said a word.

Sage screamed. "That lady's going to shoot us!"

Detective Strait pulled his gun and pointed it at Amy. "Mrs. Douglas, put down that rifle."

Amy carefully moved the rifle and pointed it at Sage. "No. You drop your gun. Unless you all want to go to another burial very soon." Amy's voice was much too calm. "I said, drop that gun."

Shirley screamed, and Maggie, still facing Amy, heard Detective Strait's gun hit the floor.

"Amy, don't do anything foolish. Put down the rifle." Maggie voice was calm, although her mind was anything but.

"Why should I? What does it matter?" Amy waved the rifle around the room, pointing at one person after another. "They can't put me in jail for more than one lifetime, can they?"

"Amy, put down the rifle. It isn't worth it."

"She wasn't worth it. That lying schemer. I cried over that poor baby we buried today, but I won't cry over Crystal Porter. Whoever that baby was, he was too young to have betrayed anyone. Crystal was a liar and a cheat. She was ruining my life. She deserved to die."

"Amy!" Drew tried to get up and move toward her, but stumbled on his cast.

Amy pointed the rifle directly at him. "You and I agreed. We had it all figured out. But she changed her mind. She wouldn't go along. I did it to protect you, Drew. I wanted you to love me."

Maggie moved forward slightly, leaning against the table. With her right hand she reached down and picked up a glass of iced tea and threw the tea into Amy's face, while she threw her body against the table and pushed it— hard—toward Amy. The movement caught Amy off-balance, and she stumbled backward against the windows. As she did, Maggie moved around the table and grabbed the rifle. The two women struggled with it. Maggie vaguely heard movements behind her. The metal of the rifle was rough; her hands were scratched, she realized, and the rifle had hit the side of her face. Amy's strength was greater than she had expected. She hoped the people in back of her were getting out. Taking the girls away. She pushed hard, and Amy fell against the window. The rifle butt caught in the lace curtain and ripped it. The table moved farther away as Tom reached over them and put both hands on the rifle, while Will, the bigger of the two men, pushed Amy down. They all ended up in a tangle on the ground until, suddenly:

"Stop it! Everyone!"

The rifle was gone, Maggie realized. She and Will were both on top of Amy on the ground, while spilled glasses of iced tea dripped down on them.

"Let her up. Slowly." It was Detective Strait. He had his gun. And he was holding a pair of handcuffs. Maggie and Will rose, pulling Amy with them. Without the rifle, which Tom held across the room, Amy stopped fighting. They moved her to a chair, where Nick Strait put the cuffs on. Maggie glanced around quickly. Good. The children had gone into the kitchen. With what they'd seen today they'd be having nightmares for a month.

"Mrs. Douglas, you're going to come with me, now. Quietly." Detective Strait read Amy her rights while Maggie stepped backward and felt Will's arms go around her. She leaned back slightly, grateful for the comforting gesture, as Detective Strait and Amy left the room.

As they reached the doorway, Nick Strait turned around. "An interesting party. Thank you for inviting me, Ms. Summer. I may have a few more questions for you, and for you, Mr. Douglas, later. First I'm going to find Mrs. Douglas a nice quiet place where she can think."

The door closed behind them.

Chapter 36

—◡𝒮◡—

Thanksgiving Day—Hanging Up the Musket. *Winslow Homer wood engraving published in* Frank Leslie's Illustrated News Paper, *December 23, 1865. Man standing on chair, hanging Civil War–vintage rifle over fireplace. Rifle is labeled 1861 and is hanging beneath an earlier rifle, with a powder horn labeled 1776. 9.13 x 14.13 inches. Price: $260.*

The Learys lived only a few blocks away and left almost immediately after Detective Strait took Amy away. Brian looked pale. Shirley too wanted to remove her girls from the scene and promised French fries and ice cream on their way home, which seemed to lessen their trauma considerably. "Chocolate?" Sorrel asked as they left. "Can the ice cream be chocolate?" Rachel broke down and left with a woman Maggie didn't know.

Aunt Nettie sat on a high Queen Anne chair and surveyed

her living room. Iced tea was still dripping slowly onto the floor. She had mopped up some of it, but had missed one spot. That tablecloth will have to be bleached, Maggie thought. And the curtains mended. Drew sat on a straight Hitchcock chair stenciled in gold and red. His injured foot stuck out into the room; his face was white with shock. Will and Maggie held hands and settled on an upholstered, blue-flowered couch that was so much lower than Aunt Nettie's seat that Maggie kept thinking she should stand up. Tom Colby paced from one side of the room to the other.

Aunt Nettie spoke first. "Would anyone else like a real drink? I think some Jack Daniel's would go down right well just now."

Tom and Drew joined her, Maggie poured herself some sherry, and Will found a beer in the refrigerator.

"All right, now would one of you explain just what went on here?" Aunt Nettie looked from one to the other. "I'm not daft. I understand Amy Douglas killed Crystal. But I don't have a clue as to why."

Maggie looked at Drew. "I'm so sorry, Drew. Did you have any idea?"

He shook his head. "I wondered. But, no, I didn't know. I kept hoping not." He looked at Maggie. "How did you know?"

"I wasn't positive. But the pieces fit. Amy told me how much you both wanted a child."

He nodded.

"And how you didn't want to adopt. You wanted a child biologically yours. Amy was afraid she couldn't have a child. She was afraid to tell you; she thought it might end your marriage."

Drew looked at Maggie incredulously. "It wouldn't have ended our marriage! And I knew she might not be able to have children. Her doctor told me everything." Drew looked around the room. "I guess it doesn't make a difference anymore. Amy's stepfather raped her repeatedly when she was a teenager; she got pregnant. He arranged an abortion, but it was botched, and as a result she probably couldn't have children." Drew sighed. "She didn't tell me about the abortion, but her doctor thought I knew, and he referred to it once. I knew if she hadn't told me herself, she was embarrassed about it, so I never told her I knew. She had told me about the stepfather and the rapes, just after we were married."

"I didn't realize." Maggie shook her head slowly. "She told me about the abortion, but not about the stepfather. So that's why she stayed close to home in college?"

Drew nodded. "He would only pay for a college close to home so she would be—available. Her mother had no clue, and Amy was too afraid of hurting her to tell. And she didn't have the self-confidence to leave home and get a job or scholarship somewhere else."

"The poor girl," said Aunt Nettie. "That's a horrible thing to have to live through. But what had Amy's past to do with Crystal?"

Drew answered, "Amy knew I wanted a biological child. It was really important to me." He took a sip of the Jack Daniel's. "Not important enough to kill for, though. But without telling me, Amy worked out a deal with Crystal."

Maggie looked at him. "Crystal was going to have your child, wasn't she?"

"At first I thought it was crazy, but then it began to make more sense. Crystal agreed to get pregnant. To have my child. After the child was born she would relinquish parental rights to Amy and me and we would give her enough money to start a new life in New York, which is what she wanted."

The room was silent.

"It would be an open adoption; she could have come home and seen the child anytime she wanted to. And her son or daughter would have all the advantages Amy and I could provide."

"And Crystal did get pregnant."

"Yes."

"What went wrong?" asked Will.

"She changed her mind. She told me right after . . . you saw us together, Maggie. We didn't want you to know what we were doing, but you found out. What you didn't know was that Amy had arranged the whole thing. She wasn't embarrassed, except by the fact that you knew. But that afternoon Crystal told me she had changed her mind; she wanted to keep the baby." Drew took another deep drink of the liquor. "She also told me it might not be my baby, anyway. It might be Brian's."

Maggie nodded. She decided not to point out that there was no need for Drew to have kept sleeping with Crystal after he'd known she was pregnant. At this point, was it even important? So far this made sense. Horrible sense, but sense. "How did you feel?"

"I was shocked. I know that sounds stupid under the circumstances, but it never occurred to me Crystal might be sleeping with anyone else. She was cheating Amy and me out of the only child we might have who would be related to me. I was furious. I was disappointed. I didn't know what to do." Drew blanched a bit. "When Amy came home that afternoon, I told her, and then I got drunk. It seemed the only reasonable thing to do at the time."

Maggie nodded. "I remember. Amy said she had some work to do in her study, and when she was finished, she and I took a walk. And when we got home, you were a bit under the weather. That was the night Crystal didn't make it home."

"But then when did Amy do it?" Will asked.

"It must have been when I was in my room. Drew, you were drinking on the front porch, and Amy said she was going to her study." Maggie put it all together. "She went to tell Crystal she could go home. The Learys had already left for the day because they needed to pick up some supplies. So Amy and Crystal were alone."

"Amy was furious," added Drew. "I knew that. I was furious too. But I never thought of anything like murder! But Amy had planned the pregnancy and the adoption. She had talked Crystal into it. She had talked me into agreeing. She had already spoken with our lawyer in New York about the legalities regarding open adoption, and about our helping Crystal to make a start in the city."

Amy would have done that, Maggie thought. Amy wouldn't have wanted anything to get in the way of her plans. It would have been illegal to pay Crystal for the adoption, but, from what she'd seen in the adoption books, Amy and Drew could have paid for her pregnancy and birth expenses. No doubt Amy's lawyer would have come up with some way of getting Crystal started in New York, perhaps arranging for an apartment, and a job. The details didn't matter now.

Drew sat and looked at the wall. "I saw her leave the house with Crystal. She wasn't yelling; she wouldn't have wanted you to hear, Maggie, and you were upstairs. But I knew she was really giving it to Crystal. 'Betrayer, liar, whore.' I saw them walk around the barn, back toward where Crystal's body was found the next day."

"I wonder why they did that? Amy told me Crystal usually walked through the other field to go home."

"I can answer that," Tom spoke up from the corner. "Crystal was coming to see me. I had promised to find out about the rifle, and tell her."

269

Drew frowned. "The rifle?"

Maggie looked over at Aunt Nettie, who also looked confused. "We found five Civil War–era rifles hidden in the floor of the attic. Will suspected there had been six, but we didn't know for sure until Tom told me. Crystal had found them and taken one to Tom, asking him to get it appraised. She wanted to sell the rifles."

"That must have been what she meant when she told me she didn't need our checks; she had her own way of making money." Drew looked around. "Of course. She and Amy cleaned the attic. She found the loose board there."

"So you expected Crystal, Tom?"

"I did. I waited for her. But she didn't come. I even called Rachel, but by then Crystal was missing. I drove around looking for her that night. It never occurred to me to look in the back field."

"And you didn't tell anyone you'd expected to see her that day."

Tom shook his head. "I suppose now that I should have. But at the time I didn't think it was important. And I didn't want Crystal to get into trouble about the rifle."

"Or for you to get in trouble, Tom Colby. You were helping that girl steal rifles!" Aunt Nettie shook her finger at him.

Tom didn't answer. But he shrugged acceptance. "I made a mistake. A bad mistake."

Will picked up the thread. "So most likely Amy followed Crystal out into the field. They were still talking. Amy was furious. And she must have picked up a rock and hit Crystal."

"And then she came back to her study, where I found her forty minutes later." Maggie shook her head, remembering how calm Amy had been. "She had changed the bandage on her arm. I remember thinking the blood had seeped through.

She must have stressed it when she knocked Crystal down. So she came back and cleaned herself up, but the wound from the window a few days before had opened. Or," Maggie said suddenly, "it might have been Crystal's blood."

Drew pulled himself up from the chair. "Why did we ever come to this place? We weren't wanted here. All those stories about ghosts, and the baby crying, and the fire, and my accident, and now Crystal is dead, and Amy's in jail. And there will be no child, and I have no wife, and . . ." Drew sat down suddenly and burst into wracking sobs.

"That's right. What was all that with the ghosts and the baby crying? And the telephone calls. And . . ." Maggie looked around the room.

"All right, all right! That was Shirley. And me." Tom came and sat down with the rest of them. "Shirley was real angry when the house was sold. She thought it should have been hers. And, I'll admit, I had hoped she'd get the house too. I missed the peace of living alone. Shirley is my sister, but those kids of hers are a real handful. Anyway, she thought we could scare those city folks right back to the city, and that maybe then they'd sell the house for about what they'd paid for it. More than we could really afford, but we might be able to swing it, if Shirley could get a settlement from her ex-husband. I figured it wouldn't do no harm to try. There had always been stories about a woman and a baby at that house. So I went and made a tape recording of Sue Smithson's baby crying, down the road, and put it on a timing device. If the batteries are holding up, it'll still be playing two or three times a week. The recorder is hanging down in the chimney flue near the master bedroom fireplace. Brian thought it was a fun game; he helped me rig it up." Tom hesitated a moment. "Crystal knew about it too. She used to talk about what a great job we were doing, scaring

Mrs. Douglas. Course, I guess by then she knew how important babies were to the Douglases."

"And the phone calls?" Maggie leaned toward Tom.

"Shirley did that part. She isn't a good sleeper. She thought that would drive them crazy."

"The ghost?"

"Don't know nothing about any ghost. Seems to me Amy probably dreamed that one up herself."

With a baby crying in the walls and strange phone calls, she might have, Maggie agreed to herself.

Will now asked, "And the fire?"

Tom looked sheepish. "That was me too. I didn't intend for it to burn down the house, or hurt anyone. I just wanted to scare them."

Drew looked up at him incredulously.

"That was before I got to know you, Drew. I wouldn't do it now."

"You dropped the fire down the ell flue?"

"Right! It was easy to walk in through the barn during the day and leave the oven open there." He looked at Aunt Nettie, as though she would understand. "The Douglases didn't spend much time in that part of the house."

"And I suppose you cut my brake line too? As something else that would be amusing?" Drew pushed his leg toward Tom as if to demonstrate the damage.

"Nope. Didn't do that. You might have gotten hurt! Shirley and me was trying to scare you folks a little. Not hurt anyone."

The room was silent.

"I think," said Maggie, "I think Amy cut the brake line. Maybe we'll find out for sure sometime in the future. But she knew something about auto mechanics. I think she cut the line to make it look as though her family was being targeted, maybe by the same person who'd killed Crystal. To take the spotlight off her and Drew."

"But she might have killed me!"

Maggie shook her head. "She knew most of your errands were to Waymouth, and that your brakes would give out at that corner. You wouldn't have been going fast enough to kill yourself. Although you did, of course, mess your leg up pretty well."

Will reached over and took Maggie's hand again. "You figured it all out. And you were brave enough to grab that rifle from Amy. I thought for sure you were going to be shot!"

"She wouldn't have been," said Tom.

"I knew that," agreed Maggie. "But I don't think Amy knew."

"Knew what, Maggie?" Aunt Nettie shook her head. "I'm trying very hard to follow along and understand all these crazy things, but Amy looked dangerous. Why wouldn't she have shot anyone?"

"Because she had Tom's rifle. When we were looking up and asking about rifles the other day, I thought back over what I knew about Civil War–era weapons. And I went to see Walter English this morning, to confirm my suspicion that it had been Tom who had taken the rifle in for an appraisal. He mentioned that one of the reasons the Sharps rifles were especially valuable during the Civil War was because they could fire more cartridges than other rifles without reloading. I thought of that when Tom fired a salute at the cemetery. I assumed that, for safety's sake, he hadn't reloaded. There was no reason for him to do so. So I took a chance. I assumed the rifle wouldn't have fired."

Aunt Nettie shook her head. "Will, your new friend seems to know all too much about everything." She turned to

Maggie. "And I suppose you know who that poor baby was that we buried this afternoon?"

"No. I have no idea about that baby," said Maggie. "But at least he or she is resting in peace with the rest of the family now."

She raised a glass to the child, and the rest of the group joined her.

"To peace," said Aunt Nettie. "The good Lord knows, this family could use some."

Chapter 37

—◡—

Moll Pitcher at Monmouth, *1860 wood engraving used as illustration for history book. Molly Pitcher, 1744–1832, born Mary Ludwig, was the wife of Revolutionary War soldier John Hays and carried water to her husband and other soldiers during the Battle of Monmouth, where legend says that after her husband was shot, she manned his cannon, earning her the nickname "Molly Pitcher." Engraving shows her dying husband, the bucket she has cast aside, and Moll loading the cannon. Signed W. H. Van Ingen, possibly the father of noted nineteenth-century mural painter William Brantley Van Ingen, who was known for his historical murals painted in government buildings. Foxed. 5 x 6.5 inches. Price: $35.*

"When will you go back to Jersey, Maggie?" Will asked. The sunset was a brilliant design of purples and reds as they shared a chaise on the Douglas porch and sipped Chablis.

Drew was inside, telephoning local lawyers Aunt Nettie had suggested. Amy was at the Lincoln County Jail.

"I'll stay another day or so and make sure there is nothing I know that the police don't. I don't think there should be. But then I have to head back and get my schedules and class list set for the fall semester. I'm still a professor. And you're leaving?"

"In two days. What do you think Drew will do?"

"He said he'll stay here, at least for now, to help Amy. He really does love her, Will. Maybe he'll look for a job teaching. He talked about that before all this happened."

"Sometimes talking about the past makes the present easier to understand."

"It might," said Maggie. "The past is always a good place to start."

She put down her glass and cuddled against Will's shoulder. A red sunset meant a clear day ahead. She hoped their tomorrows would bring clarity and answers to Amy and Drew.

"When am I going to see you again, Maggie Summer?" Will said softly. "My life always seems more exciting when we're together."

"The early part of the fall semester is always hectic. But there are a lot of antiques shows in New Jersey then. I'll bet a few of them could find a booth for a dealer in early-fireplace equipment." Maggie looked up at him.

Their kiss, like the sunset, promised a bright tomorrow.

The following document was among papers donated to the Waymouth Library archives by Mr. and Mrs. Andrew Douglas. The papers were found in the Douglas home, which was originally owned by the Brewer family. There is no date on this document, and no attribution.

Transcription by Ms. Rachel Porter, Waymouth Librarian.

As a child there was only one place on this island I was forbidden to go, and therefore that place was where I most longed to be. About an hour's walk through the pines was Jewett's Cove. After Widow Jewett's husband was claimed by the sea, she was left only a house and barn. She was a big woman, in body and in spirit. When she determined to turn her house and barn into a seaman's inn no one questioned her ability to run a tight house. Widow Jewett could raise a barrel of cider to her mouth and drink without spilling a drop. She was known to take a fist to any man who'd had too much rum and decided to make something of it. A man might drink too much at Widow Jewett's, but he didn't make trouble.

Most important to me, she listened to my dreams. And she helped me find ways to stay in this house, even after Father's ship was lost at sea, my sisters married, and Mother was lost to nightmares. She taught me to bake bread, and to grow vegetables, and to care for the chickens and the cows, even in their sicknesses. And she bought what other supplies Mother and I had need of. After Mother's death, Aunt Tempe tried to convince me it was not proper for a young woman to stay alone; that I should join her family in Belfast. But I had no desire to care for her children—seven then, and more coming—and I stayed. A woman cannot own prop-

erty, so this house was held by her husband. But no one in Belfast had need of it, and times were not prosperous; one more house on an island was not thought of value. There was no one to care what I did, so I suited myself, and remained where I had always been.

And one summer a mariner staying to Widow Jewett's took my fancy, and he mine, and there was no one on the island to see or care what was done. The man left, as Widow Jewett had said he would, since men are restless as the tides, and come and go as often. But he did not leave me alone.

Who was to know, alone in the winter cold of an island? Who was to know what shape my body or my mind took?

But when spring came, and my time with it, I knew a child would not be safe with me. A child without a father would be worse off than if he had never been. And so I made my choice, and Widow Jewett helped me do what had to be done.

And ever since I have lived here with my baby who would never be a child.

But although the child did not age, I have. Now Aunt Tempe's oldest boy is marrying and has claimed this house as his own. He will move the house to the mainland of Madoc when the river freezes. I will not go with it. My life has not been one shared with others, and this is not the time to begin doing so.

But my child has known no other home than this one, and he shall stay here. He shall be safe. I will find a way. And then I fear I will walk on ice too thin to bear weight. A simple mistake, made by a simple old woman.

And it will be over. I will not be remembered, and my child was never known. But as long as this house shall stand, we will be a part of it.

Afterword

During the 1950s my parents and grandparents bought a run-down Colonial home in a riverside community on the midcoast of Maine. We were the first to own the house outside the family that had built it in 1774, and then, four generations later, had moved it from Westport Island onto the mainland, where the ell and the barn were added. When I was a child, I helped my mother and grandmother tear down the plaster wall in the old kitchen to reveal the original fireplace, where we found its crane still intact. You can see the fireplace on my website, *www.leawait.com*.

The house is locally known as The Marie Antoinette House, because of a legend that Stephen Clough, its second owner, masterminded a plot to rescue Queen Marie Antoinette during the French Revolution and bring her to live in Maine. When the plot was discovered, Clough left France quickly, bringing with him a shipload of exquisite French clothing and furniture. Clough did have business connections with members of the French court, and he was in France when Marie Antoinette was executed. Was he ever really involved in a plot to free Marie Antoinette? No one will ever know for sure. But he was, no doubt, trying to help some fleeing French aristocrats. Clough named his youngest daughter Hannah Antoinette, and ever since there has been an Antoinette in each generation of their family.

Today I live and write in that house, and its history has inspired not only this book, but several of my historical novels for children. (Stephen Clough's daughter Sally is a character in *Stopping to Home*.) So far as I know, no one living here has ever seen a ghost, or heard a baby crying in the night, or found a skeleton in the chimney or rifles in the attic. . . . But sometimes, especially when the river winds blow down the chimney on dark winter days, the howling sound is almost a human cry.

And in the early nineteenth century Widow Jewett did run an inn for mariners on nearby Westport Island.

Lea Wait

Interested in learning more about the antique prints in Maggie Summer's business? The following books and periodicals will give you additional information.

American Historical Print Collectors Society (publication: *Imprint*). Post Office Box 201, Fairfield, Connecticut 06430

Beam, Philip C. *Winslow Homer's Magazine Engravings*. Harper & Row Publishers, New York, 1979

Blum, Ann Shelby. *Picturing Nature: American Nineteenth-Century Zoological Illustration*. Princeton University Press, Princeton, New Jersey, 1993

Blunt, Wilfrid, and William T. Stearn. *The Art of Botanical Illustration*. Antique Collectors' Club in association with The Royal Botanic Gardens, Kew, England, 1994

Book Source Monthly. 2007 Syossett Drive, Cazenovia, New York 13035

Cikovsky, Nicolai Jr., and Franklin Kelly. *Winslow Homer*. National Gallery of Art, Washington, D.C., and Yale University Press, New Haven and London, 1995

Hamilton, James. *Arthur Rackham: A Life With Illustration*. Pavilion Books Limited, London, 1990

Harthan, John. *The History of the Illustrated Book: The Western Tradition*. Thames and Hudson, Ltd., London, 1981

Hults, Linda C. *The Print in the Western World: An Introductory History*. University of Wisconsin Press, Madison, 1996

Journal of the Print World, Inc. Post Office Box 978, Meredith, New Hampshire 03253

The Magazine Antiques. Brant Publications, Inc., 575 Broadway, New York, New York 10012

Maine Antique Digest. Post Office Box 1429, Waldoboro, Maine 04572

Meyer, Susan E. *A Treasury of the Great Children's Book Illustrators*. Harry N. Abrams, Inc., Publishers, New York, 1983

St. Hill, Thomas Nast. (Introduction to) *Thomas Nast's Christmas Drawings*. Dover Publications, Inc., New York, 1978

About the Author

Lea Wait comes from a long line of antiques dealers, including her mother, her grandmother, and her great-grandfather. She has owned her antique-print business for more than twenty-five years. She now lives in Edgecomb, Maine, where she runs her antique-print business and writes historical novels for young readers as well as the Maggie Summer series.